DRAWING THE LINE

Drawing the Line: Technical Hand Drafting for Film and Television is the essential resource for students and aspiring professionals studying and working in film and television design. The book covers all aspects of scenic drafting by hand – a technique still used in film and television because of its unparalleled emotive and aesthetic qualities.

Discover how to draw the iconic scroll of a classical column or learn the difference between Flemish bond and English bond brickwork – it is all here!

Other key features include the following:

- *Beautifully illustrated, approachable, step-by-step instructions for every aspect of scenic drafting – specific to film and television;*

- *Illustrated explanations of camera lenses, including calculating aspect ratios and projections;*

- *Coverage of the four types of drafting projection: isometric, oblique, orthographic and axonometric;*

- *A comprehensive glossary of terms, including an illustration of each entry.*

This beautiful book is clear, accessible, and a must-have for any student aspiring to work in film and television design.

David McHenry studied Theatre Design in London at the Central School of Art and Design, and has worked in Theatre, Television and Film for 40 years as Designer, Art Director, Storyboard Artist, Draftsman and Lecturer. McHenry's recent work includes *Game of Thrones* and *Black Sails*. He teaches at the University of the Arts, Wimbledon in the Screen Design Department and also runs three courses at the London Film School.

DRAWING THE LINE
HAND DRAFTING FOR FILM AND TELEVISION

DAVID McHENRY

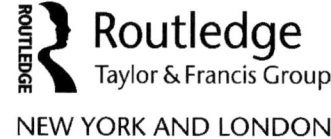

NEW YORK AND LONDON

First published 2018
by Routledge
711 Third Avenue, New York, NY 10017

and by Routledge
2 Park Square, Milton Park, Abingdon, Oxon OX14 4RN

Routledge is an imprint of the Taylor & Francis Group, an informa business

© 2018 Taylor & Francis

The right of David McHenry to be identified as the author of this work has been asserted by him in accordance with sections 77 and 78 of the Copyright, Designs and Patents Act 1988.

All rights reserved. No part of this book may be reprinted or reproduced or utilised in any form or by any electronic, mechanical, or other means, now known or hereafter invented, including photocopying and recording, or in any information storage or retrieval system, without permission in writing from the publishers.

Trademark notice: Product or corporate names may be trademarks or registered trademarks, and are used only for identification and explanation without intent to infringe.

Library of Congress Cataloging in Publication Data:

Names: McHenry, David, author.
Title: Drawing the line : technical hand drafting for film and television / David McHenry.
Description: New York : Routledge, 2018. | Includes index.
Identifiers: LCCN 2017050940| ISBN 9781138290327 (hardback) | ISBN 9781138290334 (pbk.) | ISBN 9781315266282 (e-book)
Subjects: LCSH: Mechanical drawing--Technique. | Theaters--Stage-setting and scenery.
Classification: LCC T357 .M33 2018 | DDC 777--dc23
LC record available at https://lccn.loc.gov/2017050940

ISBN: 978-1-138-29032-7 (hbk)
ISBN: 978-1-138-29033-4 (pbk)
ISBN: 978-1-315-26628-2 (ebk)

Publisher's Note: This book has been prepared from camera-ready copy provided by the author

David McHenry started his career as a Theatre Designer.
He has worked as Production Designer, Art Director,
Storyboard Artist and Draftsman in Television and Feature Films.

His credits as Draftsman include
BLACK SAILS, RUSH, GAME OF THRONES, DREDD and OUTLANDER

David lectures at the London Film School,
University of the Arts, London, and at the
Norwegian National Film School
and the Film School, Bergen.

CONTENTS

```
BIOGRAPHY..................................v
INTRODUCTION AND ACKNOWLEDGEMENTS..................ix
EQUIPMENT - THE BASICS............................1
SCALE............................................5
THE PLAN.........................................7
REFLECTED CEILING PLAN..........................19
LAYING OUT THE PAGE.............................20
LETTERING AND LABELLING.........................24
THE TITLE BLOCK.................................26
PAPER SIZES.....................................27
FOLDING DRAWINGS................................28
TRIANGLES.......................................32
THE CIRCLE......................................33
DIVIDING A LINE INTO EQUAL PARTS................34
POLAR POINT.....................................36
THE ARCH........................................37
DOORS...........................................50
WINDOWS.........................................55
STAIRCASES......................................58
BRICKS..........................................64
MOULDINGS.......................................65
ISOMETRIC PROJECTION............................69
AXONOMETRIC PROJECTION..........................70
OBLIQUE PROJECTION..............................71
PROJECTIONS OF CIRCLES..........................72
PERSPECTIVE GRID - SINGLE POINT.................73
2 POINT MEASURED PERSPECTIVE GRID...............77
SETTING UP A CAMERA PROJECTION..................84
REFLECTIONS IN A MIRROR........................103
BACKINGS: CALCULATING SIZE.....................106
FORCED PERSPECTIVE - SET FORESHORTENING........110
THE CLASSICAL ORDERS...........................116
ENTASIS OF COLUMN SHAFTS.......................124
IONIC VOLUTE...................................126
SPIRAL BASED ON QUADRANTS......................127
THE FIBONACCI SPIRAL...........................128
THE GOLDEN SECTION.............................129
THE SPIRAL (HELIX).............................130
SURVEYING......................................131
GLOSSARY.......................................139
INDEX..........................................160
```

This is a Manual, a Text book and a Reference book combined.

It is for students of Film and Television Design
and those starting out in the Art Department.

There are no long pages of text and written explanations
here, only diagrams and drawings with brief concise notes.

With many thanks to Alby Bailey
for all her help and talent and to
Maureen for her endless encouragement.

David McHenry
Glasgow, September 2017

Dedicated to
Ted McHenry, my father.

EQUIPMENT – THE BASICS

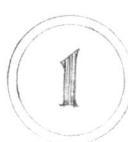

PLASTIC COATED BOARDS (MELAMINE) ARE TOO UNFORGIVING TO DRAW ON. DRAUGHTING MATS ARE NECESSARY BUT WHITE MOUNT CARD IS A GOOD SUBSTITUTE

PARALLEL MOTION DRAWING BOARDS

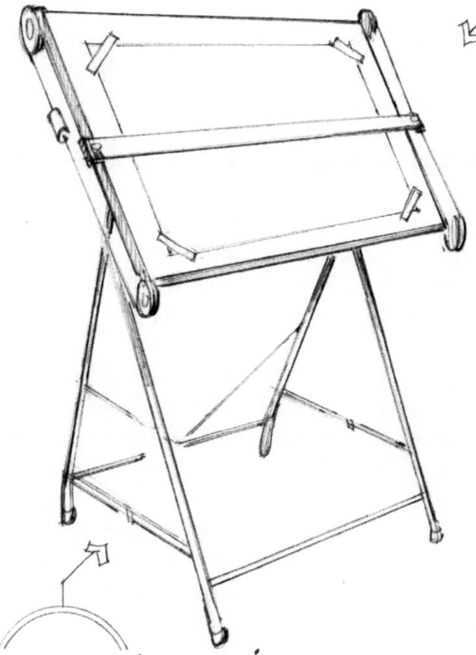

FLOOR STANDING

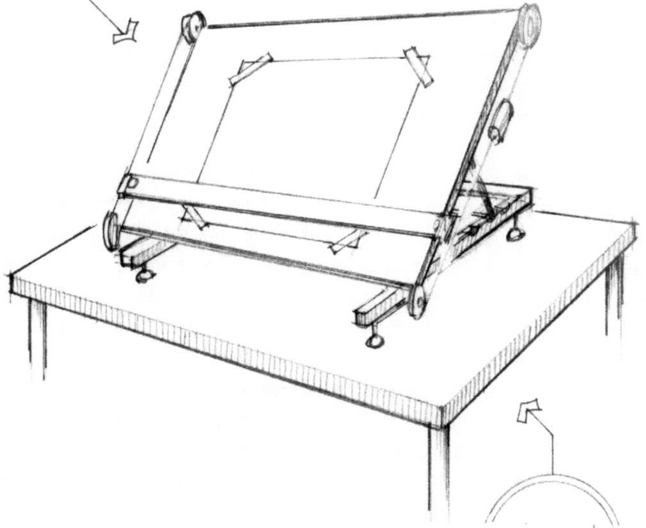

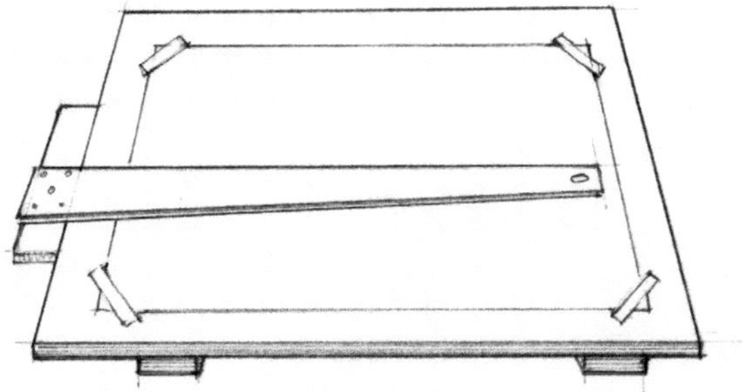

"THE ORIGINAL" WITH 'T' SQUARE

TABLE TOP

EQUIPMENT - THE BASICS

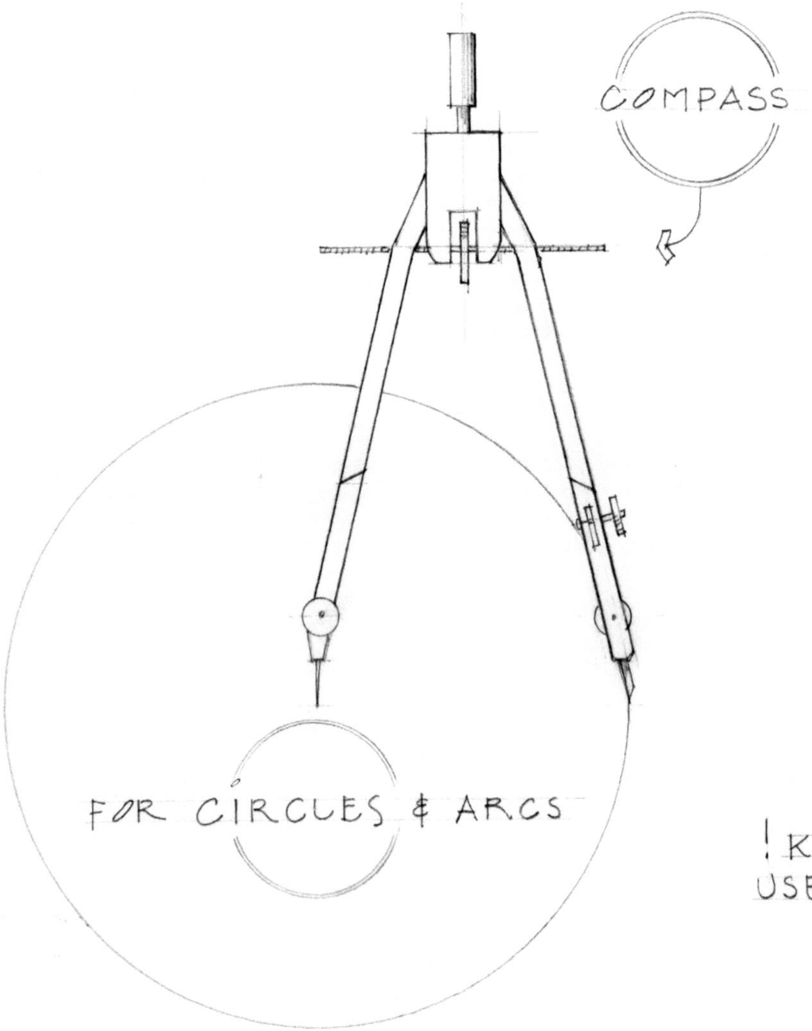

COMPASS

FOR CIRCLES & ARCS

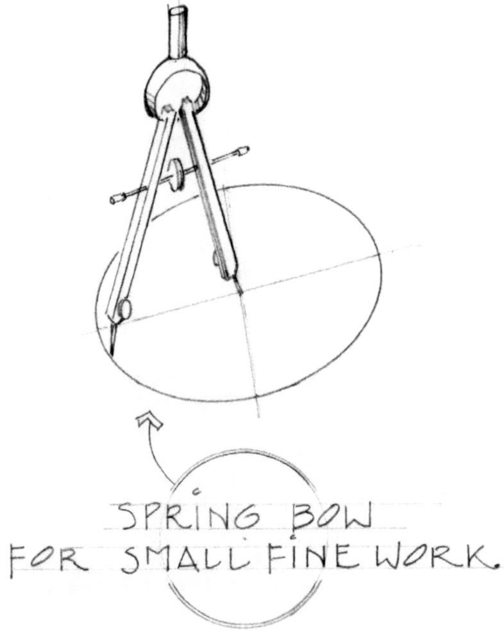

SPRING BOW FOR SMALL FINE WORK.

! KEEP LEADS SHARP !
USE AN EMERY BOARD

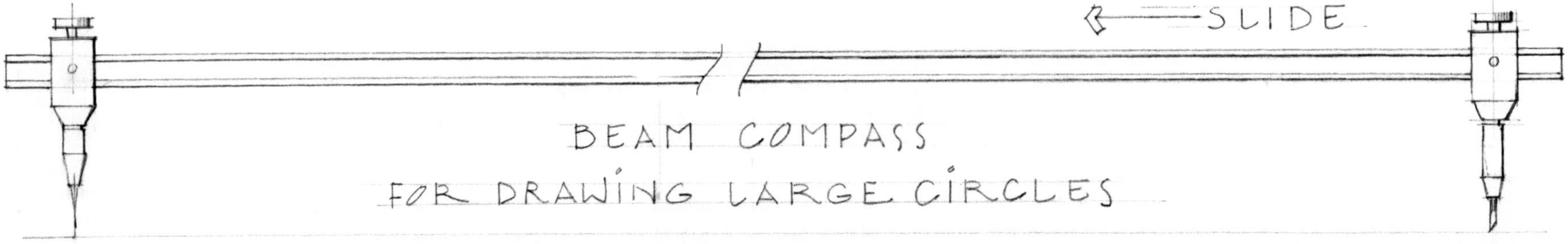

← SLIDE

BEAM COMPASS
FOR DRAWING LARGE CIRCLES

EQUIPMENT - THE BASICS

ADJUSTABLE SET SQUARE ESSENTIAL!

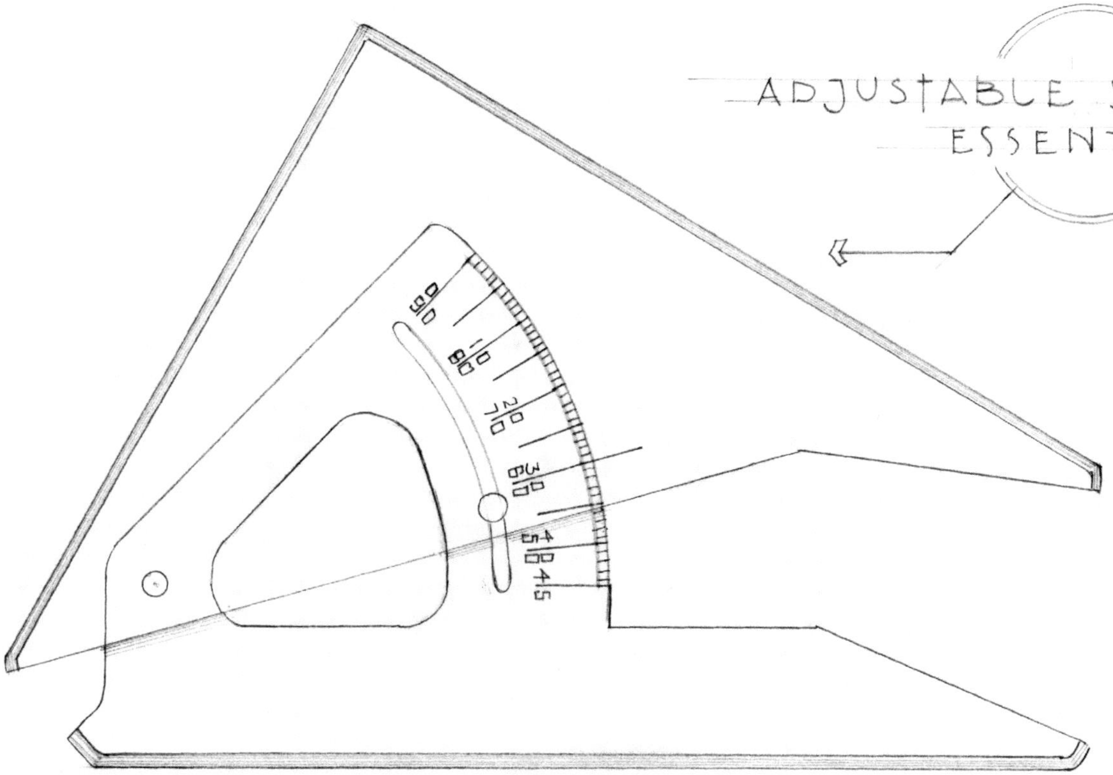

2 USEFUL SET SQUARES

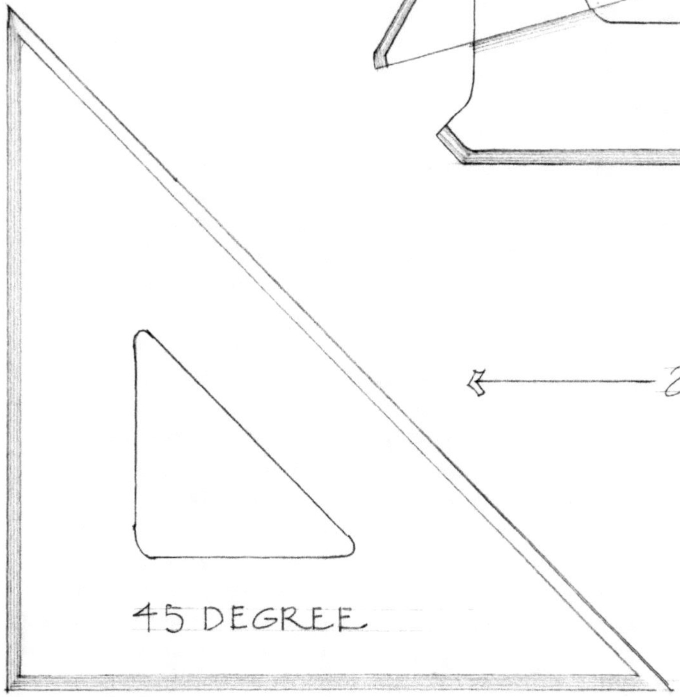

45 DEGREE

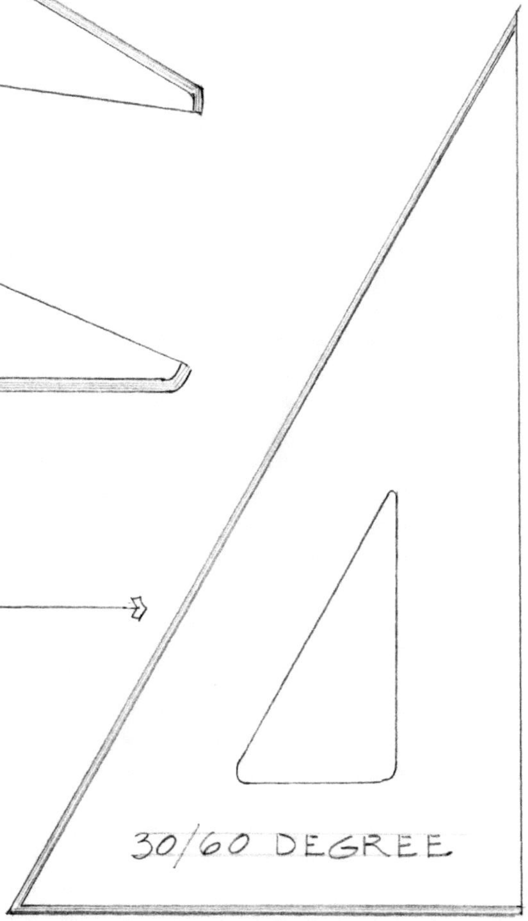

30/60 DEGREE

EQUIPMENT - THE BASICS

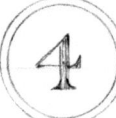

MECHANICAL PENCILS

STENCIL TEMPLATE[S]

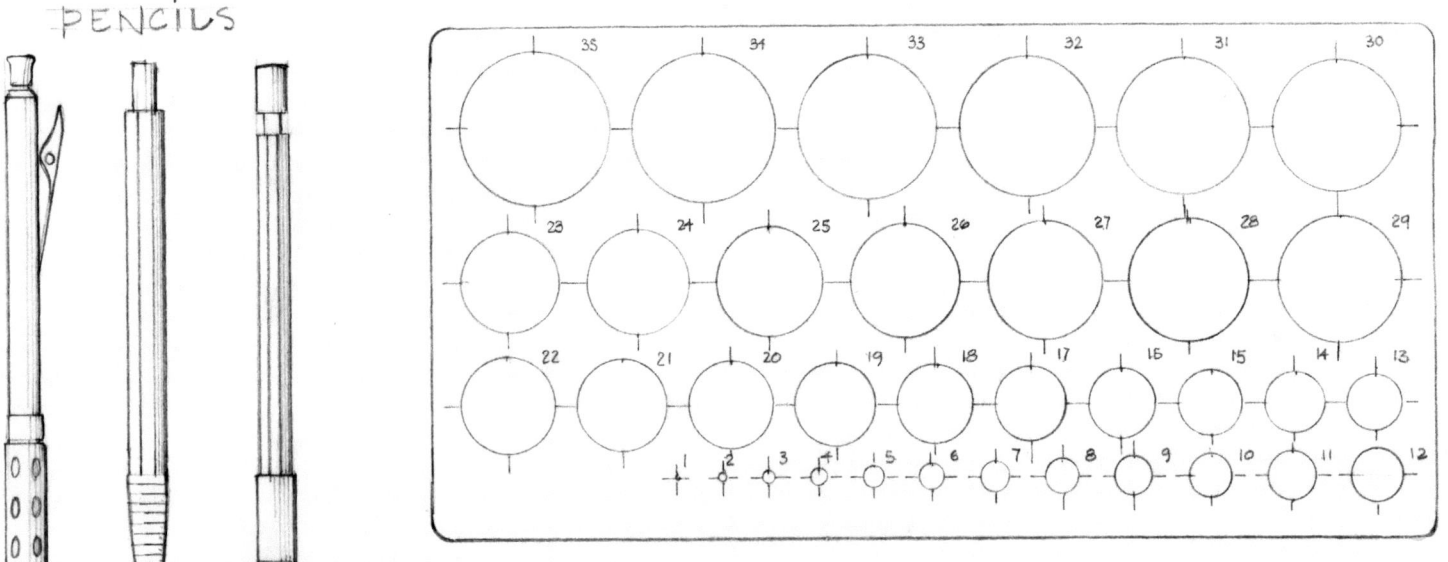

0.5 PENCIL FOR BASIC WORK
0.3 PENCIL FOR FINE DETAIL
0.9 PENCIL FOR OUTLINES ETC.

ERASER SHIELD

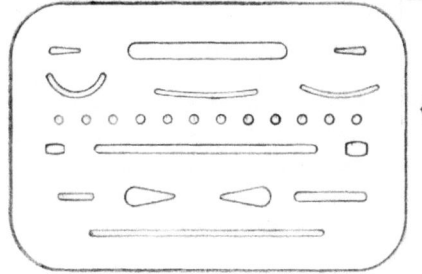

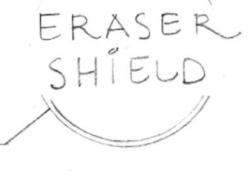

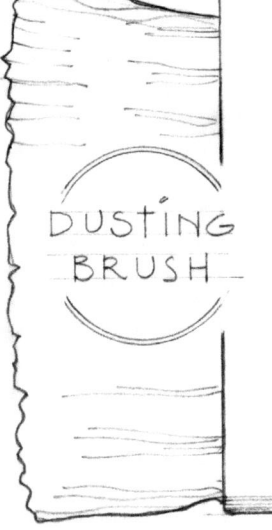

DUSTING BRUSH

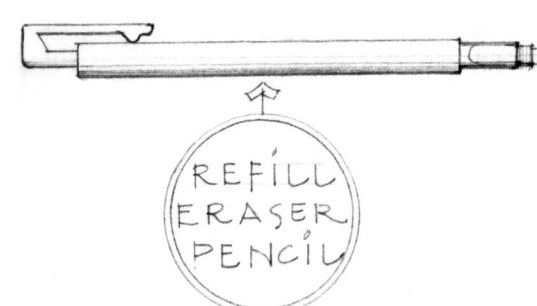

REFILL ERASER PENCIL

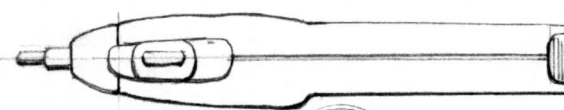

BATTERY POWERED ERASER.

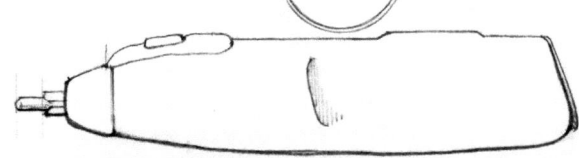

SCALE : IMPERIAL [U.S.]

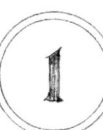

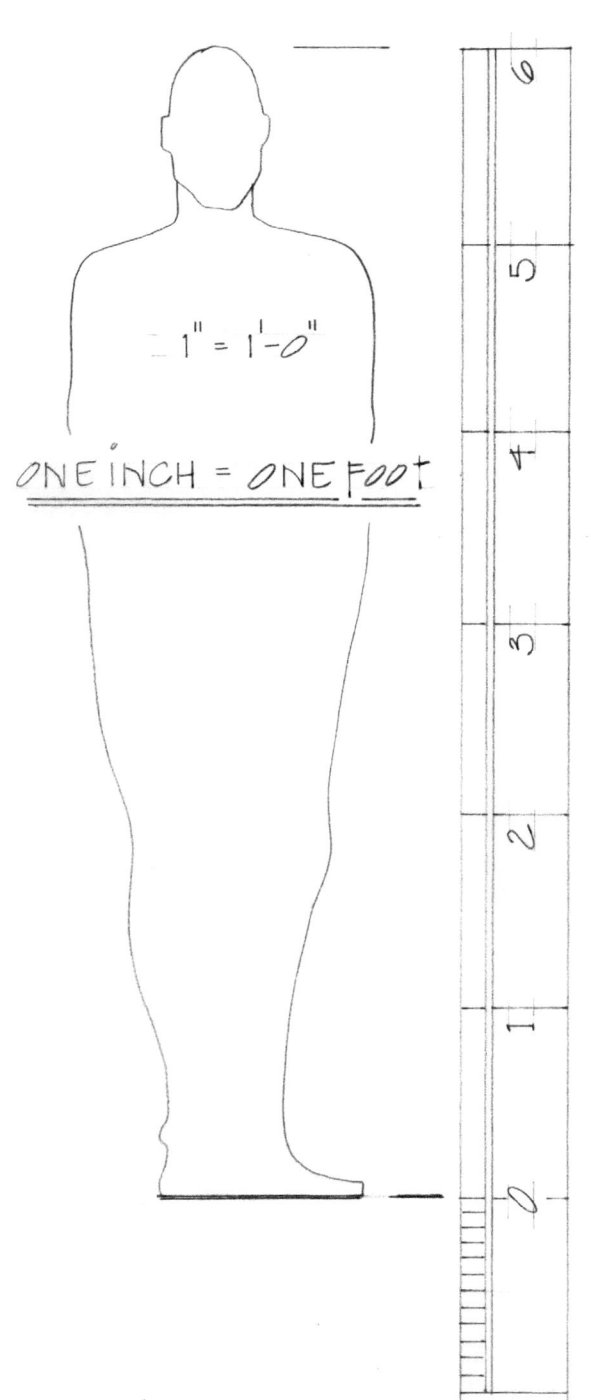

1" = 1'-0"

ONE INCH = ONE FOOT

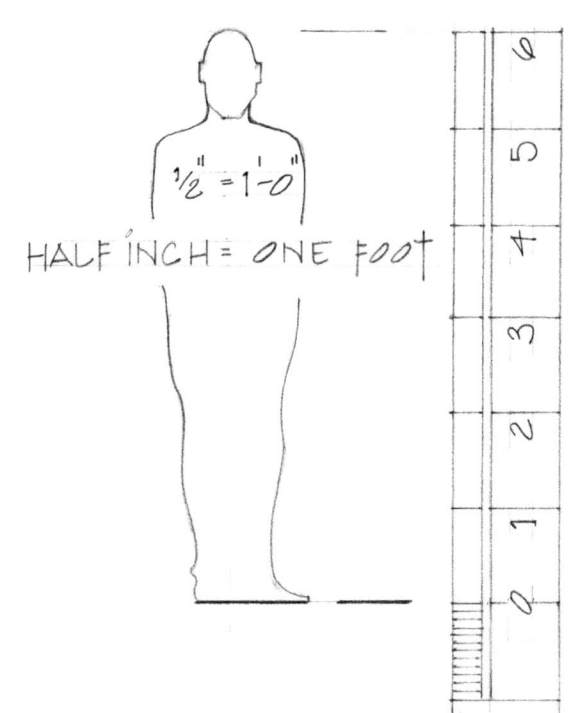

1/2" = 1'-0"

HALF INCH = ONE FOOT

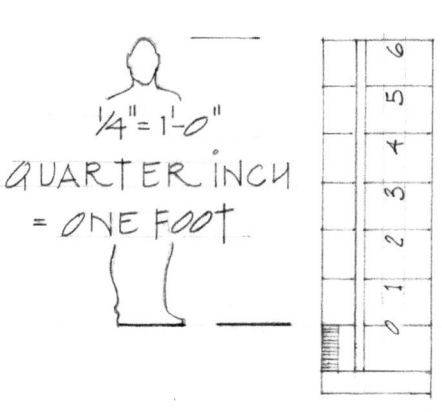

1/4" = 1'-0"

QUARTER INCH = ONE FOOT

SCALE : METRIC

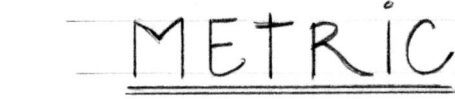

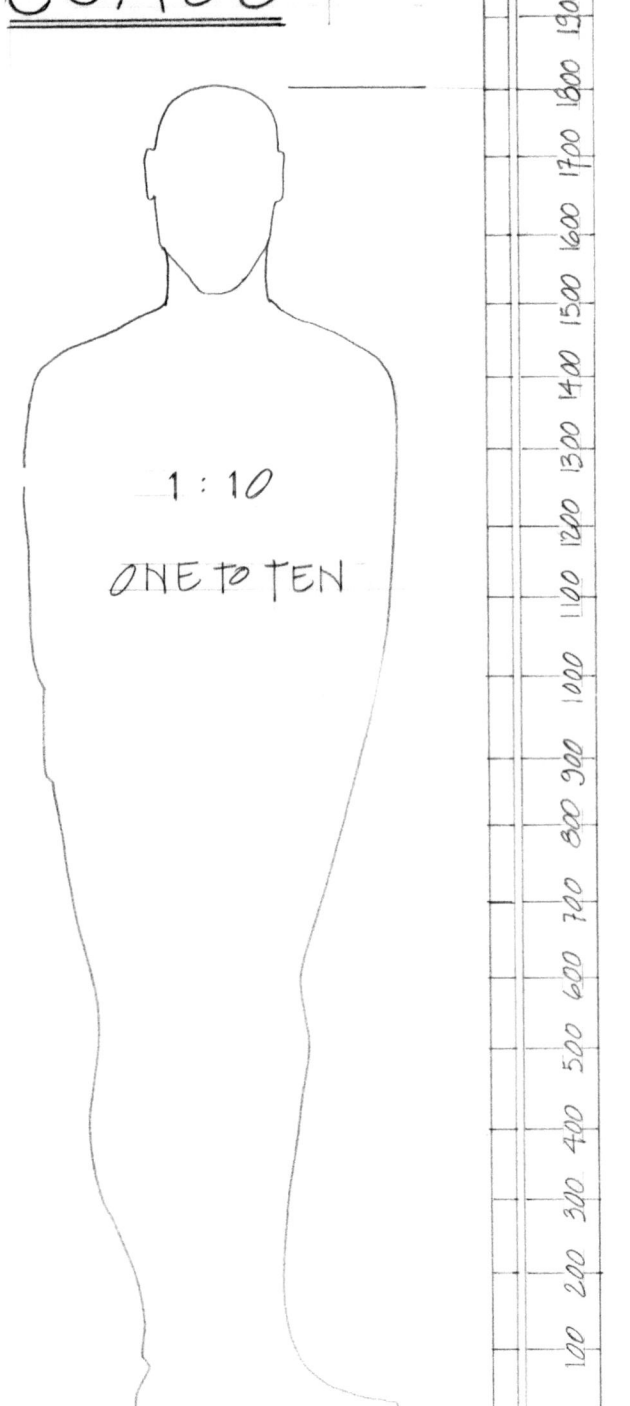

1 : 10
ONE TO TEN

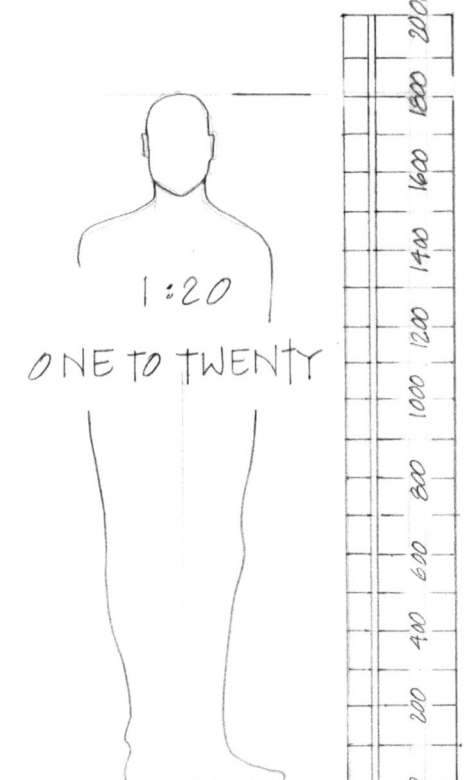

1 : 20
ONE TO TWENTY

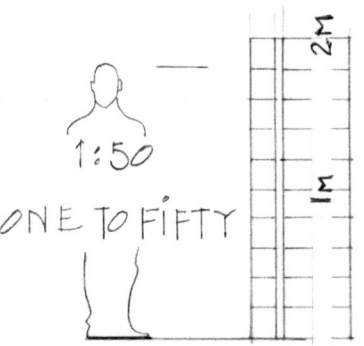

1 : 50
ONE TO FIFTY

THE PLAN

- THE PLAN IS LIKE A MAP — A BIRDS EYE VIEW
- "THE PLAN IS THE GENERATOR" — LE CORBUSIER
- THE PLAN IS THE FOOTPRINT WHERE THE SET MEETS THE STAGE FLOOR.

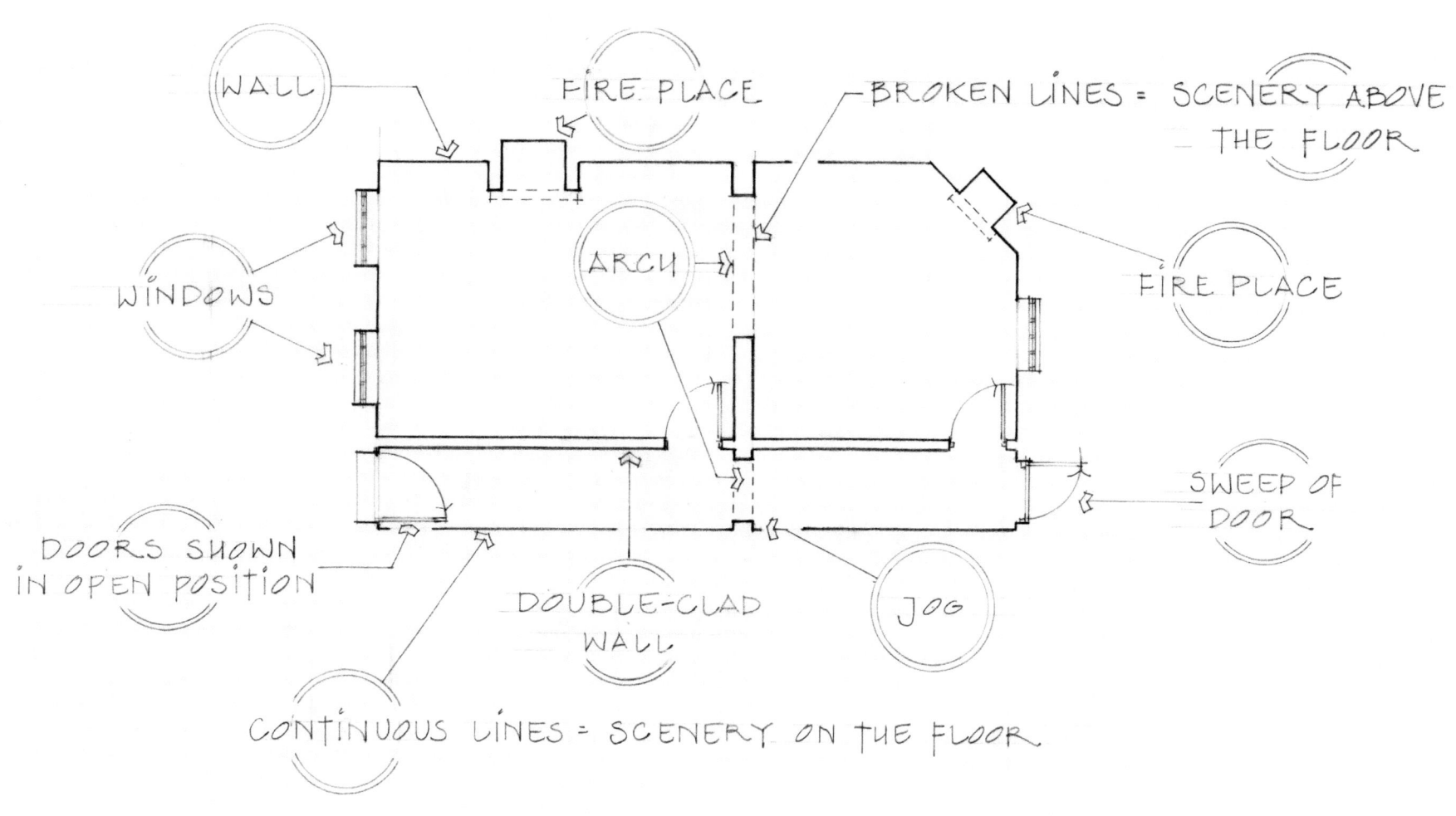

THE PLAN IS AN IMAGINARY HORIZONTAL SLICE THAT CUTS THE SET AT CONVENTIONALLY 1·0 METRE OR 3'-0" ABOVE THE FLOOR

THE PLAN — HATCHING: 3 TYPES

(2)

HATCHING INDICATES THE BACK [UNSEEN SIDE] OF THE SET/SCENERY

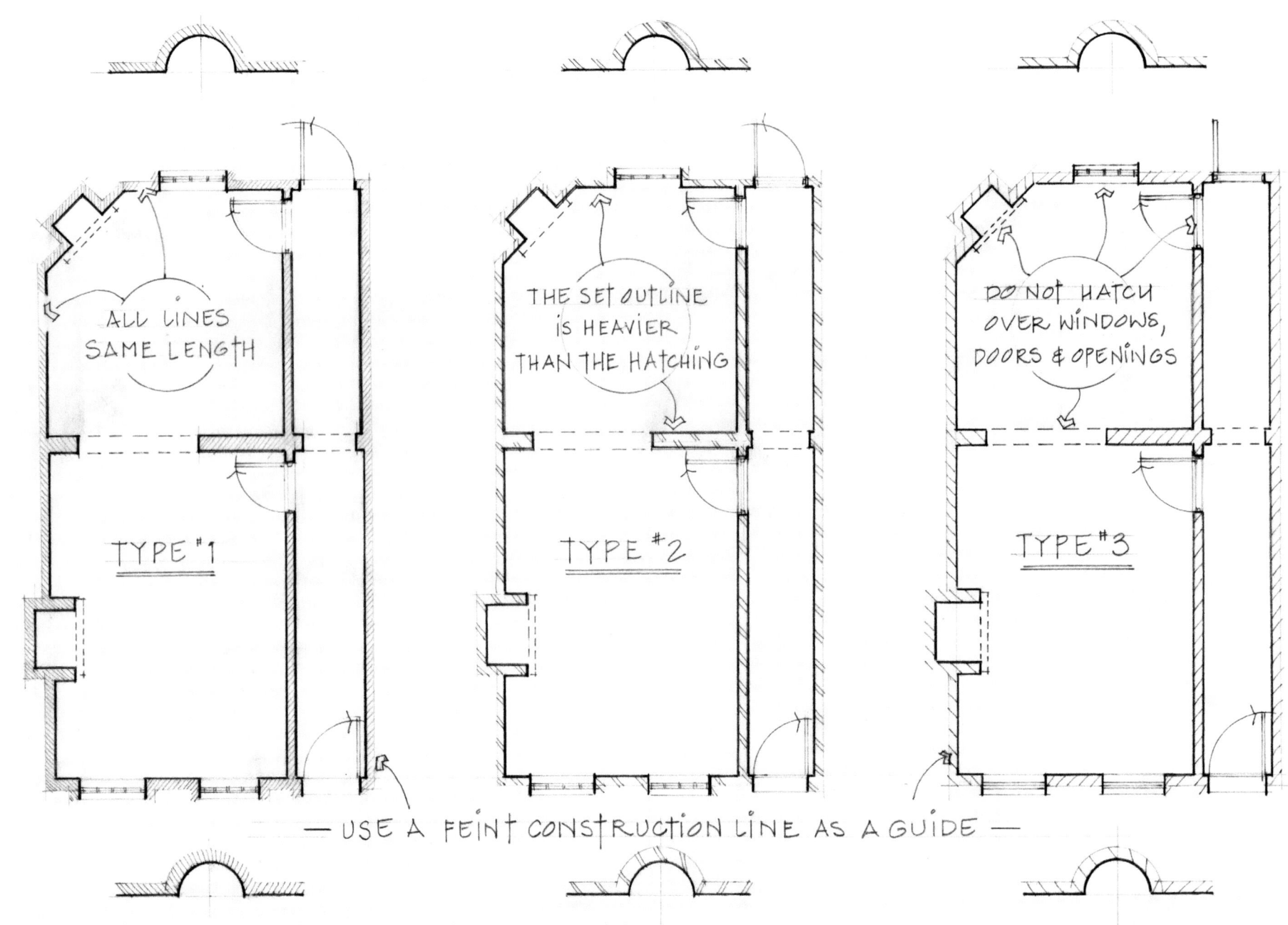

TYPE #1 — ALL LINES SAME LENGTH

TYPE #2 — THE SET OUTLINE IS HEAVIER THAN THE HATCHING

TYPE #3 — DO NOT HATCH OVER WINDOWS, DOORS & OPENINGS

— USE A FEINT CONSTRUCTION LINE AS A GUIDE —

THE PLAN   ③

- THE SAME PRINCIPLES APPLY WHEN DRAWING IN IMPERIAL [FEET & INCHES]

- REMEMBER TO KEEP ALL DIMENSIONS THE SAME SIZE

MEASUREMENTS SHOWN ON THIS PAGE ARE IN IMPERIAL [FEET & INCHES]

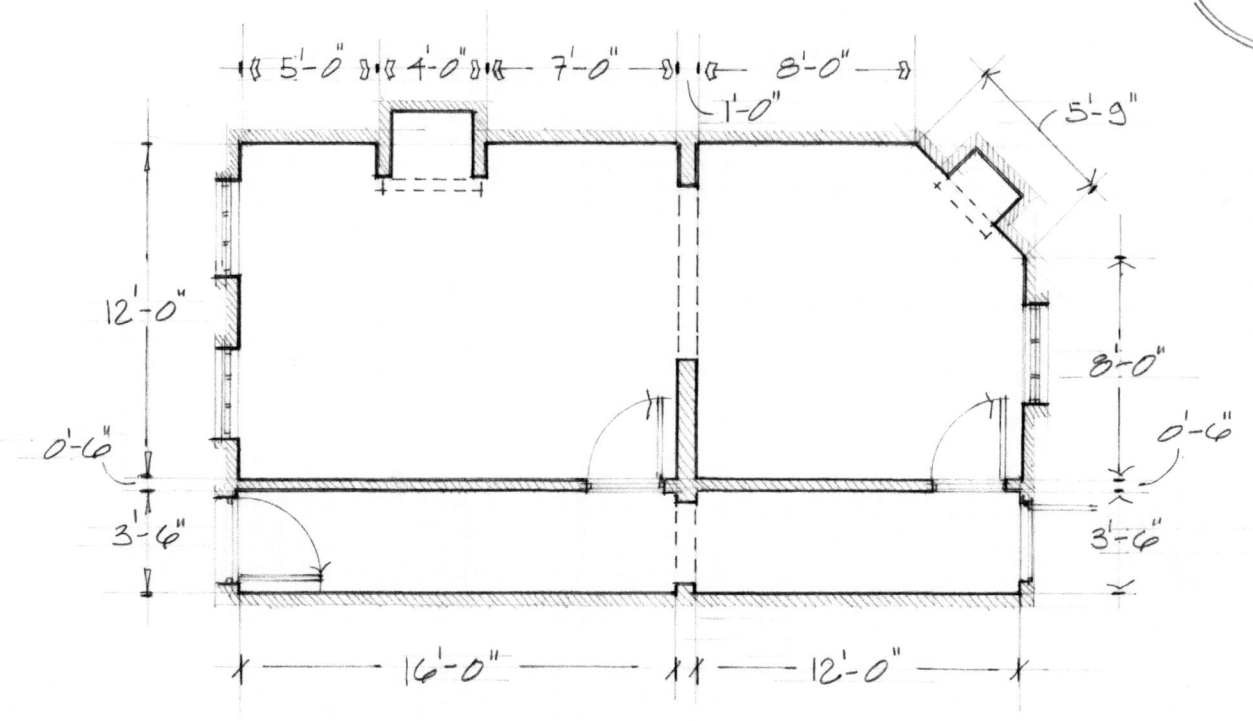

DIMENSION LINES VARY IN STYLE FOR ILLUSTRATION PURPOSES ONLY
! USE ONE TYPE ONLY !

THE PLAN: VERTICAL DIMENSION LINES

THERE ARE SEVERAL OPTIONS OF DIMENSION LINE STOPS.

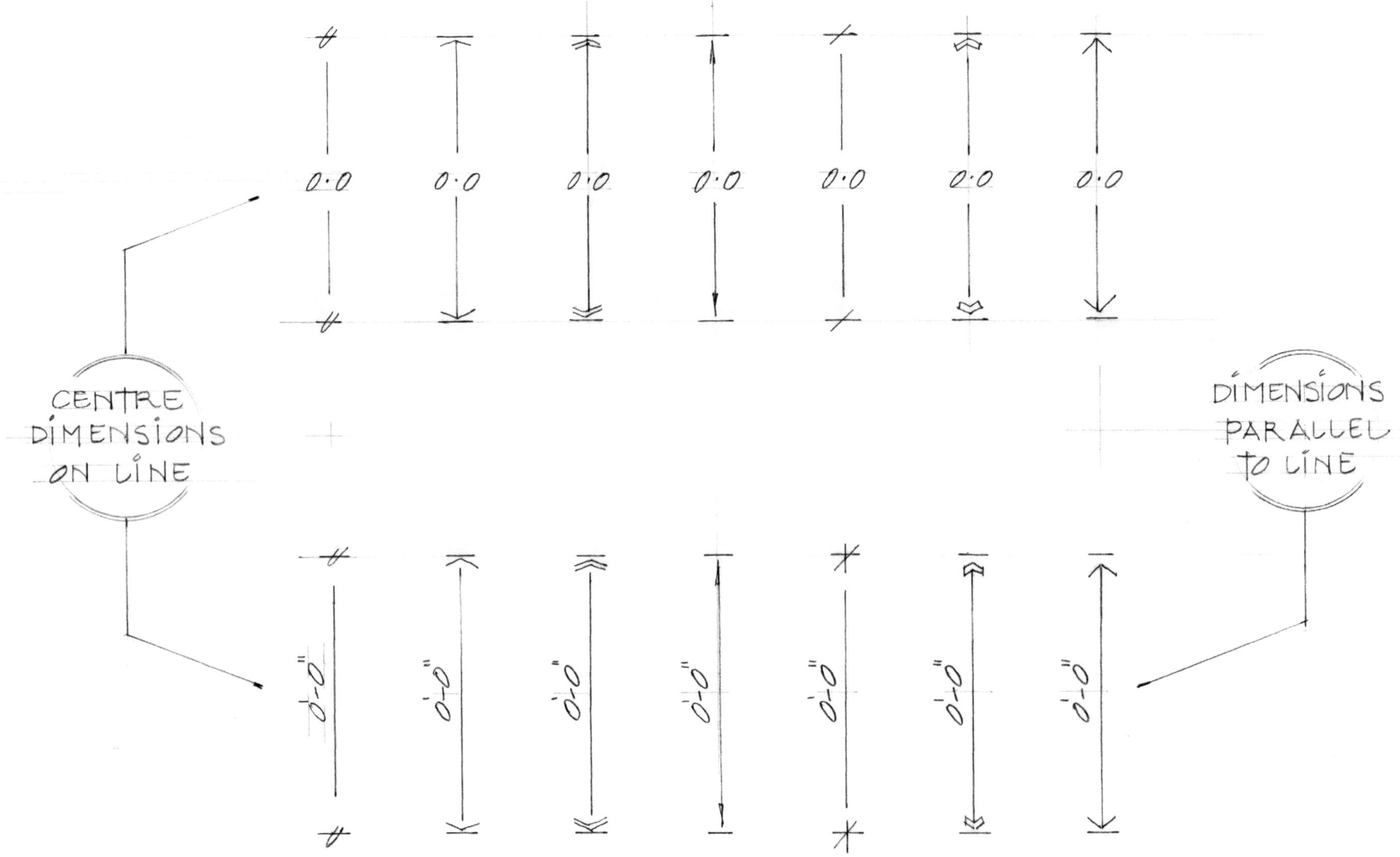

CENTRE DIMENSIONS ON LINE

DIMENSIONS PARALLEL TO LINE

NB! USE METRIC OR IMPERIAL FOR EITHER

THE PLAN : HORIZONTAL DIMENSION LINES

THERE ARE SEVERAL OPTIONS OF DIMENSION LINE STOPS

DIMENSIONS IN THE MIDDLE	DIMENSIONS ON TOP
✳——— 0.0 ———✳	✳——— 0'-0" ———✳
⫸——— 0.0 ———⫷	⫸——— 0'-0" ———⫷
✕——— 0.0 ———✕	✕——— 0'-0" ———✕
⟵——— 0.0 ———⟶	⟵——— 0'-0" ———⟶
⟨——— 0.0 ———⟩	⟨——— 0'-0" ———⟩
⟪——— 0.0 ———⟫	⟪——— 0'-0" ———⟫
⟵——— 0.0 ———⟶	⟵——— 0'-0" ———⟶

NB! USE METRIC OR IMPERIAL FOR EITHER

THE PLAN: SECTION LINE INDICATORS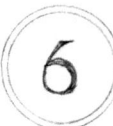

— 5 EXAMPLES OF THE MOST COMMONLY USED TYPES —

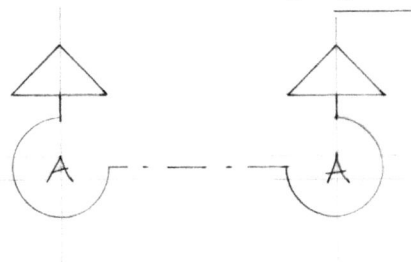 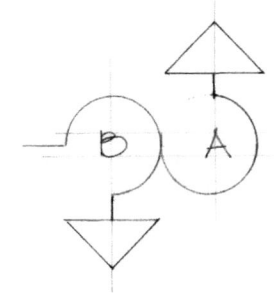 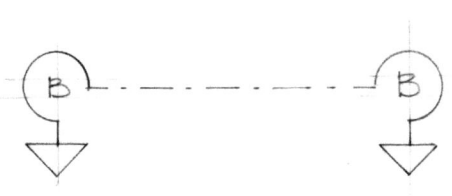 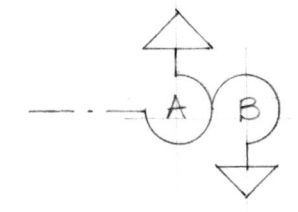

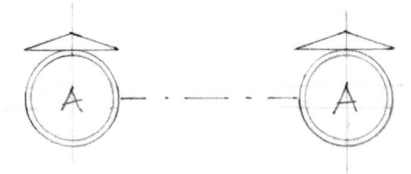 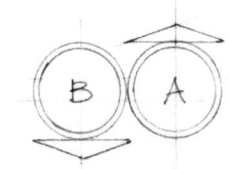  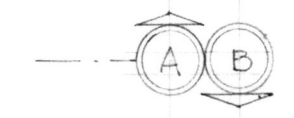

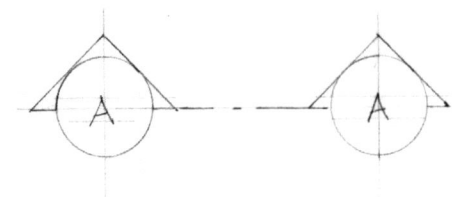 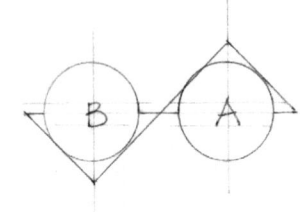  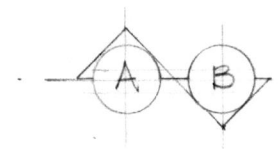

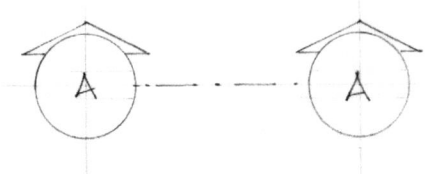 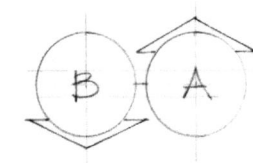 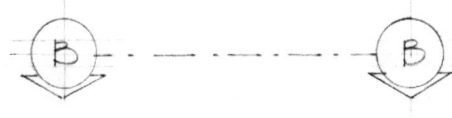 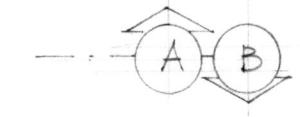

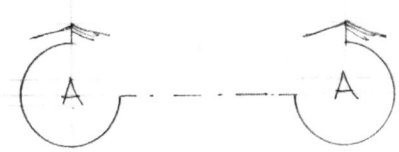 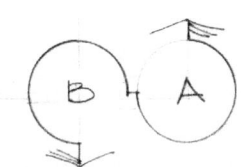 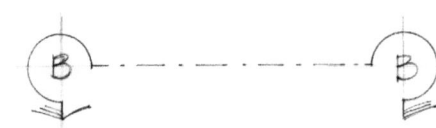 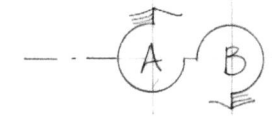

THE PLAN

- DIMENSION LINES PLACED ON OUTSIDE OF SET.
- KEEP SAME DISTANCE AWAY FROM SET LINES

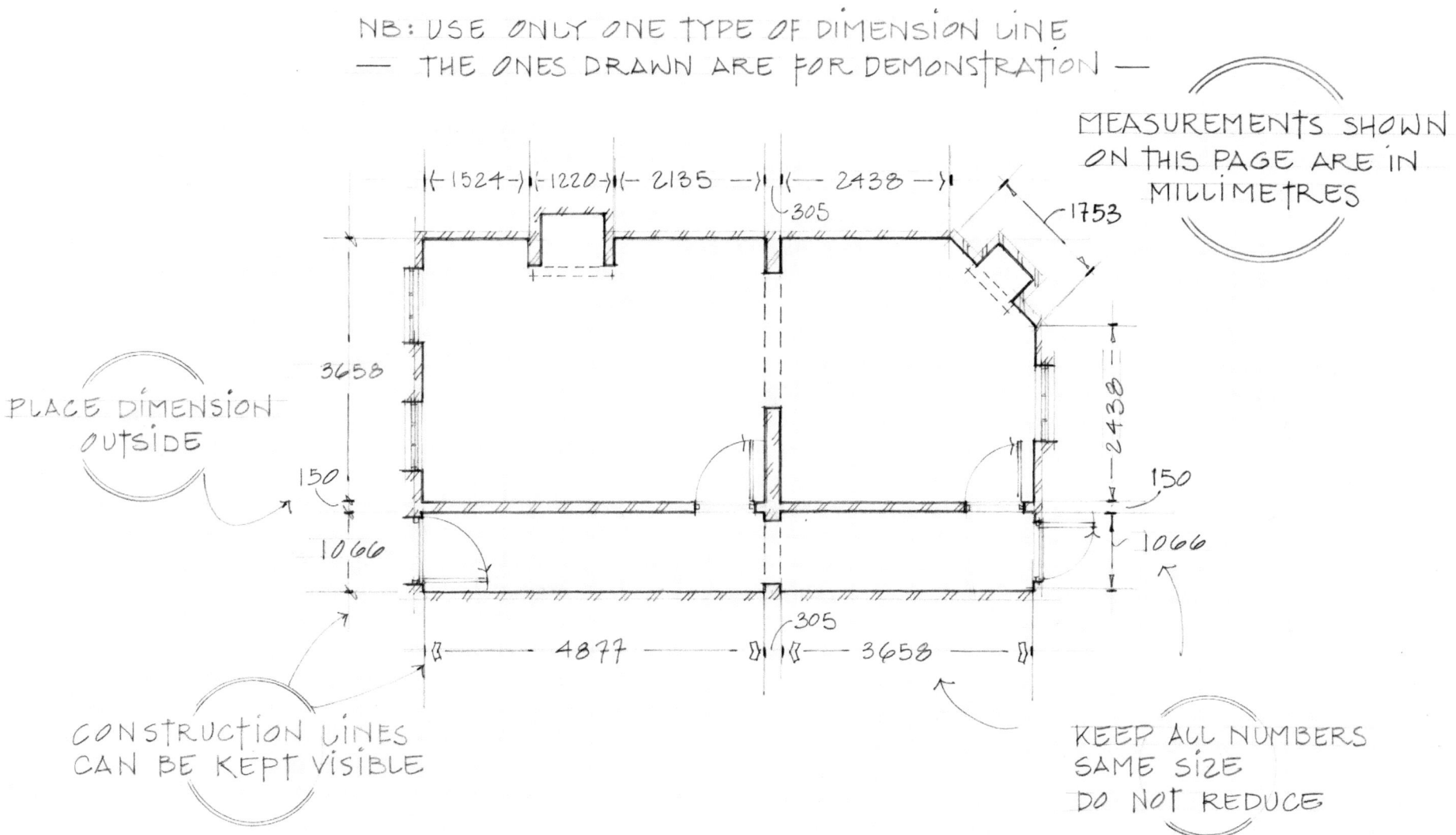

— DO NOT TRY & PUT ALL DIMENSIONS ON THE PLAN —
THEY WILL BE ON THE ELEVATIONS & SECTIONS

THE PLAN : SECTIONS

A SECTION IS A CUT MADE THROUGH THE SET WALLS & OPENINGS

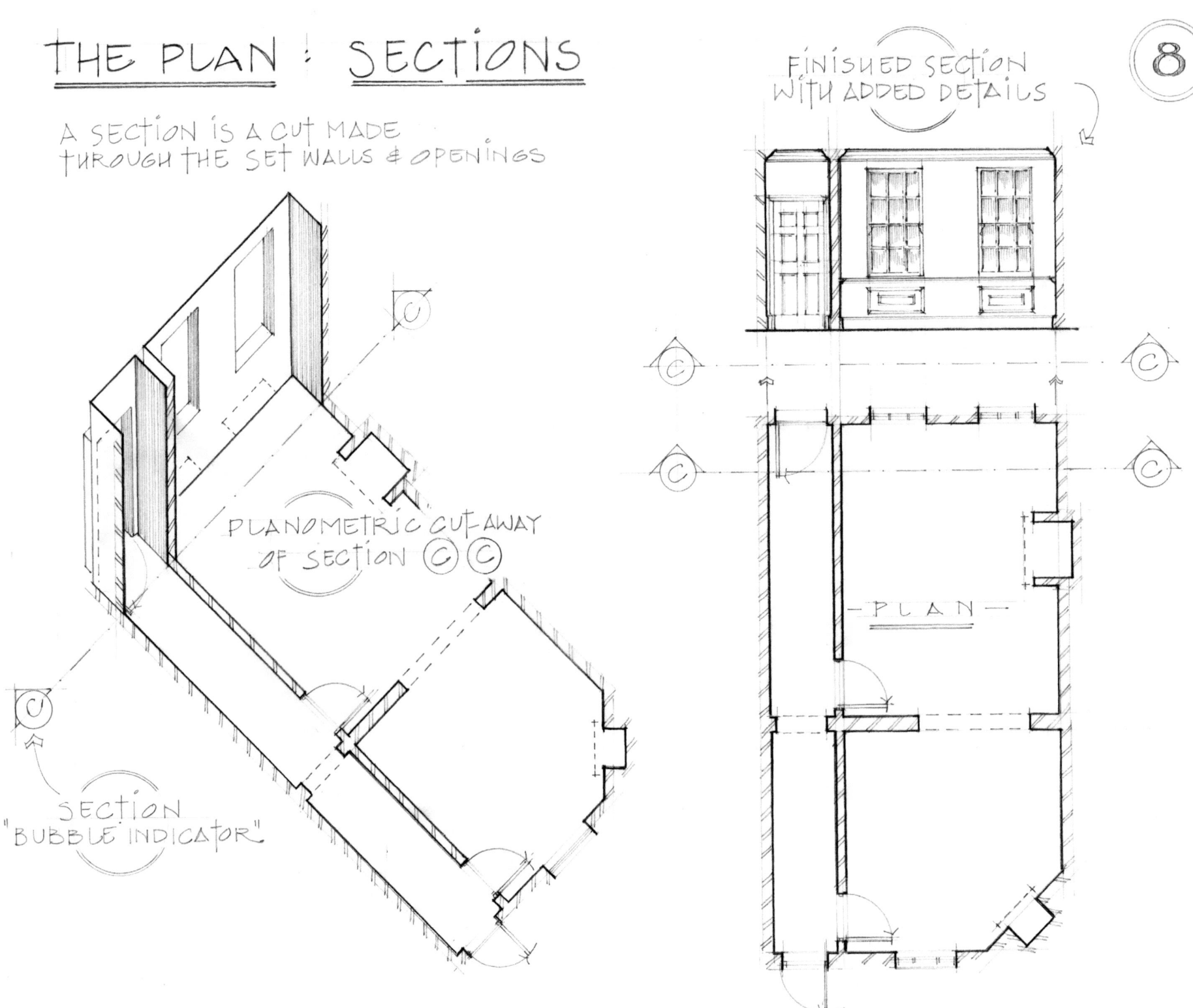

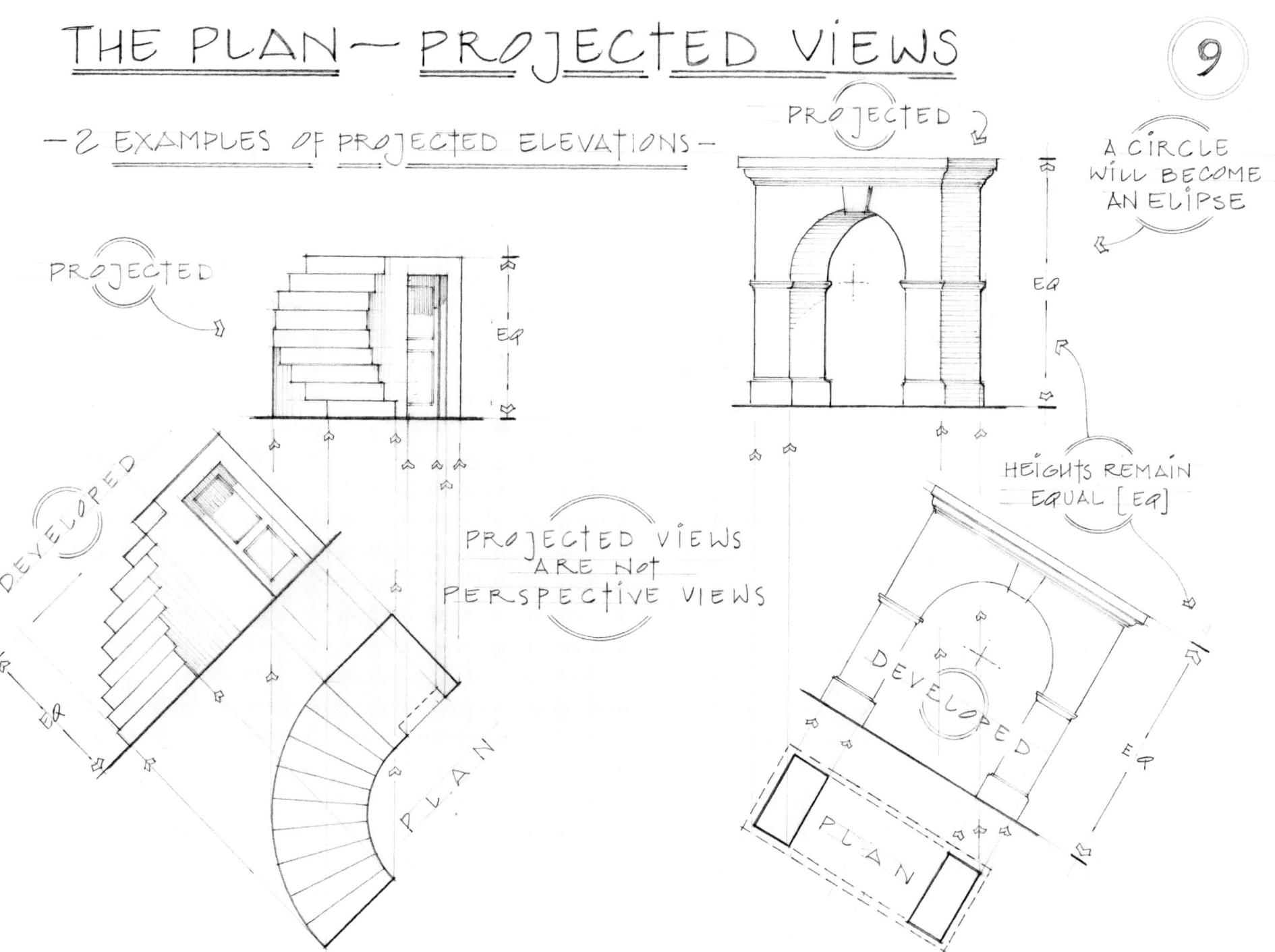

THE PLAN: SECTION LINES

CUTTING PLANES THROUGH THE SET

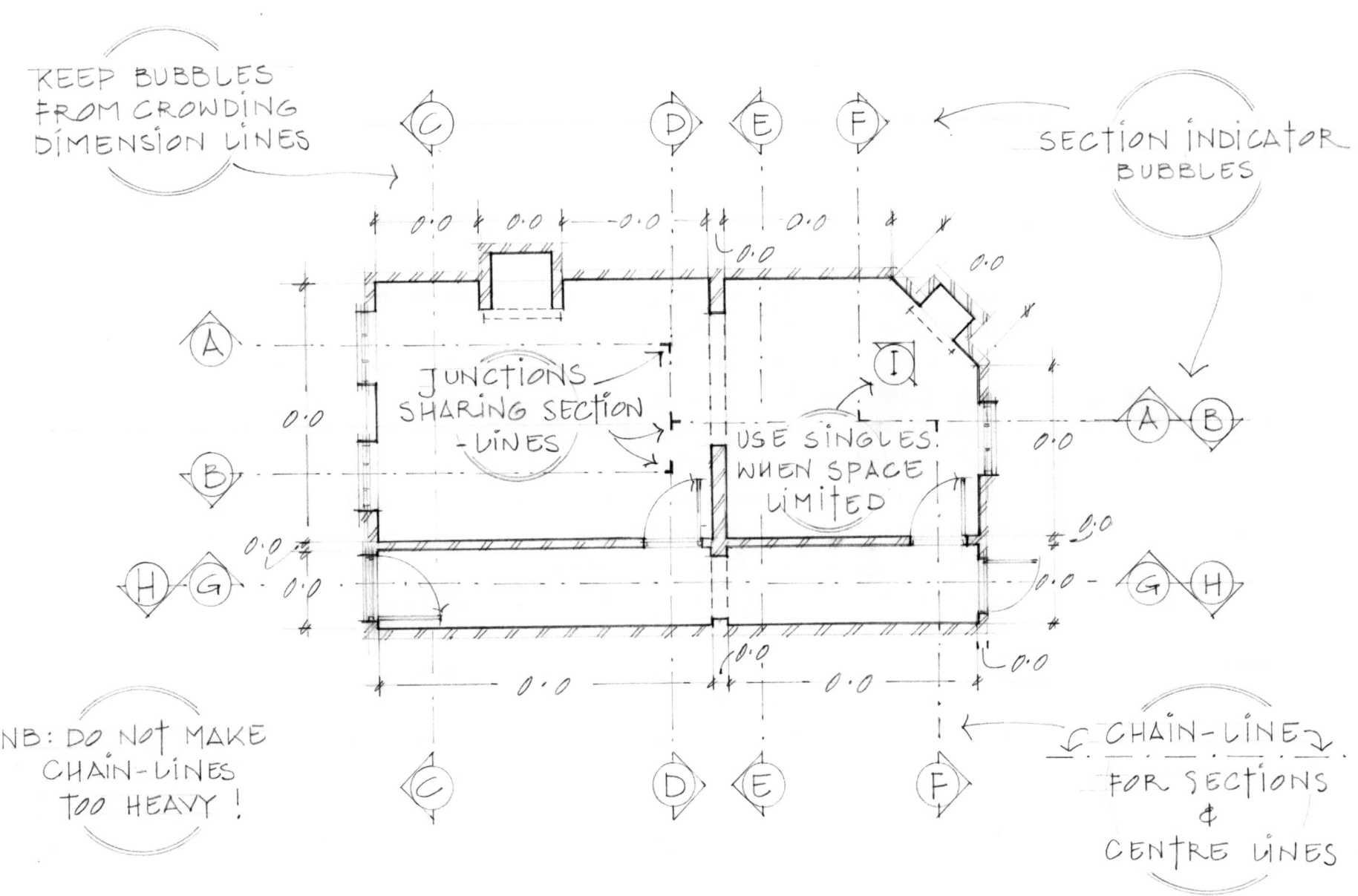

THE PLAN — PROJECTED SECTIONS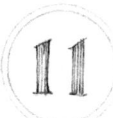

THE PROJECTED VIEW IS AN OBLIQUE ELEVATION i.e. IT IS CONDENSED IN ITS WIDTH BUT NOT ITS HEIGHT

ONLY USE VERTICAL DIMENSIONS FOR MEASUREMENTS

THIS IS <u>NOT</u> PERSPECTIVE

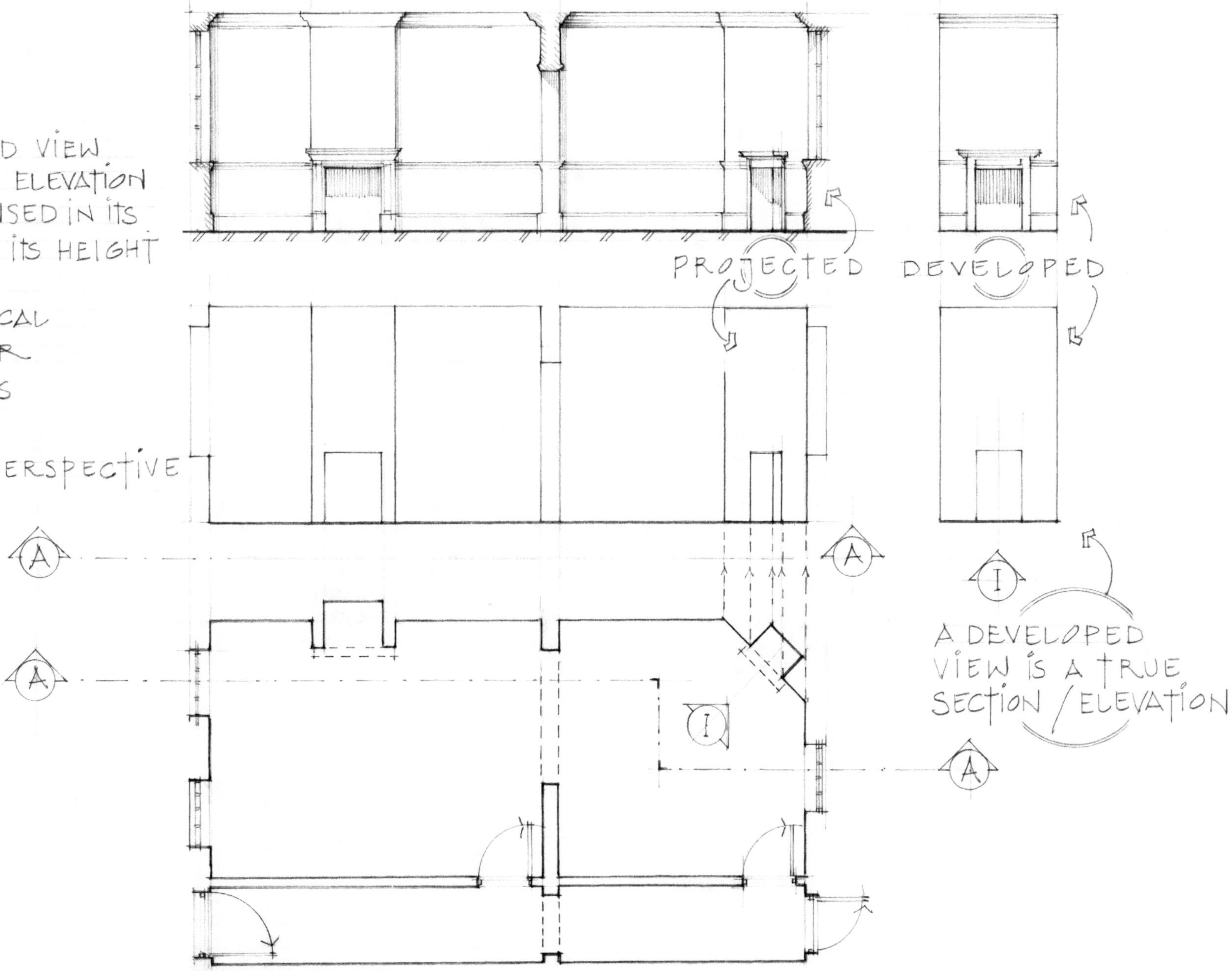

PROJECTED   DEVELOPED

A DEVELOPED VIEW IS A TRUE SECTION / ELEVATION

THE PLAN: COMPLETED

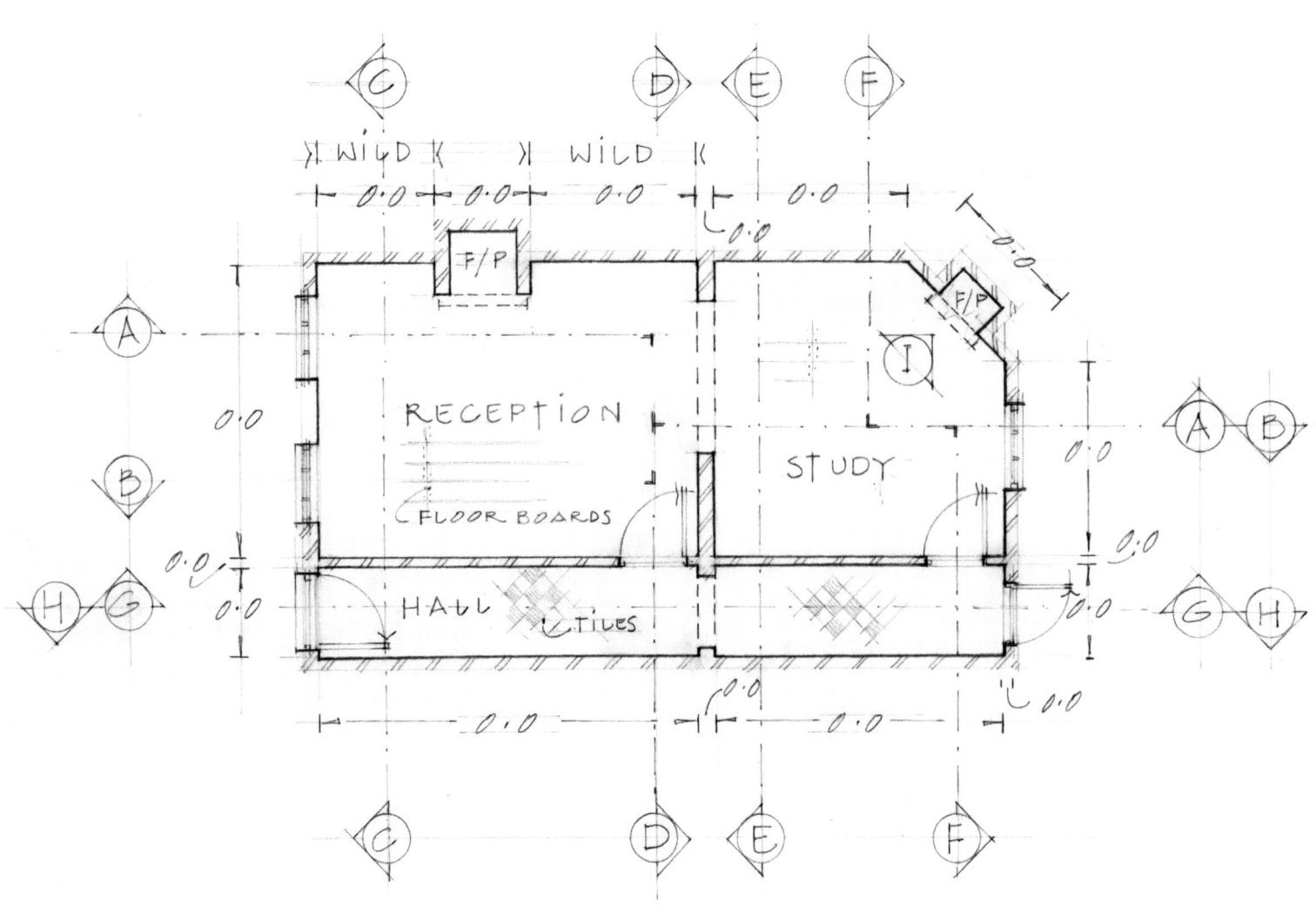

WILD [U.S.] = FLOAT
F/P = FIRE PLACE

REFLECTED CEILING PLAN

THE SET FLOOR BECOMES A MIRROR

SHOWS THE CEILING IN SAME ORIENTATION AS THE FLOOR PLAN

THE CEILING IS REFLECTED IN THE FLOOR PLAN

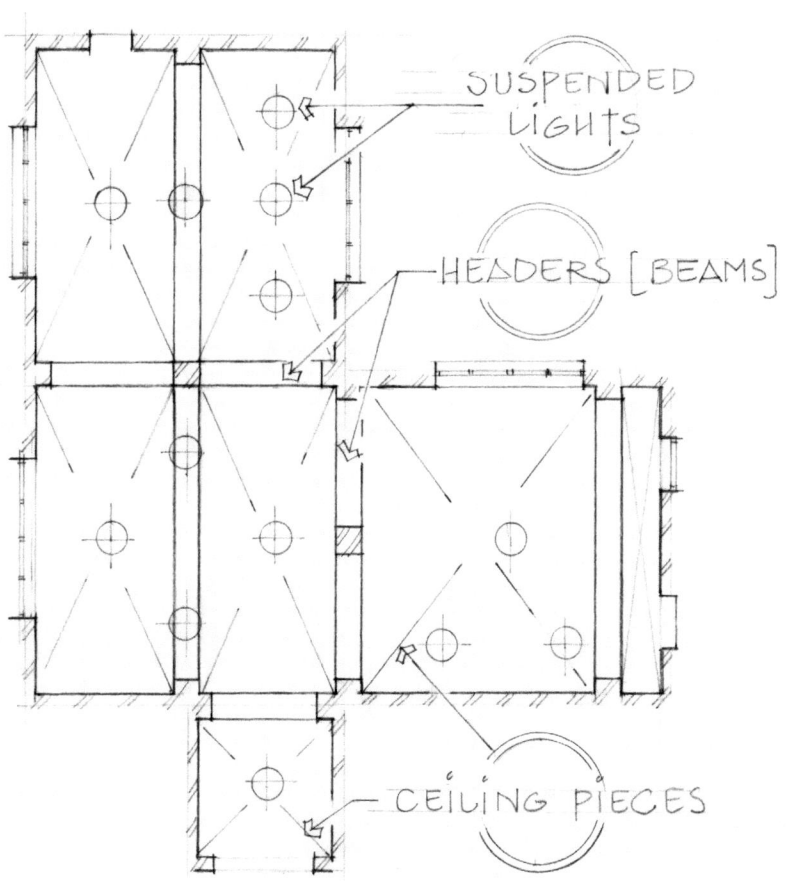

EASIER TO READ THE OVERHEAD OPENINGS, FIXTURES, BEAMS ETC. THEY CAN BE DIRECTLY LINED UP WITH THE SET DRESSING BELOW.

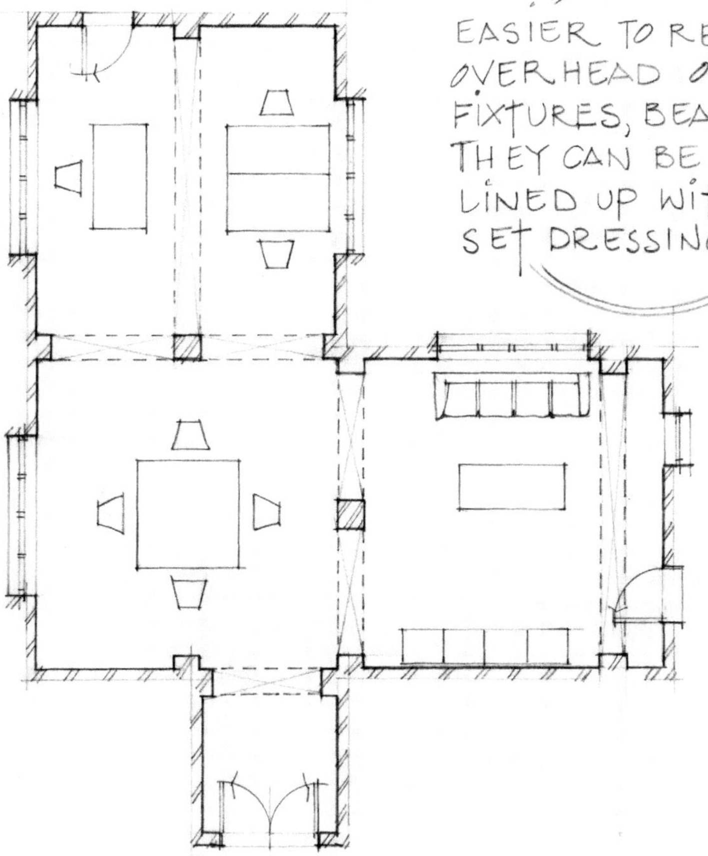

FLOOR PLAN WITH DRESSING

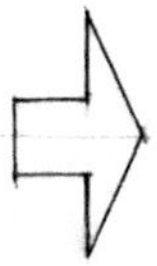

REFLECTED PLAN SHOWING LIGHT FITTINGS IN CEILING & HEADERS [BEAMS]

LAYING OUT THE PAGE ①

PARALLEL LINES FOR TITLE & SCALE INFO.

MASKING TAPE ON CORNERS ONLY!

— SELECT A PAPER SIZE THAT SUITS THE DRAWING —

BE AWARE THAT U.S. STANDARD PAPER SIZES
DIFFER FROM
INTERNATIONAL 'A' SIZES

EDGE OF PAPER

LAYING OUT THE PAGE

DRAW EACH SECTION BY ROTATING THE PLAN HORIZONTALLY AND PROJECT THE LINES UPWARDS

HEIGHTS OF WINDOWS & DOORS ETC. ARE DECIDED BEFOREHAND.

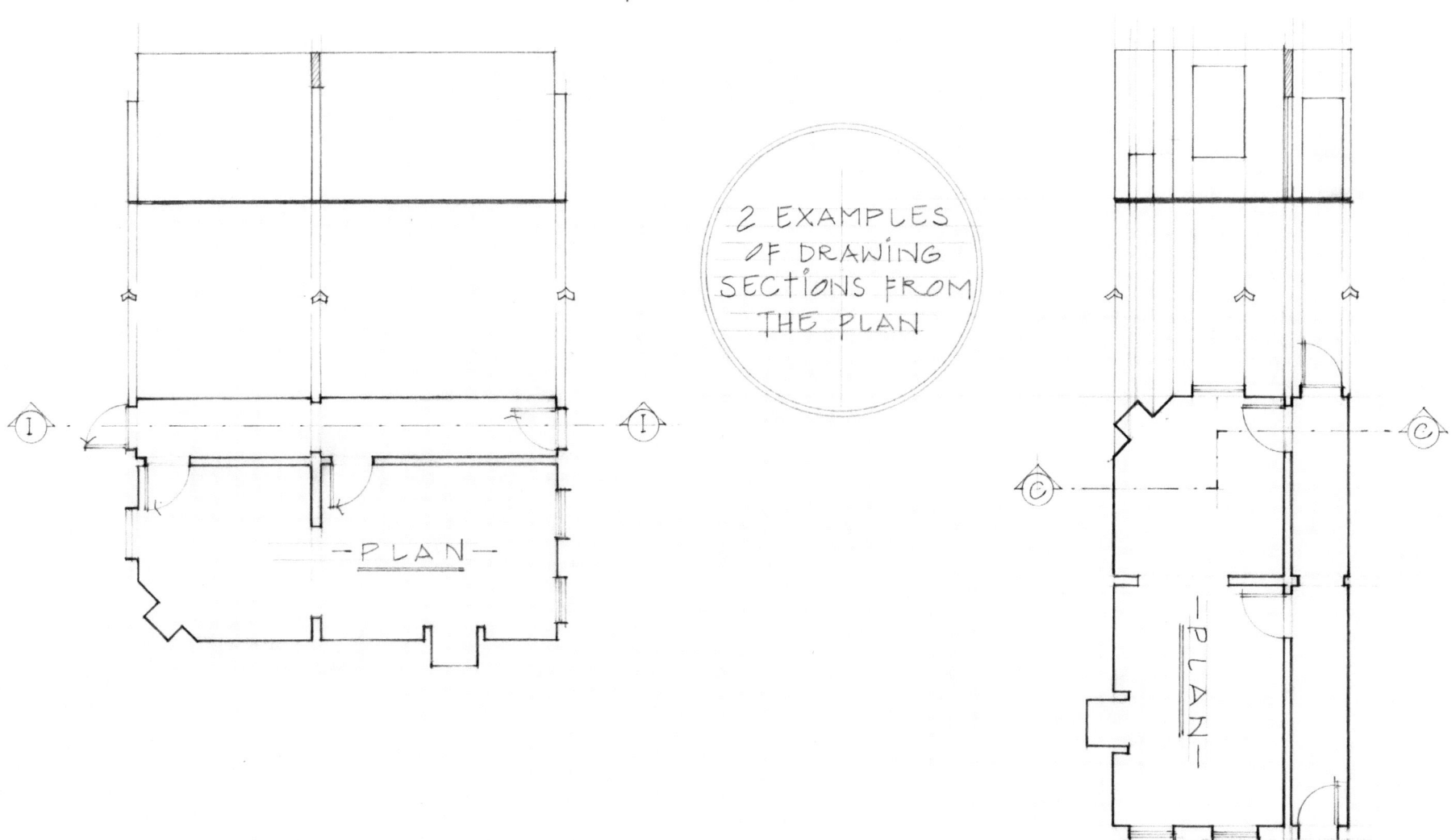

2 EXAMPLES OF DRAWING SECTIONS FROM THE PLAN

LAYING OUT THE PAGE

ARRANGE ALL ELEMENTS INDIVIDUALLY UNTIL SATISFIED WITH LAYOUT. MAKE SPACE FOR DIMENSIONS & LABELLING

③

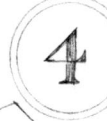

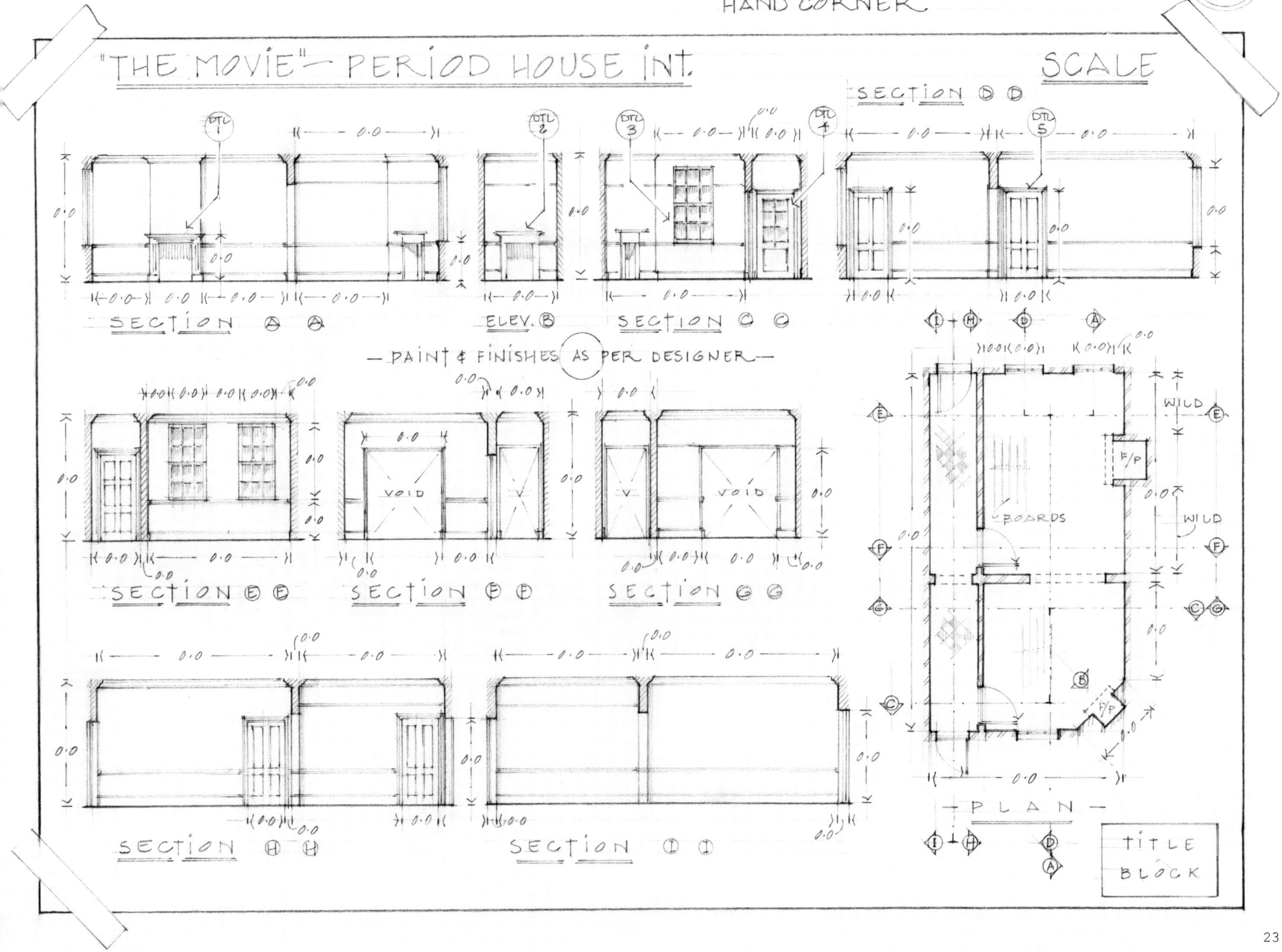

LETTERING & LABELLING

ABCDEFGHIJKLMNOPQRSTUVWXYZ

THE ALPHABET FROM TRAJANS COLUMN IN ROME 114 A.D.

GUIDE LINES WILL HELP

UPRIGHT OR SLOPING — UPRIGHT OR SLOPING
IT IS YOUR CHOICE   IT IS YOUR CHOICE
UPPERCASE ONLY [CAPITALS]   UPPERCASE ONLY [CAPITALS]

GOOD DRAUGHTSMANSHIP IS EASILY RUINED BY BAD LETTERING
GOOD DRAUGHTSMANSHIP IS EASILY RUINED BY BAD LETTERING

MAINTAIN THE SAME HEIGHT THROUGHOUT
MAINTAIN THE SAME HEIGHT THROUGHOUT

SIZE MATTERS   SIZE MATTERS
TOO SMALL IS ILLEGIBLE   TOO SMALL IS ILLEGIBLE

THE QUICK BROWN FOX JUMPS OVER THE LAZY DOG

LETTERING & LABELLING

TRY THREE LINES — UPPER THIRDS
OR LOWER THIRDS :—
ABCDEFGHIJKLMNOPQRSTUVWXYZ
1234567890
ABCDEFGHIJKLMNOPQRSTUVWXYZ
1234567890

NUMERALS ARE AS IMPORTANT AS LETTERING
NUMERALS ARE AS IMPORTANT AS LETTERING
1 2 3 4 5 6 7 8 9 0
1 2 3 4 5 6 7 8 9 0

! LEGIBILITY — CLARITY — PRACTICE !

THE TITLE BLOCK

ENLARGED FOR CLARITY

— PRODUCTION TITLE & LOGO —		
DIRECTOR:	LOC/STAGE:	DATE DRAWN:
PRODUCTION DESIGNER:	SCALE:	DATE ISSUED:
DRAWING BY:	ART. DEPT. APPROVAL:	RE-ISSUED:
SET:	NOTE:	DRAWING NO.
DRAWING TITLE:	SET NO.	

DISTRIBUTION:

DIRECTOR ☐	PROD DESIGNER ☐	LOCATIONS ☐	CONSTR MANAGER ☐
PRODUCER ☐	ART DIRECTOR ☐	D.O.P. ☐	CARPENTERS ☐
PRODUCTION ☐	ART DEPT ☐	GAFFER ☐	PLASTERERS ☐
1ST AD ☐	SET DEC ☐	SFX SUPERVISOR ☐	METAL ☐
UPM ☐	PROP MASTER ☐	VFX SUPERVISOR ☐	PAINTERS ☐
2ND UNIT ☐	GREENS ☐	STUNT CO-ORDINATOR ☐	RIGGERS ☐
	PROP MAKER ☐		SUB-CONTRACTORS ☐

EVERY DRAWING MUST HAVE A TITLE BLOCK, SIZED TO SUIT THE PAPER USED.

PRINT ONTO ADHESIVE BACKED PAPER

POSITION TITLE BLOCK IN BOTTOM RIGHT-HAND CORNER OF DRAWING

PAPER SIZES

— COMPARITIVE PROPORTIONS —

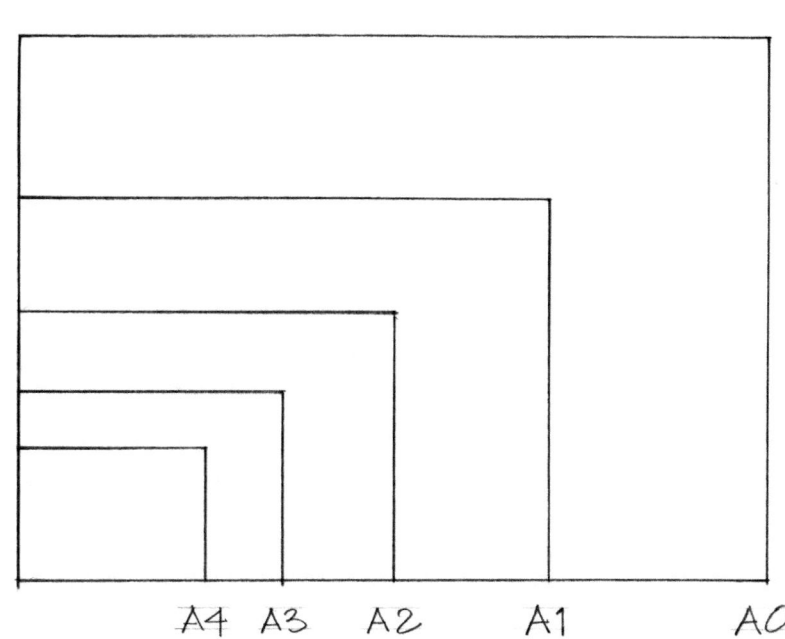

A4 A3 A2   A1   A0

INTERNATIONAL 'A' SERIES

```
A0: 841 × 1189
A1: 594 ×  841
A2: 420 ×  594
A3: 297 ×  420
A4: 210 ×  297
```

[MILLIMETRES]

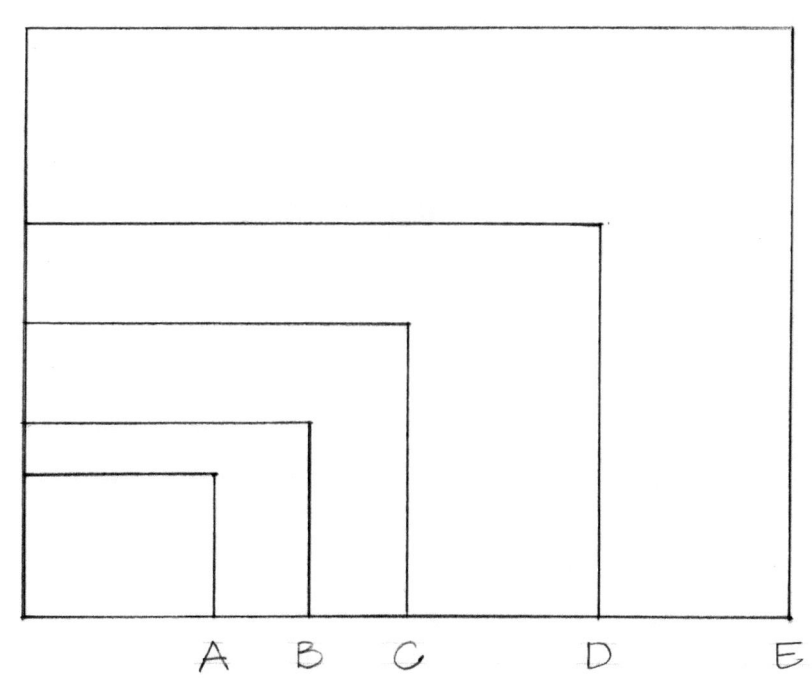

A   B   C   D   E

U.S. ARCHITECTURAL SERIES

```
A:  9 × 12
B: 12 × 18
C: 18 × 24
D: 24 × 36
E: 36 × 48
```

[INCHES]

FOLDING DRAWINGS [U.S. ARCHITECTURAL]

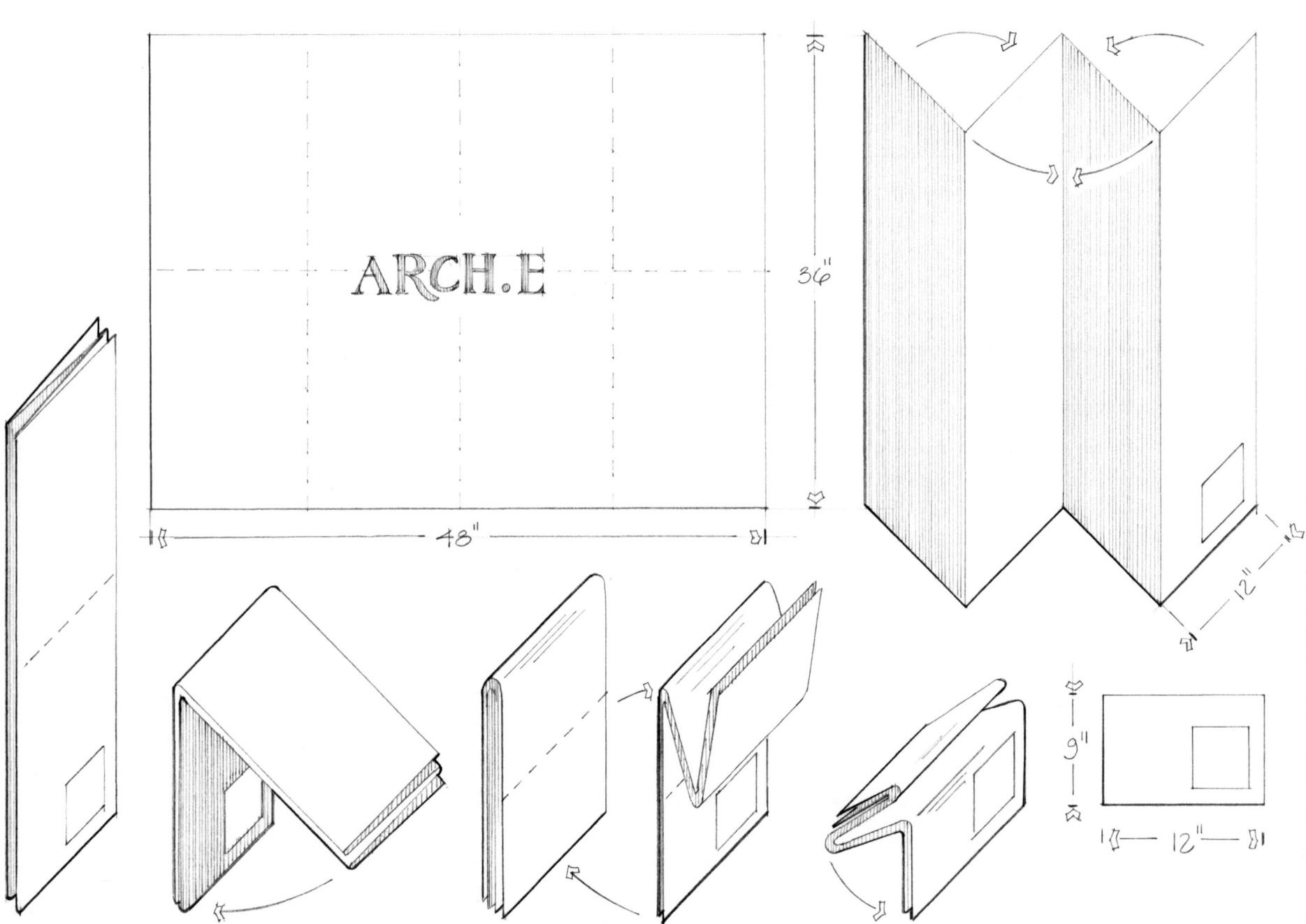

FOLDING DRAWINGS [U.S. ARCHITECTURAL]

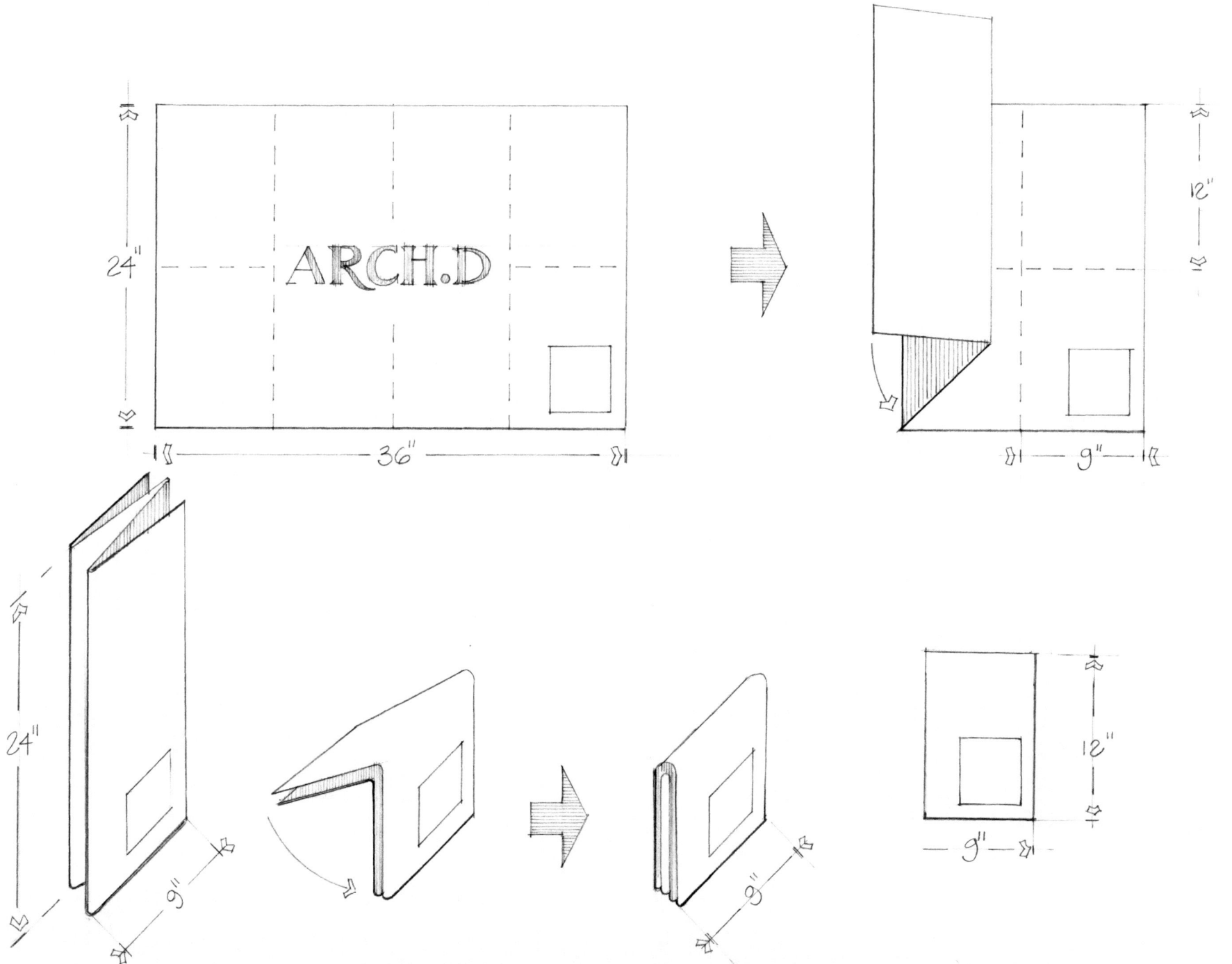

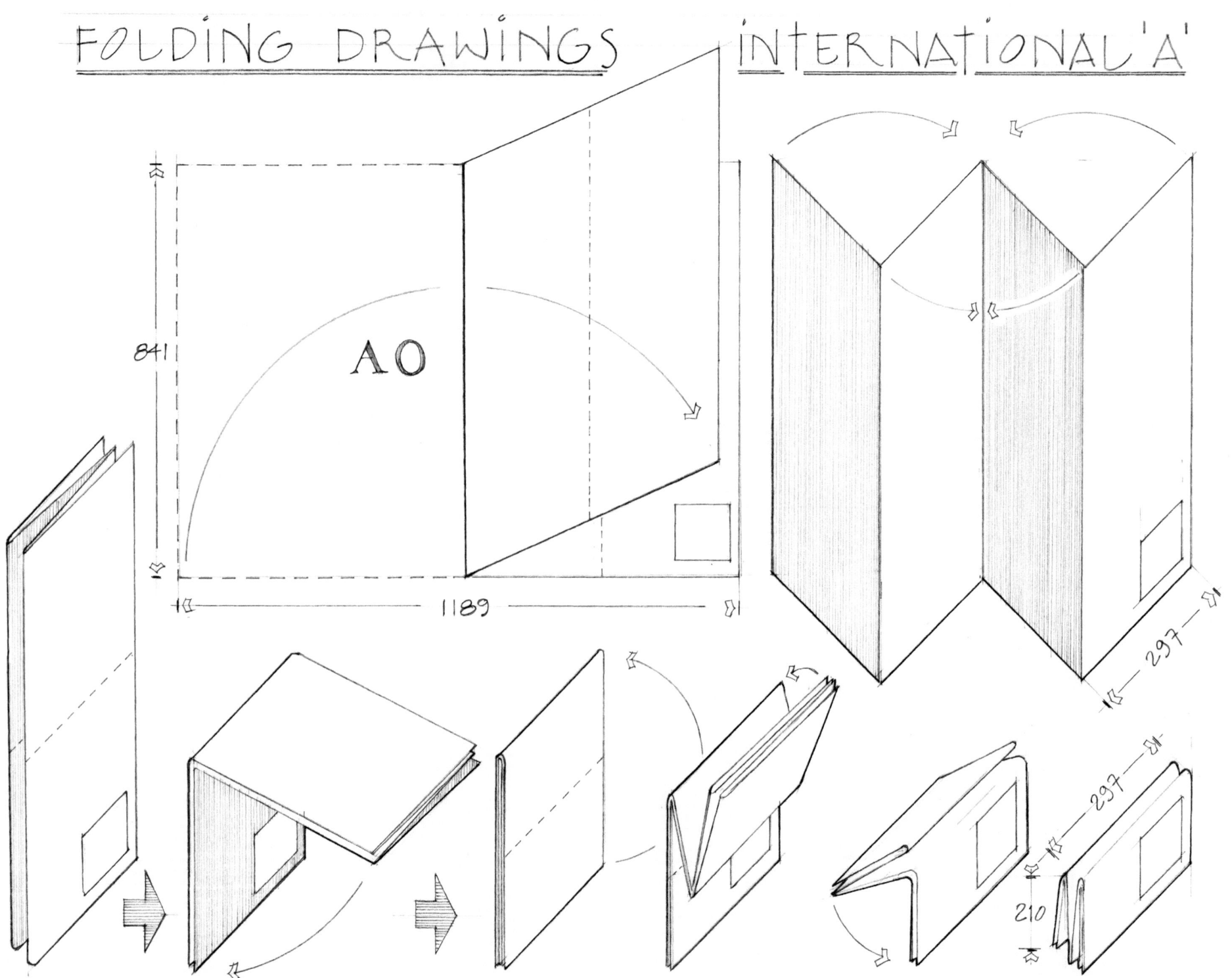

FOLDING DRAWINGS — INTERNATIONAL 'A'

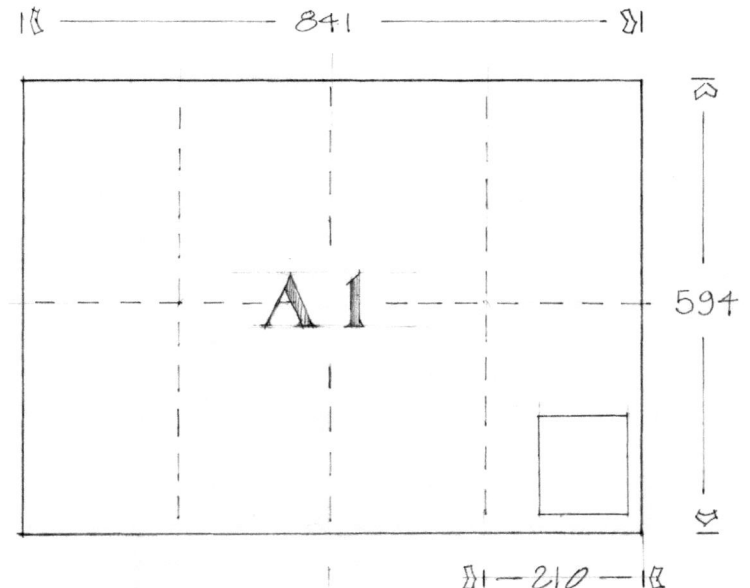

This example is for 'A1' size papers folded to 'A4' size

Drawings must be folded to the same size for filing

Note the position of the title block in bottom right-hand corner

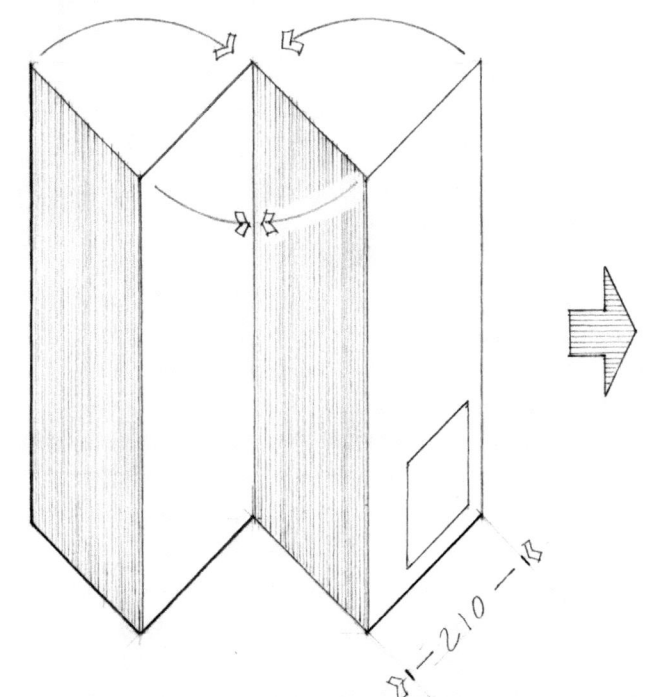
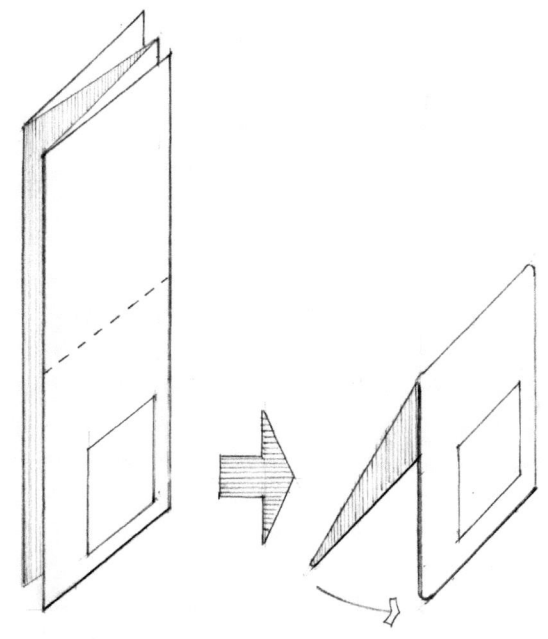
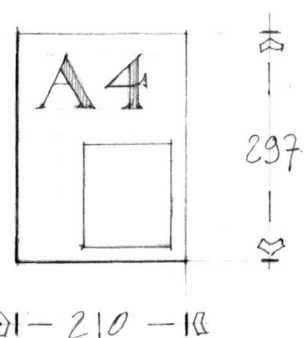

TRIANGLES

A TRIANGLE IS A FLAT SURFACE BOUNDED BY 3 STRAIGHT LINES

IT HAS 3 SIDES & 3 ANGLES

ALL 3 ANGLES EQUAL 180°

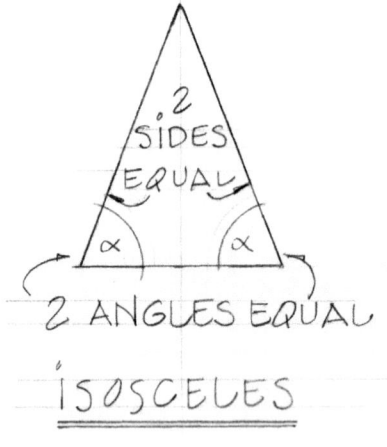

2 ANGLES EQUAL

ISOSCELES

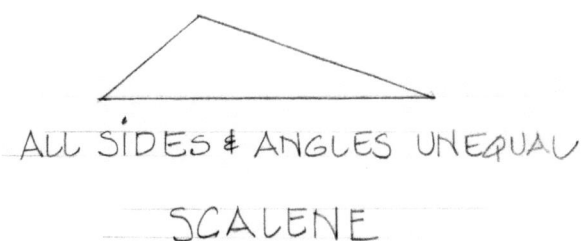

ALL SIDES & ANGLES UNEQUAL

SCALENE

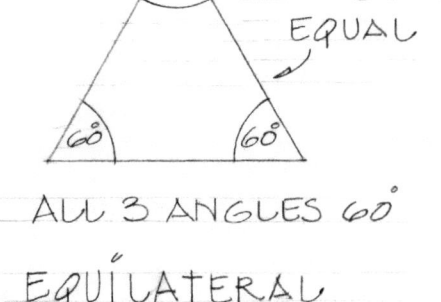

ALL 3 ANGLES 60°

EQUILATERAL

WHAT TYPE OF ANGLE?

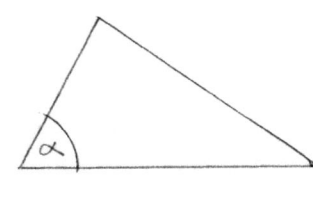

ACUTE
ALL ANGLES LESS THAN 90°

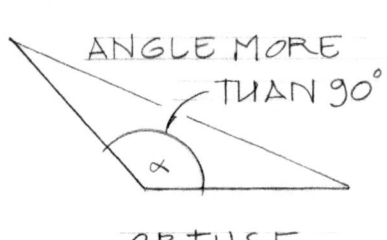

OBTUSE

RIGHT ANGLE

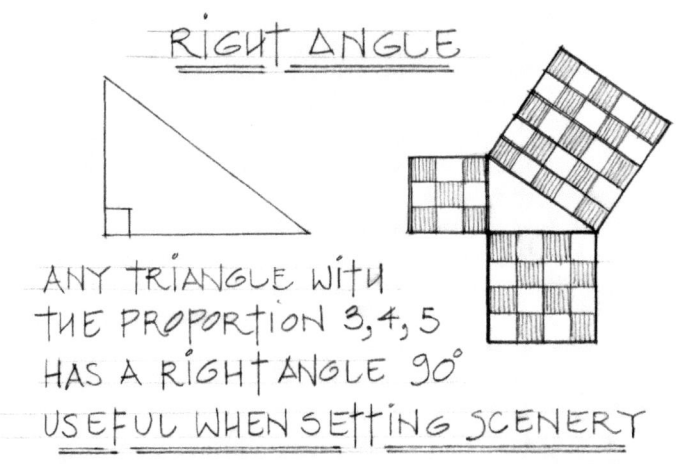

ANY TRIANGLE WITH THE PROPORTION 3, 4, 5 HAS A RIGHT ANGLE 90°
USEFUL WHEN SETTING SCENERY

THE CIRCLE

THE CIRCUMFERENCE OF A CIRCLE = 3.1416 [π] × DIAMETER

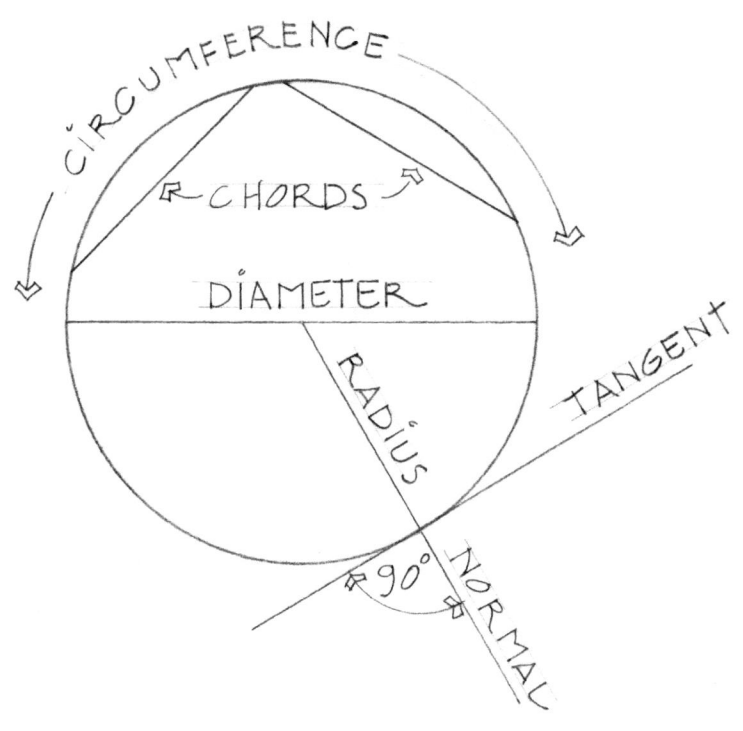

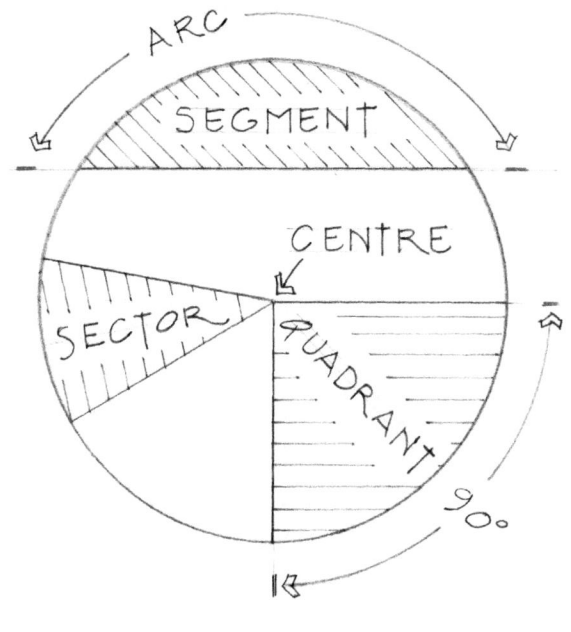

— TO FIND THE CENTRE OF A CIRCLE —

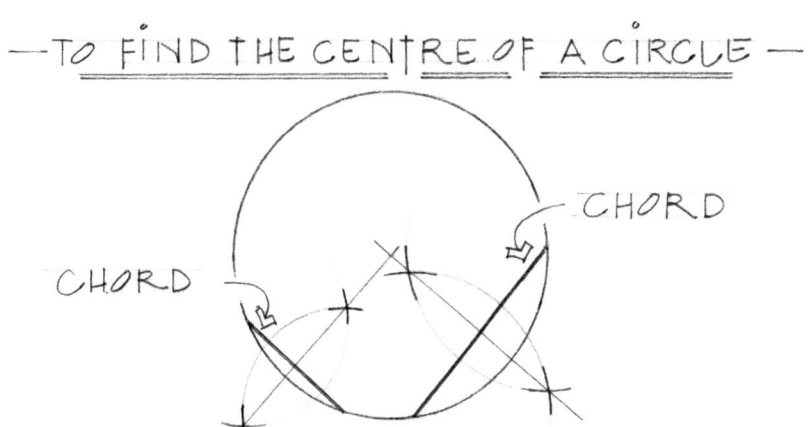

DIVIDING A LINE INTO EQUAL PARTS

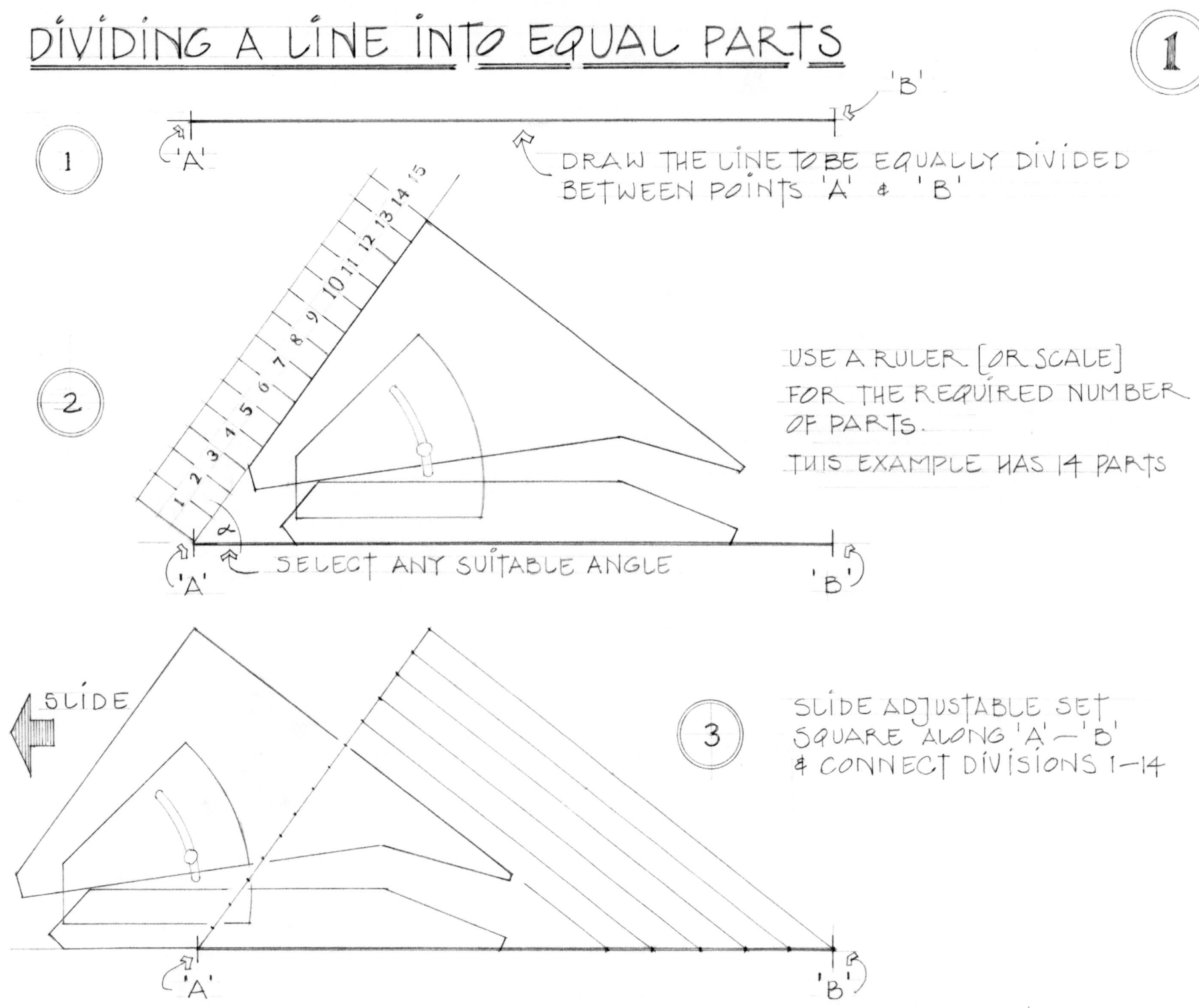

DIVIDING A LINE INTO EQUAL PARTS

NOTE: 'A'–'B' LINE IS THE SAME LENGTH ON ALL EXAMPLES

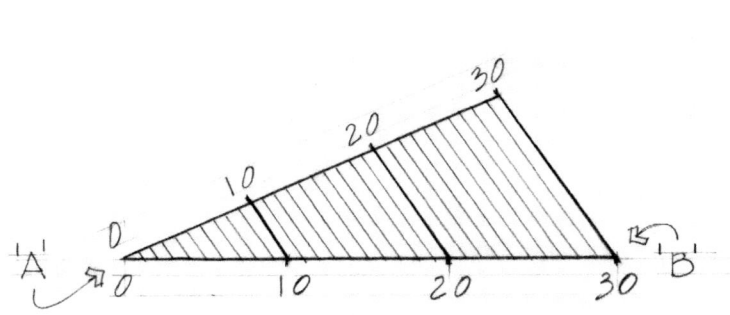
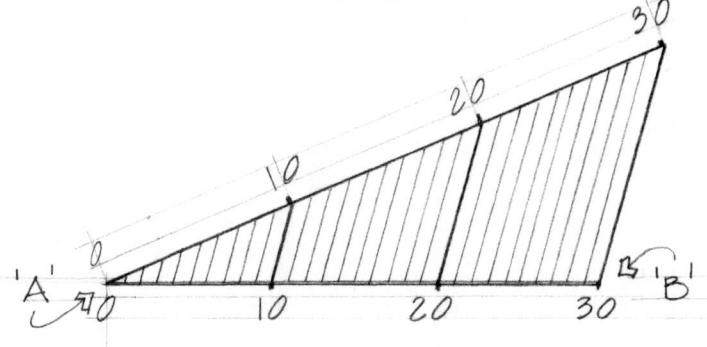

DIFFERENT ANGLE = SAME RESULT !

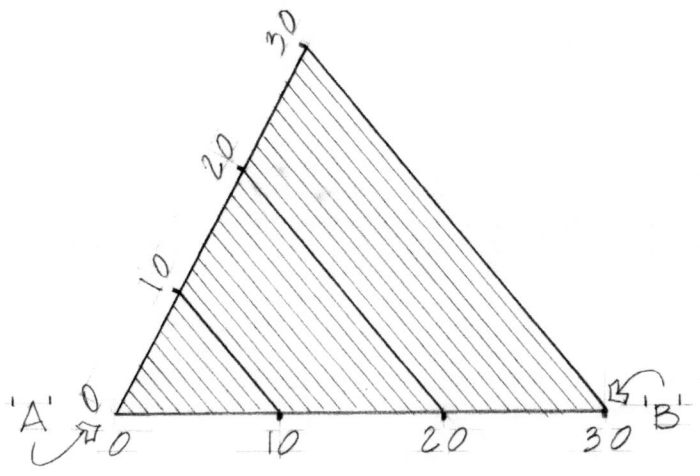
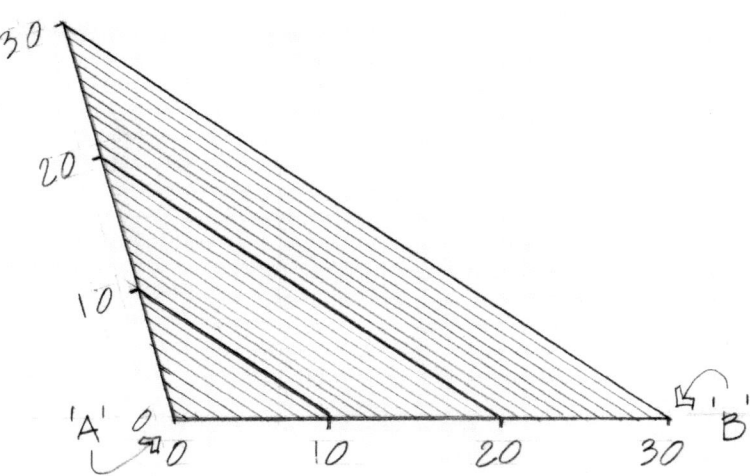

USEFUL FOR CALCULATING THE SPACING FOR PANELLING, FENCING, BALUSTRADING ETC.

POLAR POINT: REDUCTION & ENLARGEMENT

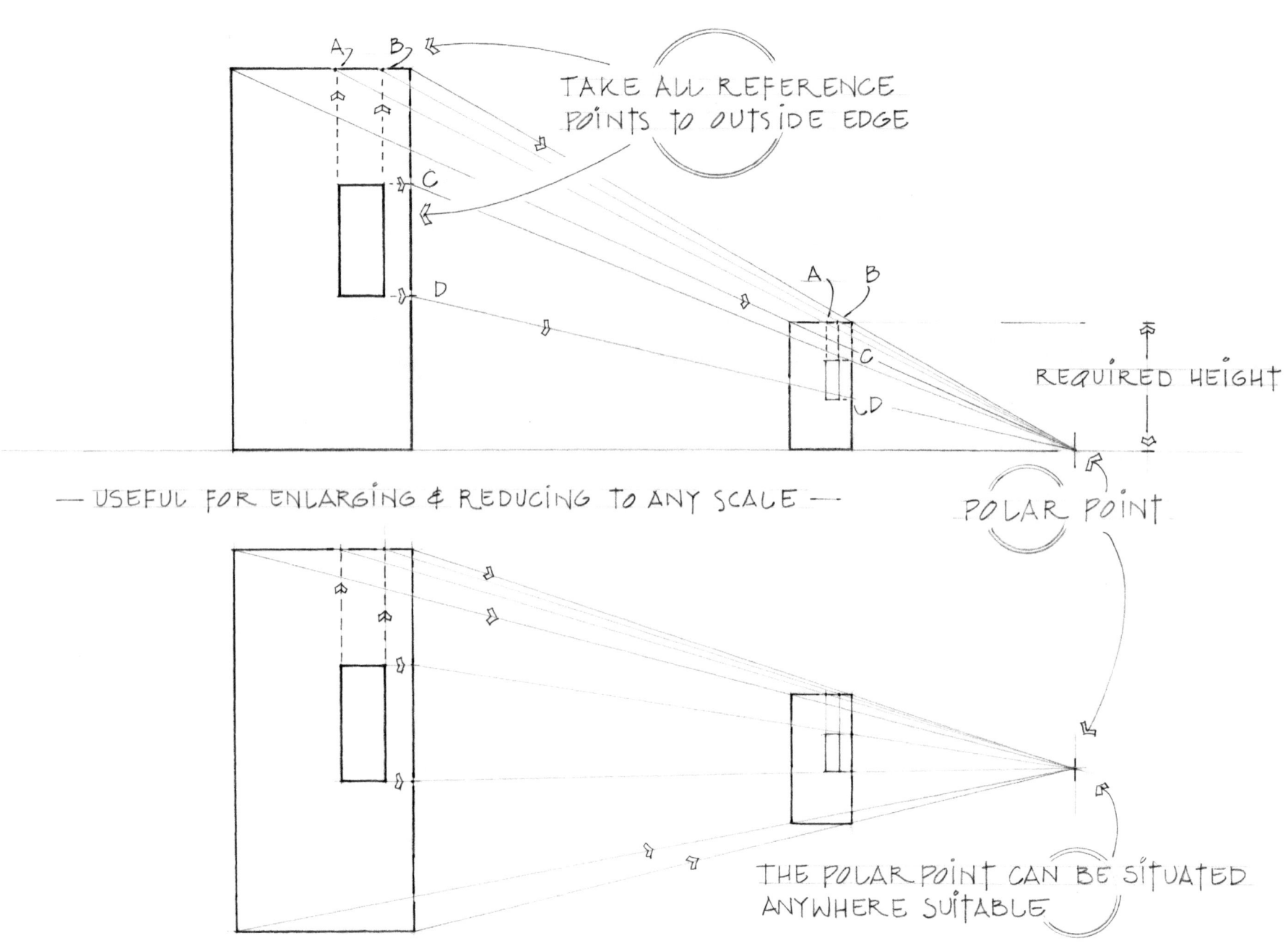

THE ARCH — SEMI-CIRCULAR

THE SEMI-CIRCULAR ARCH WAS FIRST COMMONLY USED & DEVELOPED BY THE ROMANS

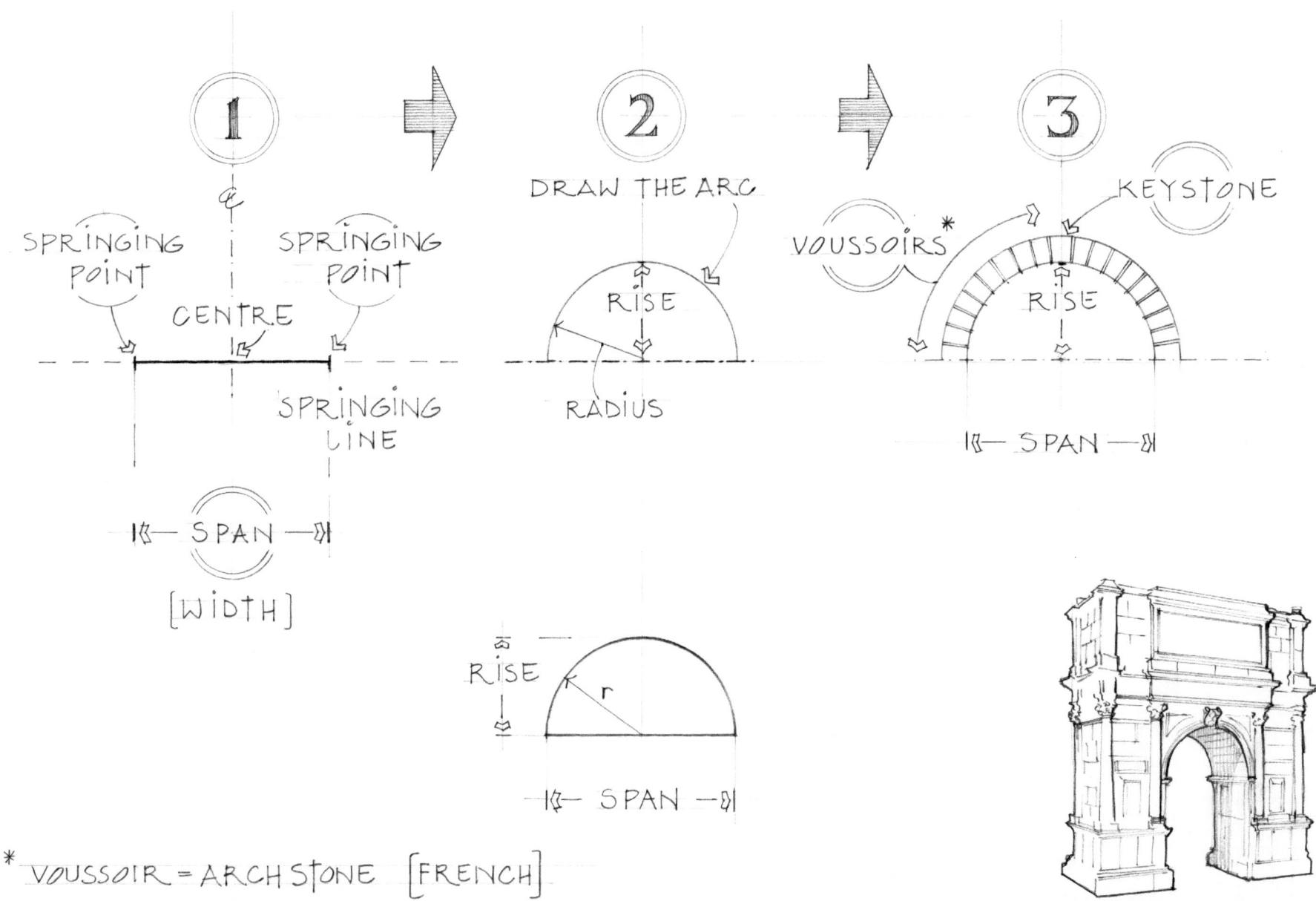

* VOUSSOIR = ARCH STONE [FRENCH]

THE ARCH — HORSE-SHOE

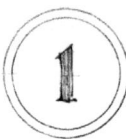 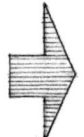 

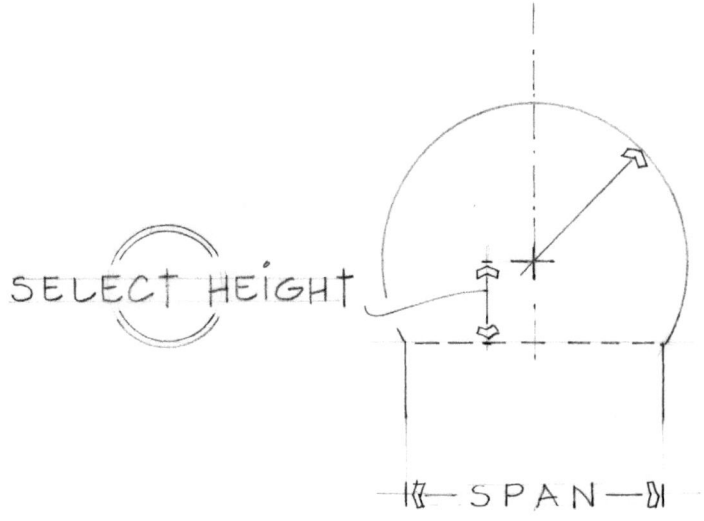

SELECT HEIGHT

SPAN

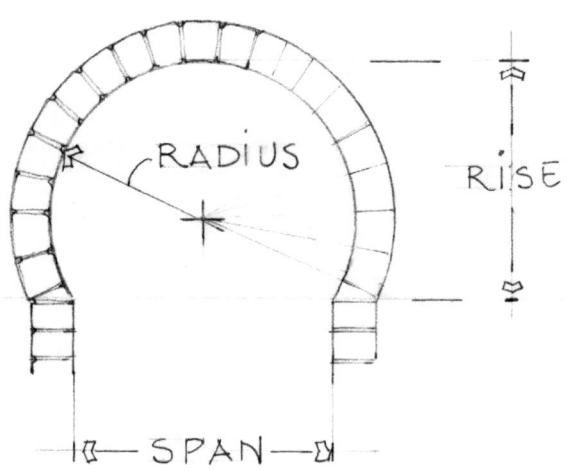

RADIUS

RISE

SPAN

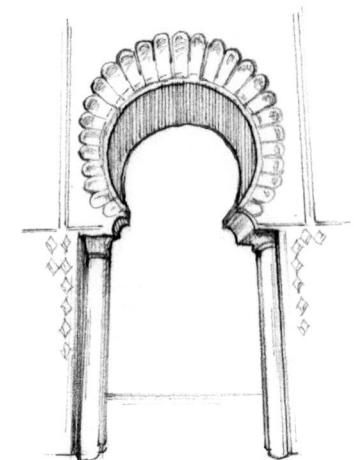

THE ARCH — SEGMENTAL

THIS ARCH IS BASED ON THE SEGMENT OF A CIRCLE

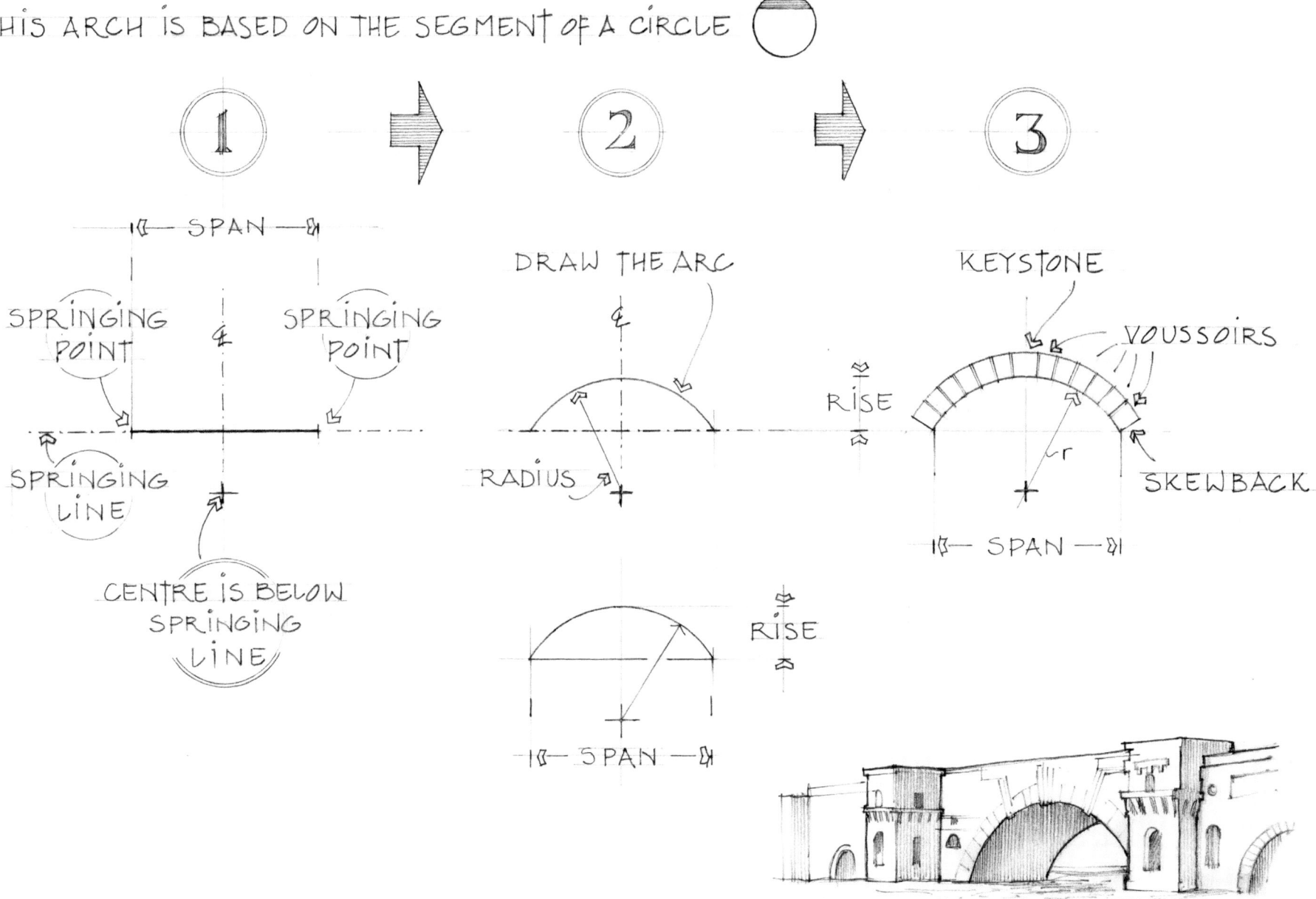

THE ARCH — TUDOR [4 CENTRED] TYPE 1

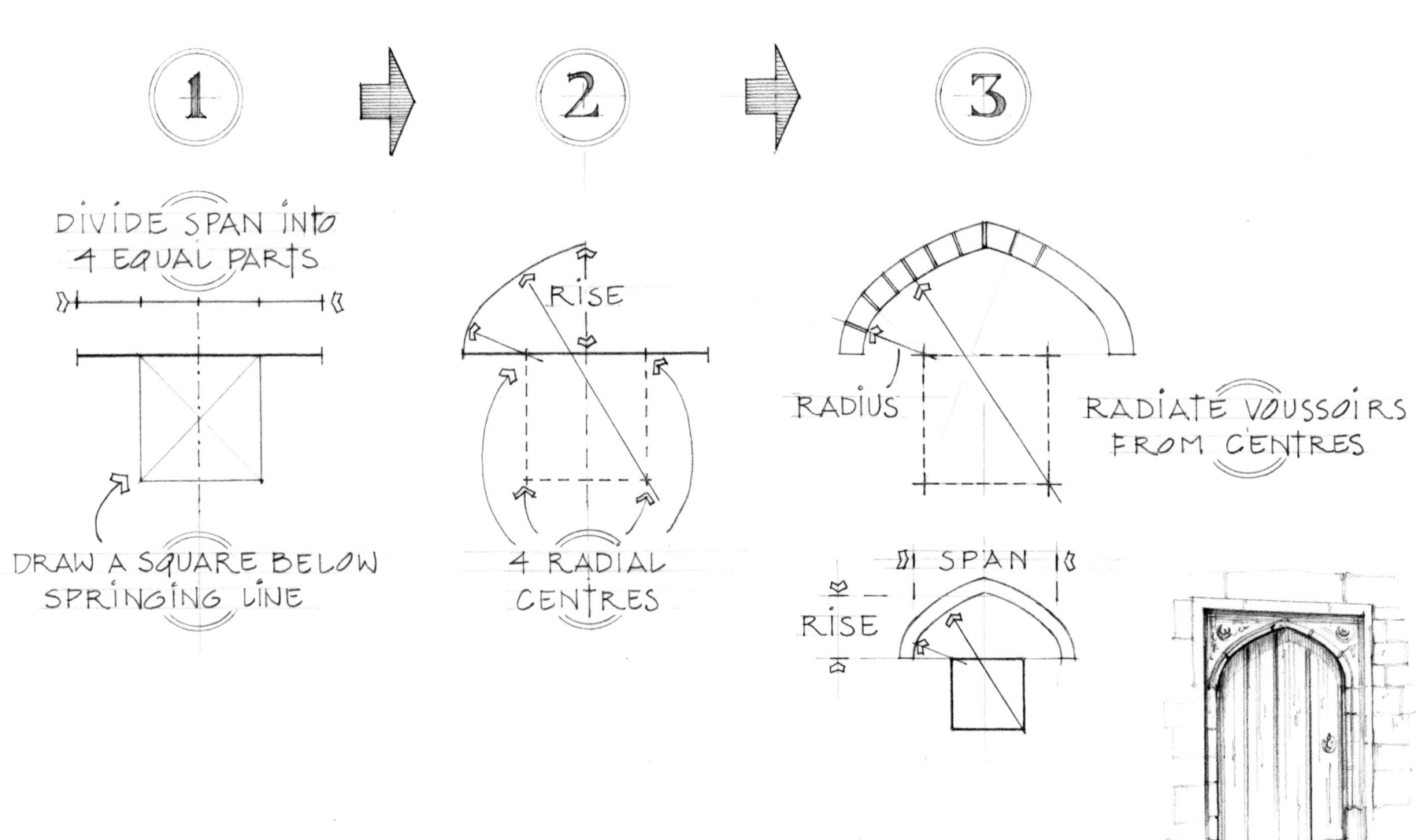

THE ARCH — TUDOR [4 CENTRED] TYPE 2

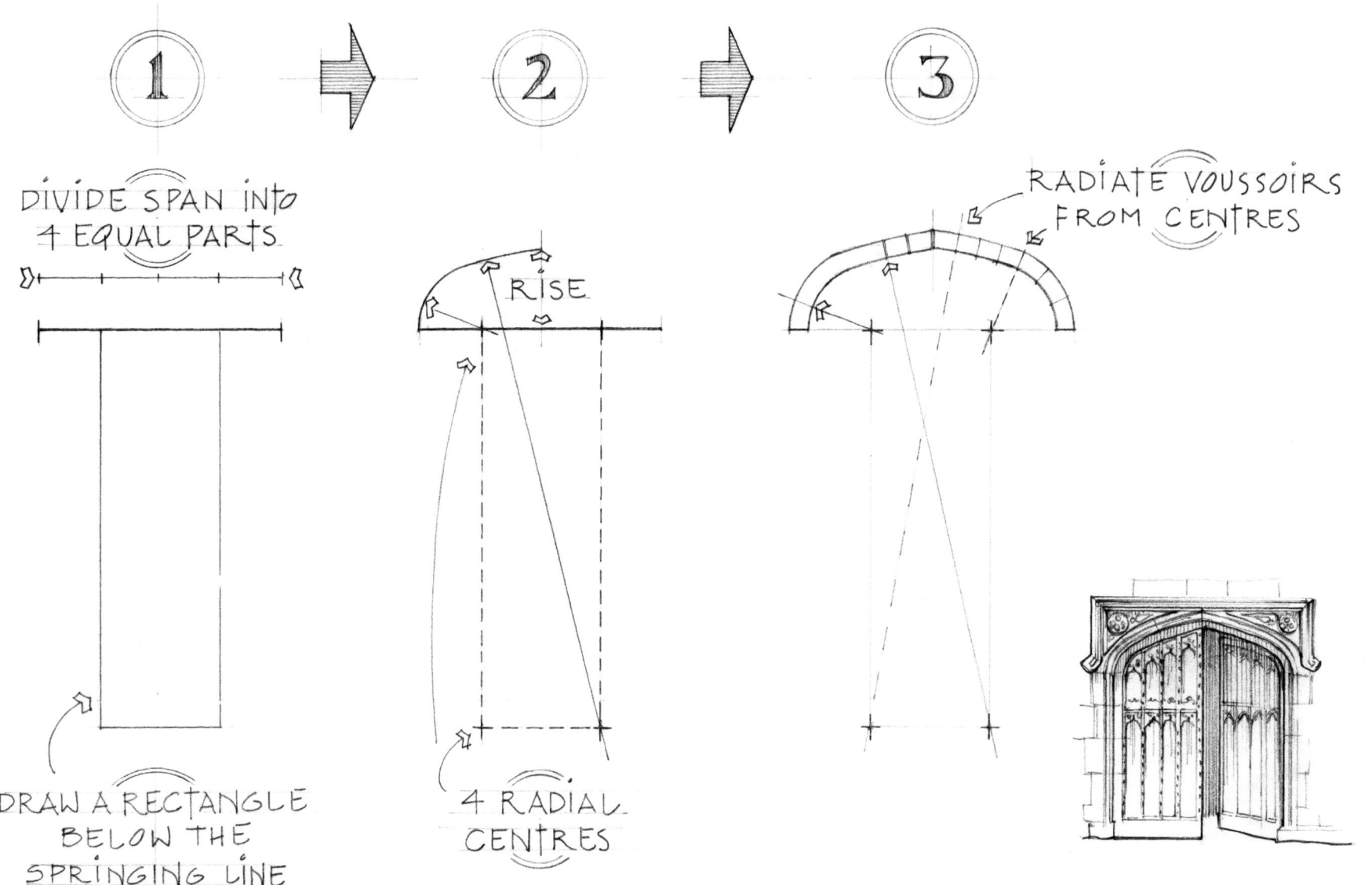

THE ARCH — THREE CENTRED

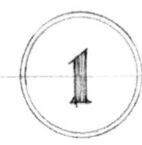 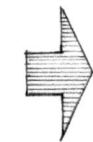 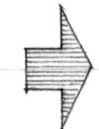

DRAW A SEMI-CIRCLE

USING RISE AS CENTRE
DRAW A CIRCLE

BISECT LINE

DRAW THE 3 ARCS

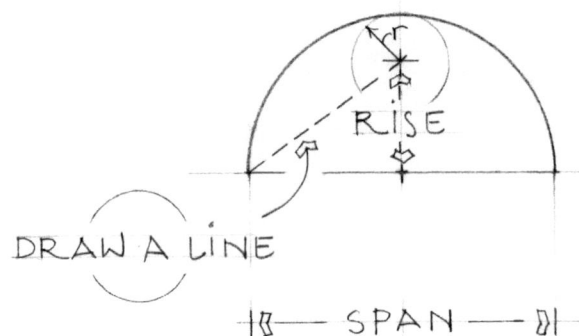

DRAW A LINE

|◁— SPAN —▷|

RADIAL POINTS

3 RADIAL POINTS

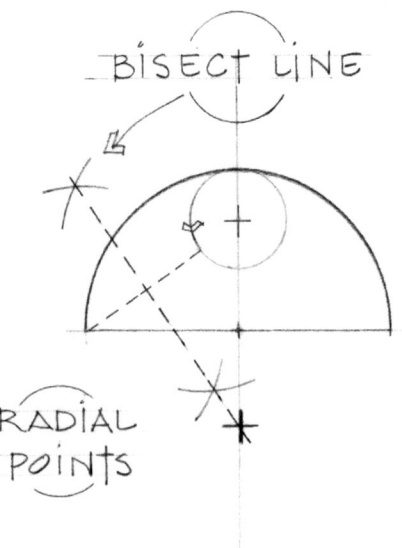

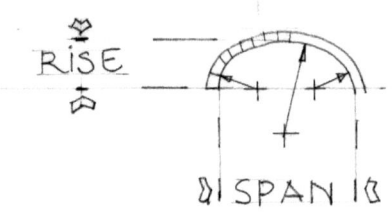

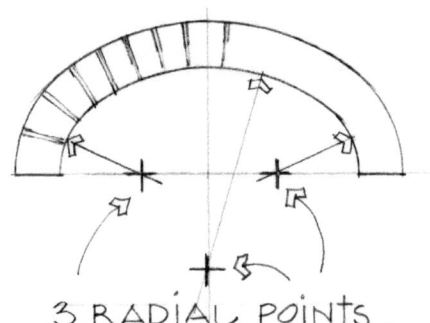

CURVE APPROXIMATES AN ELIPSE

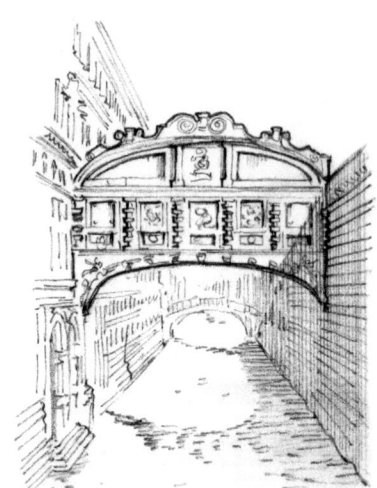

THE ARCH – LANCET

GOTHIC: EARLY ENGLISH PERIOD

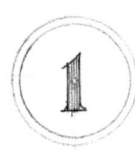 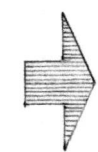  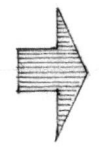 

SELECT SPAN & RISE   DRAW THE ARC

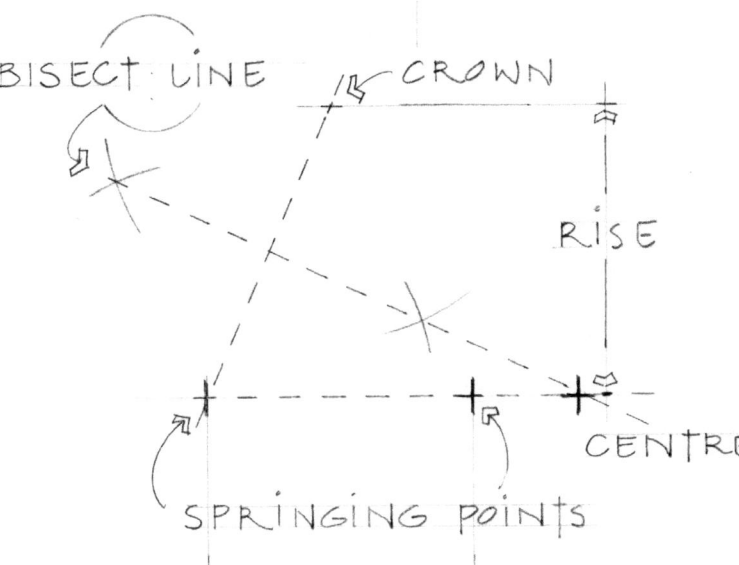

BISECT LINE — CROWN — RISE — CENTRE — SPRINGING POINTS — SPAN

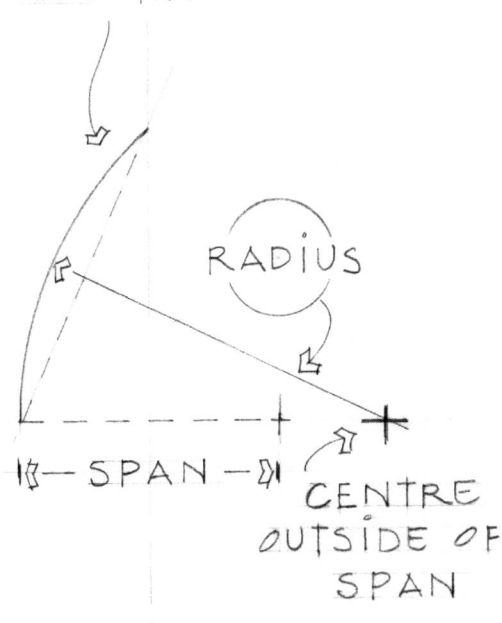

RADIUS — SPAN — CENTRE OUTSIDE OF SPAN

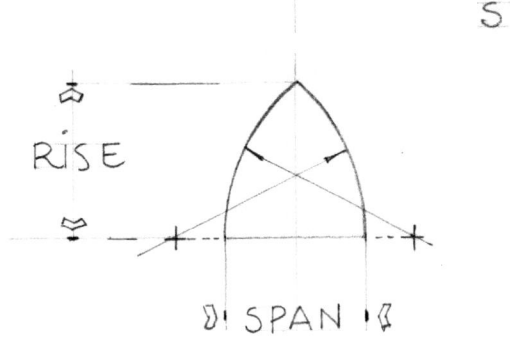

RISE — SPAN

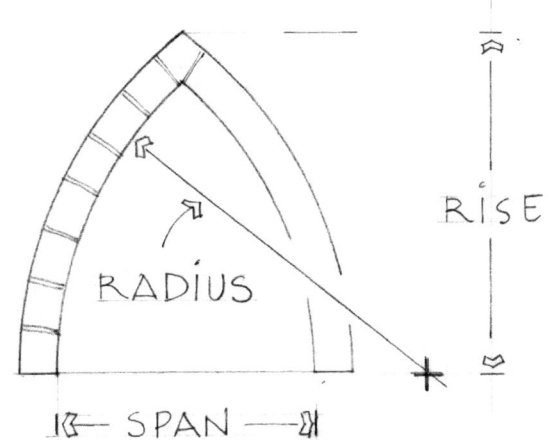

RADIUS — RISE — SPAN

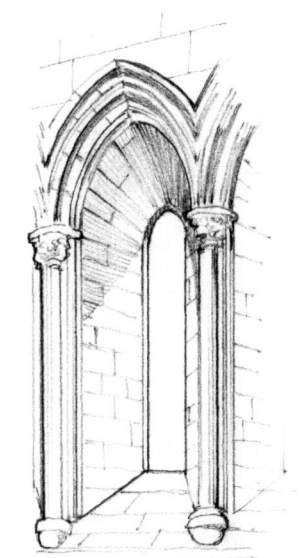

THE ARCH — OGEE [CYMA REVERSA]

 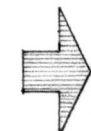  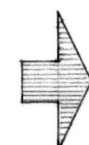 

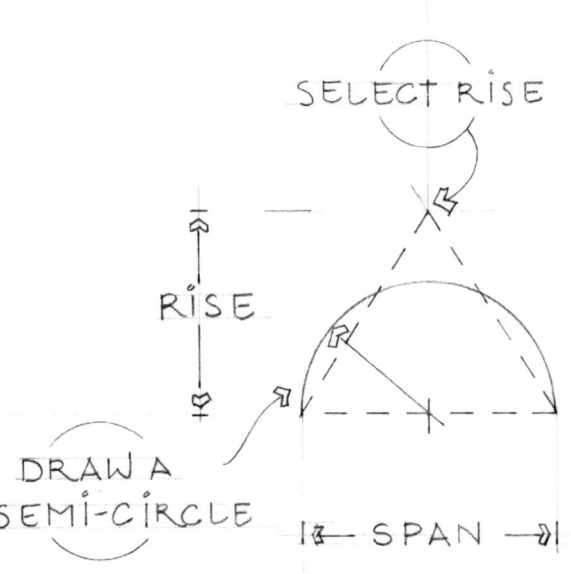

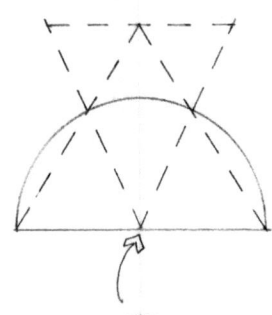

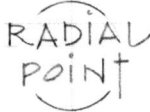

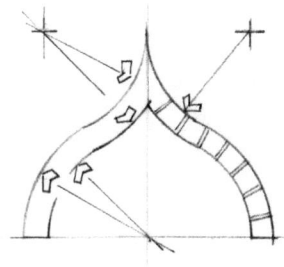

The appearance of the arch is improved by making the lower part larger

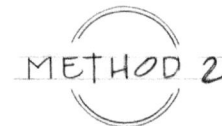 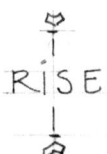 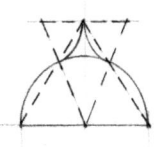

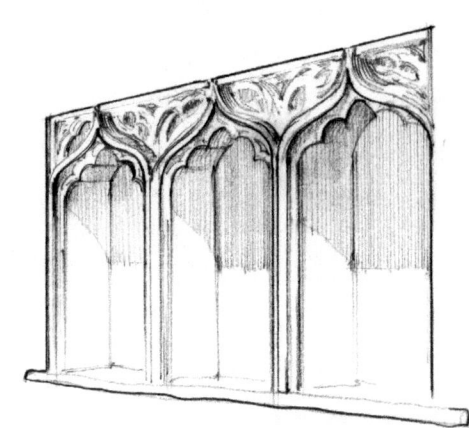

NB: NOT AN EQUILATERAL TRIANGLE

THE ARCH — EQUILATERAL GOTHIC - DECORATED PERIOD

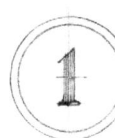 ➡  ➡

DRAW AN EQUILATERAL TRIANGLE

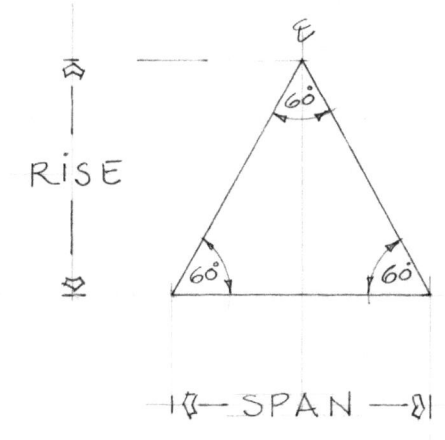

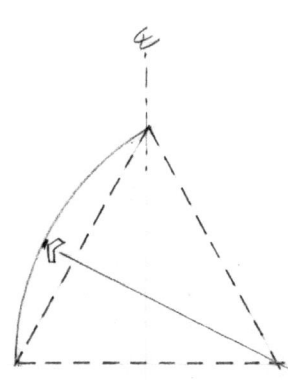

DRAW AN ARC USING SPRINGING POINTS AS CENTRES

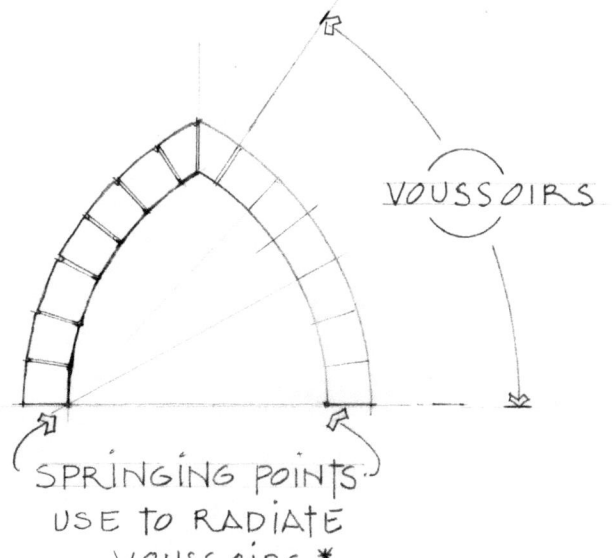

VOUSSOIRS

SPRINGING POINTS USE TO RADIATE VOUSSOIRS *

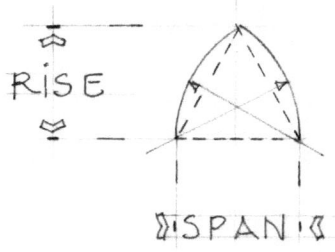

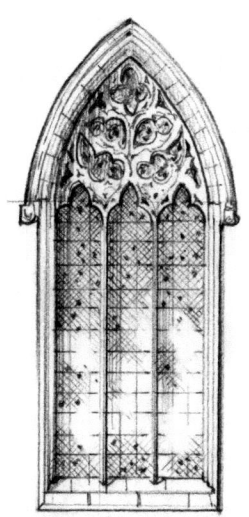

* [FRENCH ⹋ ARCH STONES]

THE ARCH — DROP   "DEPRESSED GOTHIC"

 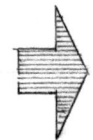 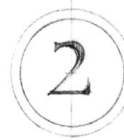 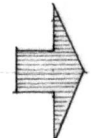 

RISE IS LESS THAN SPAN → DRAW ARC → DRAW OPPOSITE ARC

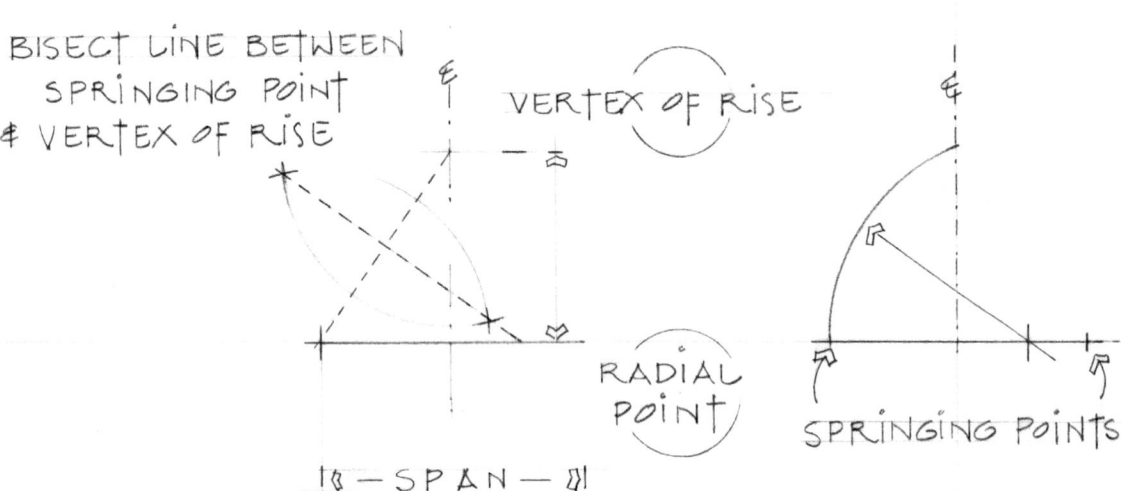

BISECT LINE BETWEEN SPRINGING POINT & VERTEX OF RISE

VERTEX OF RISE

RADIAL POINT

|←— SPAN —→|

SPRINGING POINTS

ARC CENTRES

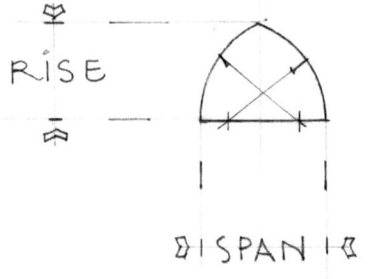

RISE

|← SPAN →|

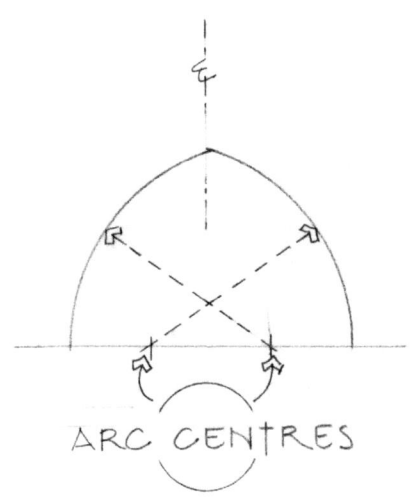

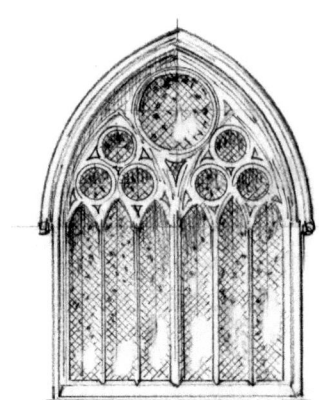

THE ARCH – OGEE [CYMA REVERSA]

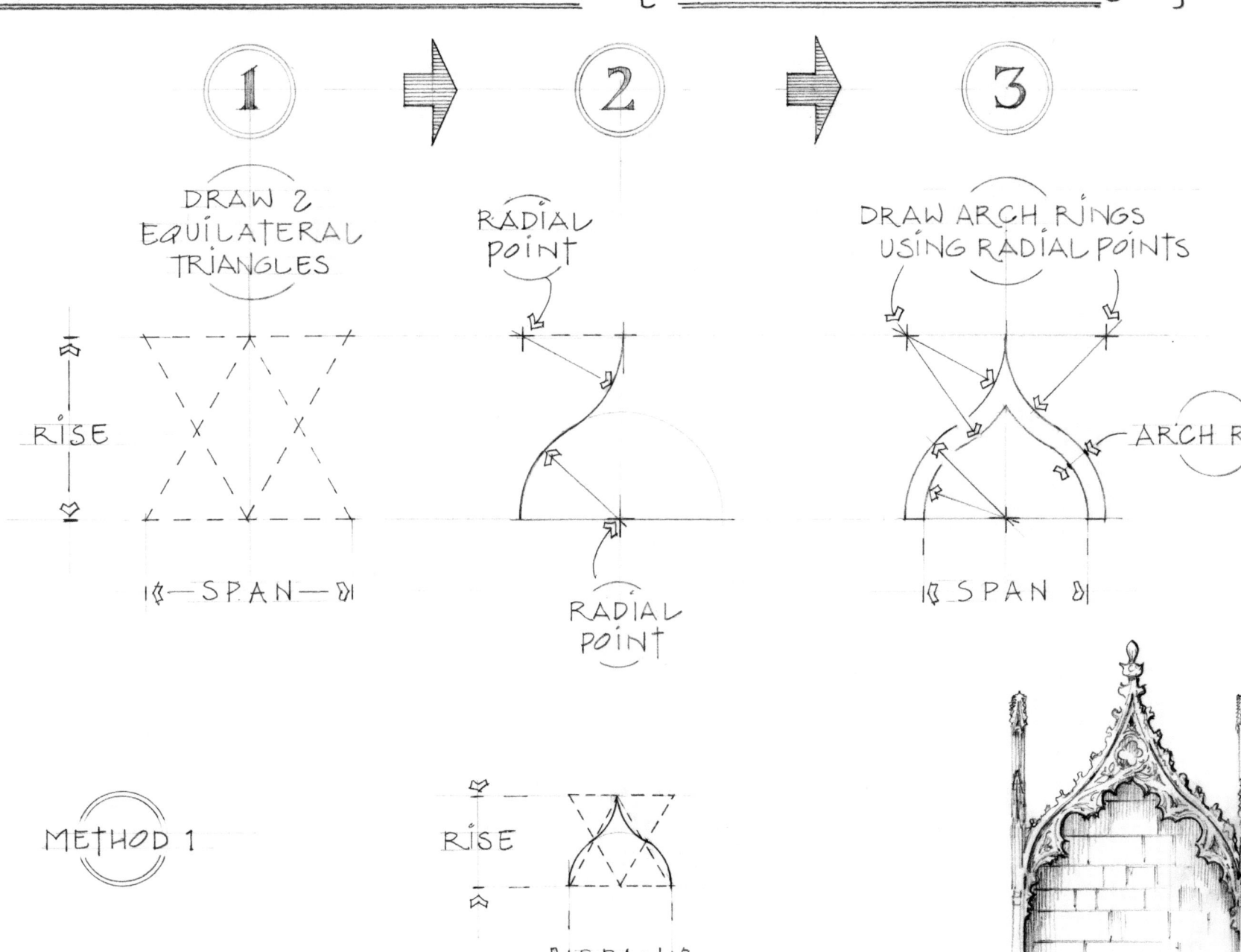

THE ARCH — MOORISH

1 ⇒ 2 ⇒ 3

VERTEX

SELECT RISE & SPAN

DRAW A LINE BETWEEN THE SPRINGING POINT & THE VERTEX

RISE

SPAN

SPRINGING POINT

BISECT LINE

RADIUS

SELECT HEIGHT

RADII

RISE

SPAN

RISE

SPAN

"THE ARCH NEVER SLEEPS" — ISLAMIC PROVERB

THE ARCH — RAMPANT

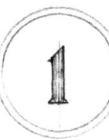 → 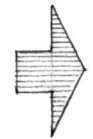 →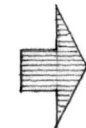

DRAW A RECTANGLE   PLACE RADIAL POINTS

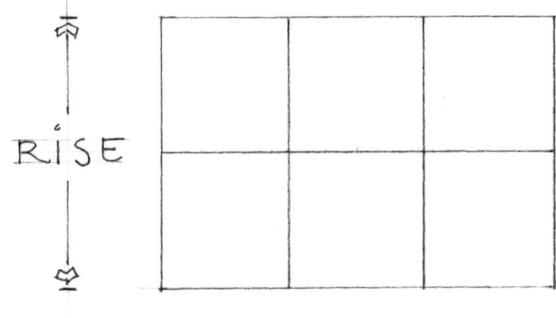

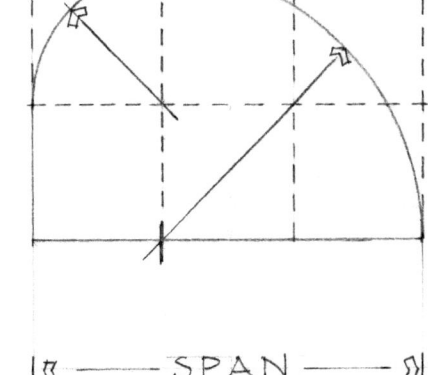

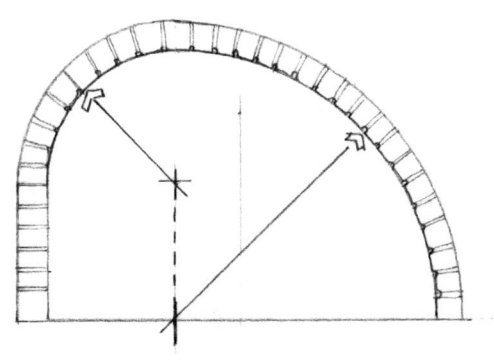

THE SETTING-OUT IS THE
SAME AS A SCOTIA MOULDING

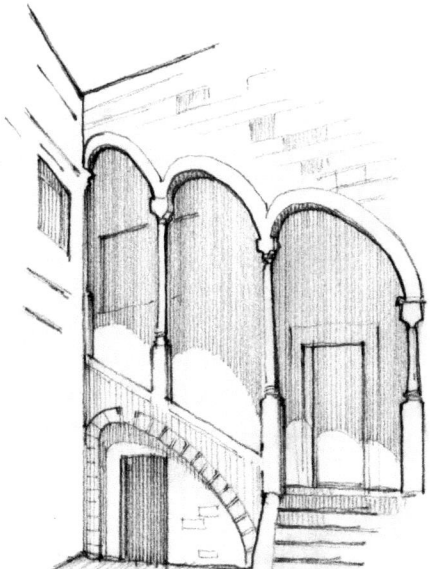

FOR SUPPORTING A FLIGHT OF SOLID STEPS

DOORS — TYPES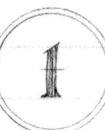

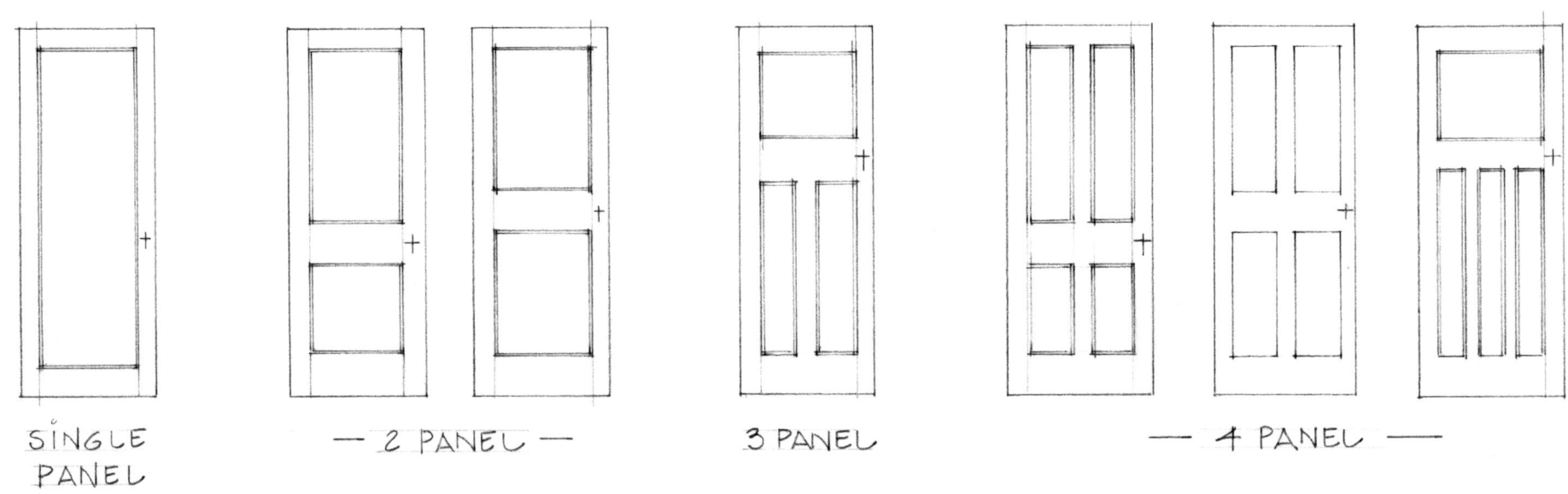

SINGLE PANEL — 2 PANEL — 3 PANEL — 4 PANEL —

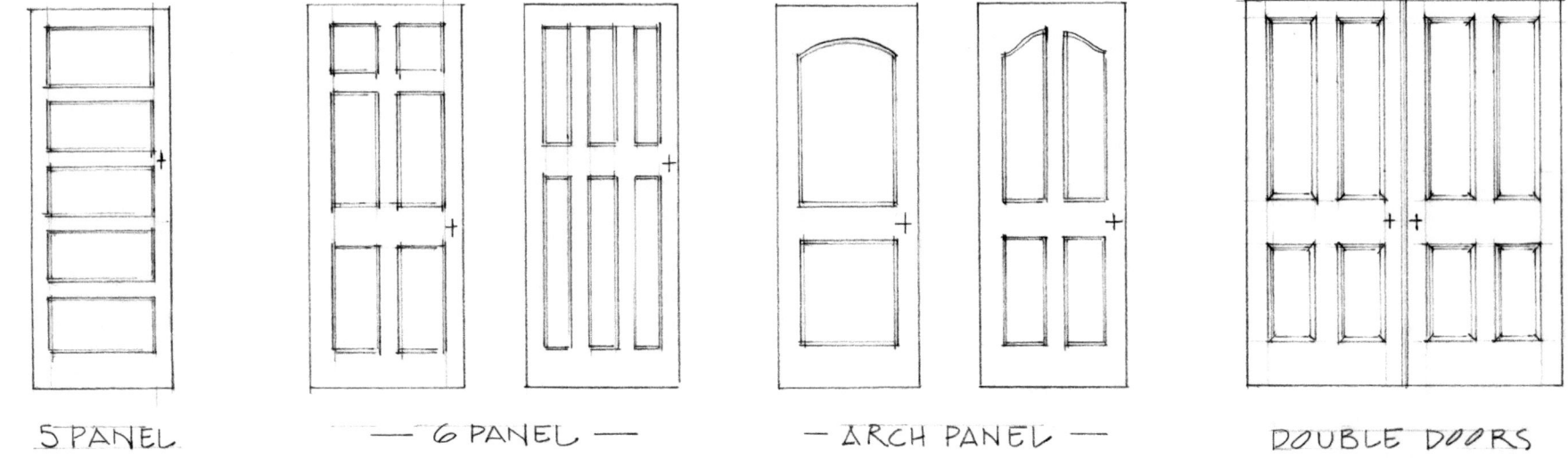

5 PANEL — 6 PANEL — — ARCH PANEL — DOUBLE DOORS

DOORS – TYPES – LEDGE & BATTEN ②

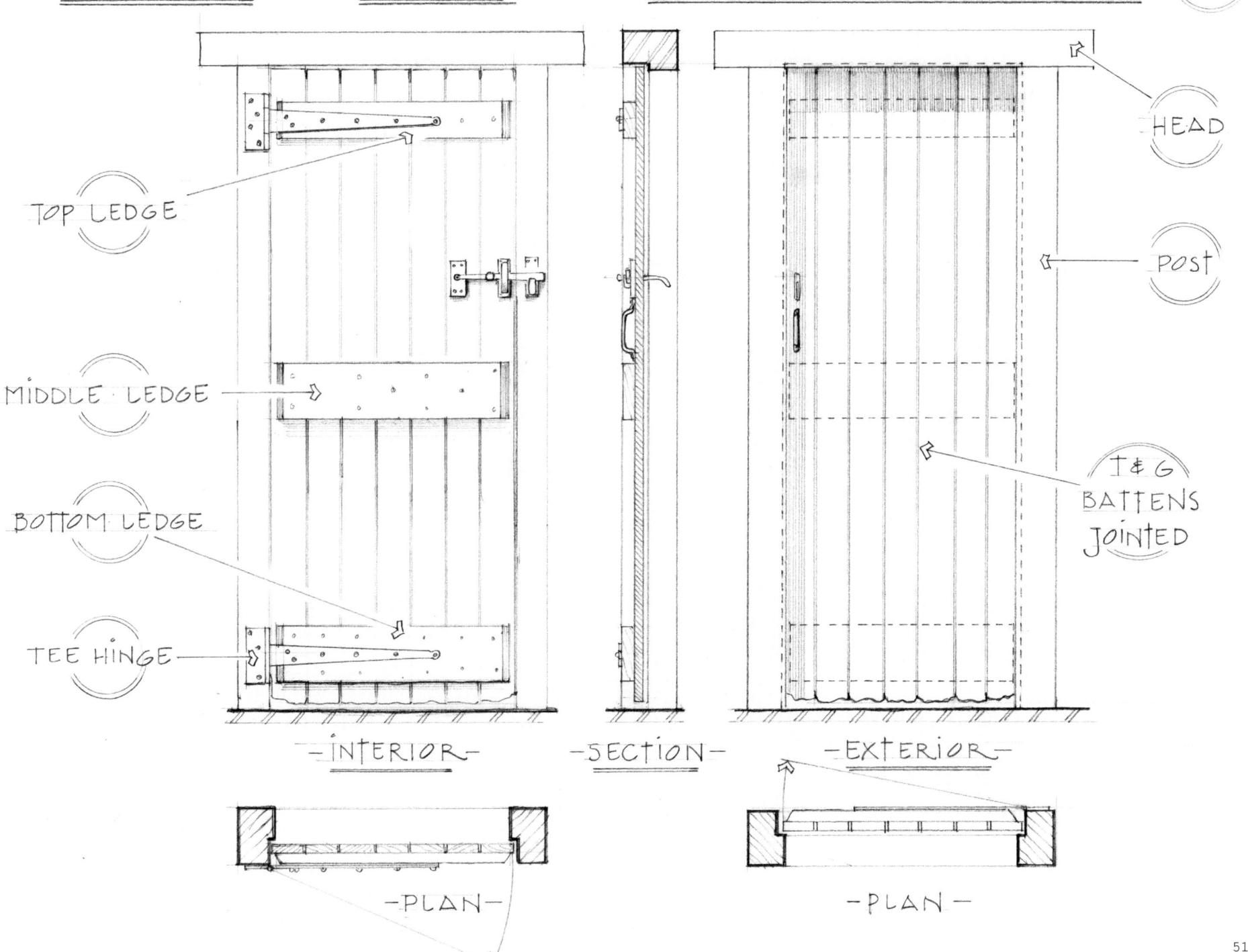

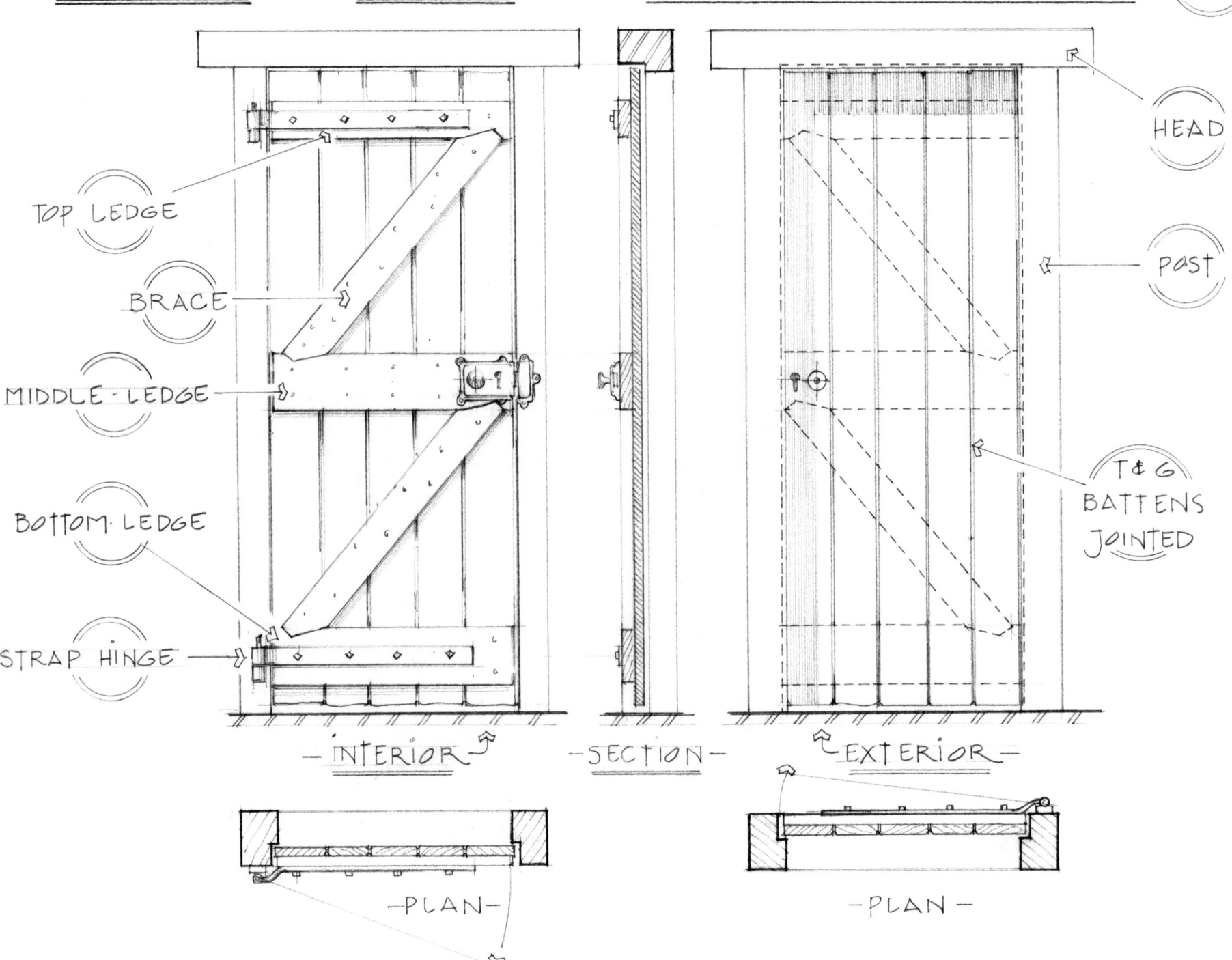

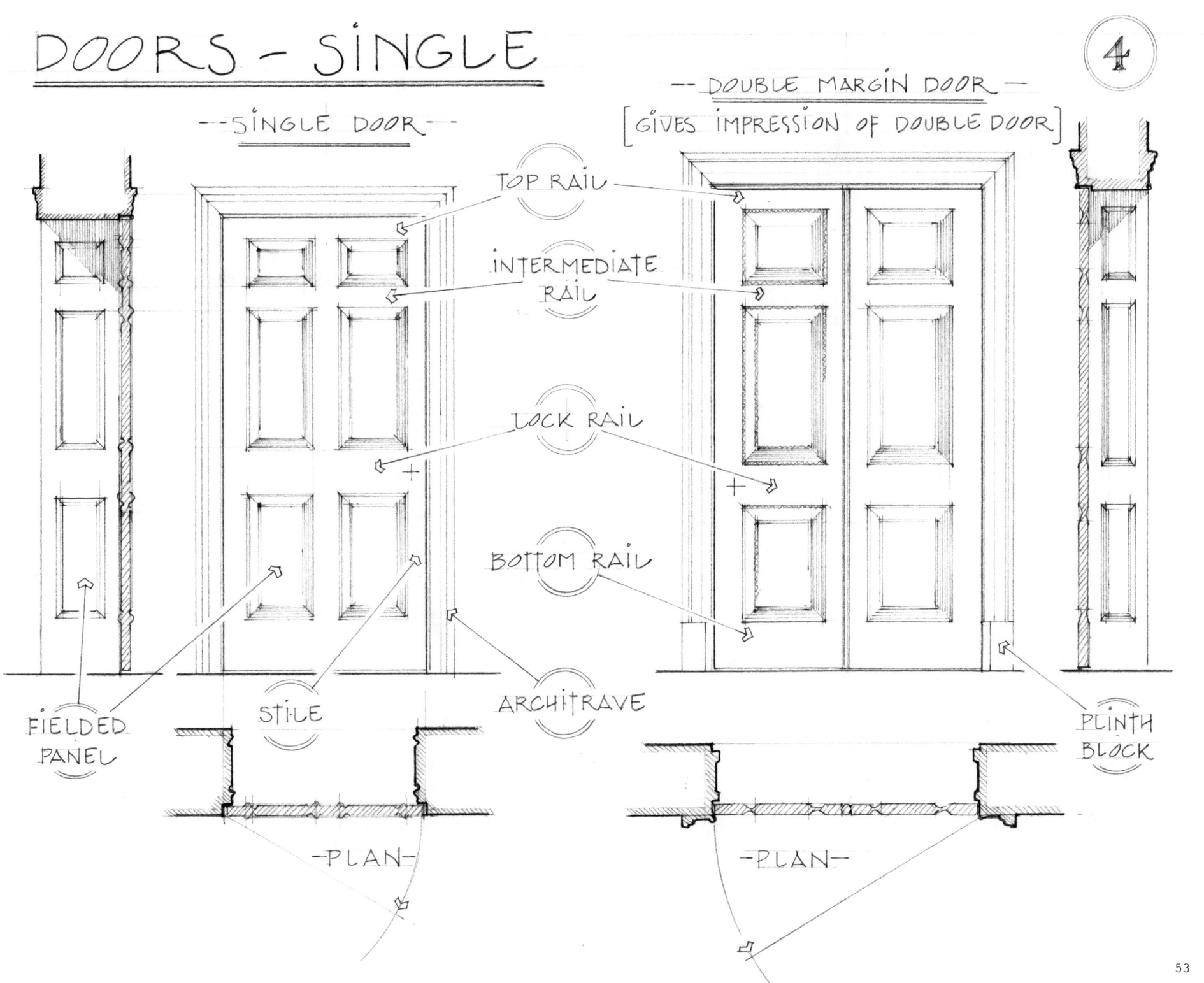

DOORS — TYPES — DOUBLE ⑤

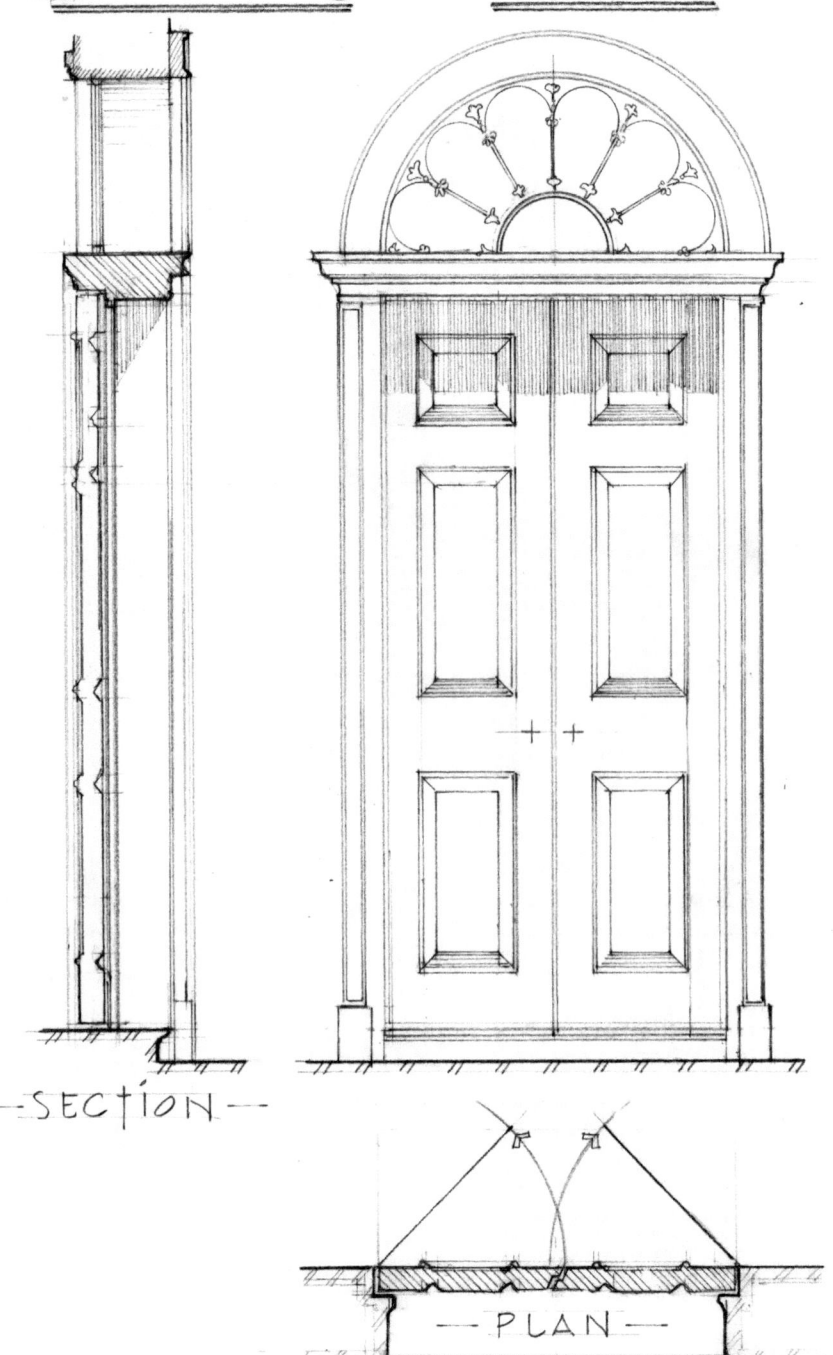

— SECTION —

— PLAN —

WITH DOUBLE DOORS THE PRIMARY DOOR IS THE "MASTER" THE SECONDARY IS THE "SLAVE"

NOTE THE ANGLED MEETING STILES

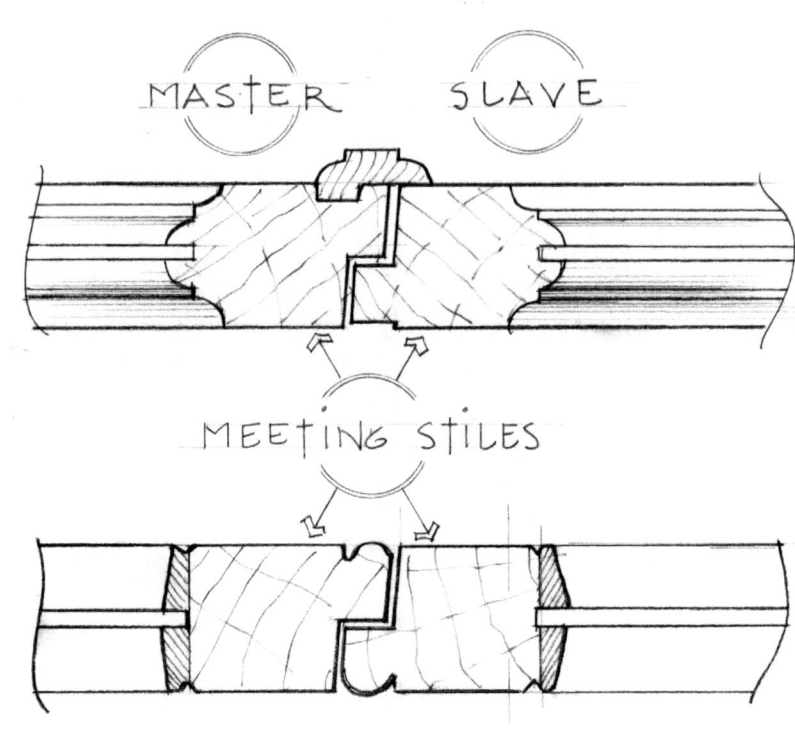

MASTER   SLAVE

MEETING STILES

WINDOWS — SLIDING SASH

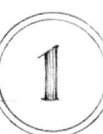

- TOP RAIL
- STILE
- TOP SASH
- HORN, JOGGLE
- MEETING RAIL
- BOTTOM SASH
- ASTRAGAL, MUNTIN, GLAZING-BAR
- BOTTOM RAIL

— SECTION —

"SIX OVER SIX"

EXTERIOR VIEW COMBINED

SECTION

GLAZING PROPORTIONS

WIDTH

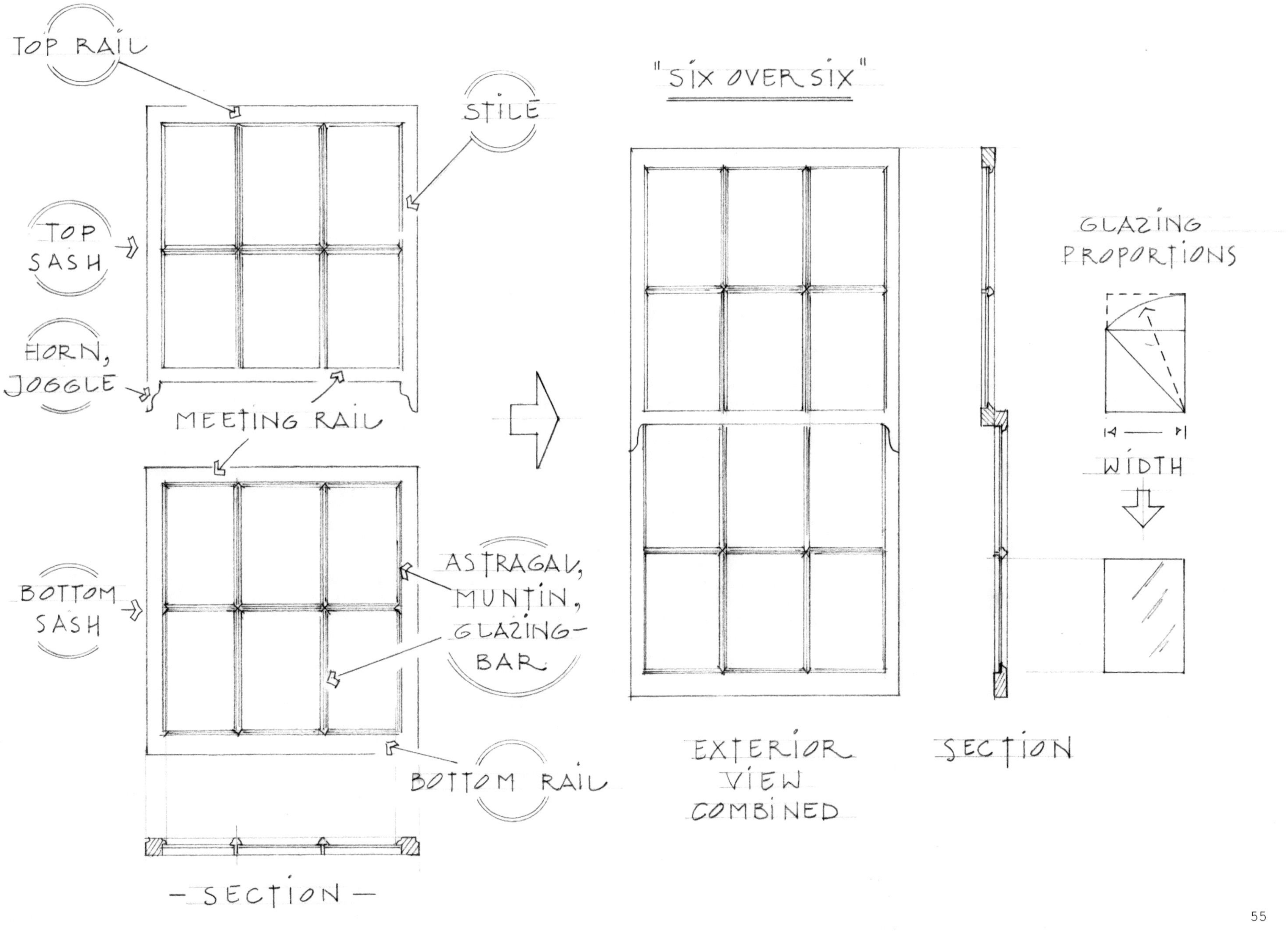

WINDOWS — SLIDING SASH

ARCHITRAVE

EXT. — INT.

GLASS

SILL

SILL

PLAN

PLAN

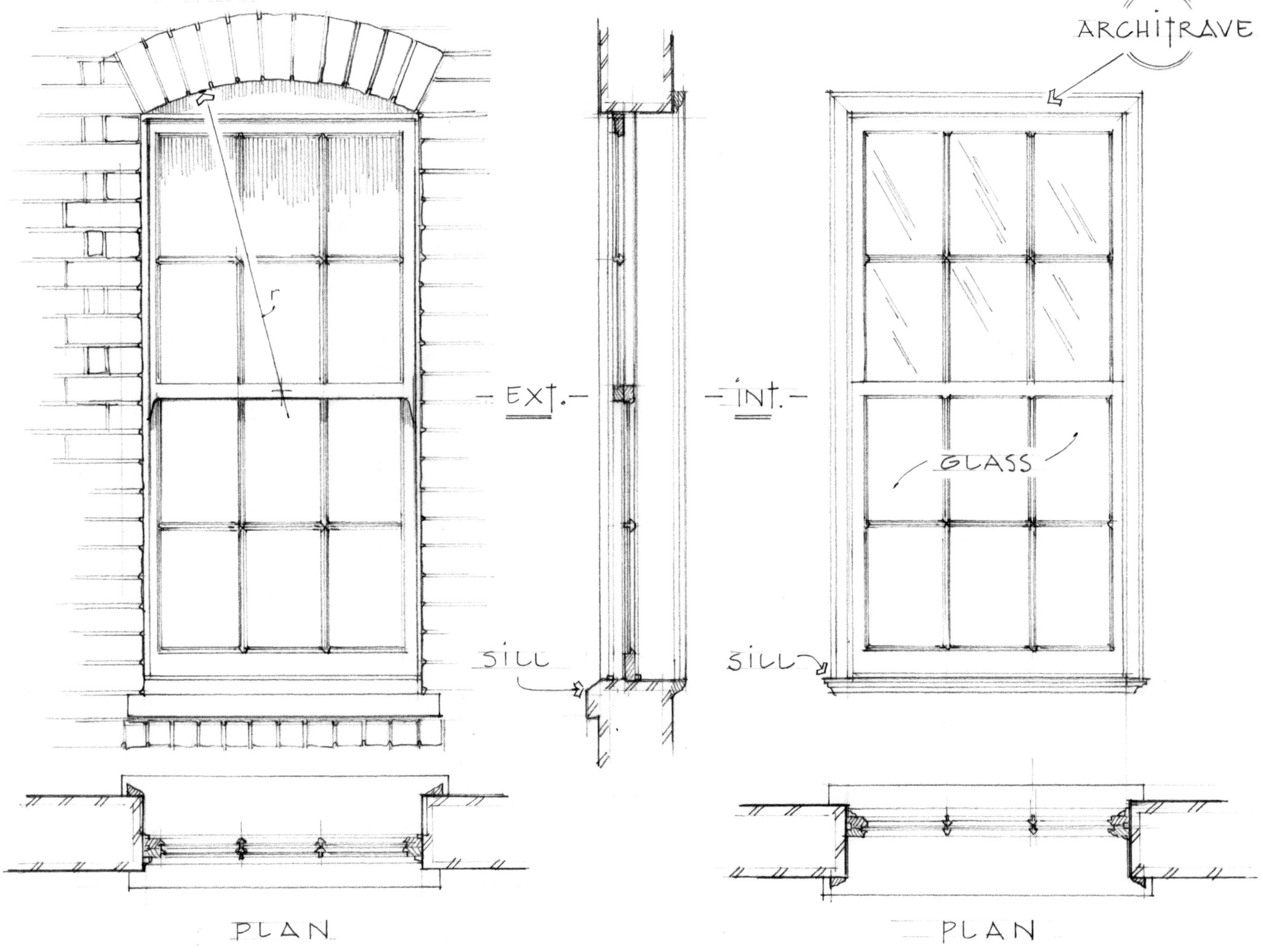

WINDOWS — CASEMENT 3

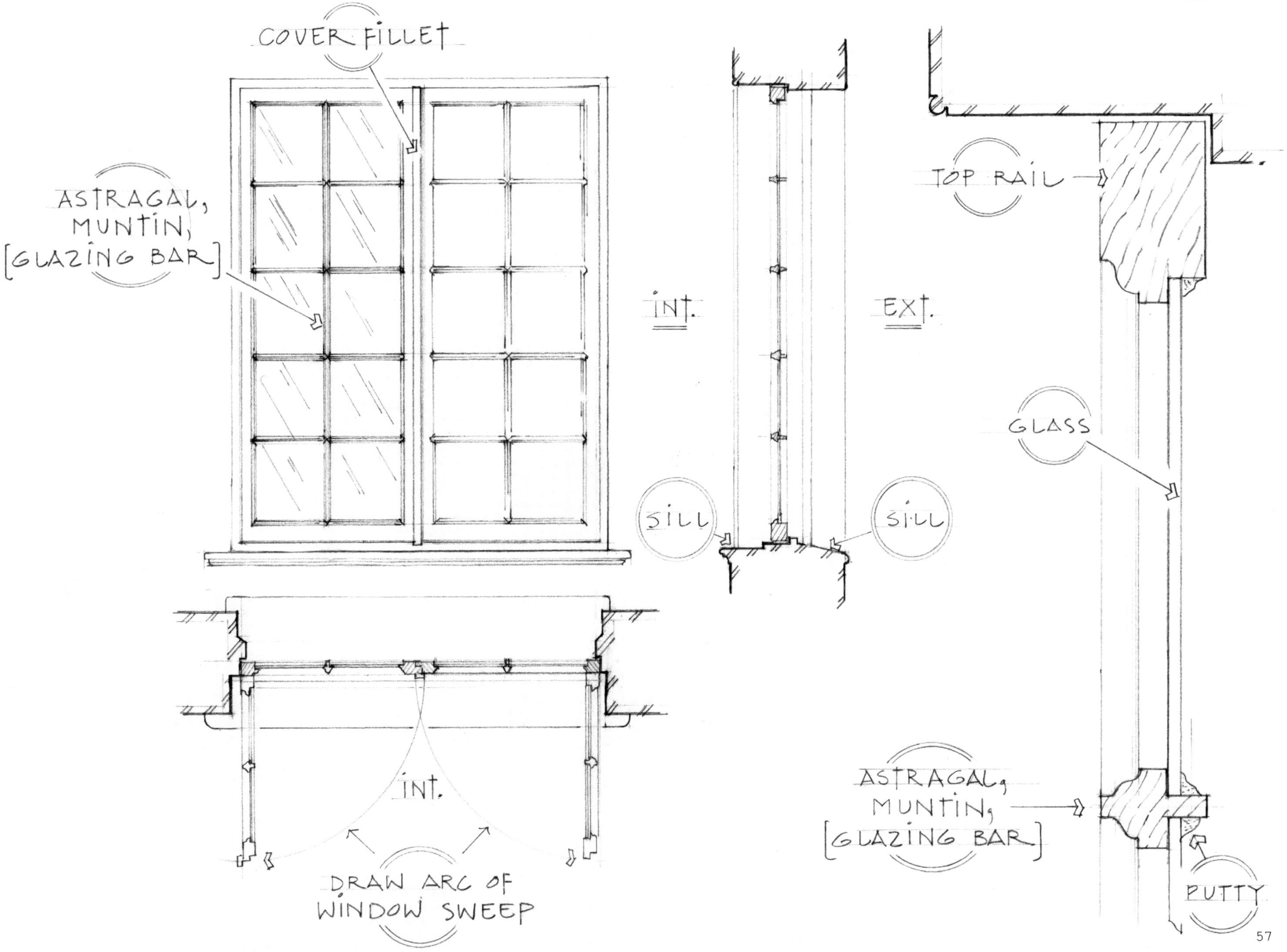

- COVER FILLET
- ASTRAGAL, MUNTIN, [GLAZING BAR]
- INT.
- EXT.
- SILL
- SILL
- TOP RAIL
- GLASS
- ASTRAGAL, MUNTIN, [GLAZING BAR]
- PUTTY
- INT.
- DRAW ARC OF WINDOW SWEEP

STAIRCASES — TYPES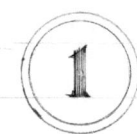

STRAIGHT FLIGHT — CONTINUOUS OVER ITS WHOLE LENGTH

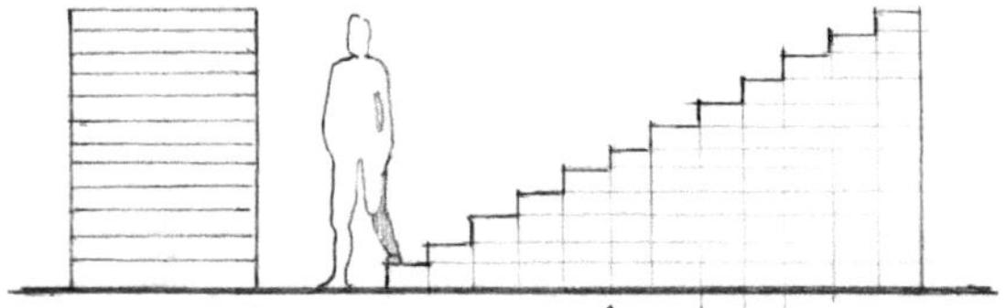

STAIRS
A SET OF STEPS LEADING FROM ONE FLOOR TO ANOTHER

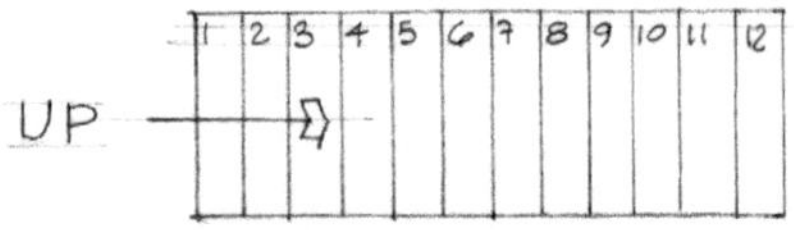

STAIRCASE
A SET OF STAIRS WITHIN A SURROUNDING STRUCTURE

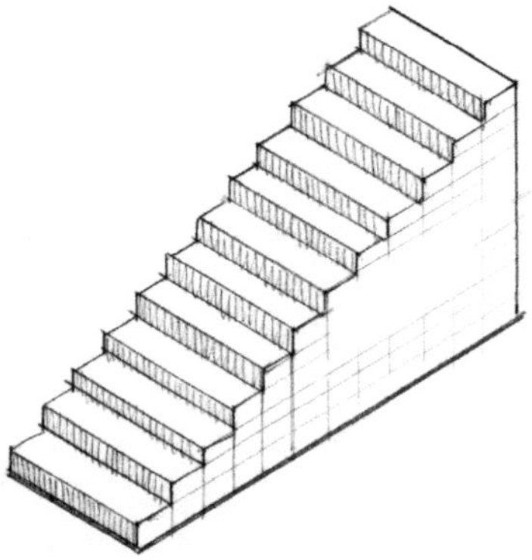

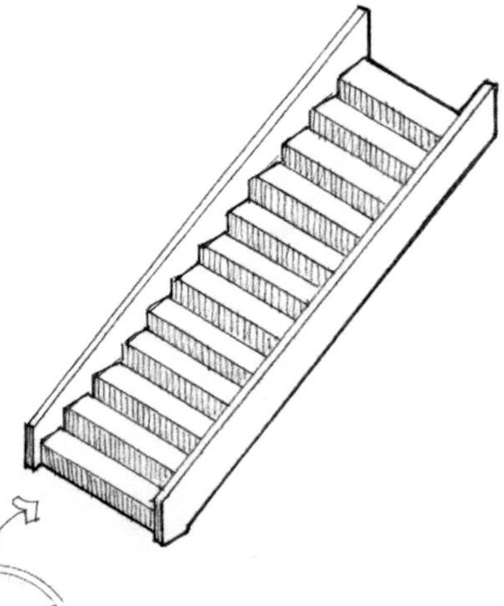

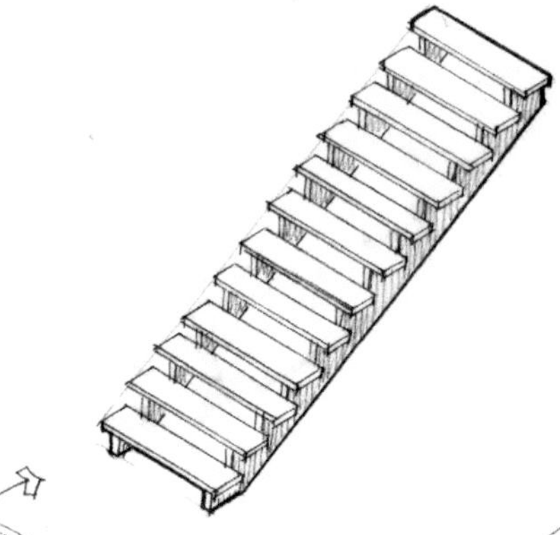

- CLOSED STRINGER CLOSED RISER
- OPEN STRINGER CLOSED RISER
- OPEN STRINGER OPEN RISER
- CLOSED STRINGER OPEN RISER 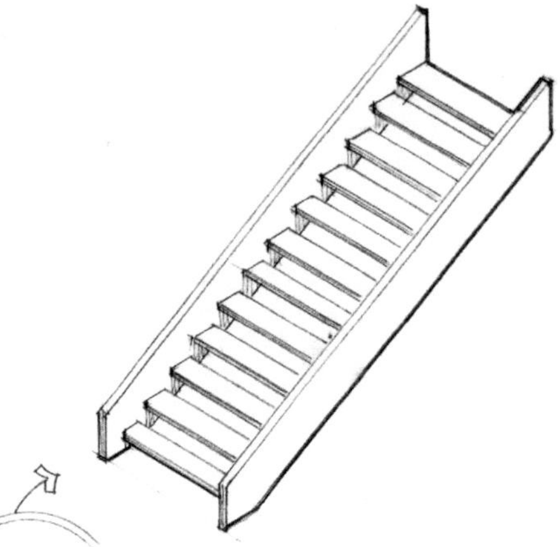
- CLOSED & OPEN STRINGERS WITH CLOSED RISERS

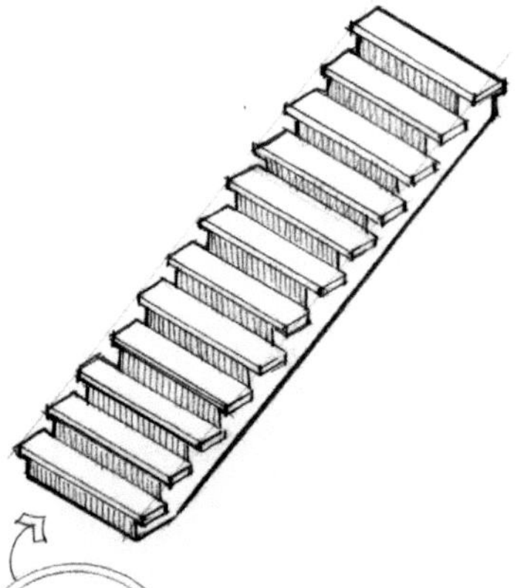

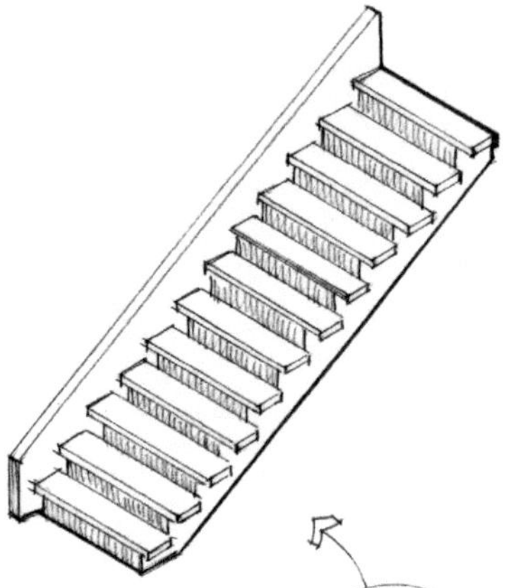

STAIRCASES — TYPES

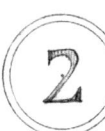

STRAIGHT FLIGHT WITH HALF-LANDING

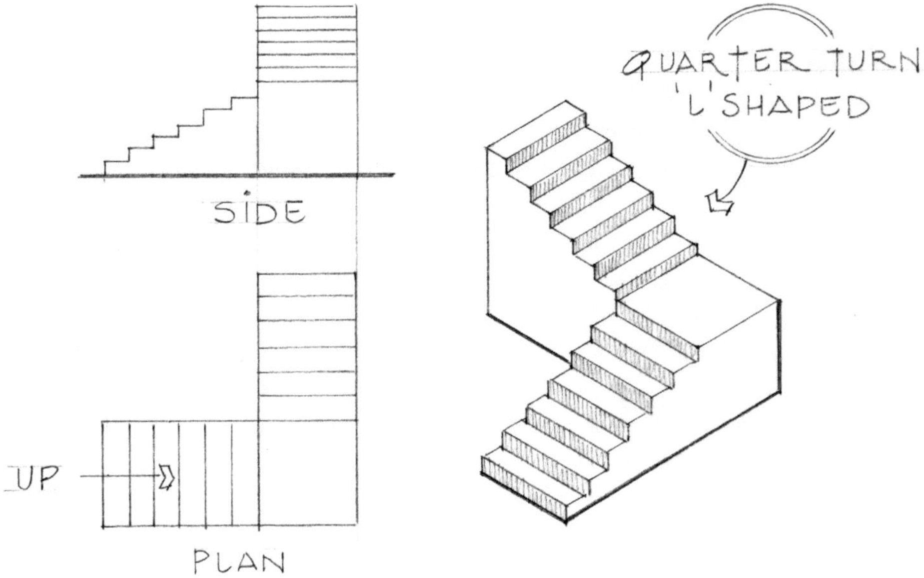

QUARTER TURN 'L' SHAPED

QUARTER TURN WITH WINDER

KITE WINDER

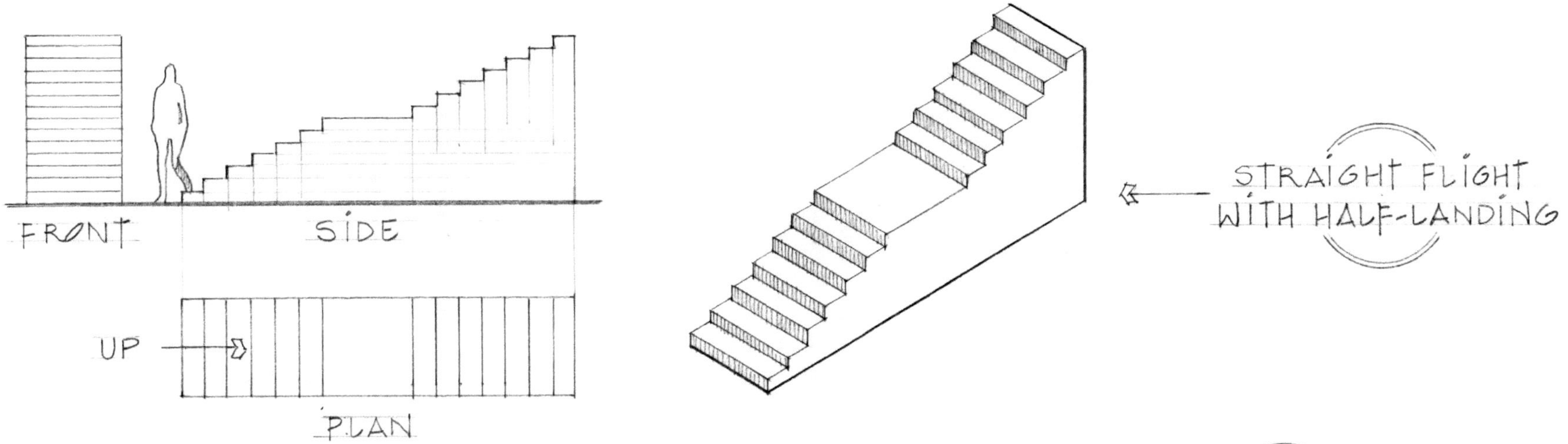

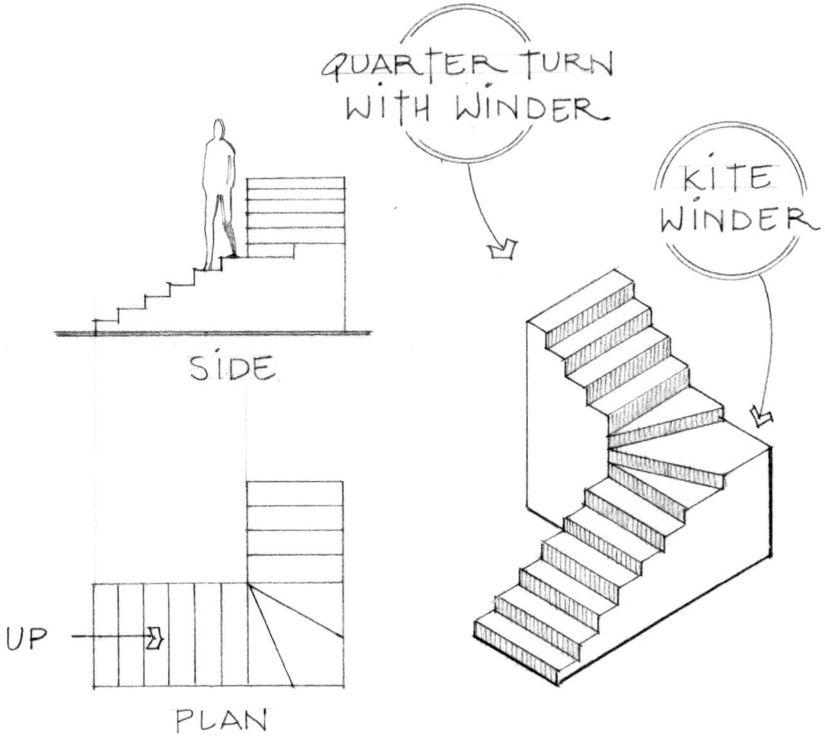

STAIRCASES — TYPES

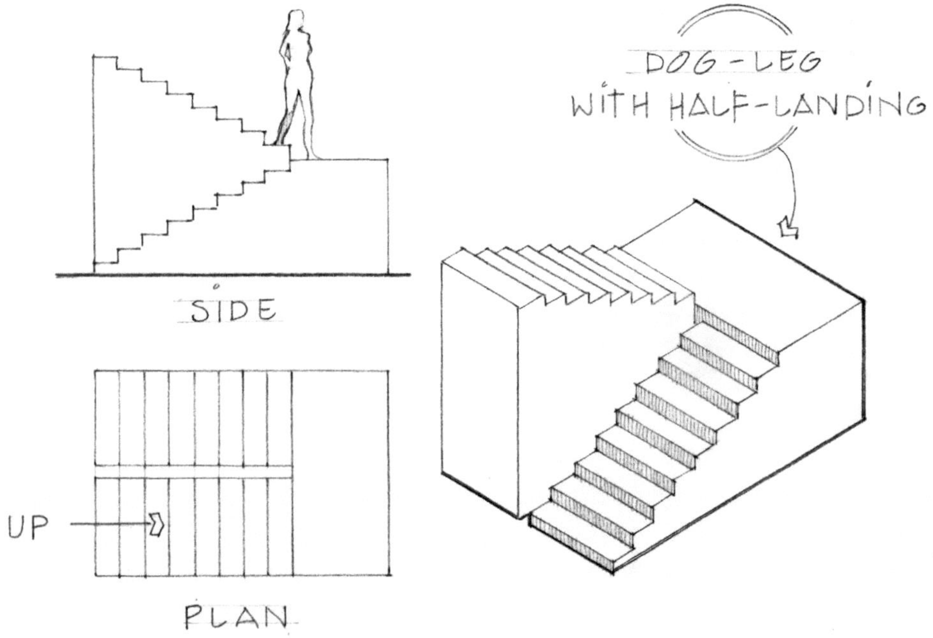

DOG-LEG WITH HALF-LANDING

SIDE

PLAN — UP

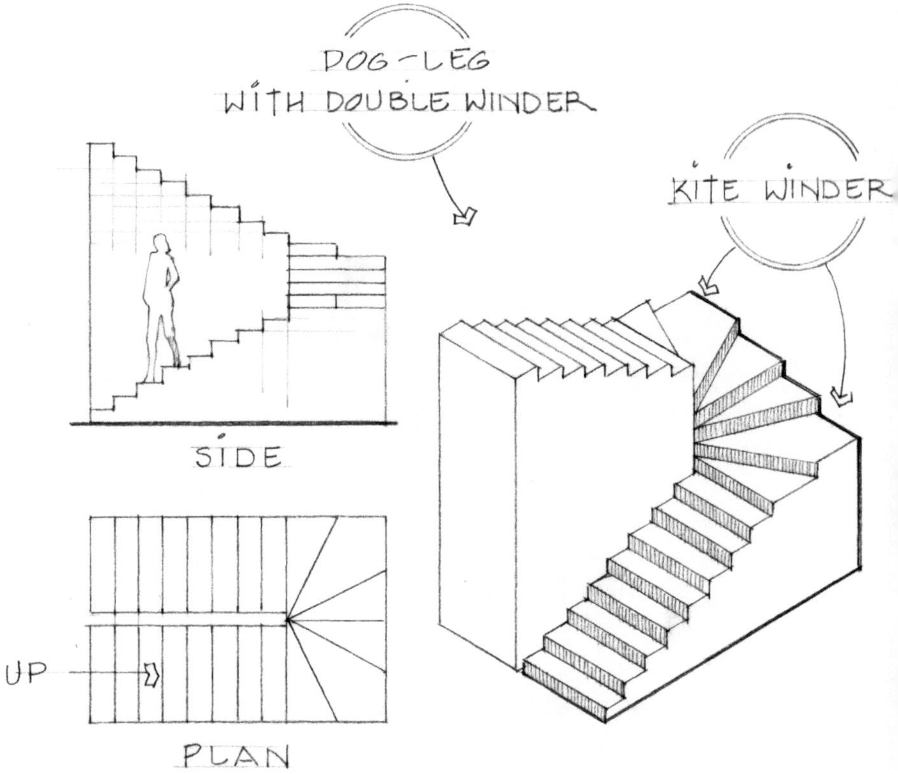

TWO QUARTER LANDING (OPEN WELL)

PLAN — UP

DOG-LEG WITH DOUBLE WINDER

KITE WINDER

SIDE

PLAN — UP

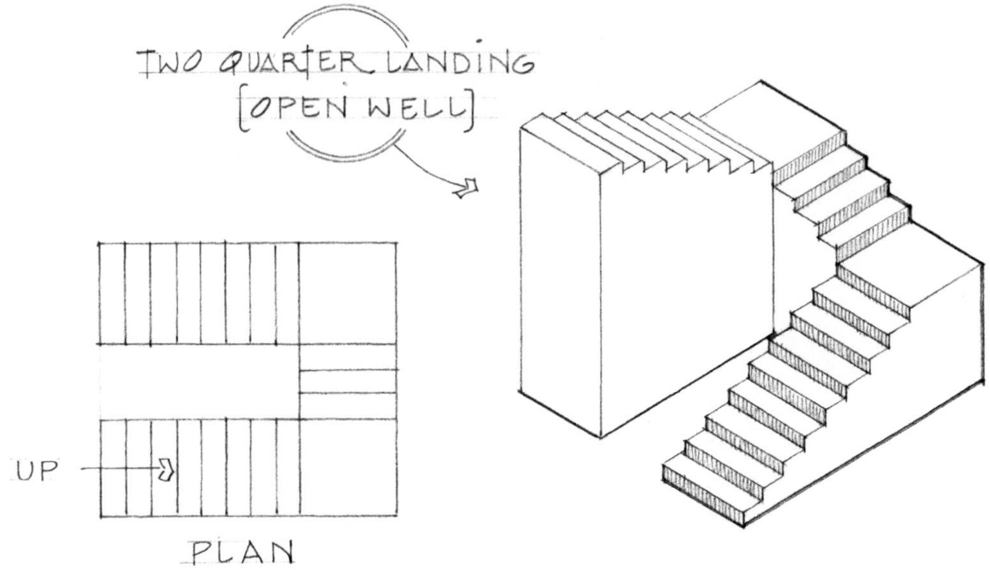

STAIRCASES — TYPES (4)

SIDE

PLAN

TWO QUARTER WINDER

FRONT

PLAN

BIFURCATED

STAIRCASES - TYPES

GEOMETRIC OR CONTINUOUS

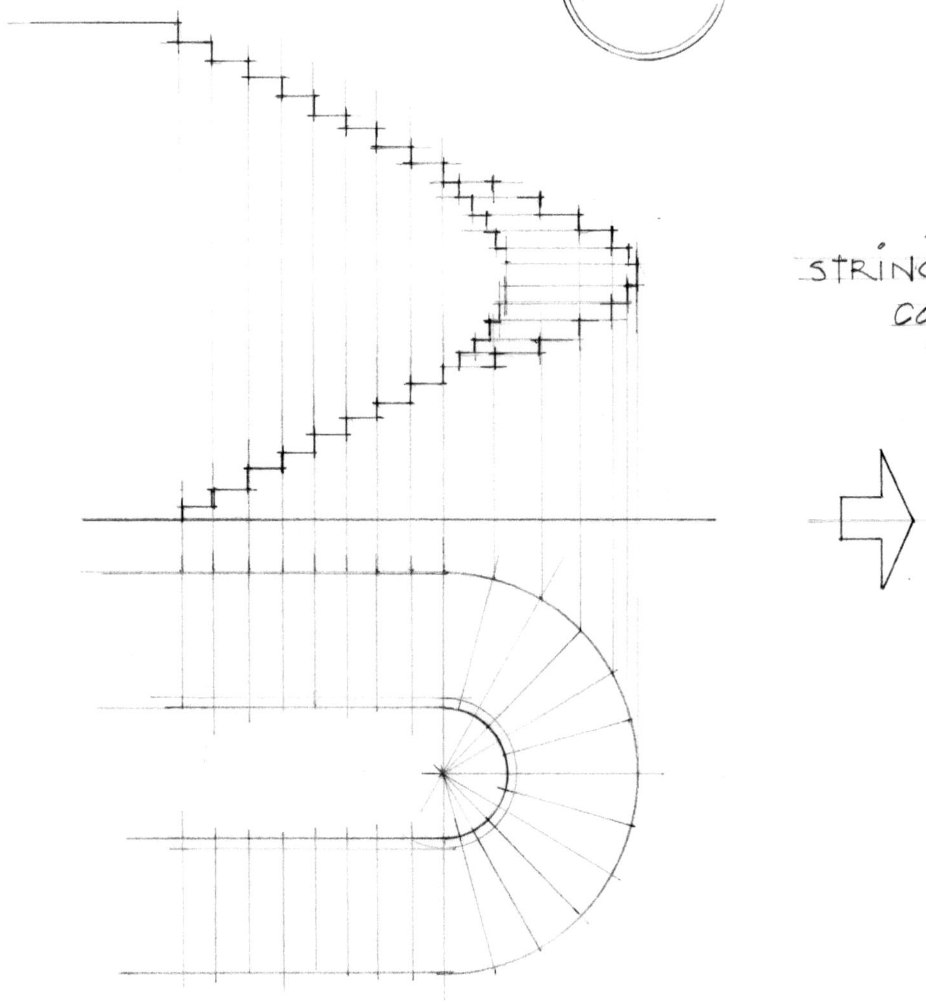

STRINGS & HANDRAILS CONTINUOUS

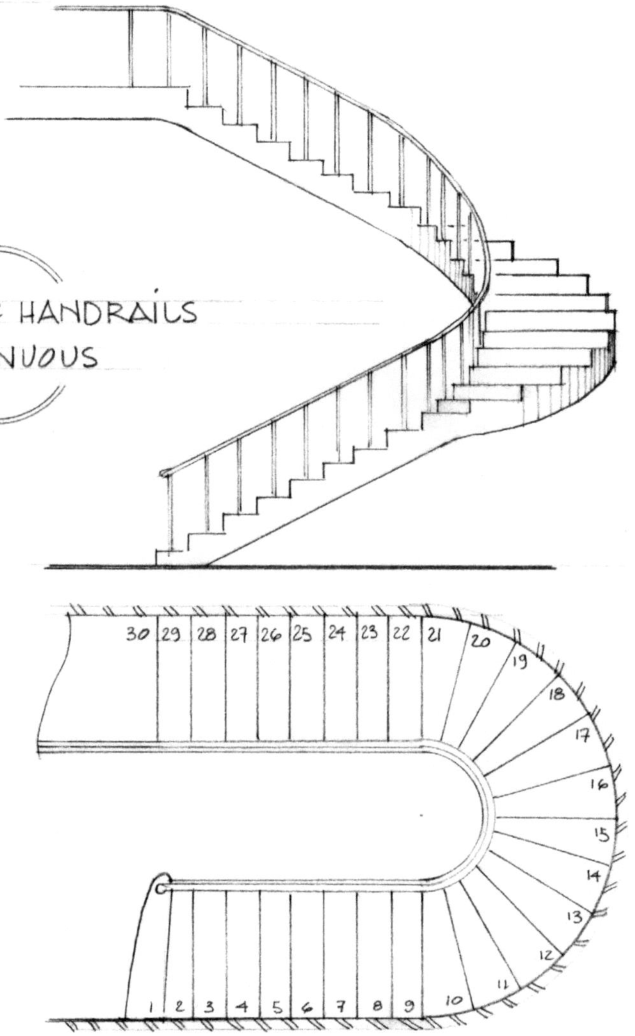

SET OUT TO GEOMETRIC RULES

NEWEL POSTS **NOT** PART OF STRUCTURE

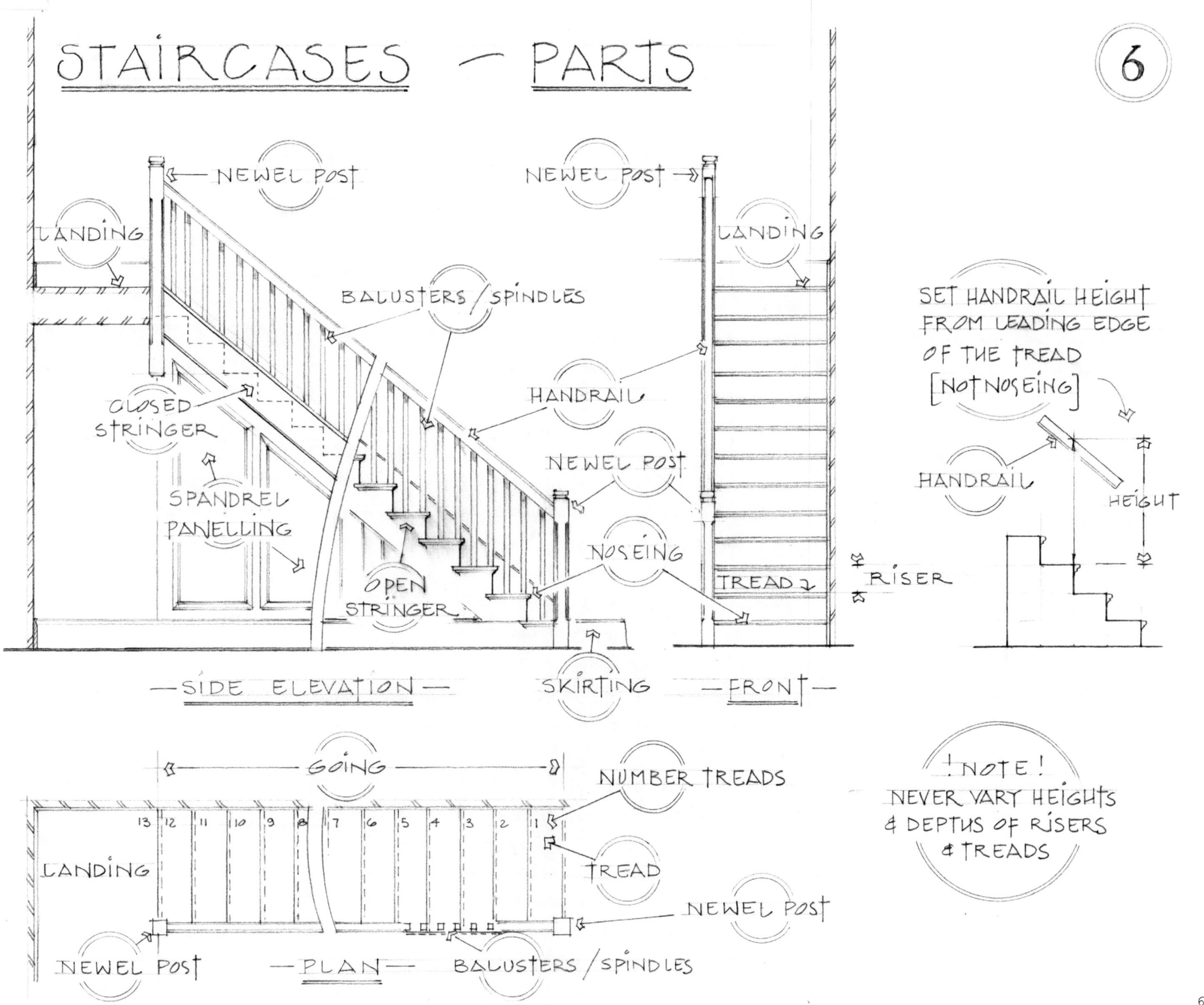

BRICKS — BONDS

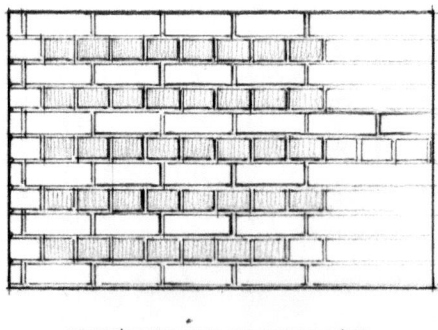
ENGLISH BOND

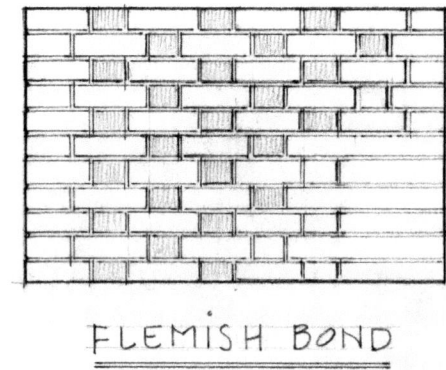
FLEMISH BOND

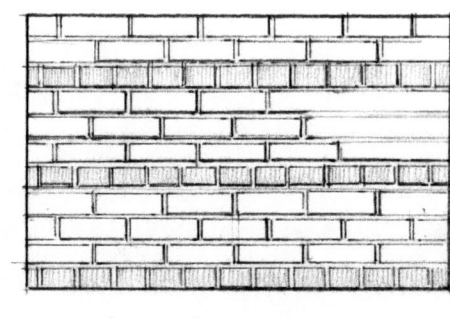
ENGLISH GARDEN BOND

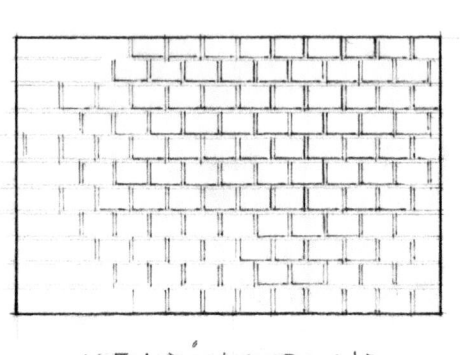
HEADING BOND

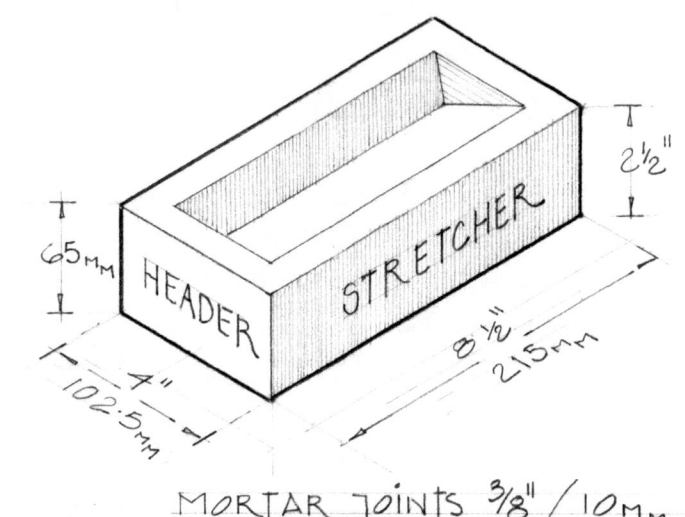
— USUAL BRICK SIZE —

MORTAR JOINTS 3/8" / 10MM

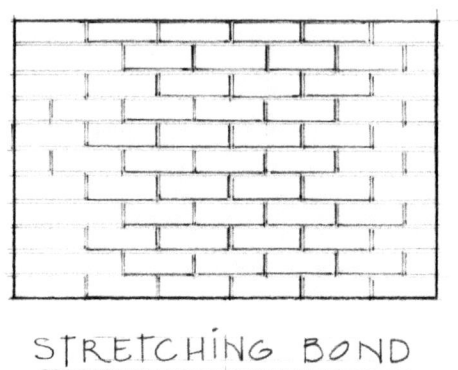
STRETCHING BOND

MOULDINGS — PARTS OF A CIRCLE

A CONTINUOUS PROFILED DECORATION CASTING STRONG SHADOWS WITH INFINITE VARIATIONS

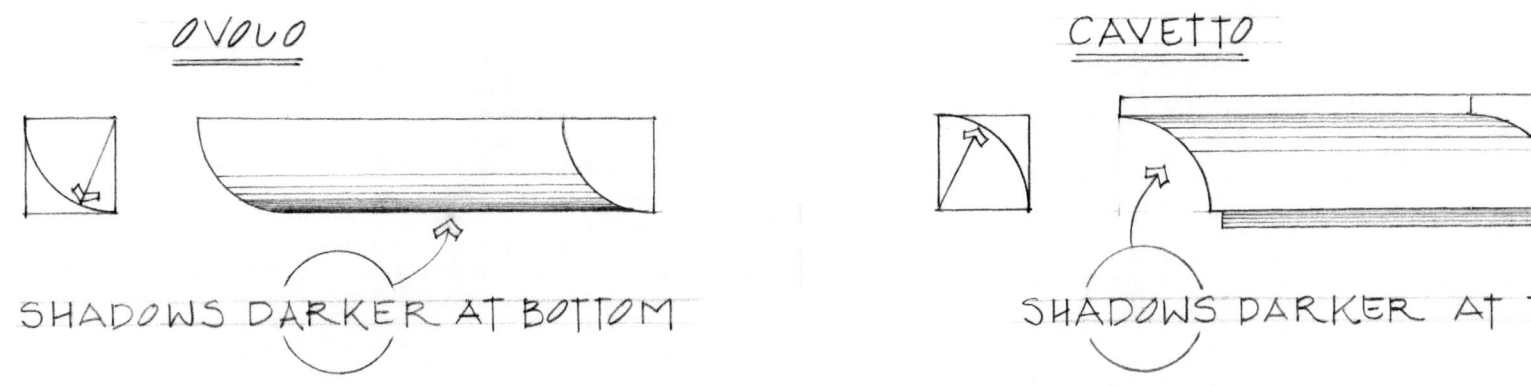

OVOLO
SHADOWS DARKER AT BOTTOM

CAVETTO
SHADOWS DARKER AT TOP

THE PORTIONS OF A CIRCLE MAKE A FULLER & STRONGER CURVE PREFERRED BY THE ROMANS

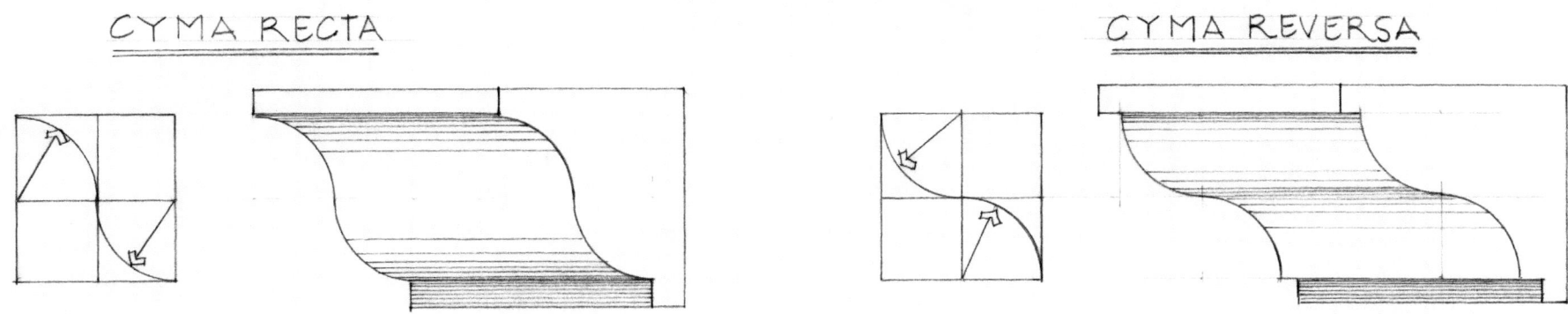

CYMA RECTA

CYMA REVERSA

MOULDINGS — PARTS OF A CIRCLE

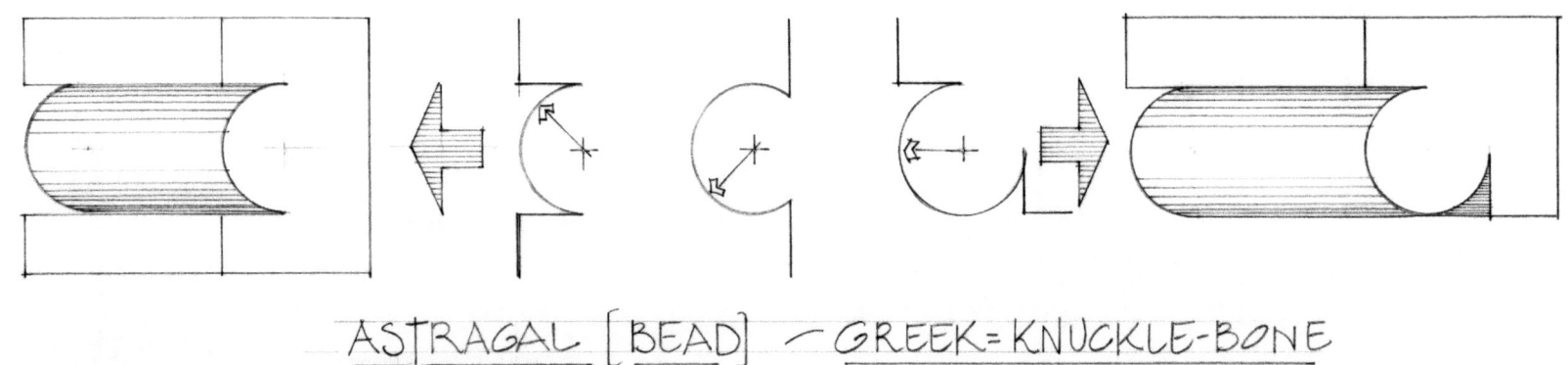

ASTRAGAL [BEAD] — GREEK = KNUCKLE-BONE

SCOTIA — USED IN THE BASES OF COLUMNS & FOR RAMPANT ARCH CONSTRUCTION

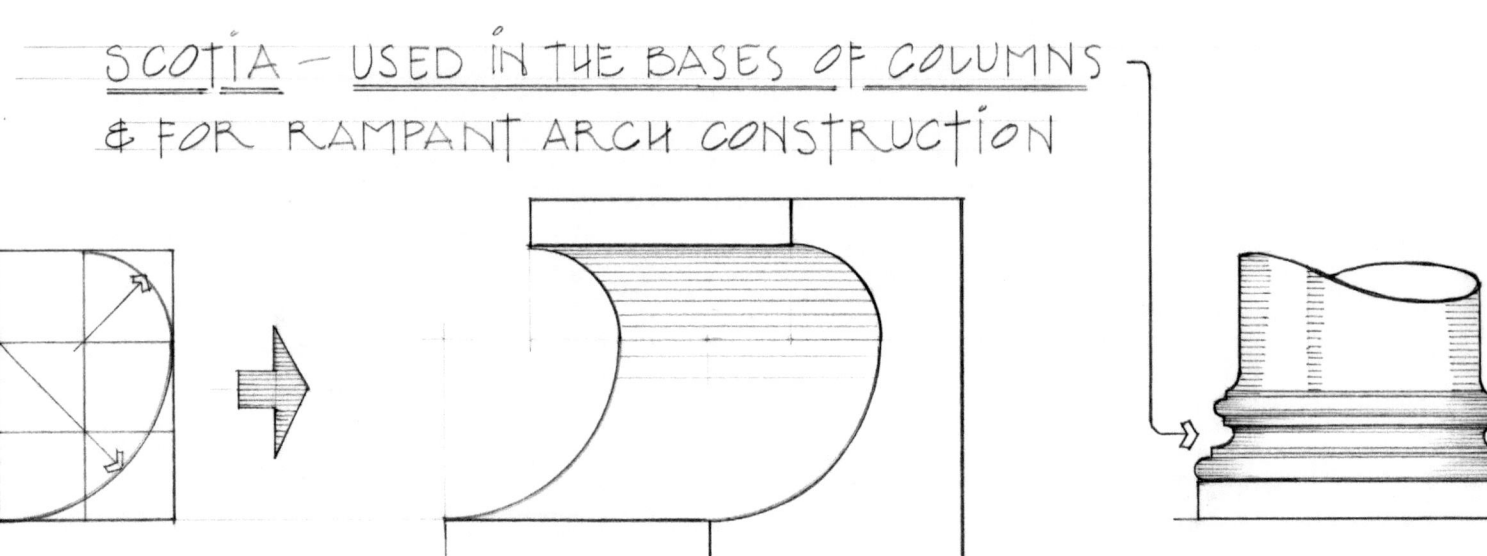

MOULDINGS — CONIC SECTIONS

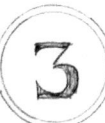

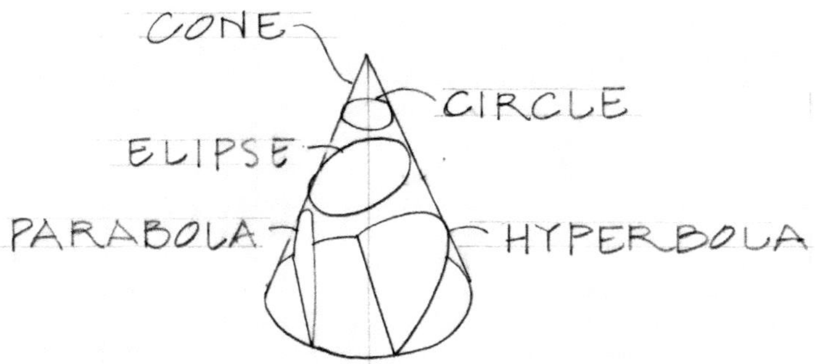

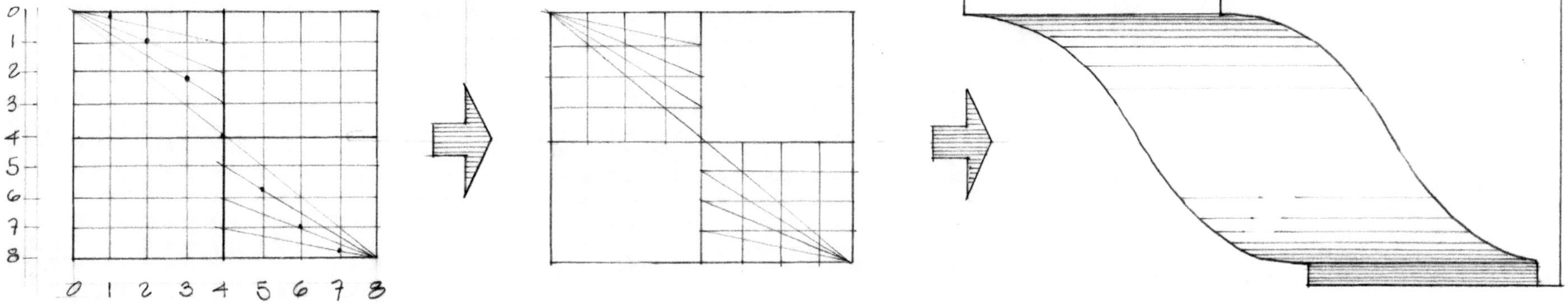

THE ELIPSE, PARABOLA & HYPERBOLA MAKE A FLATTER CURVE PREFERRED BY THE GREEKS

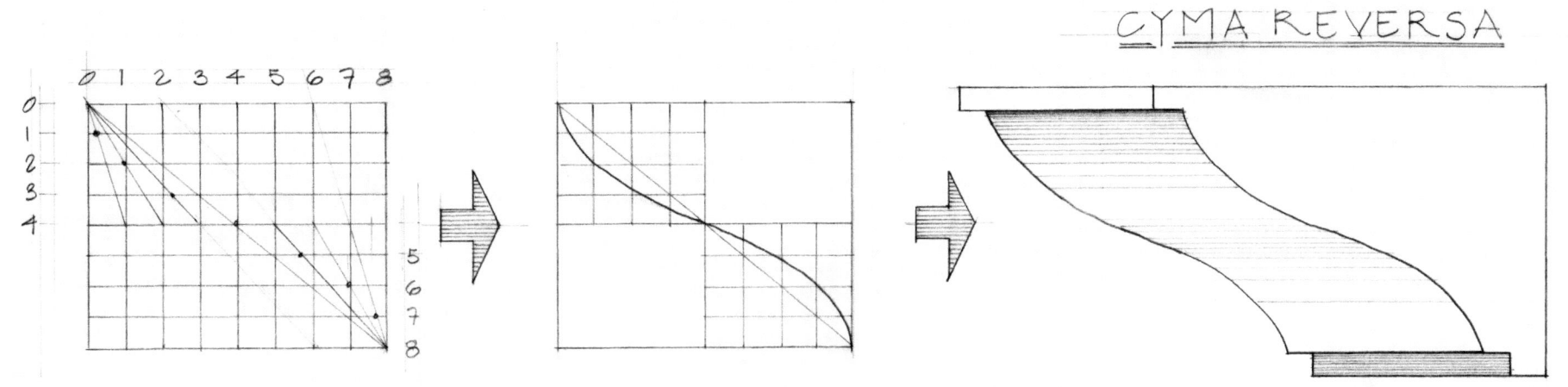

MOULDINGS — "3D" CLASSIC EXAMPLES

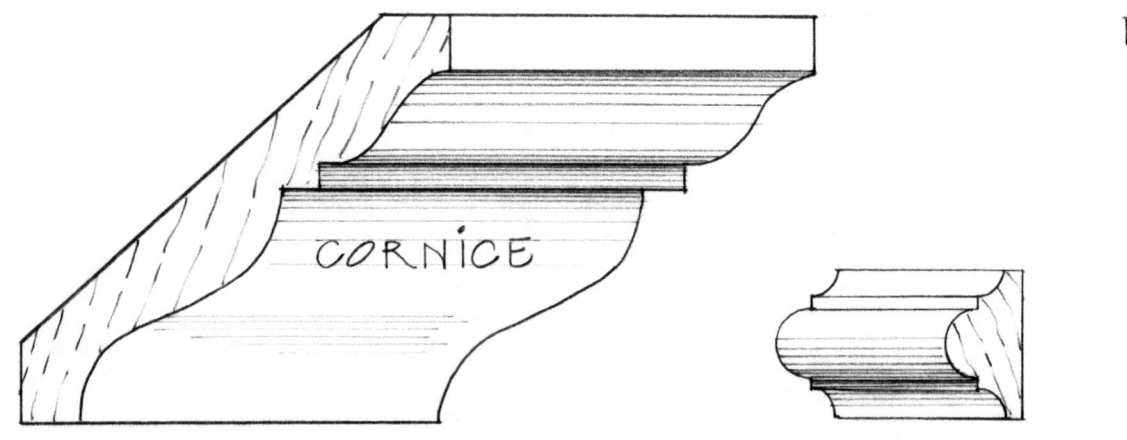

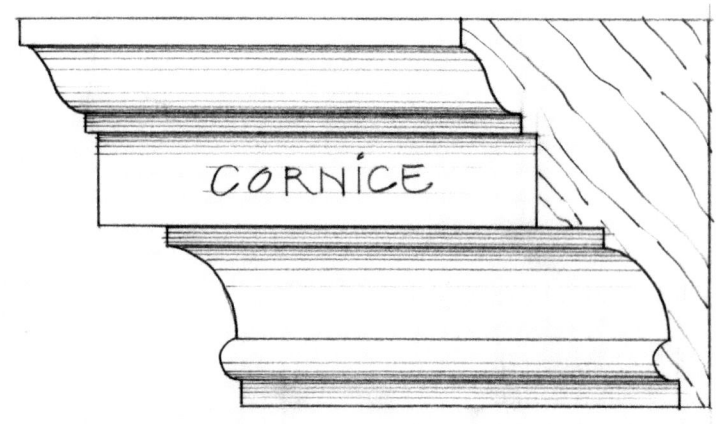

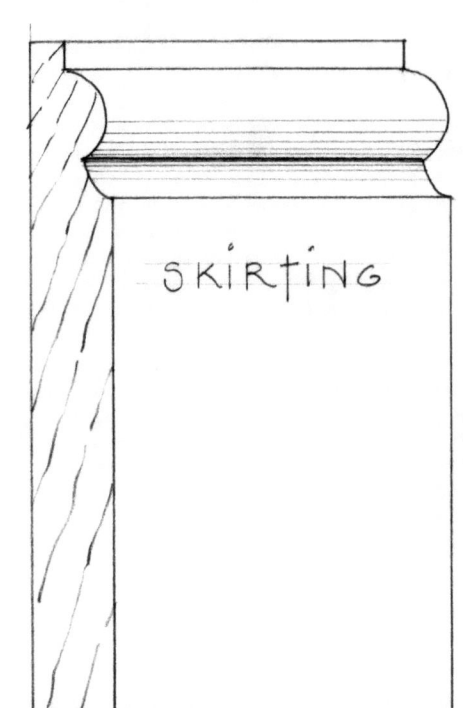

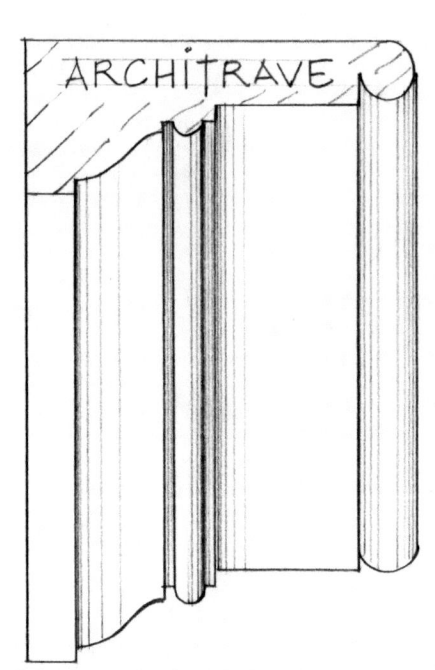

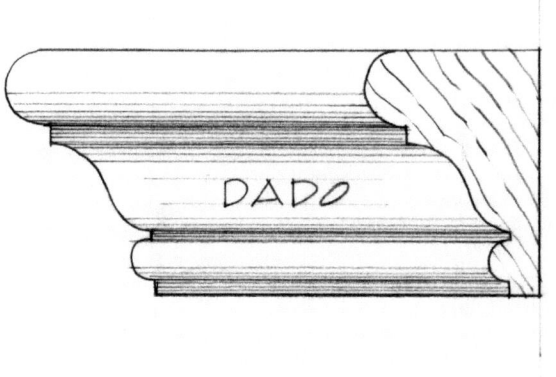

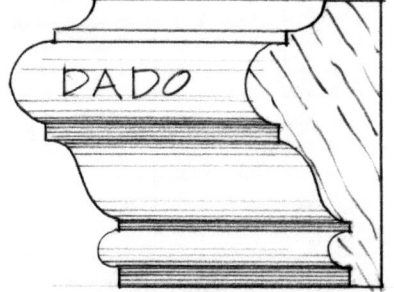

ISOMETRIC PROJECTION

ANCIENT GREEK:
"isos" MEANS "EQUAL"
"metric" MEANS "MEASURE"

MOST COMMONLY USED
SIMILAR TO AXONOMETRIC
BUT PLAN IS DISTORTED

HORIZONTAL LINES @ 30°
VERTICALS REMAIN VERTICAL
MEASUREMENTS CAN BE
TAKEN FROM ALL LINES
ON ORIGINAL (NOT SLOPING)

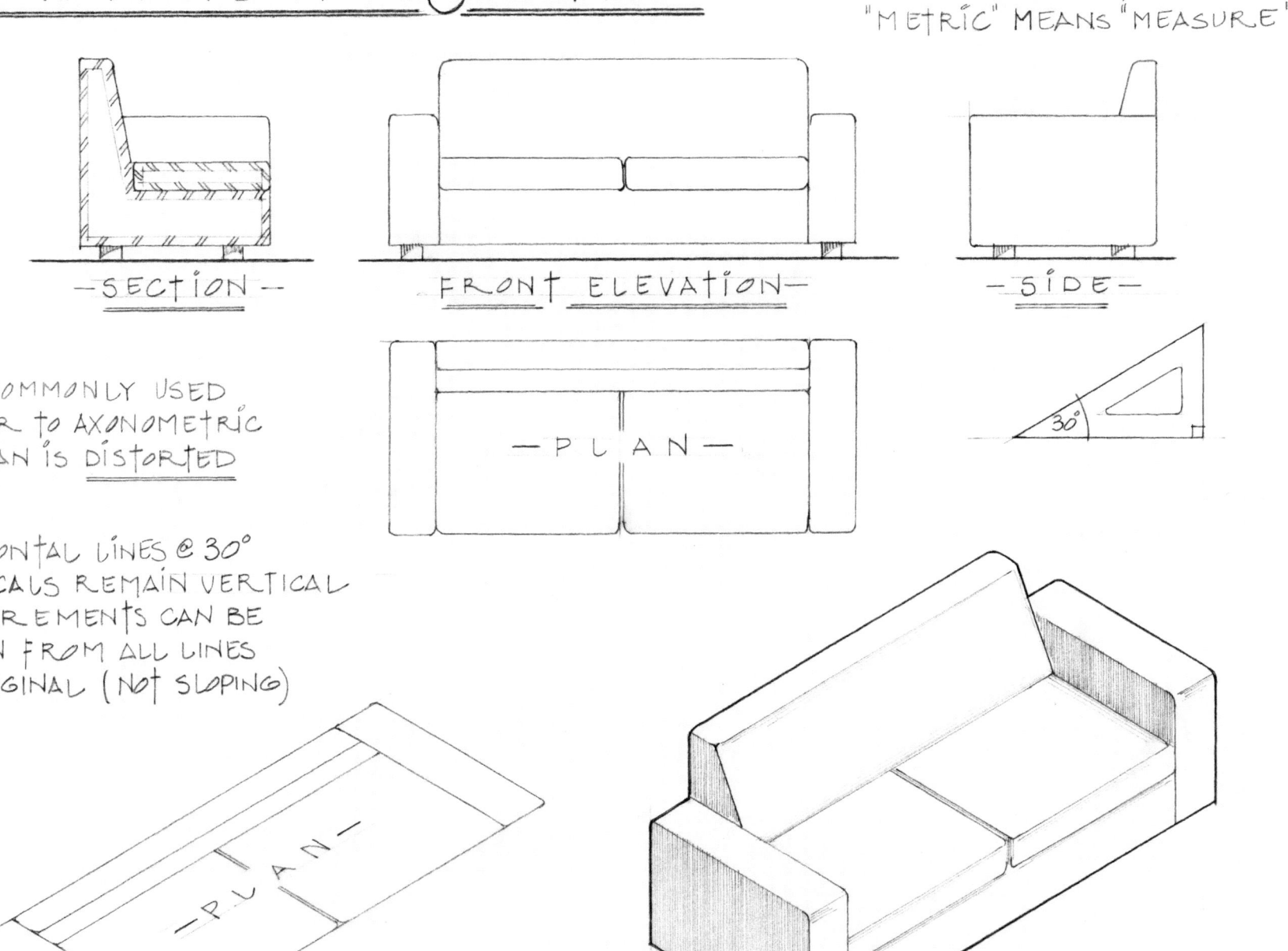

— SECTION —   — FRONT ELEVATION —   — SIDE —
— PLAN —
— PLAN —
30°   30°
30°   30°

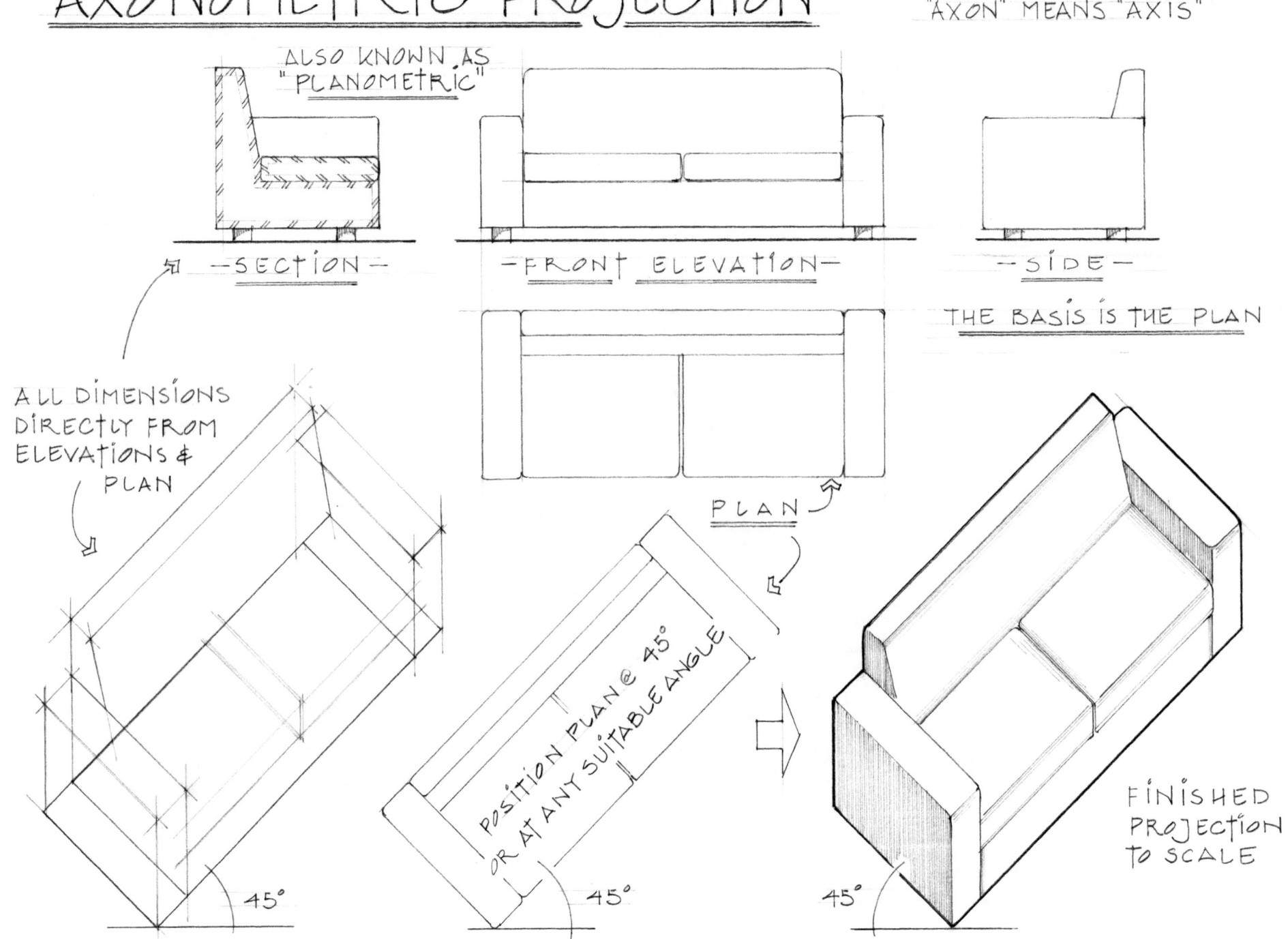

OBLIQUE PROJECTION

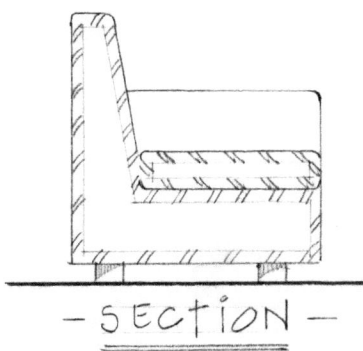
— SECTION —

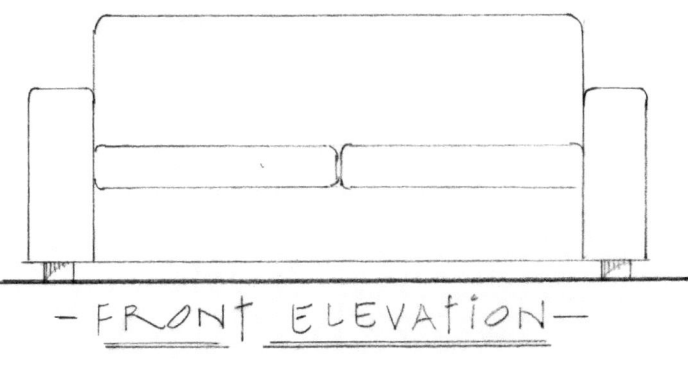
— FRONT ELEVATION —

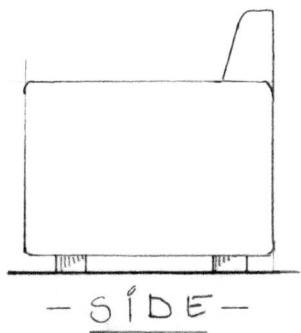
— SIDE —

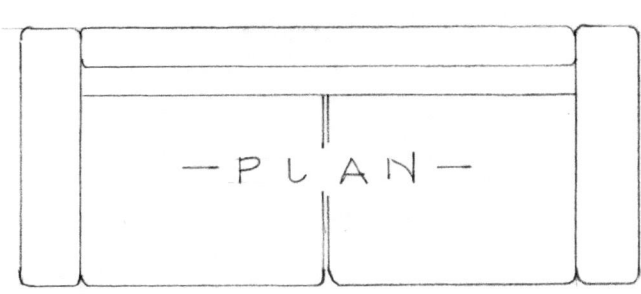
— PLAN —

USE FRONT ELEVATION & PROJECT THE DEPTH AT 30° or 45°
DEPTHS ARE ½ or ⅔ OF ACTUAL DIMENSIONS TO REDUCE ANY DISTORTION

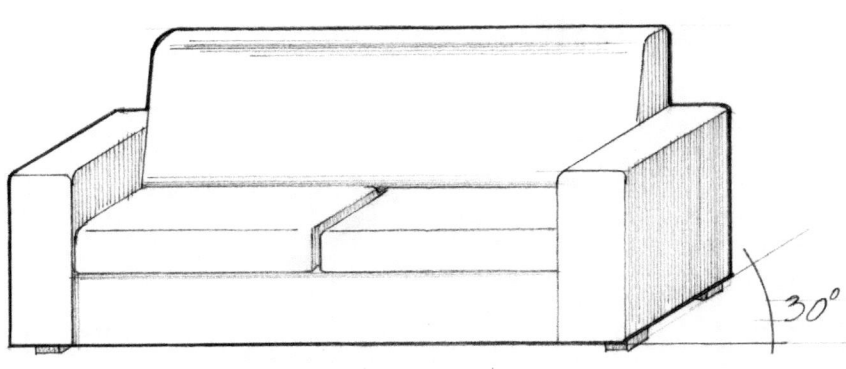
30°

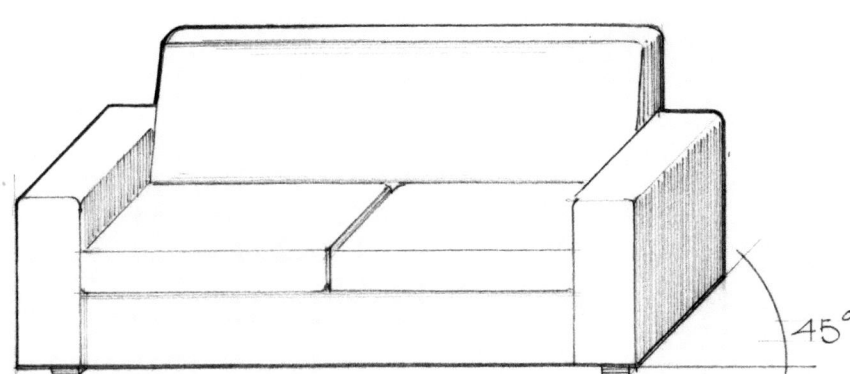
45°

PROJECTIONS OF CIRCLES

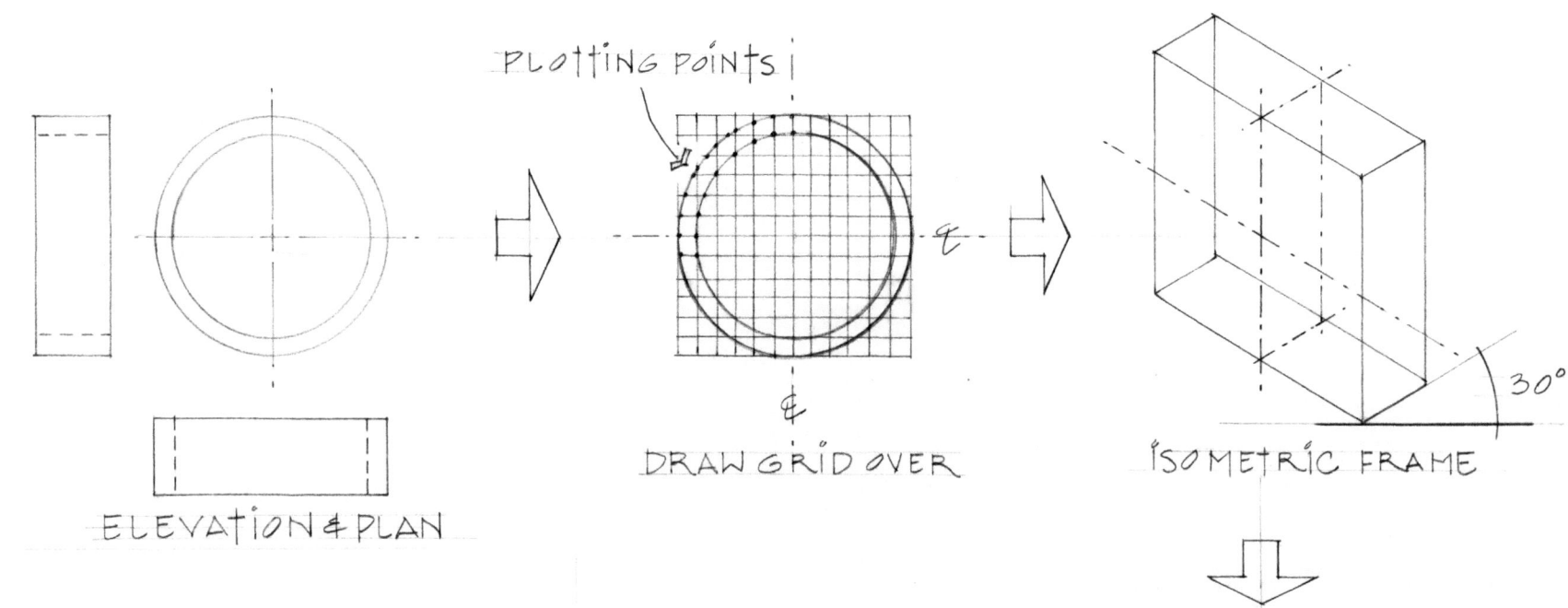

ELEVATION & PLAN

PLOTTING POINTS
DRAW GRID OVER

ISOMETRIC FRAME

DRAW ISOMETRIC GRID PLOT & JOIN BY FREEHAND, FRENCH CURVES OR FLEXICURVE

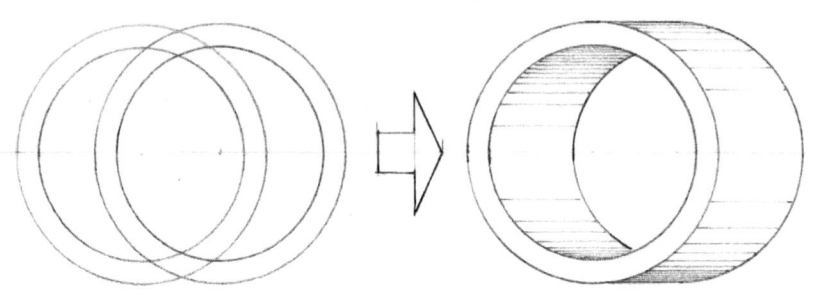

AXONOMETRIC (PLANOMETRIC)

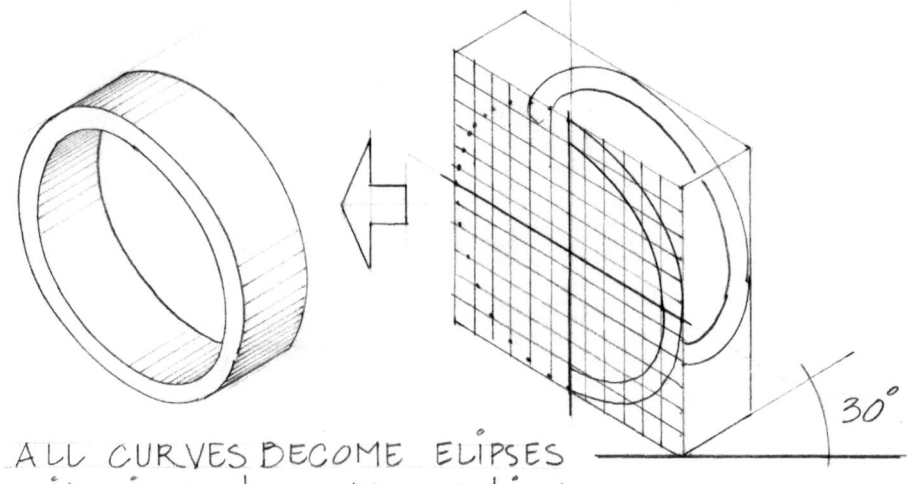

ALL CURVES BECOME ELIPSES WITH ISOMETRIC PROJECTION

PERSPECTIVE GRID — SINGLE POINT

PART ONE

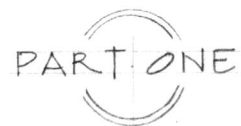

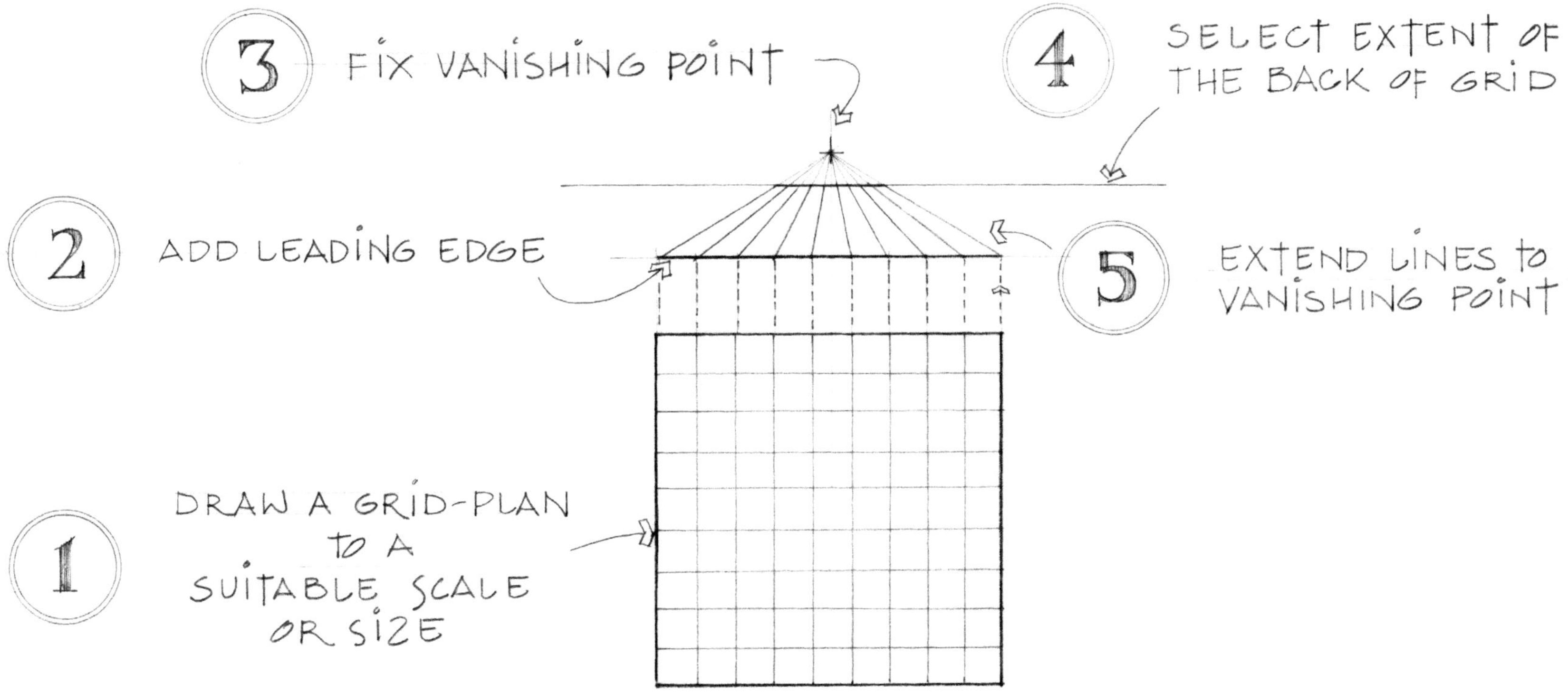

③ FIX VANISHING POINT

④ SELECT EXTENT OF THE BACK OF GRID

② ADD LEADING EDGE

⑤ EXTEND LINES TO VANISHING POINT

① DRAW A GRID-PLAN TO A SUITABLE SCALE OR SIZE

PERSPECTIVE GRID — SINGLE POINT

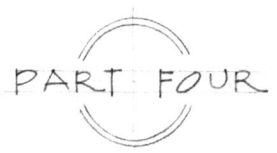

PART FOUR

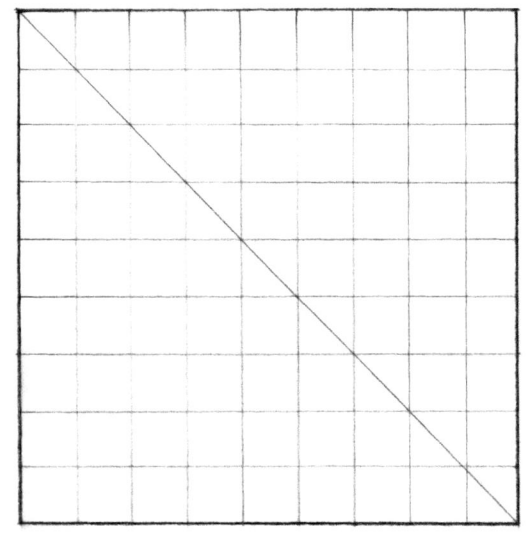

[NB: GRID ENLARGED]

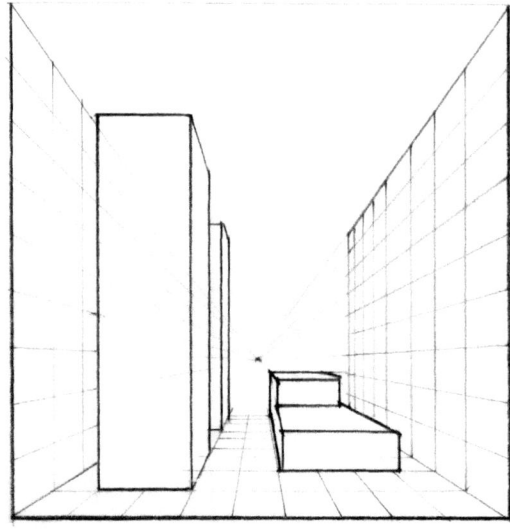

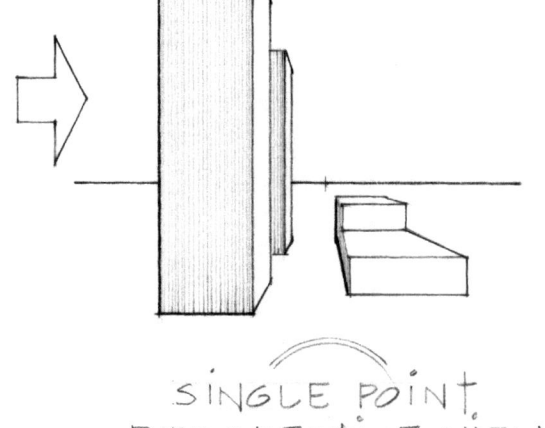

SINGLE POINT PERSPECTIVE VIEW

NB: ALL OBJECTS ARE IN THE CORRECT PROPORTION WITH EACH OTHER

 USE OF GRID WITH BASIC PLAN ADDED

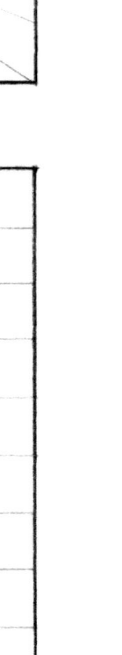

+8 UNITS
+2 UNITS
+1 UNIT
+8 UNITS

2 POINT MEASURED PERSPECTIVE GRID

PART ONE

1 FINDING THE VANISHING POINTS VP_1 & VP_2

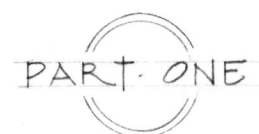

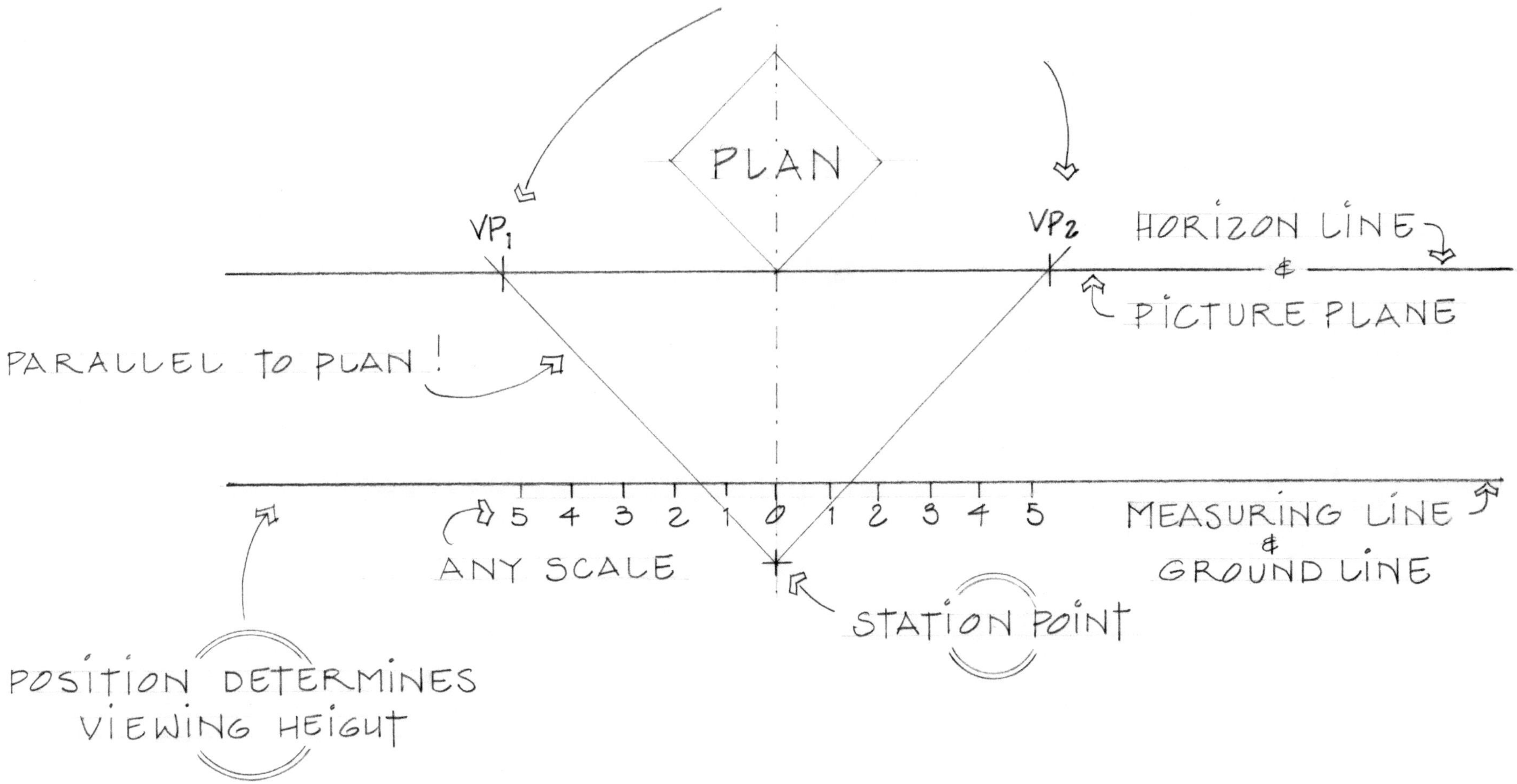

PLAN

VP_1 — VP_2 — HORIZON LINE & PICTURE PLANE

PARALLEL TO PLAN !

5 4 3 2 1 0 1 2 3 4 5 — MEASURING LINE & GROUND LINE

ANY SCALE

STATION POINT

POSITION DETERMINES VIEWING HEIGHT

THIS GIVES THE VANISHING POINTS

2 POINT MEASURED PERSPECTIVE GRID

PART TWO

② FINDING THE MEASURING POINTS MP_1 & MP_2

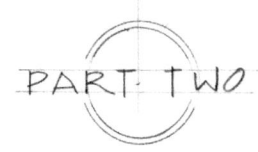

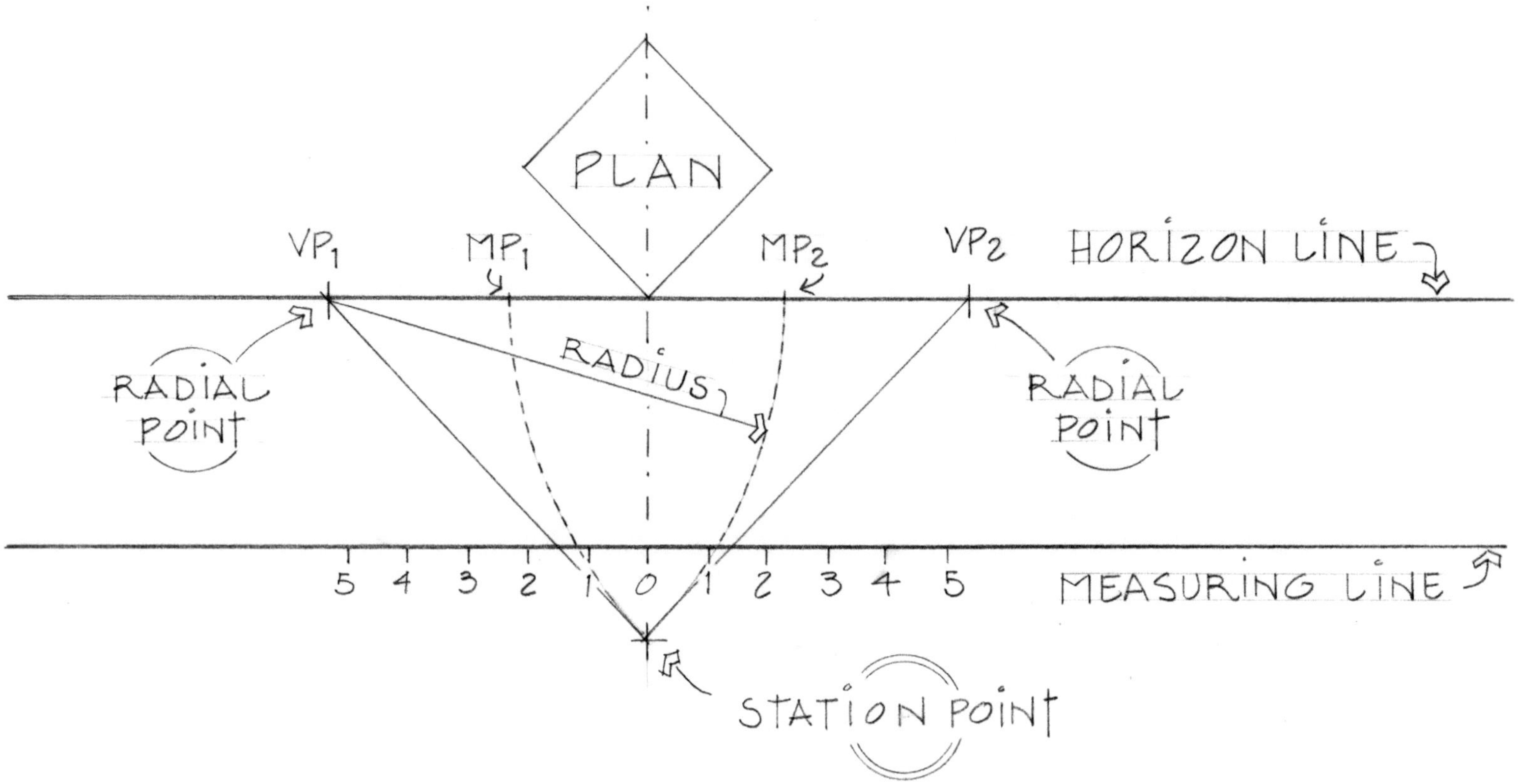

USE VP_1 TO STATION POINT AS RADIUS TO MP_2

2 POINT MEASURED PERSPECTIVE GRID

PART THREE

③ DRAW LINES FROM MEASURING LINE TO MP₁ & MP₂

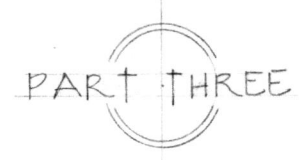

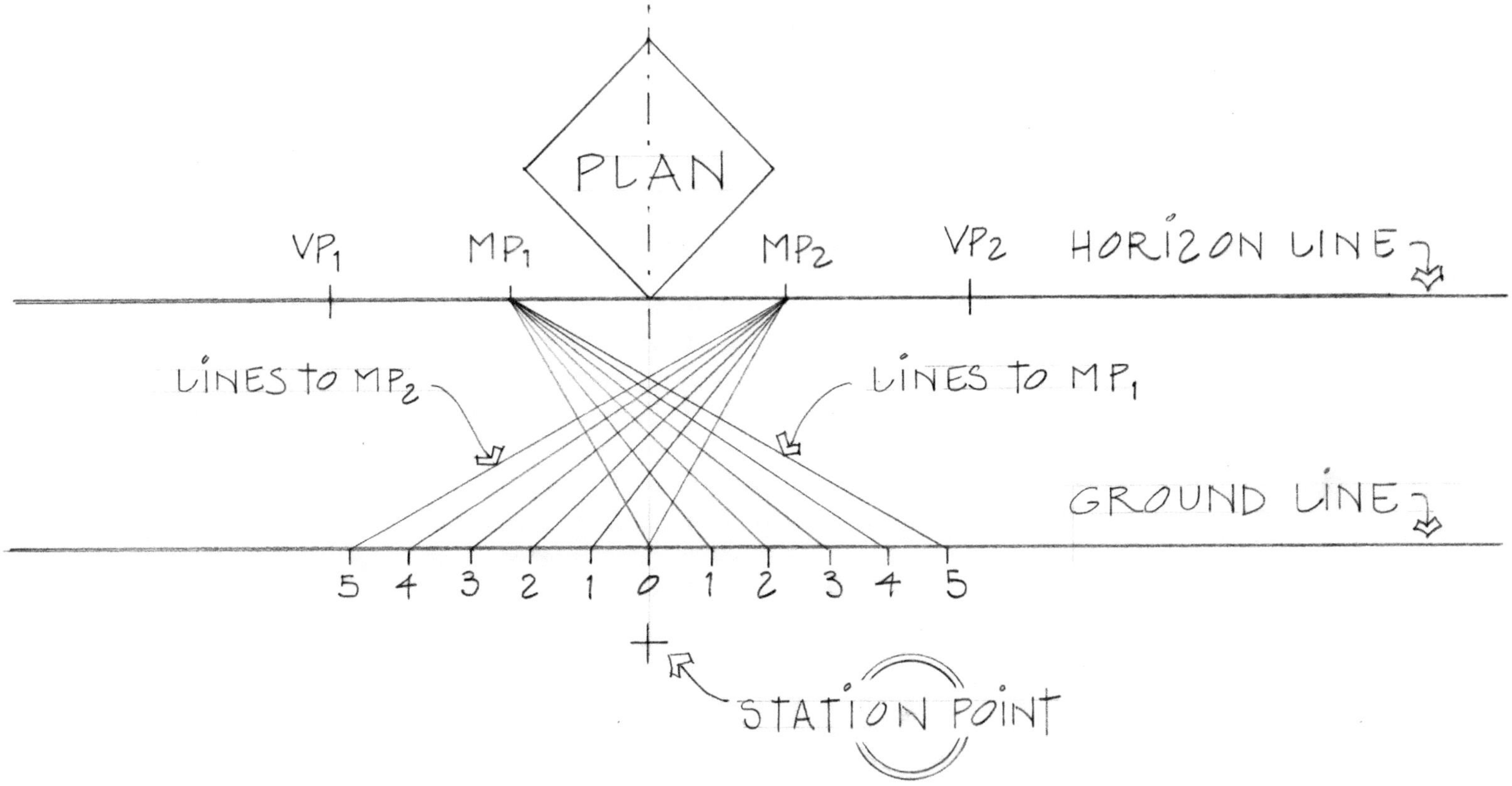

2 POINT MEASURED PERSPECTIVE GRID

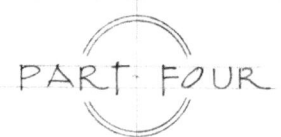

PART FOUR

④ DRAW LINES FROM VP_2 TO JUNCTION OF MP_1 & STATION POINT LINE —
— CARRY LINE THROUGH

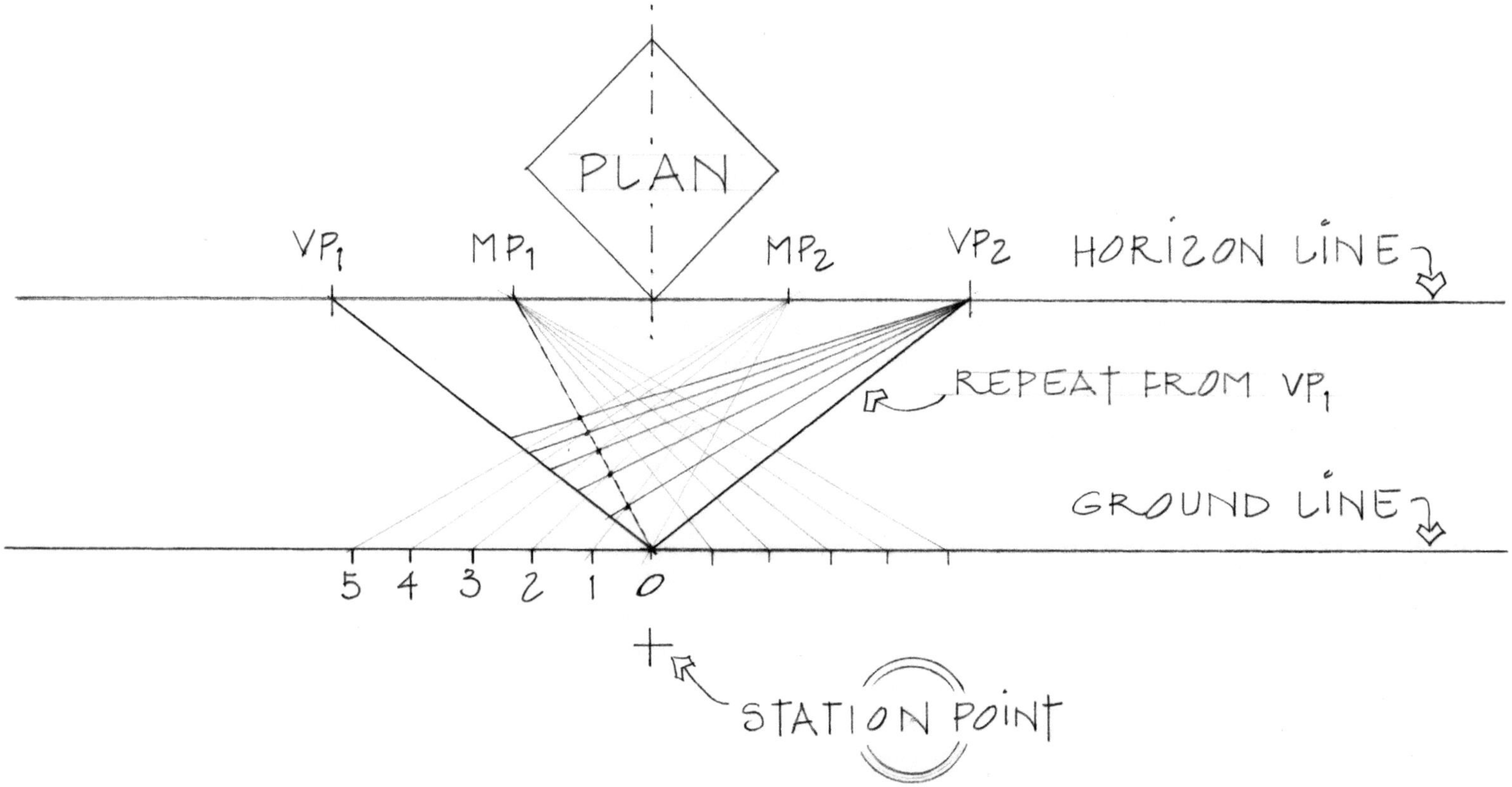

PLAN

VP_1 MP_1 MP_2 VP_2 HORIZON LINE

REPEAT FROM VP_1

GROUND LINE

5 4 3 2 1 0

STATION POINT

2 POINT MEASURED PERSPECTIVE GRID

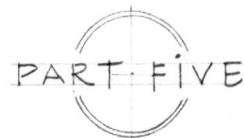

PART FIVE

⑤ COMPLETE PERSPECTIVE GRID PLAN

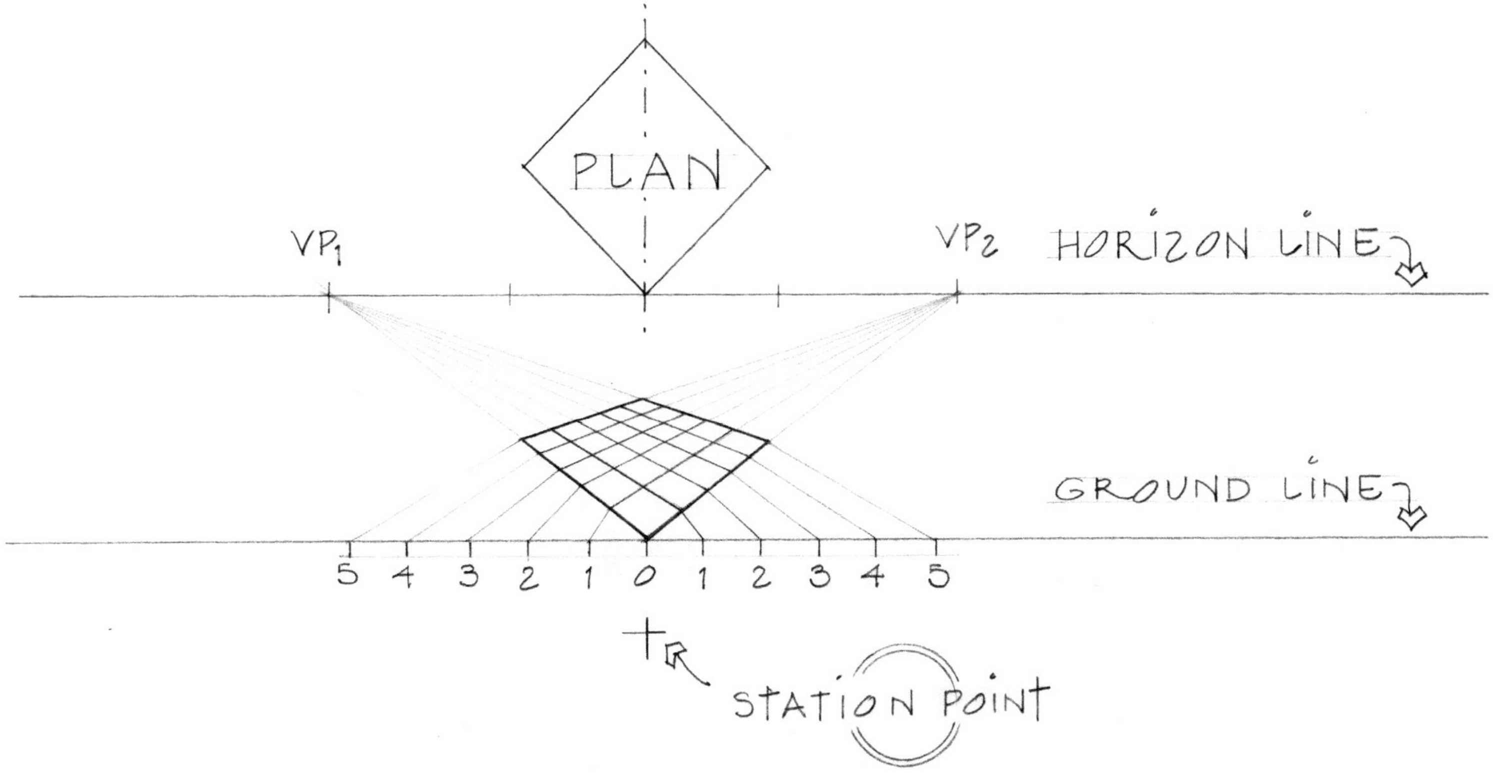

2 POINT MEASURED PERSPECTIVE GRID

PART SIX

6 COMPLETED GRID

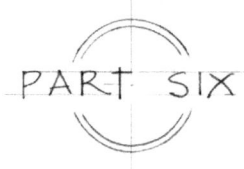

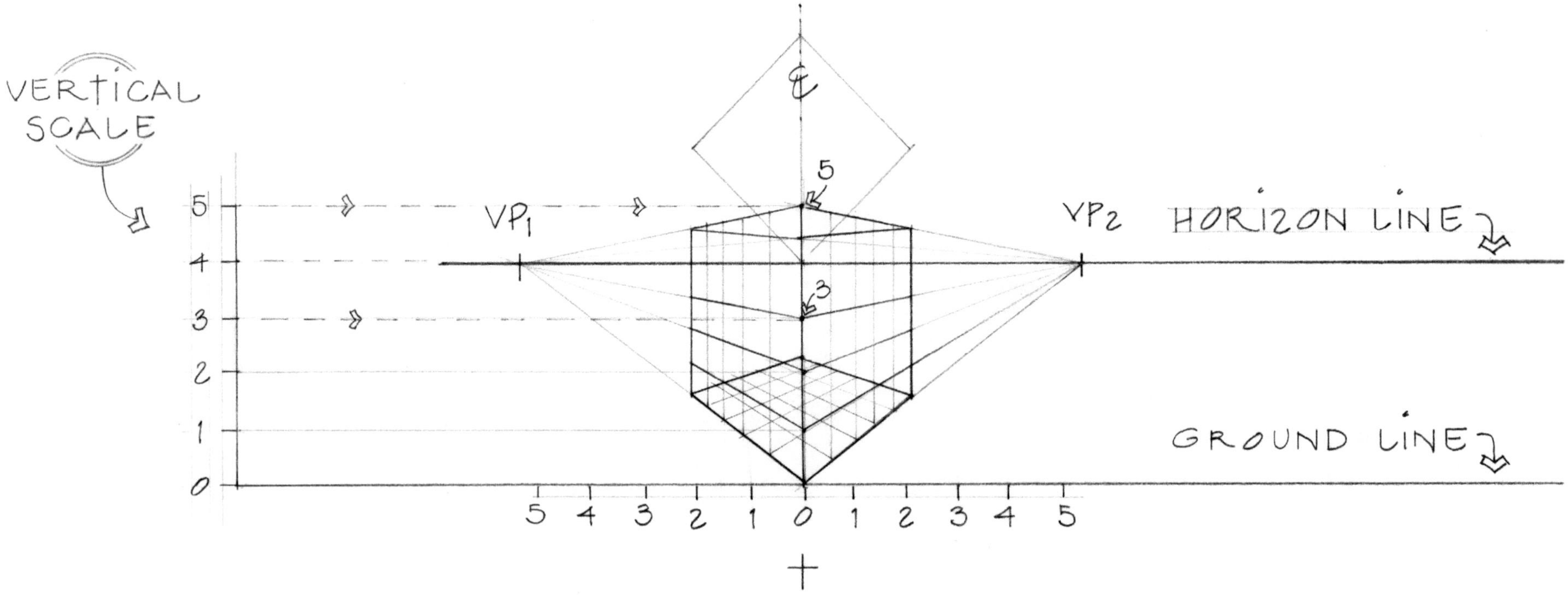

VERTICAL SCALE

VP₁ HORIZON LINE

VP₂

GROUND LINE

TRANSFER VERTICAL SCALE TO CENTRE LINE, STARTING AT ZERO ON GROUND LINE

2 POINT MEASURED PERSPECTIVE GRID

STATION POINT SET TO RIGHT OF PLAN — PART SEVEN

(7) ALTERNATIVELY USE FOR SETTING STATION POINT TO LEFT OF PLAN

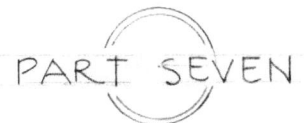

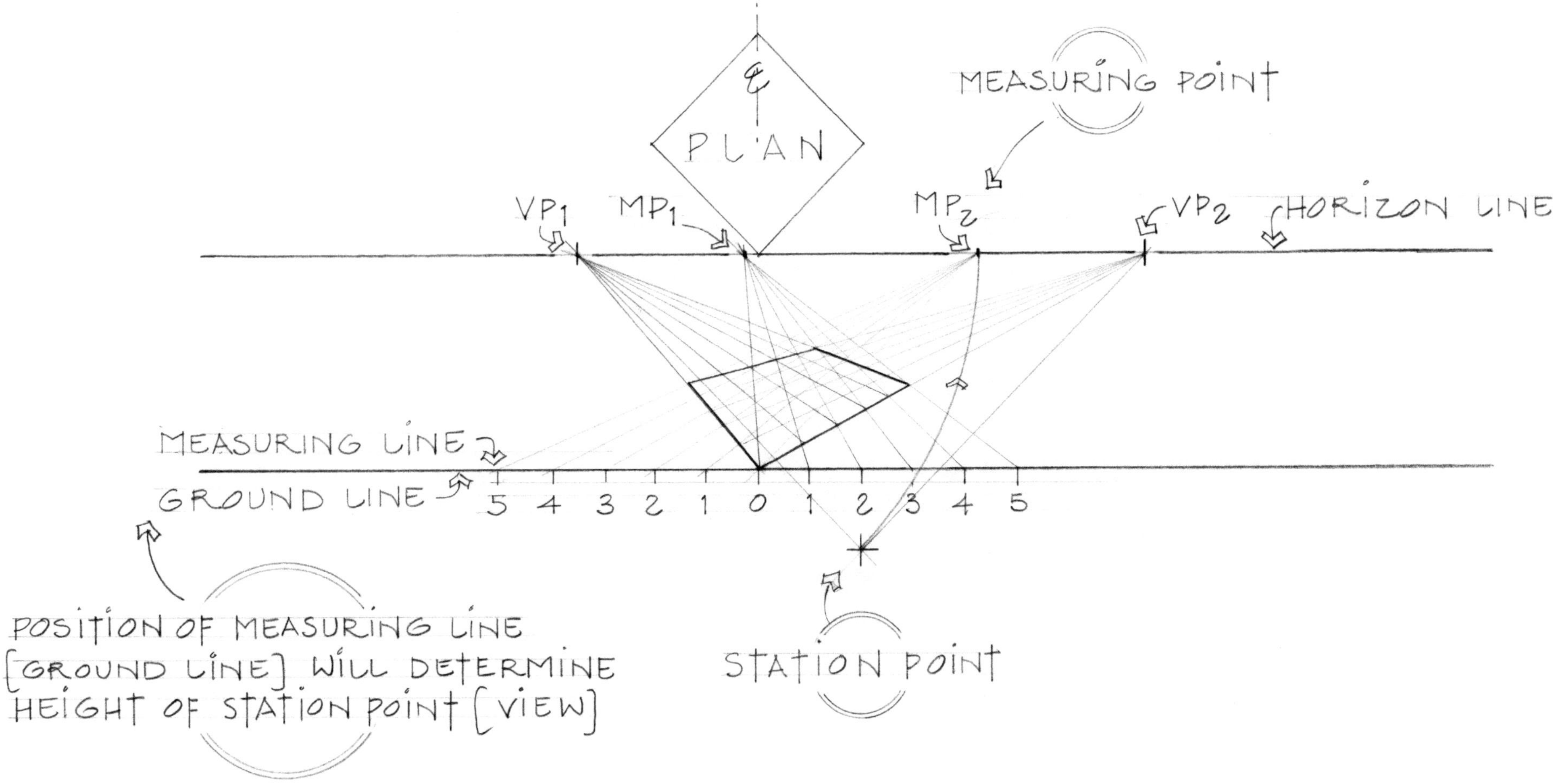

PLAN

MEASURING POINT

VP₁ MP₁ MP₂ VP₂ HORIZON LINE

MEASURING LINE
GROUND LINE — 5 4 3 2 1 0 1 2 3 4 5

STATION POINT

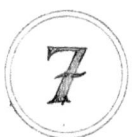

POSITION OF MEASURING LINE (GROUND LINE) WILL DETERMINE HEIGHT OF STATION POINT (VIEW)

SETTING UP A CAMERA PROJECTION

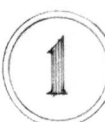

DETERMINE THE ASPECT RATIO [SCREEN FORMAT] WITH THE CINEMATOGRAPHER, DIRECTOR AND PRODUCER.

THERE ARE 3 MAJOR FORMATS IN USE:

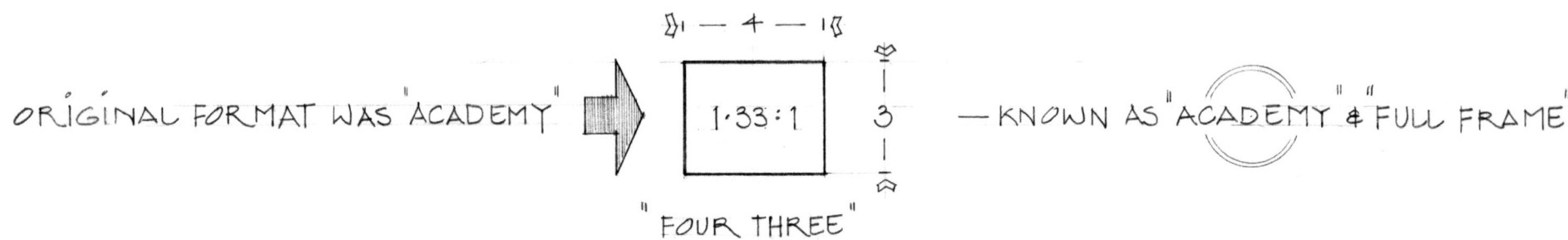

— ASPECT RATIO IS DETERMINED BY DIVIDING WIDTH OF PICTURE BY HEIGHT —

SETTING UP A CAMERA PROJECTION

SELECT A LENS — EG 50mm

SELECT AN ASPECT RATIO [AR] — EG 1·85:1

FOR AR 1·85:1 THE ACTIVE APERTURE SIZE ON THE SENSOR = 0·825" × 0·446"   0·446"

THE SENSOR CAPTURES THE IMAGE FROM THE LENS

0·825"

[NOT TO SCALE]

ASPECT RATIO = WIDTH ÷ HEIGHT   W = 0·825"   } = SENSOR SIZE
                                    H = 0·446"

$\dfrac{0.825"}{0.446"}$ OR IN METRIC $\dfrac{20.95_{MM}}{11.33_{MM}}$ = 1·8490732 — ROUNDED UP = 1·85 !

GIVEN THAT THE FOCAL LENGTH OF THE LENS IS 50mm AND THE APERTURE IS 20·95mm × 11·33mm

! THIS IS TOO SMALL TO DRAW !

ENLARGE LENS LENGTH [FOCAL LENGTH] & APERTURE [SENSOR] × 10 TIMES

THEREFORE:

50mm × 10 = 500mm   [FOCAL LENGTH]

20·95mm × 10 = 209·5mm [SENSOR WIDTH] & 11·33mm × 10 = 113·3mm [SENSOR HEIGHT]

SETTING UP A CAMERA PROJECTION (3)

TO DRAW A 50mm LENS WITH ASPECT RATIO 1·85:1

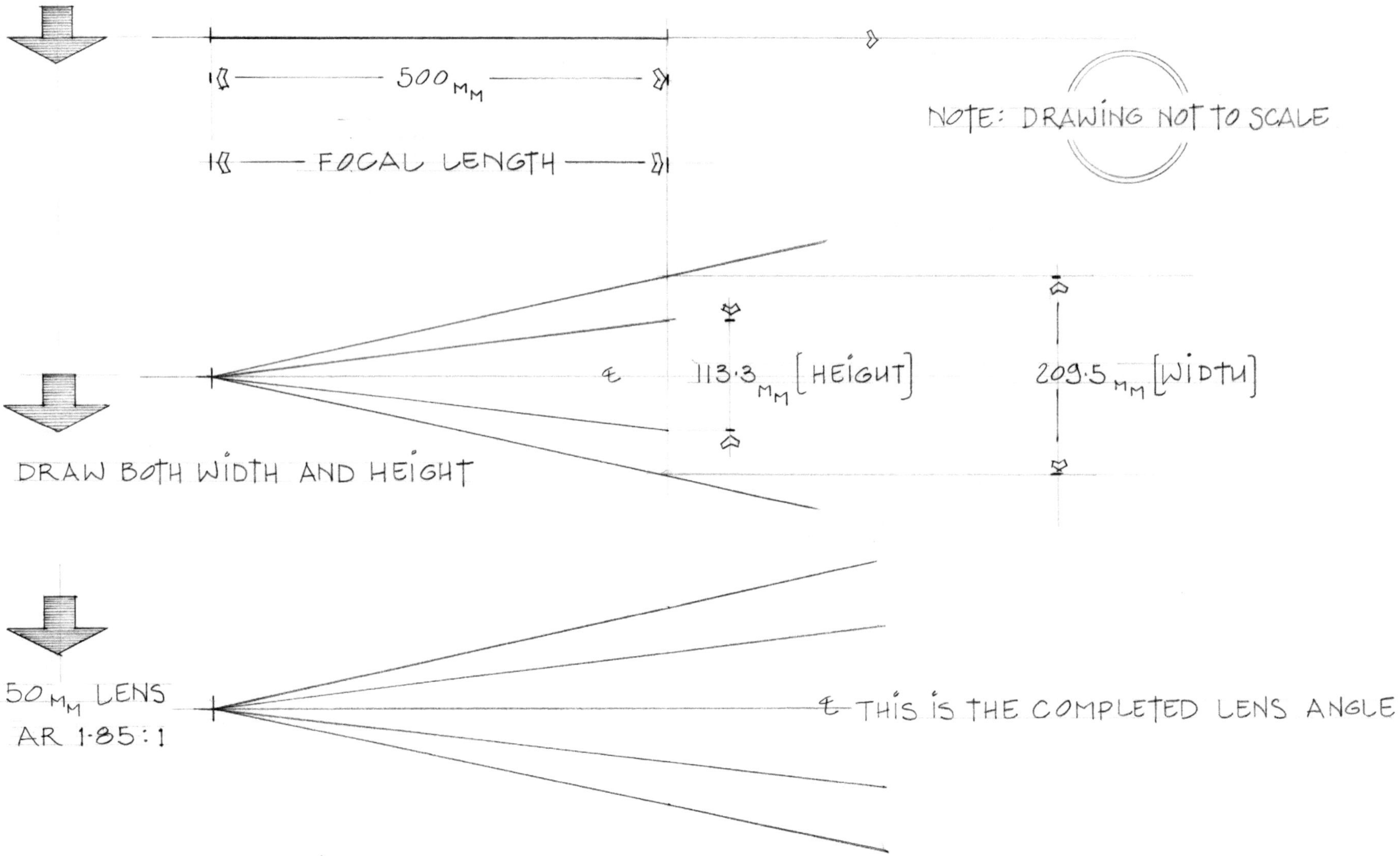

|← 500mm →|

|← FOCAL LENGTH →|

NOTE: DRAWING NOT TO SCALE

⬇ DRAW BOTH WIDTH AND HEIGHT

₵ 113·3mm [HEIGHT]   209·5mm [WIDTH]

⬇ 50mm LENS
AR 1·85:1

₵ THIS IS THE COMPLETED LENS ANGLE

SETTING UP A CAMERA PROJECTION

COPY THE LENS ANGLE ONTO A SHEET OF CLEAR ACETATE

TO INFINITY & BEYOND!

WIDTH
HEIGHT
₡ THE ANGLE IS CONSTANT WHATEVER SIZE IT IS DRAWN

50mm LENS
AR 1·85:1

LABEL THE LENS AND ASPECT RATIO

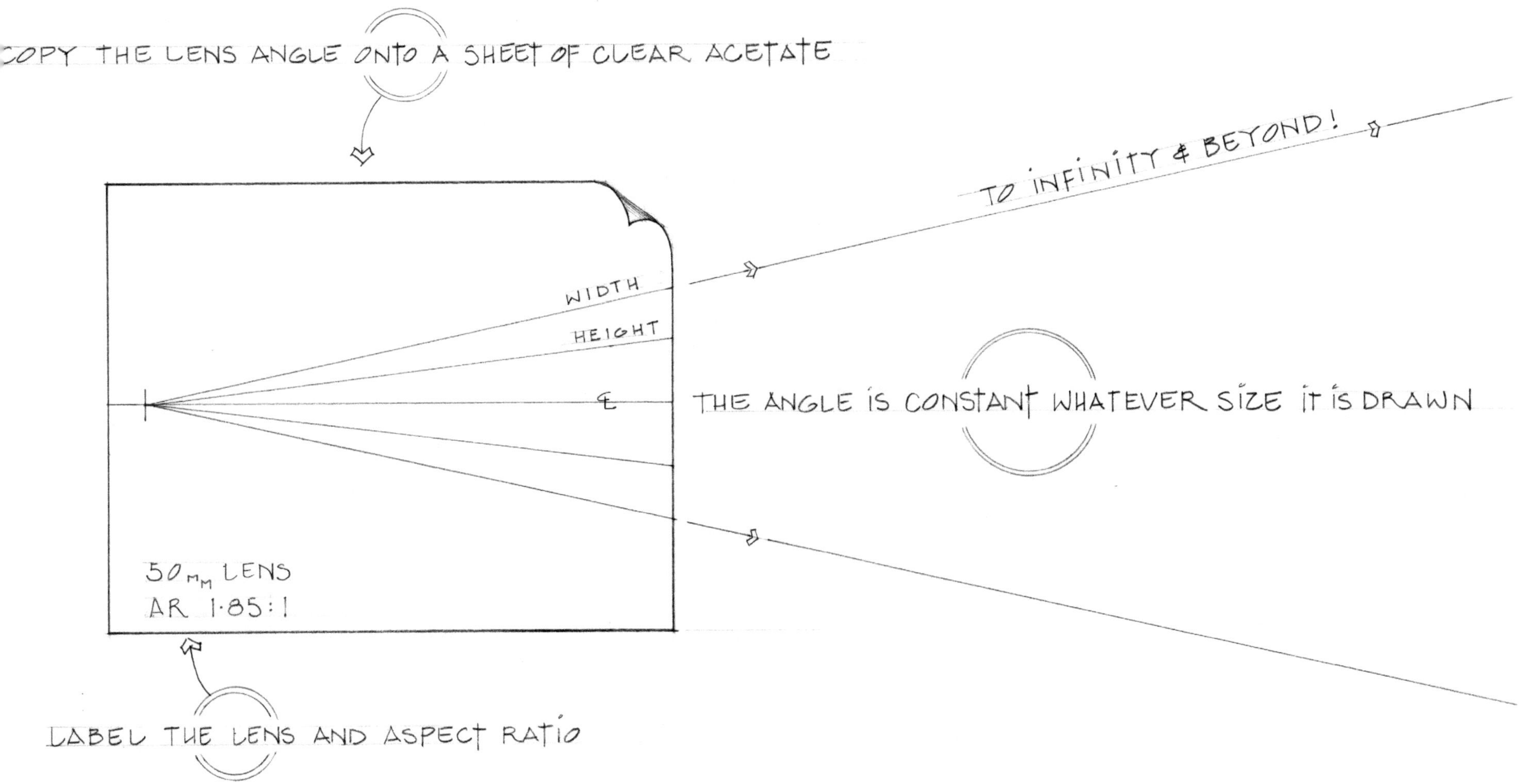

THE LENS ANGLE CAN NOW BE OVERLAID ON THE SET PLAN & ELEVATIONS CHECKING FOR SHOOT-OFFS, CEILING REQUIREMENTS AND THE POSITIONING OF BACKDROPS & DRESSING.

SETTING UP A CAMERA PROJECTION

USING A 6'-0" CUBE ON A STUDIO FLOOR @ 56'-0" FROM THE CAMERA & 2'-0" TO CAMERA RIGHT OF THE CENTRE LINE ON PLAN, POSITION BOTH HEIGHT & WIDTH LENS ANGLES AS SHOWN

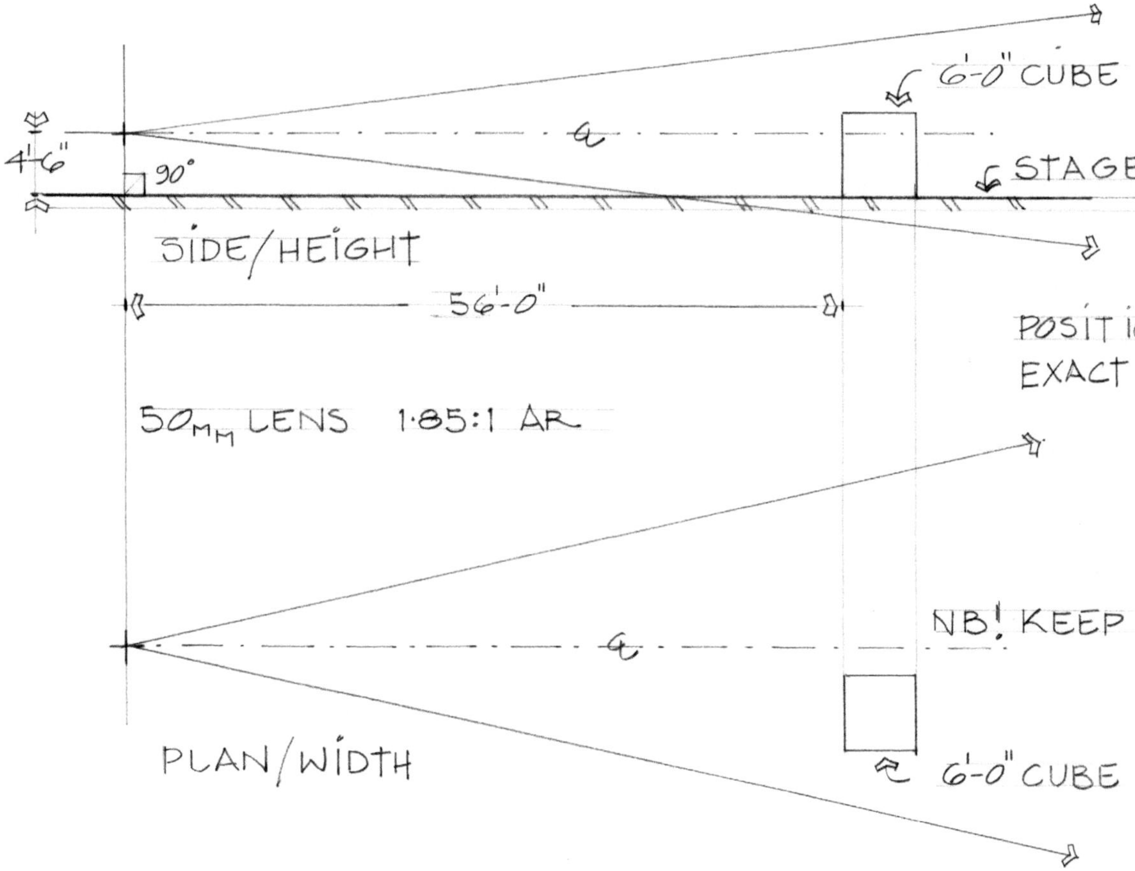

6'-0" CUBE

STAGE FLOOR

4'-6"   90°

SIDE/HEIGHT

56'-0"

50mm LENS   1·85:1 AR

POSITION PLAN & SIDE VIEW EXACTLY IN LINE — VERY IMPORTANT!

NB! KEEP BOTH CENTRE LINES PARALLEL!

PLAN/WIDTH

6'-0" CUBE

SETTING UP A CAMERA PROJECTION

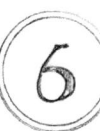

THE IMAGE AREA CAN BE AS BIG AS YOUR DRAWING BOARD ALLOWS

CAMERA

4'-6" 90°

SIDE/HEIGHT

IMAGE AREA 1·85 : 1

PICTURE PLANE

50mm LENS   1·85:1 AR

CAMERA

PLAN/WIDTH

45°

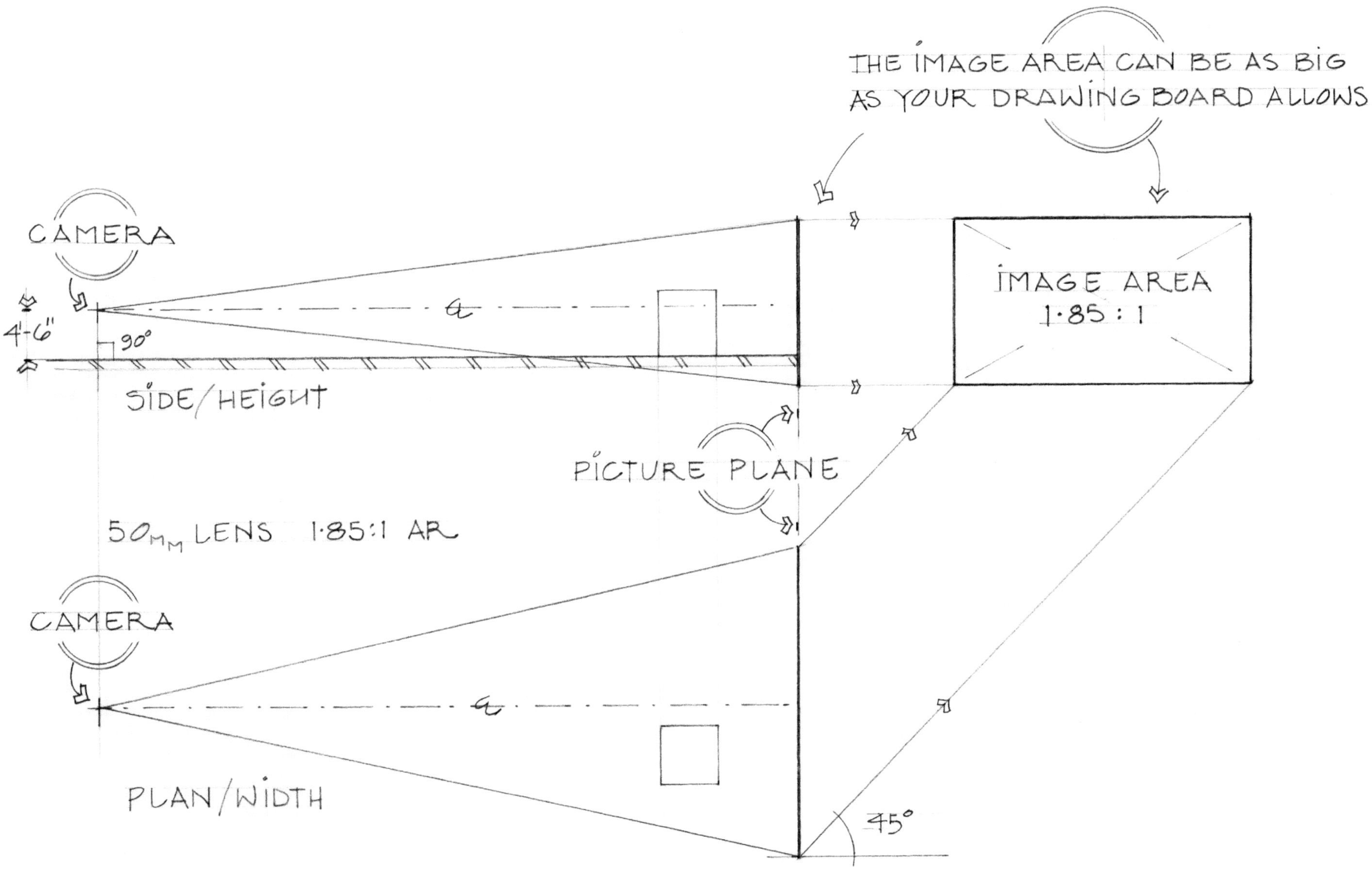

SETTING UP A CAMERA PROJECTION

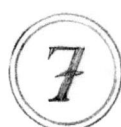

DRAW RAY LINES FROM CAMERA TO SELECTED POINTS ON THE CUBE TO THE PICTURE PLANE

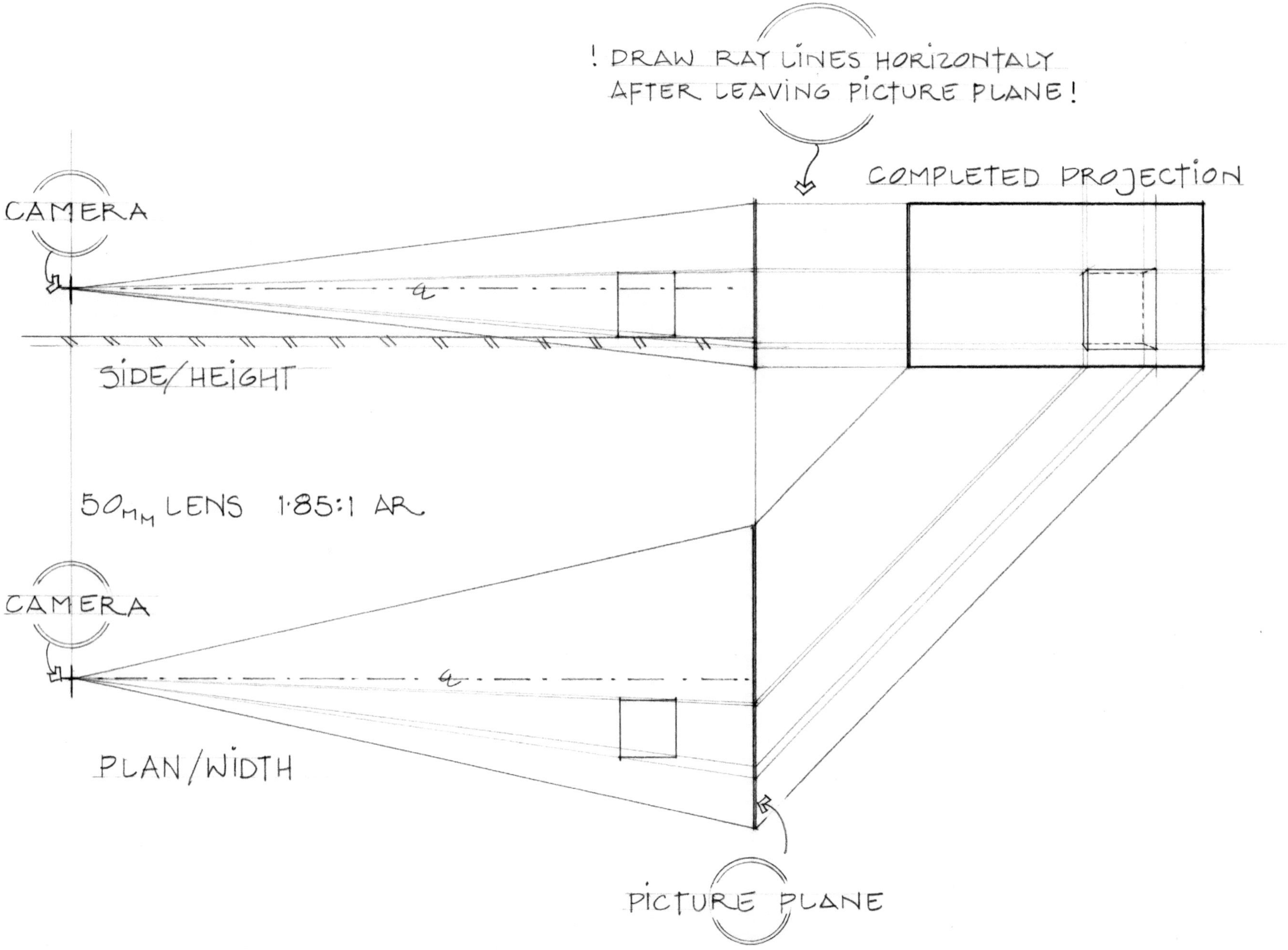

! DRAW RAY LINES HORIZONTALY AFTER LEAVING PICTURE PLANE !

COMPLETED PROJECTION

CAMERA

SIDE/HEIGHT

50MM LENS   1.85:1 AR

CAMERA

PLAN/WIDTH

PICTURE PLANE

SETTING UP A CAMERA PROJECTION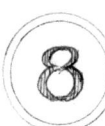

— PROJECTING OUTSIDE THE IMAGE AREA —

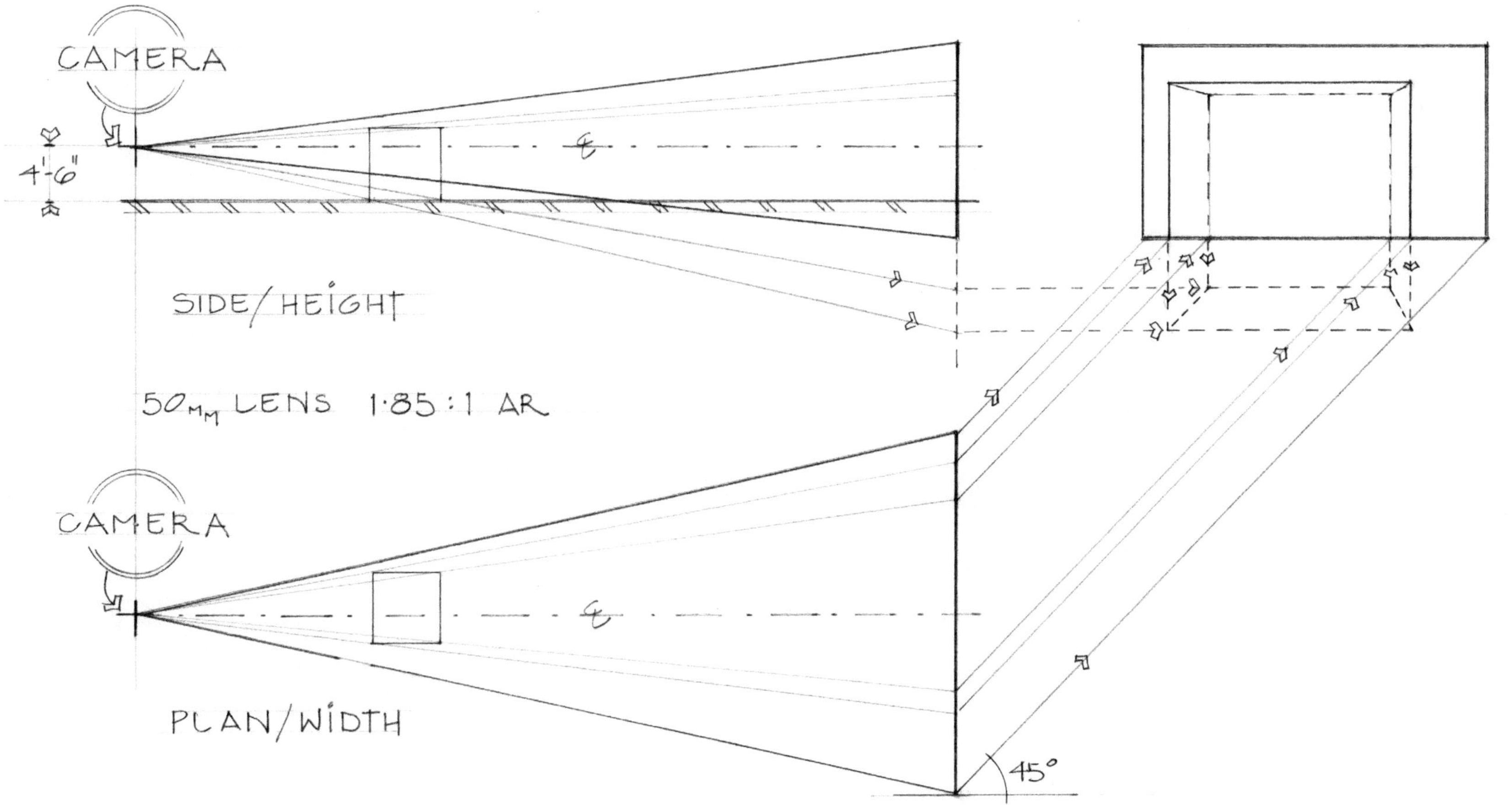

CAMERA
4'-6"
SIDE/HEIGHT

50mm LENS 1·85:1 AR

CAMERA
PLAN/WIDTH
45°

SOMETIMES IT IS NECESSARY TO ILLUSTRATE BEYOND THE IMAGE AREA

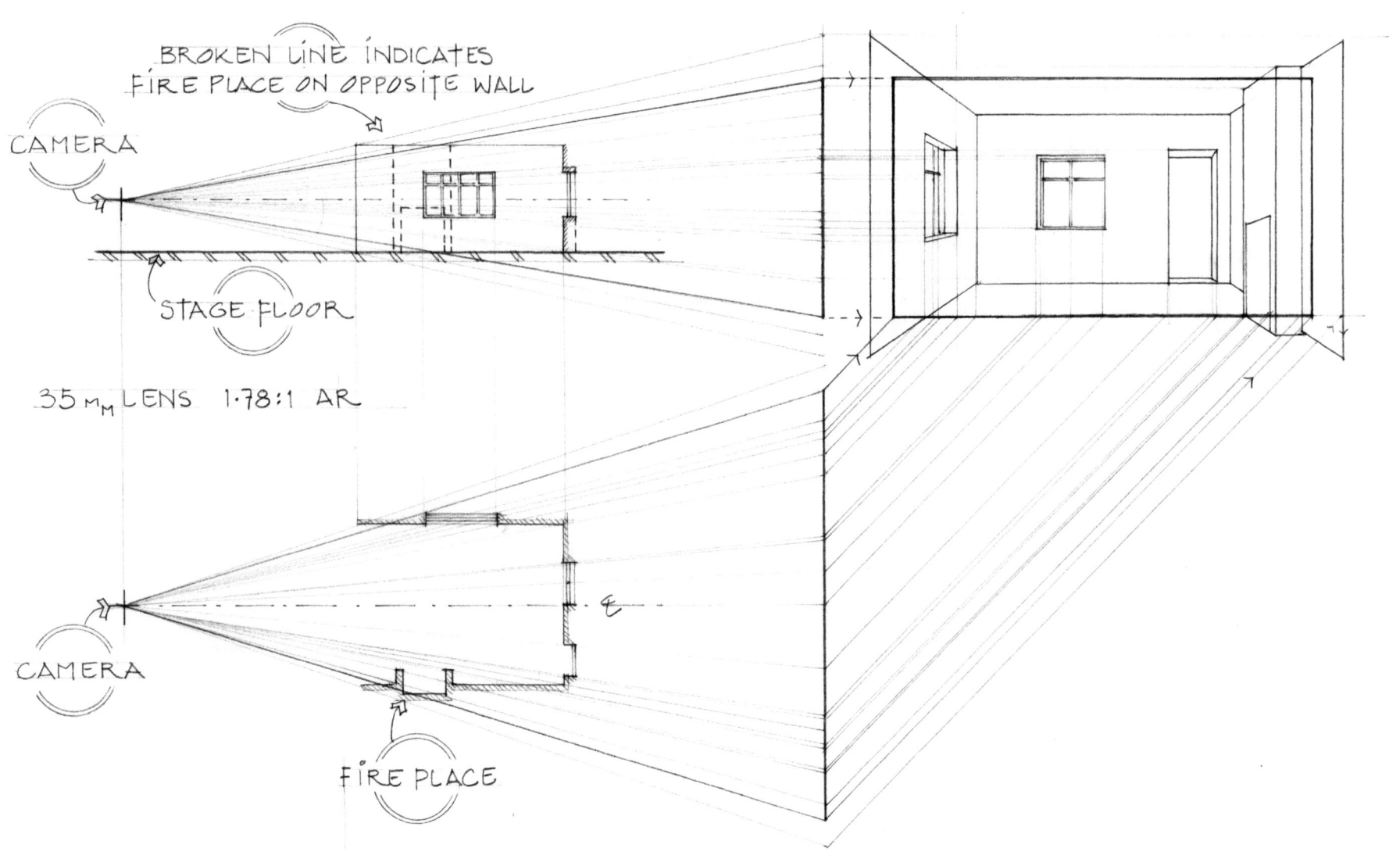

SETTING UP A CAMERA PROJECTION

HORIZONTAL ANGLE OF LENS WILL GIVE WIDTH OF IMAGE AREA

COMPLETED PROJECTION

50mm LENS
AR 1·85:1

GROUND LINE

SIDE/HEIGHT

"TILT DOWN"

TRANSFER WIDTHS TO THE IMAGE AREA

PLAN/WIDTH

RAY LINES STRAIGHT ONTO SLOPING PICTURE PLANE

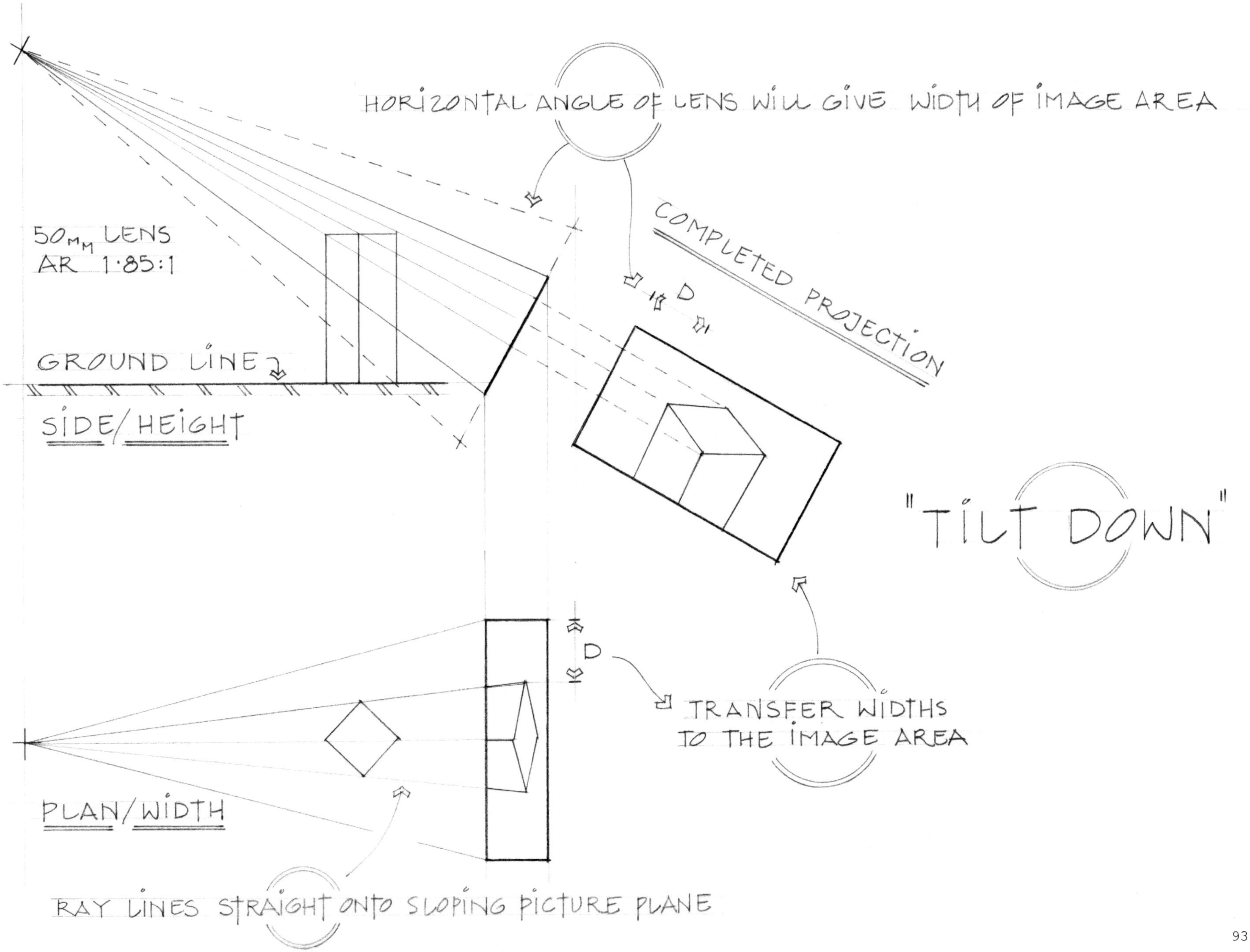

SETTING UP A CAMERA PROJECTION

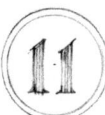

50mm LENS
AR 1.85:1

COMPLETED PROJECTION

GROUND LINE

"TILT UP"

TOP OF IMAGE PLANE

NB: THIS IS THE REVERSE SIDE

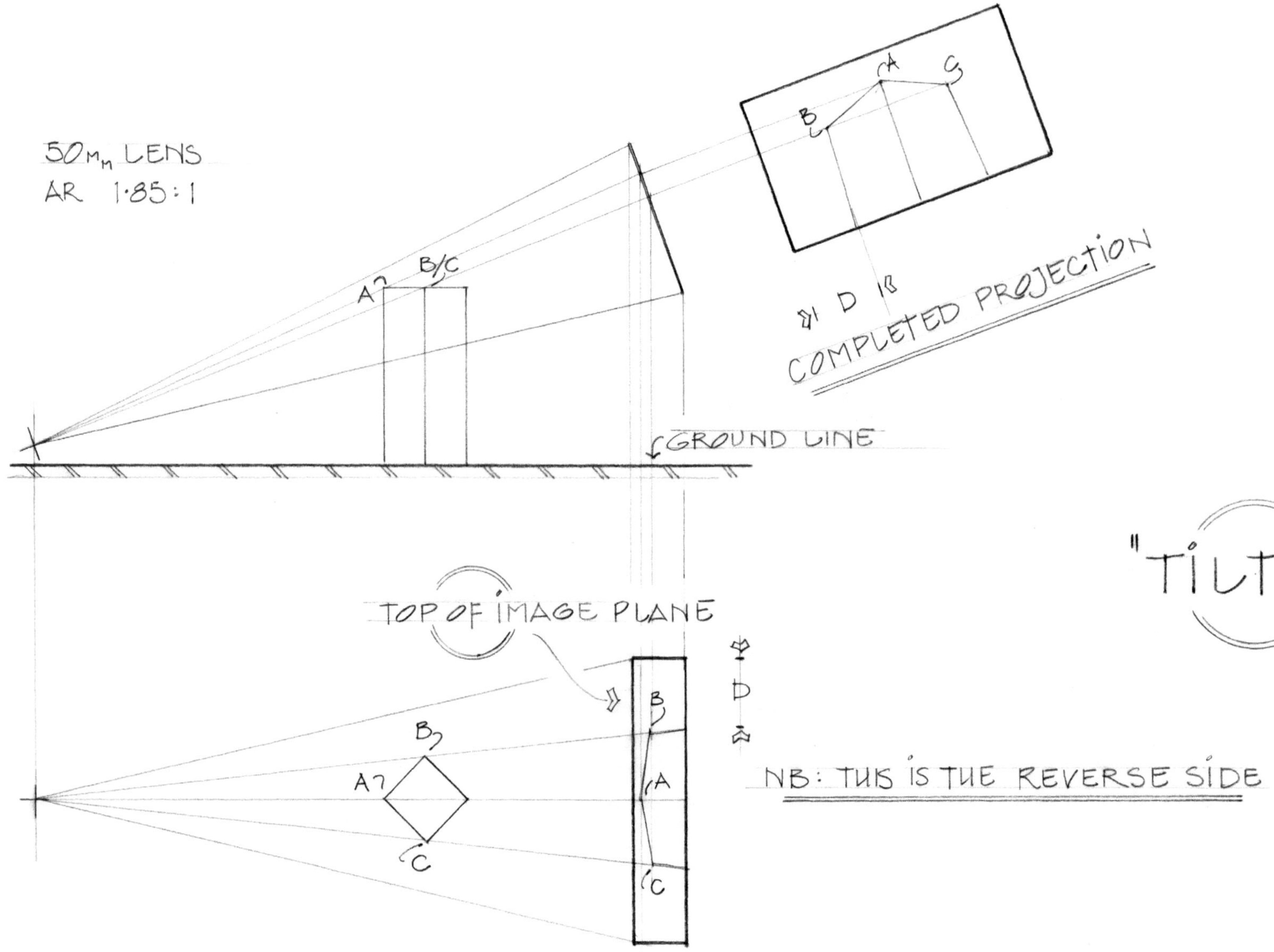

SETTING UP A CAMERA PROJECTION

TO DRAW A 35mm LENS WITH ASPECT RATIO 1·85:1

NOTE: DRAWING NOT TO SCALE

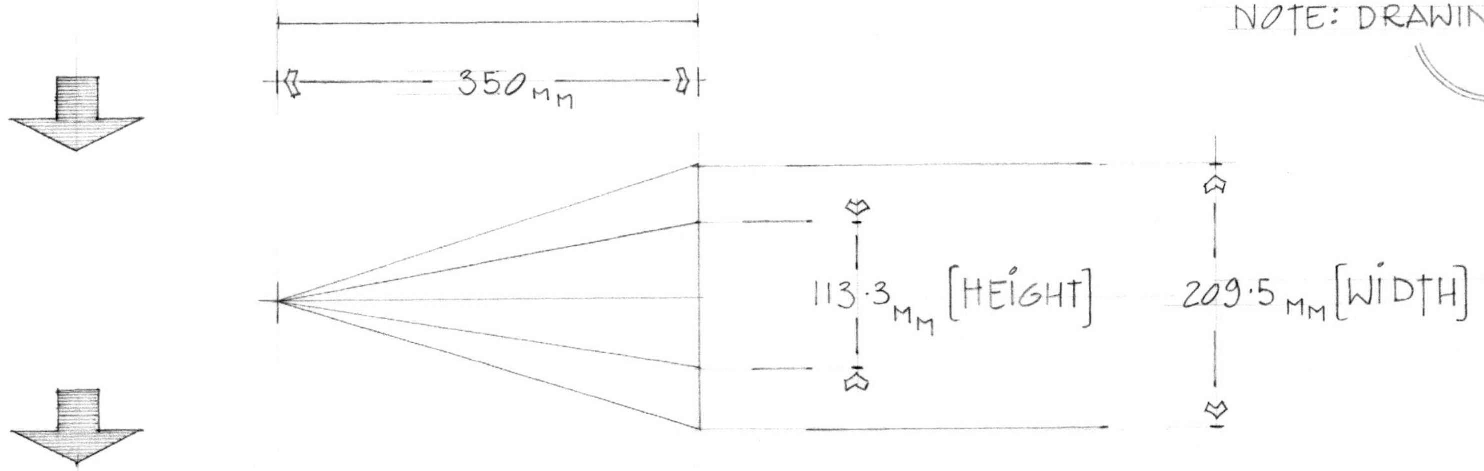

350mm

113·3mm [HEIGHT]   209·5mm [WIDTH]

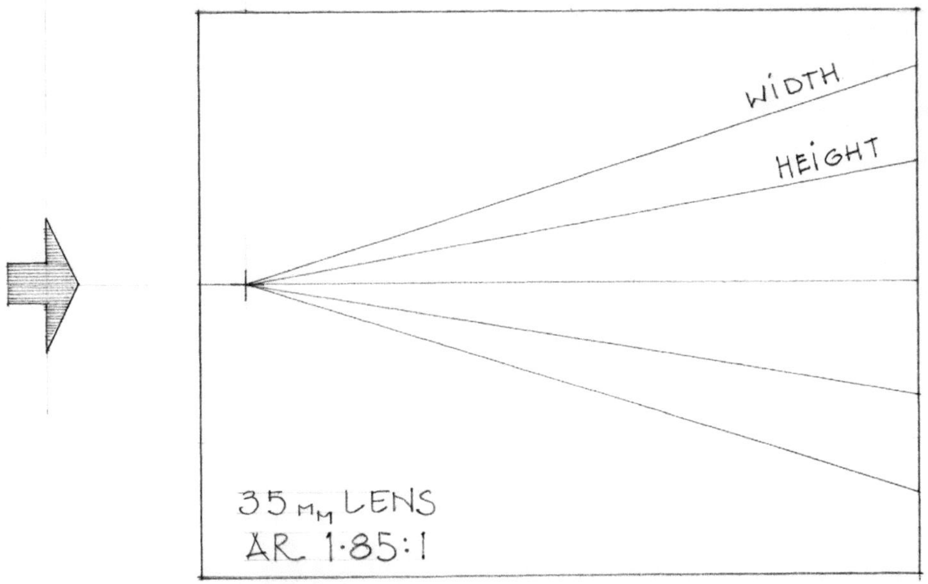

35mm LENS
AR 1·85:1

AR 1·85:1

PROJECTION APERTURE
20·95mm × 11·33mm

! MULTIPLY ×10 ALL DIMENSIONS !

SETTING UP A CAMERA PROJECTION

TO DRAW AN 85 MM LENS WITH ASPECT RATIO 1·85:1

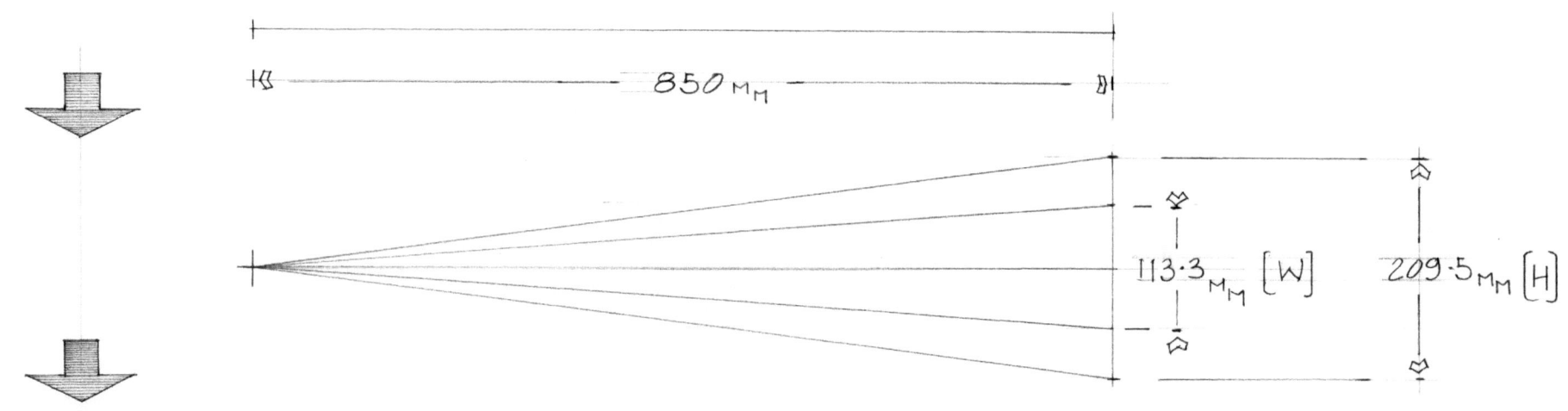

850 MM

113·3 MM [W]   209·5 MM [H]

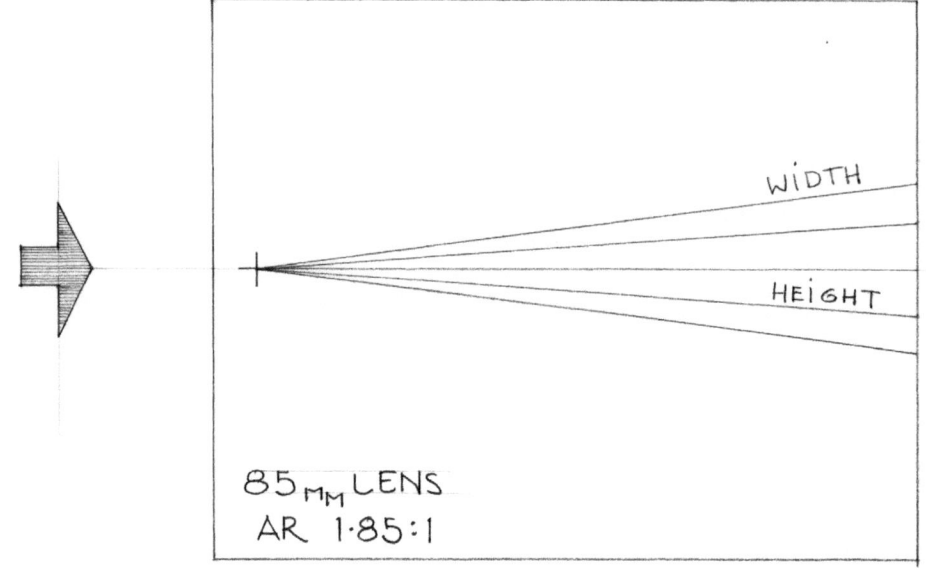

WIDTH

HEIGHT

85 MM LENS
AR 1·85:1

NOTE: DRAWING NOT TO SCALE

AR 1·85:1

PROJECTION APERTURE
20·95 MM × 11·33 MM

! MULTIPLY × 10 ALL DIMENSIONS !

SETTING UP A CAMERA PROJECTION   ⑭

TO DRAW A 35mm LENS WITH ASPECT RATIO 1·78:1 [16:9]

NOTE: DRAWING NOT TO SCALE

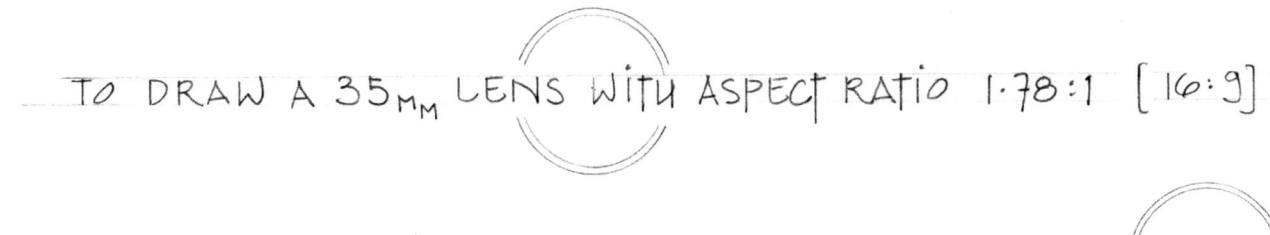

350mm

132·8mm [HEIGHT]   236·2mm [WIDTH]

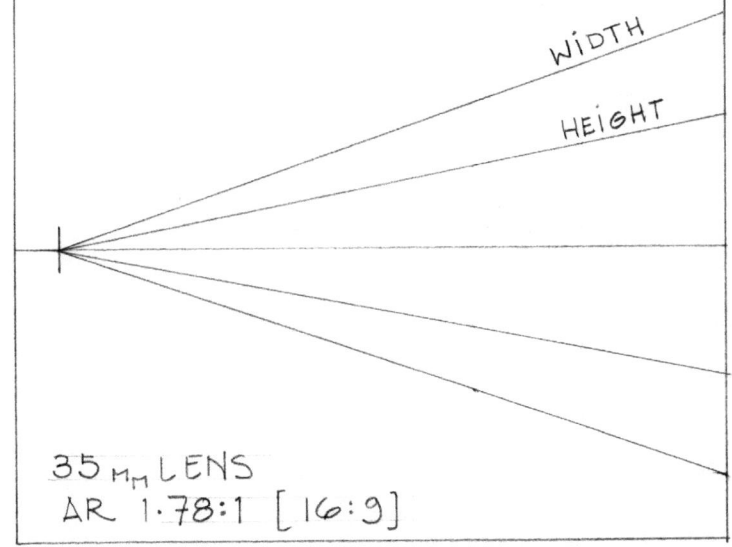

35mm LENS
AR 1·78:1 [16:9]

AR 1·78:1

ACTIVE AREA OF SENSOR
23·62mm × 13·28mm

! MULTIPLY ×10 ALL DIMENSIONS !

SETTING UP A CAMERA PROJECTION   15

TO DRAW A 50mm LENS WITH ASPECT RATIO 1·78:1 [16:9]

NOTE: DRAWING NOT TO SCALE

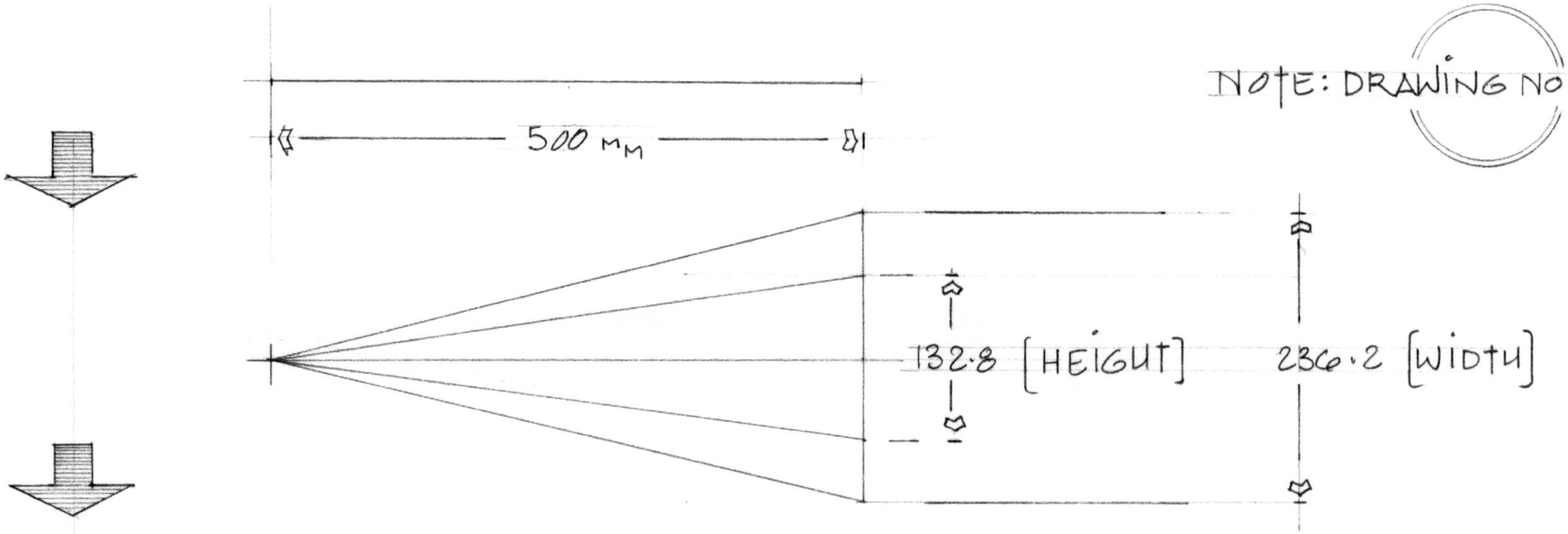

500 MM

132·8 [HEIGHT]   236·2 [WIDTH]

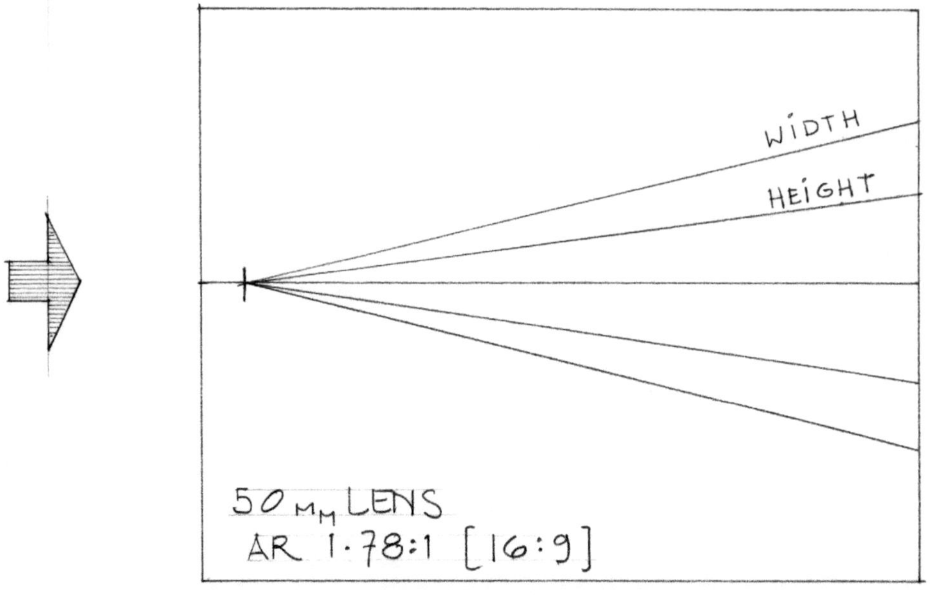

WIDTH
HEIGHT

AR 1·78:1
ACTIVE AREA OF SENSOR
23·62mm × 13·28mm

50mm LENS
AR 1·78:1 [16:9]

! MULTIPLY × 10 ALL DIMENSIONS !

SETTING UP A CAMERA PROJECTION

TO DRAW AN 85mm LENS WITH ASPECT RATIO 1·78:1 [16:9]

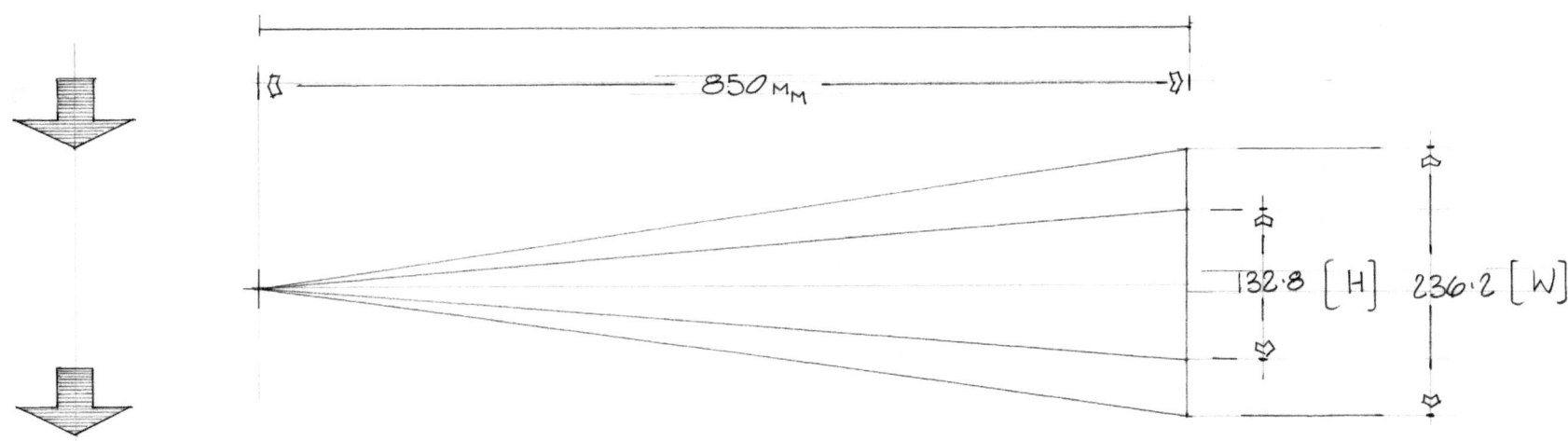

850mm

132·8 [H]   236·2 [W]

NOTE: DRAWING NOT TO SCALE

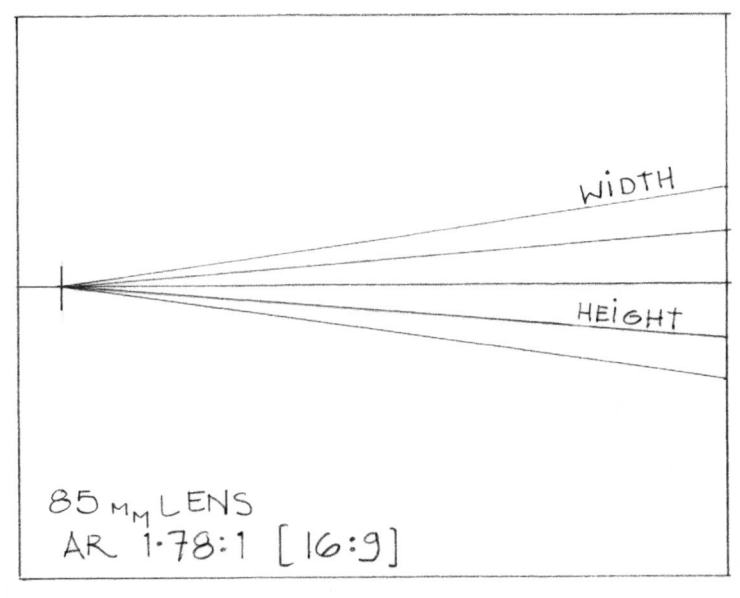

WIDTH

HEIGHT

85mm LENS
AR 1·78:1 [16:9]

AR 1·78:1

ACTIVE AREA OF SENSOR
23·62mm × 13·28mm

!MULTIPLY × 10 ALL DIMENSIONS!

SETTING UP A CAMERA PROJECTION

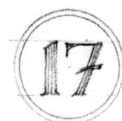

TO DRAW A 50mm LENS WITH ASPECT RATIO 2·39:1 [SCOPE]

500 MM

NOTE: DRAWING NOT TO SCALE

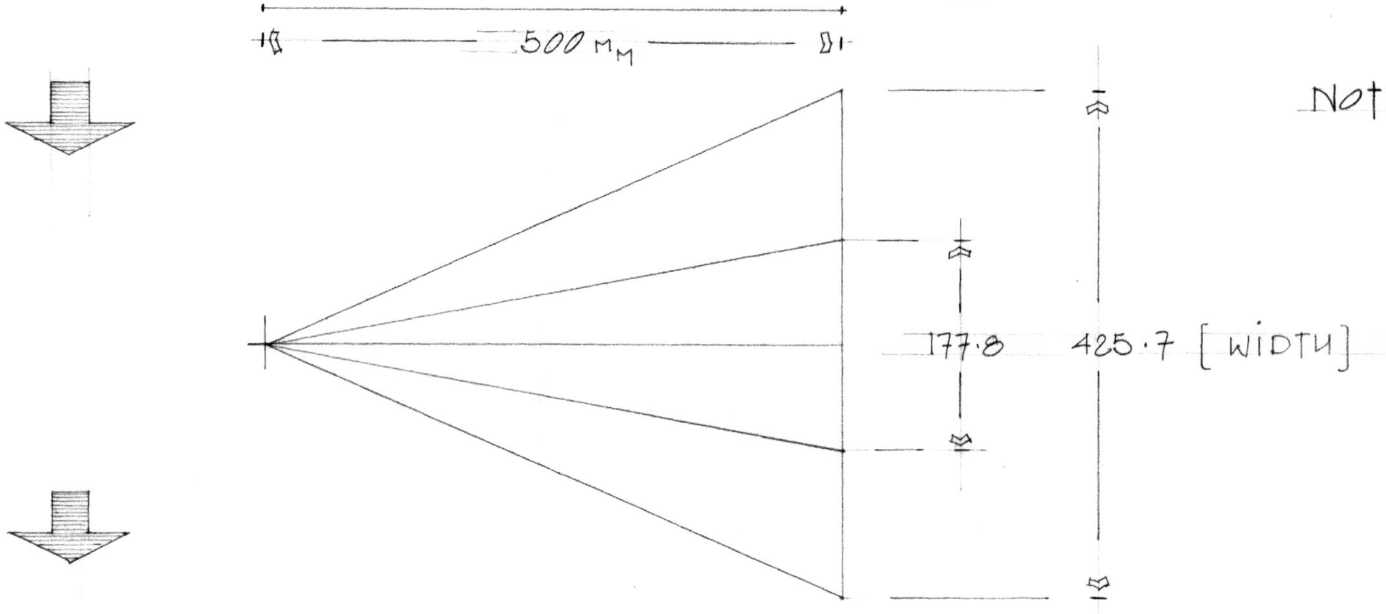

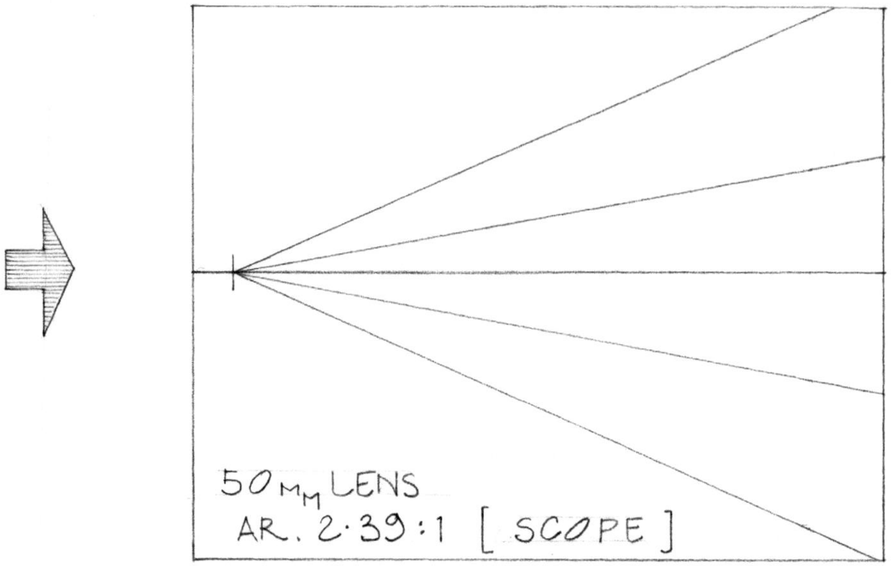

177·8   425·7 [WIDTH]

AR. 2·39:1

PROJECTION APERTURE

42·57mm × 17·78mm

50mm LENS
AR. 2·39:1 [SCOPE]

! MULTIPLY × 10 ALL DIMENSIONS !

SETTING UP A CAMERA PROJECTION

TO DRAW A 35mm LENS WITH ASPECT RATIO 2.39:1 [SCOPE]

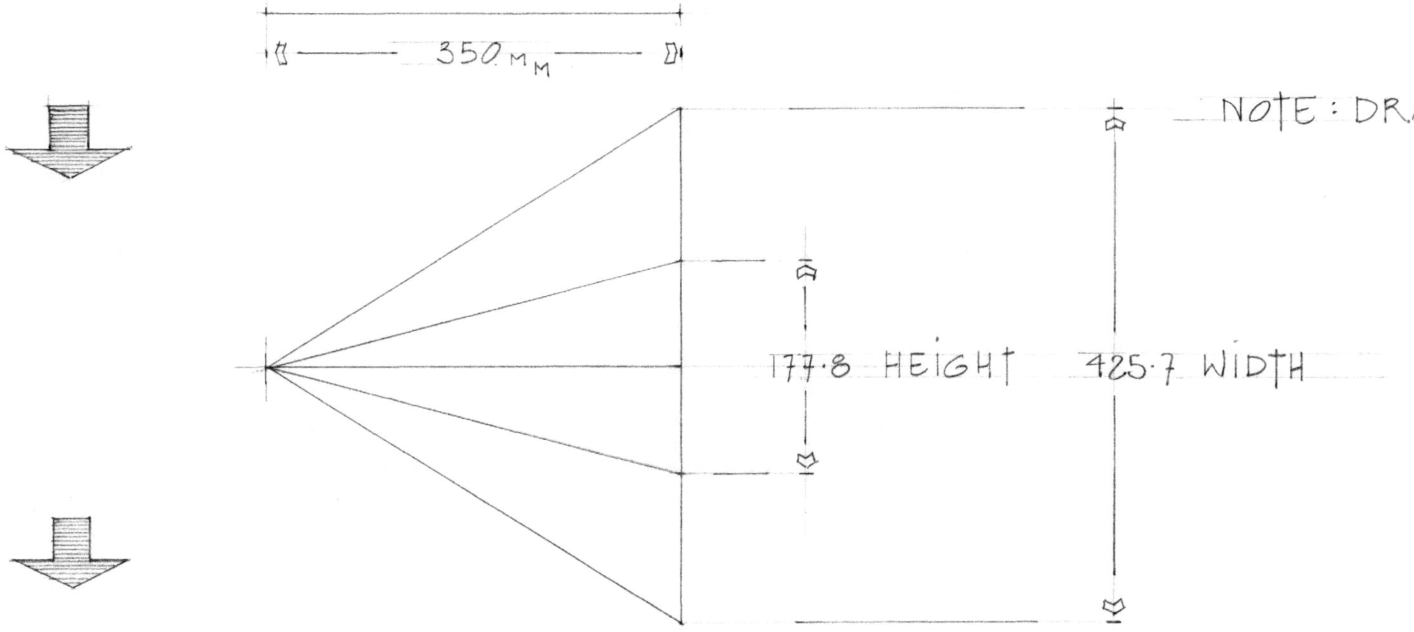

NOTE: DRAWING NOT TO SCALE

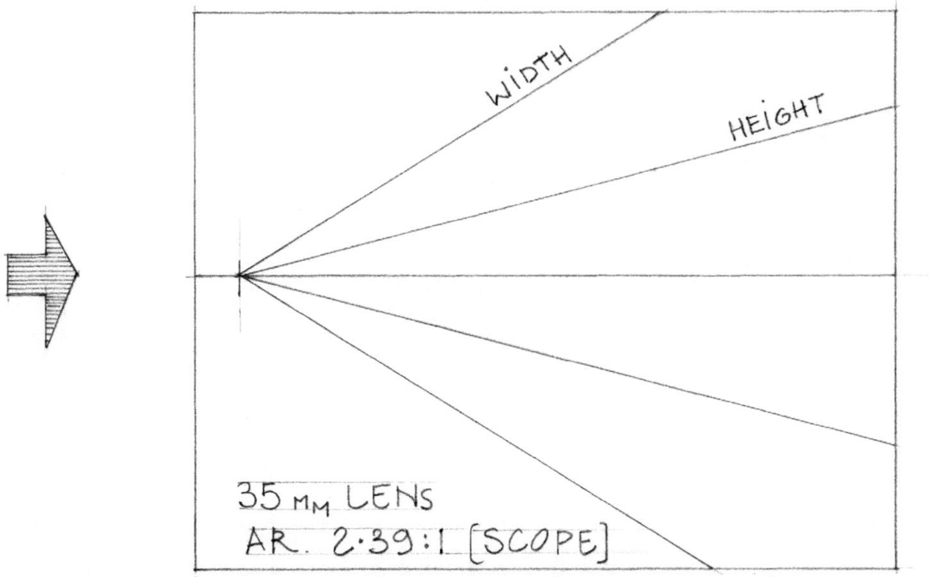

350 mm

177.8 HEIGHT   425.7 WIDTH

35 mm LENS
AR. 2.39:1 [SCOPE]

AR. 2.39:1

PROJECTION APERTURE:

42.57 mm × 17.78 mm

! MULTIPLY ×10 ALL DIMENSIONS !

SETTING UP A CAMERA PROJECTION

TO DRAW AN 85mm LENS WITH ASPECT RATIO 2.39:1 [SCOPE]

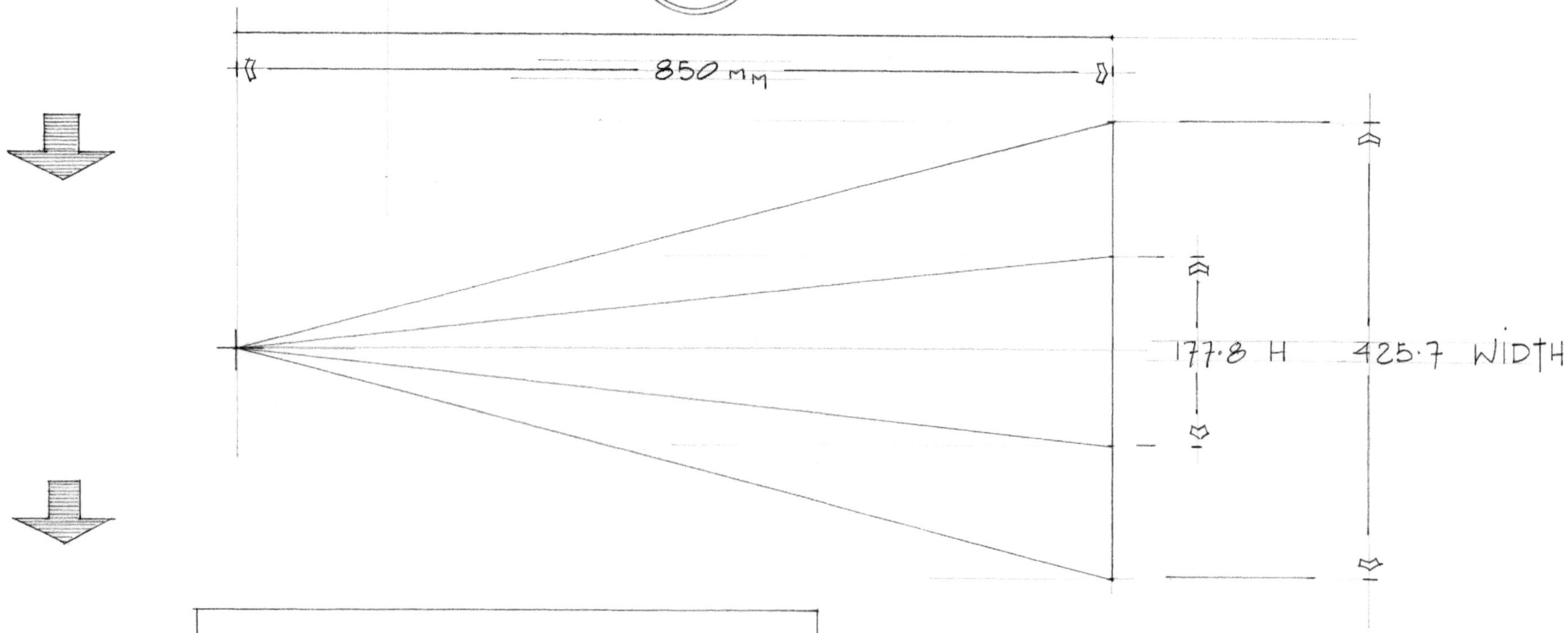

850 mm

177.8 H   425.7 WIDTH

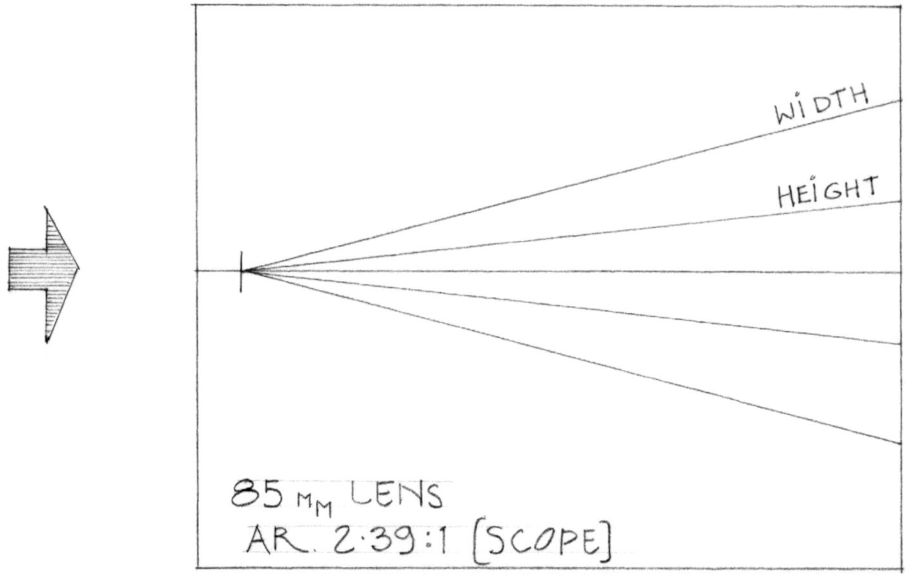

85 mm LENS
AR. 2.39:1 [SCOPE]

NOTE: DRAWING NOT TO SCALE

AR. 2.39:1

PROJECTION APERTURE:

42.57mm × 17.78mm

! MULTIPLY ×10 ALL DIMENSIONS !

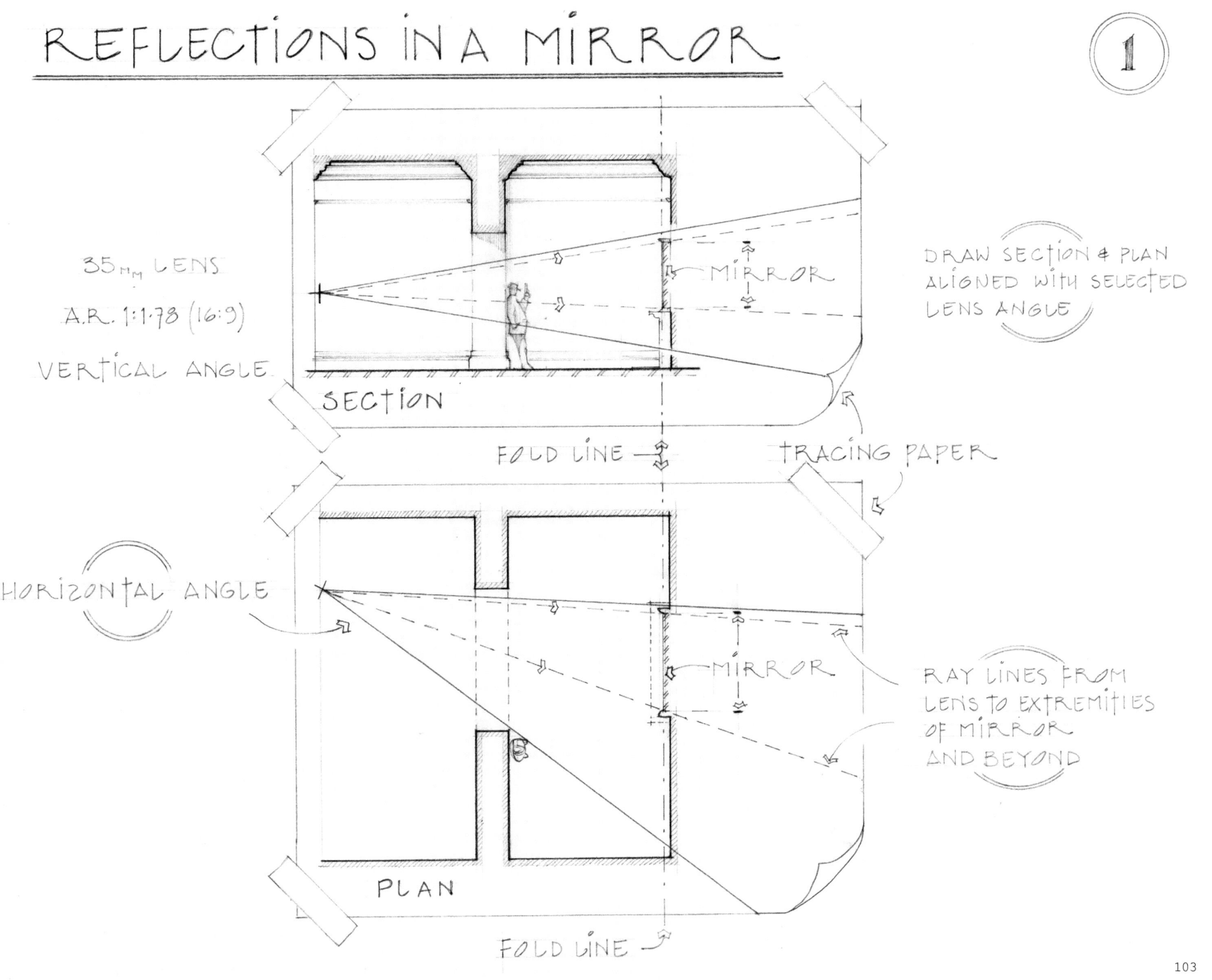

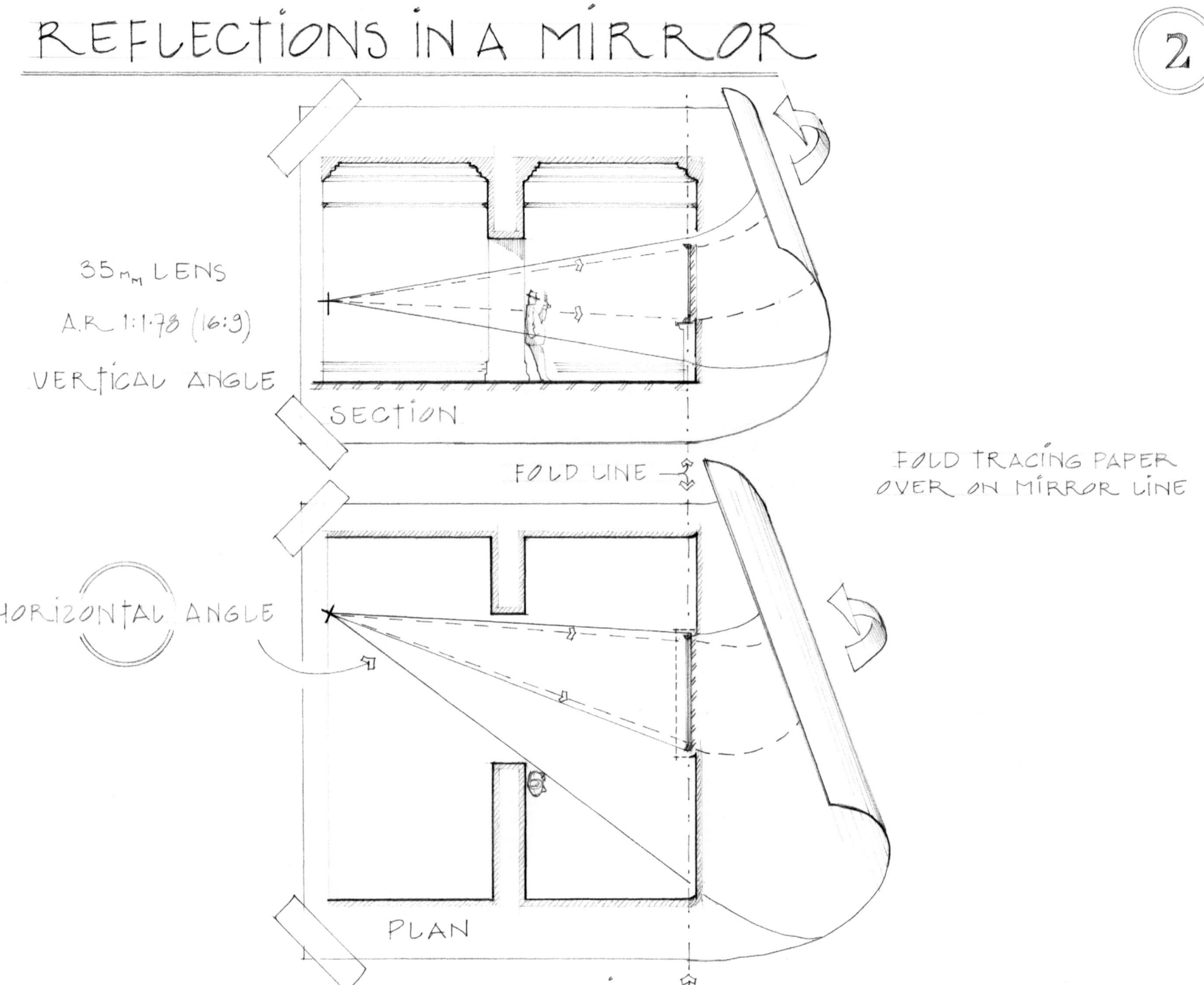

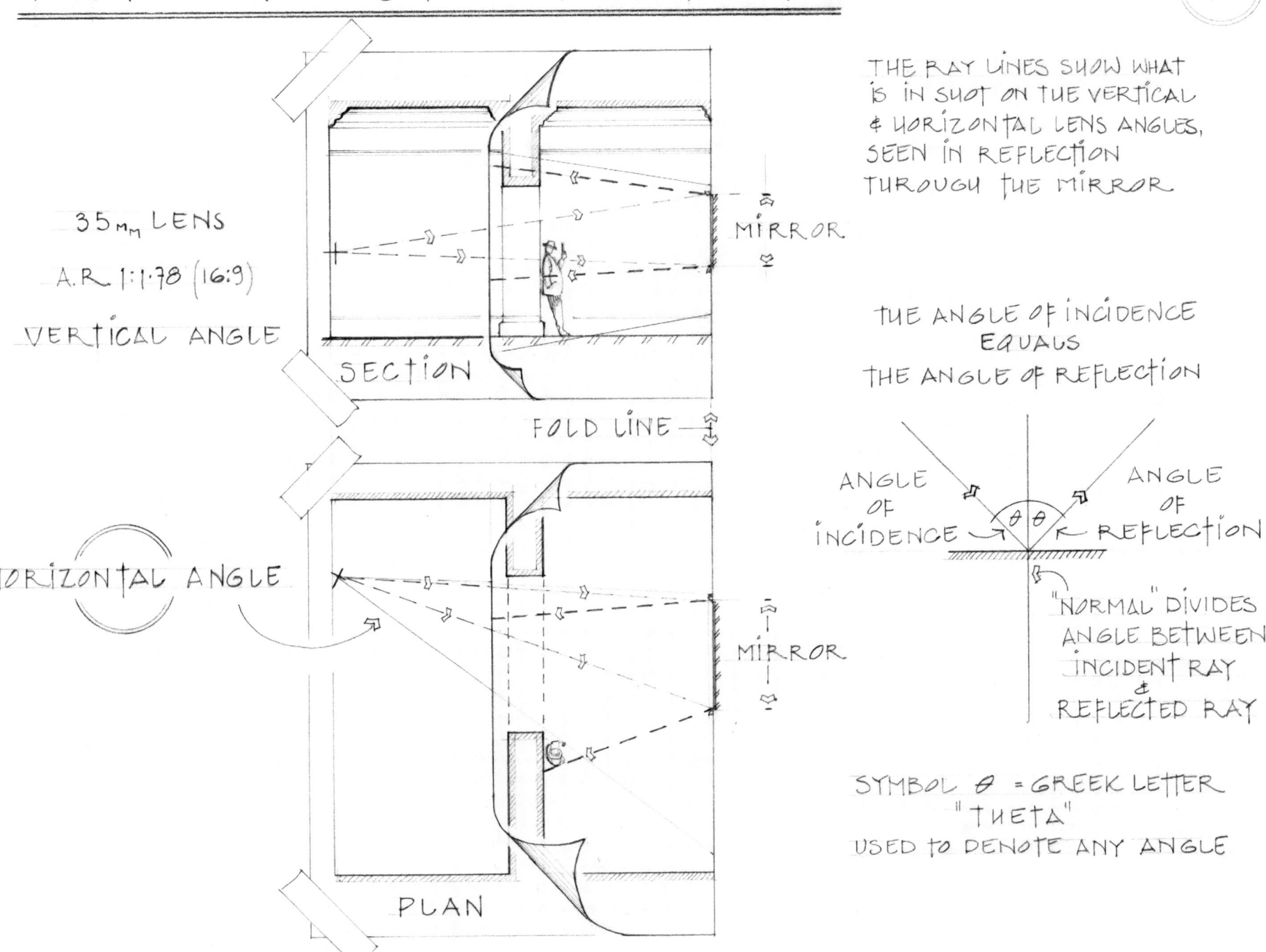

BACKINGS : CALCULATING SIZE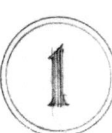

— SELECT A PHOTOGRAPH —

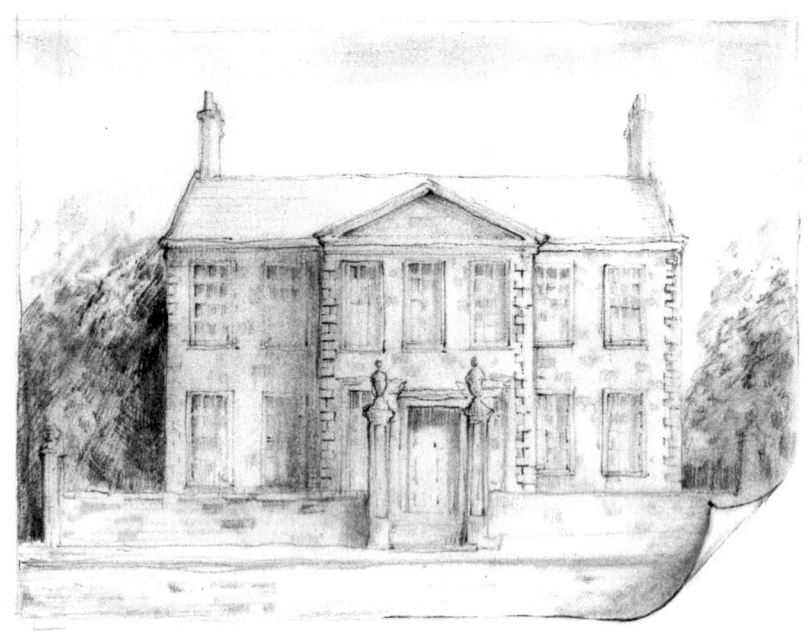

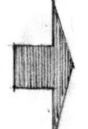

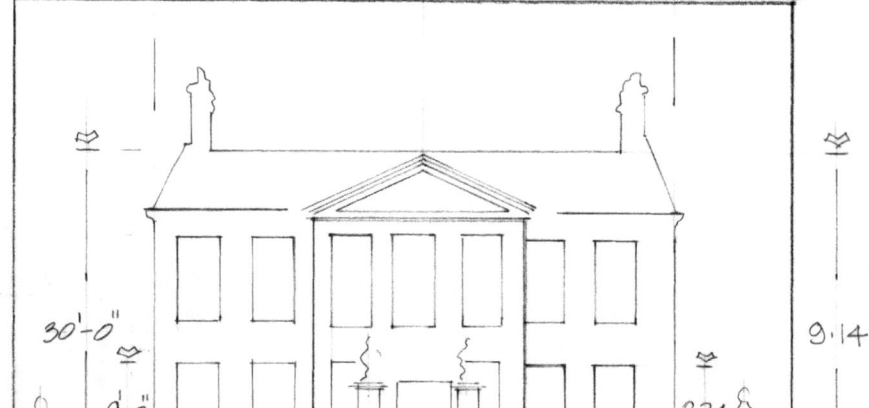

THIS CAN BE YOUR OWN OR A
CLEARED LIBRARY IMAGE

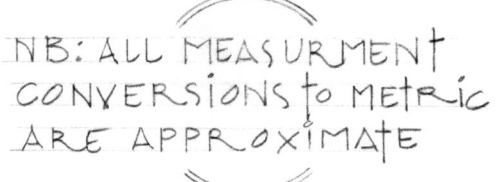
NB: ALL MEASUREMENT
CONVERSIONS TO METRIC
ARE APPROXIMATE

IF USING A LOCATION, MEASURE BASIC
OVERALL DIMENSIONS — WIDTH & HEIGHT
& WINDOWS & DOORS ETC.
IF USING A LIBRARY IMAGE ESTIMATE
DIMENSIONS USING CLUES :
BRICK SIZES & DOOR OPENINGS
FIGURES WILL GIVE APPROXIMATE
HEIGHTS

BACKINGS: CALCULATING SIZE

DRAW IMAGE IN PLAN & SECTION TO A SCALE SUITABLE TO THE DRAWING BOARD SIZE

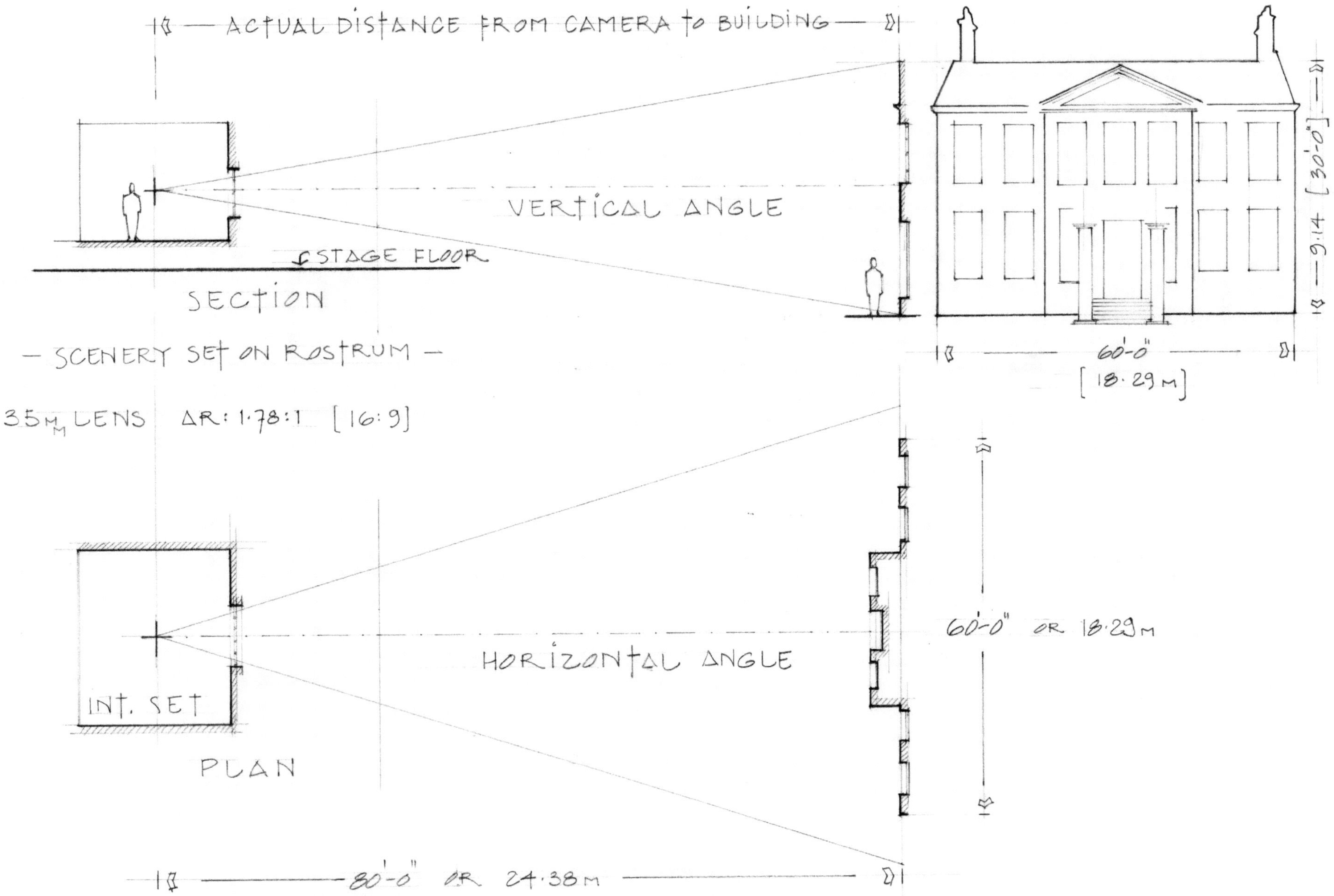

← ACTUAL DISTANCE FROM CAMERA TO BUILDING →

VERTICAL ANGLE

9.14 [30'-0"]

STAGE FLOOR

SECTION

— SCENERY SET ON ROSTRUM —

35mm LENS   AR: 1.78:1 [16:9]

60'-0" [18.29 m]

INT. SET

PLAN

HORIZONTAL ANGLE

60'-0" OR 18.29 m

← 80'-0" OR 24.38 m →

BACKINGS: CALCULATING SIZE

DRAW RAY LINES FROM SUITABLE REFERENCE POINTS ON BUILDING TO CAMERA LENS

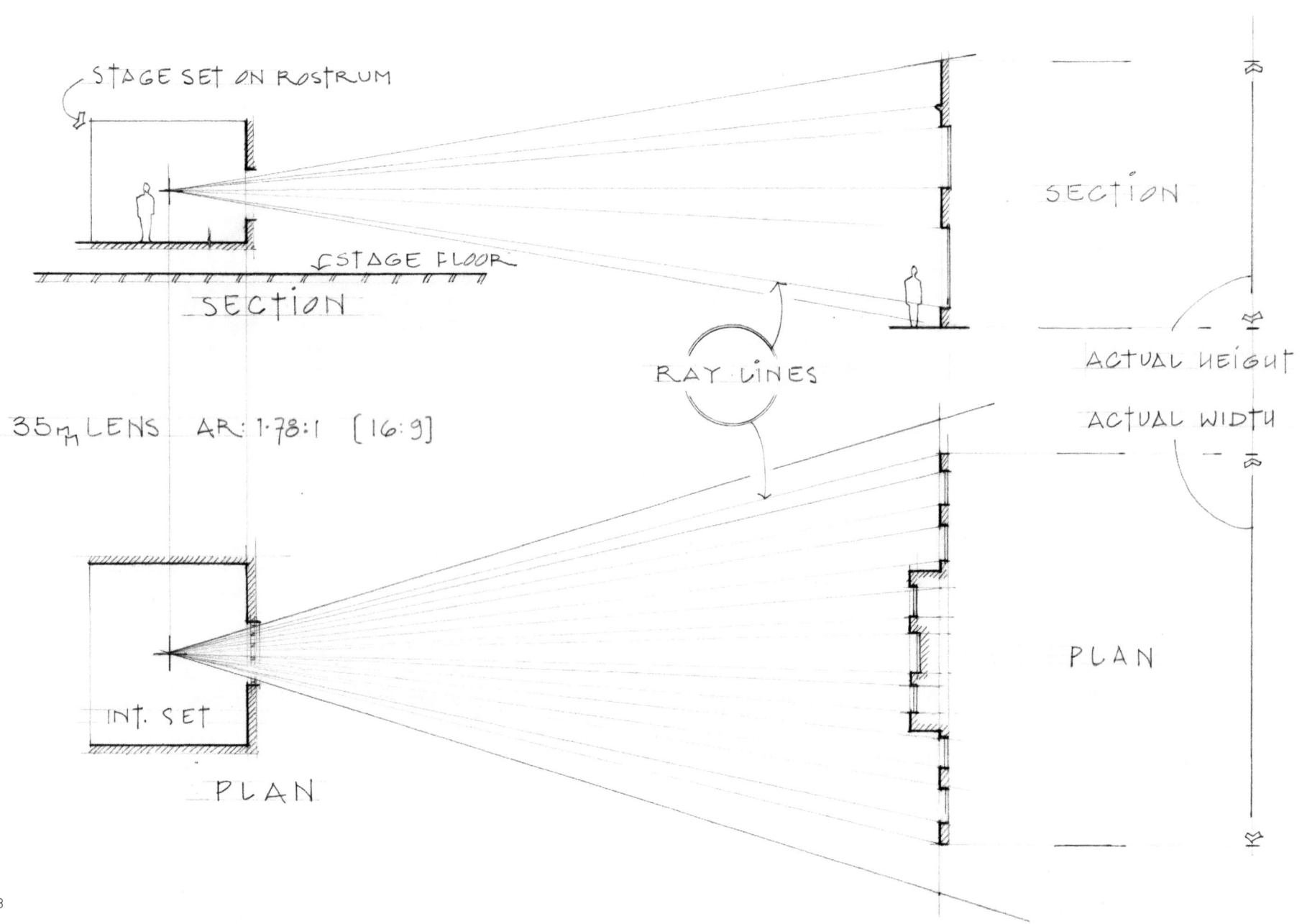

BACKINGS : CALCULATING SIZE ④

SELECT DISTANCE OF BACKING FROM SET: STAGE SPACE WILL GOVERN THIS.
ALLOW 16'-0" (APPROX 5.0m) MINIMUM FOR LIGHTING

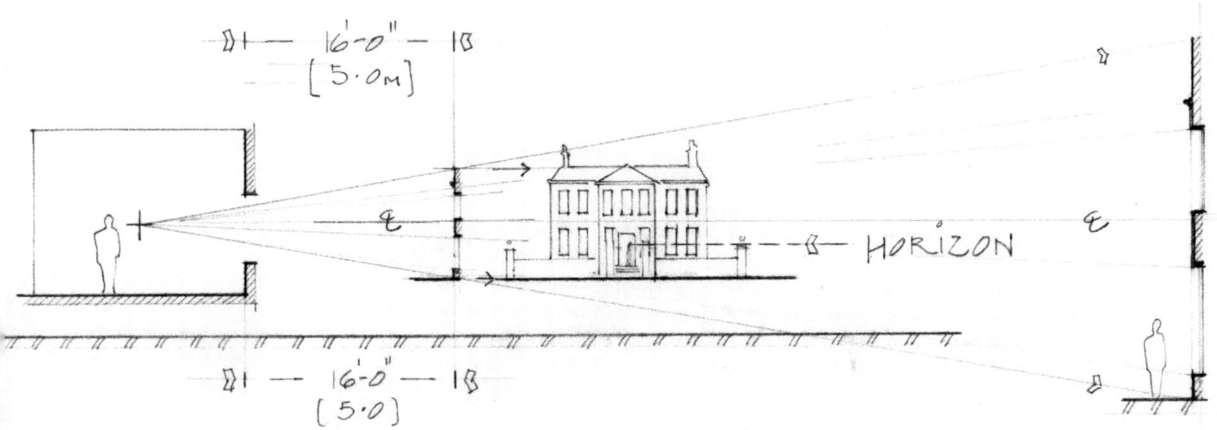

COMPLETED BACKING

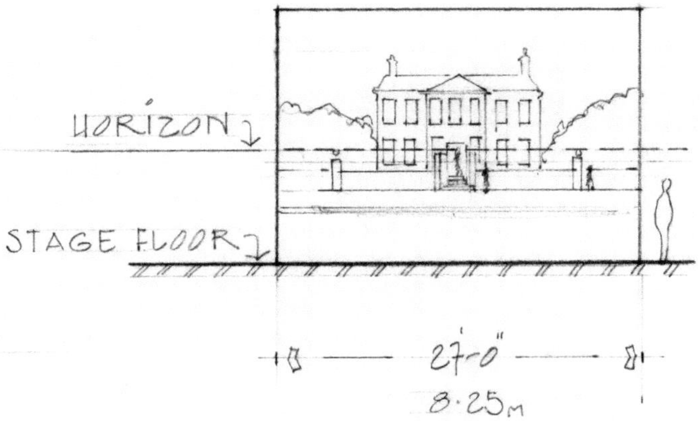

16'-0" (5.0m)

HORIZON

HORIZON

STAGE FLOOR

27'-0"
8.25m

35mm LENS   AR. 1:1.78 (16:9)

ADJUST IMAGE HORIZON LINE TO CENTRE LINE OF VERTICAL LENS ANGLE

12'-0" (3.6m) – REDUCED

60'-0"
8.3m

EXTREMITY OF POSSIBLE "SHOOT-OFF" ON WIDTH

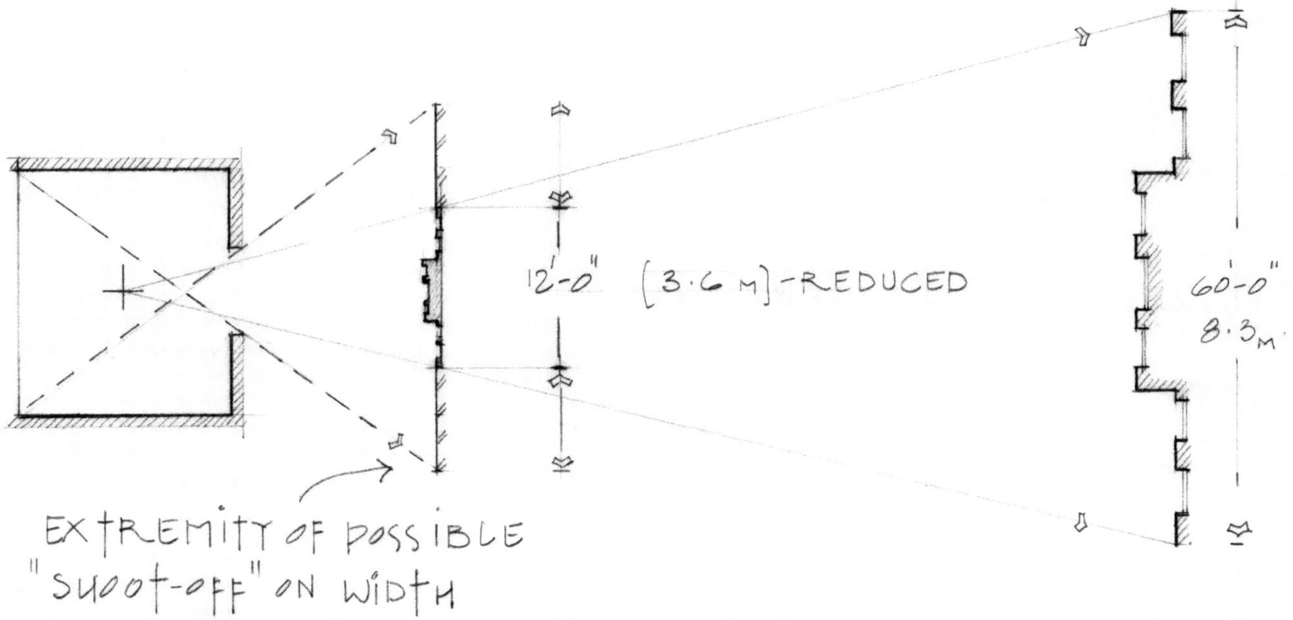

NB: ALL MEASURMENT CONVERSIONS TO METRIC ARE APPROXIMATE

FORCED PERSPECTIVE – SET FORESHORTENING

WHEN SPACE LIMITS THE LENGTH OF A SET [EG. A CORRIDOR]
A FORESHORTENED [COMPRESSED] SET CAN BE BUILT.
— IT IS AN ALTERNATIVE TO GREEN SCREEN AND POST PRODUCTION COSTS —

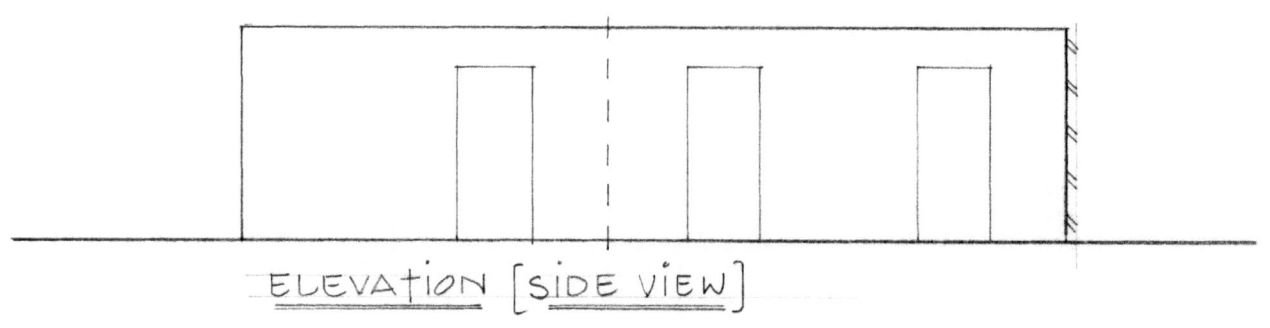

ELEVATION [SIDE VIEW]

CHOOSE WHERE THE FORESHORTENED SET-BUILD
WILL BEGIN IN RELATION TO THE NORMAL SET

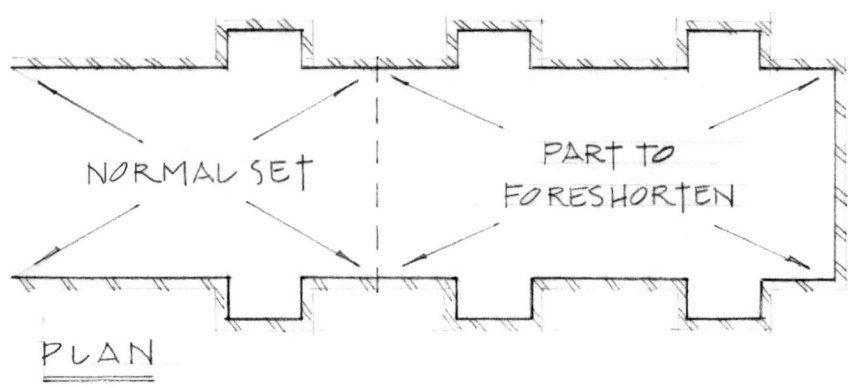

NORMAL SET   PART TO FORESHORTEN

PLAN

FORCED PERSPECTIVE – SET FORESHORTENING

②

POSITION OF FORCED PERSPECTIVE SET

|← NORMAL SET →|← SET →|

25mm LENS ANGLE

"A"

"A"

CAMERA POSITION
25mm LENS AR 1:1.78

25mm LENS ANGLE

|← IMAGINED EXTENSION →|

DRAW 2 LINES BACK TO CAMERA LENS

"A"

"A"

111

FORCED PERSPECTIVE — SET FORESHORTENING

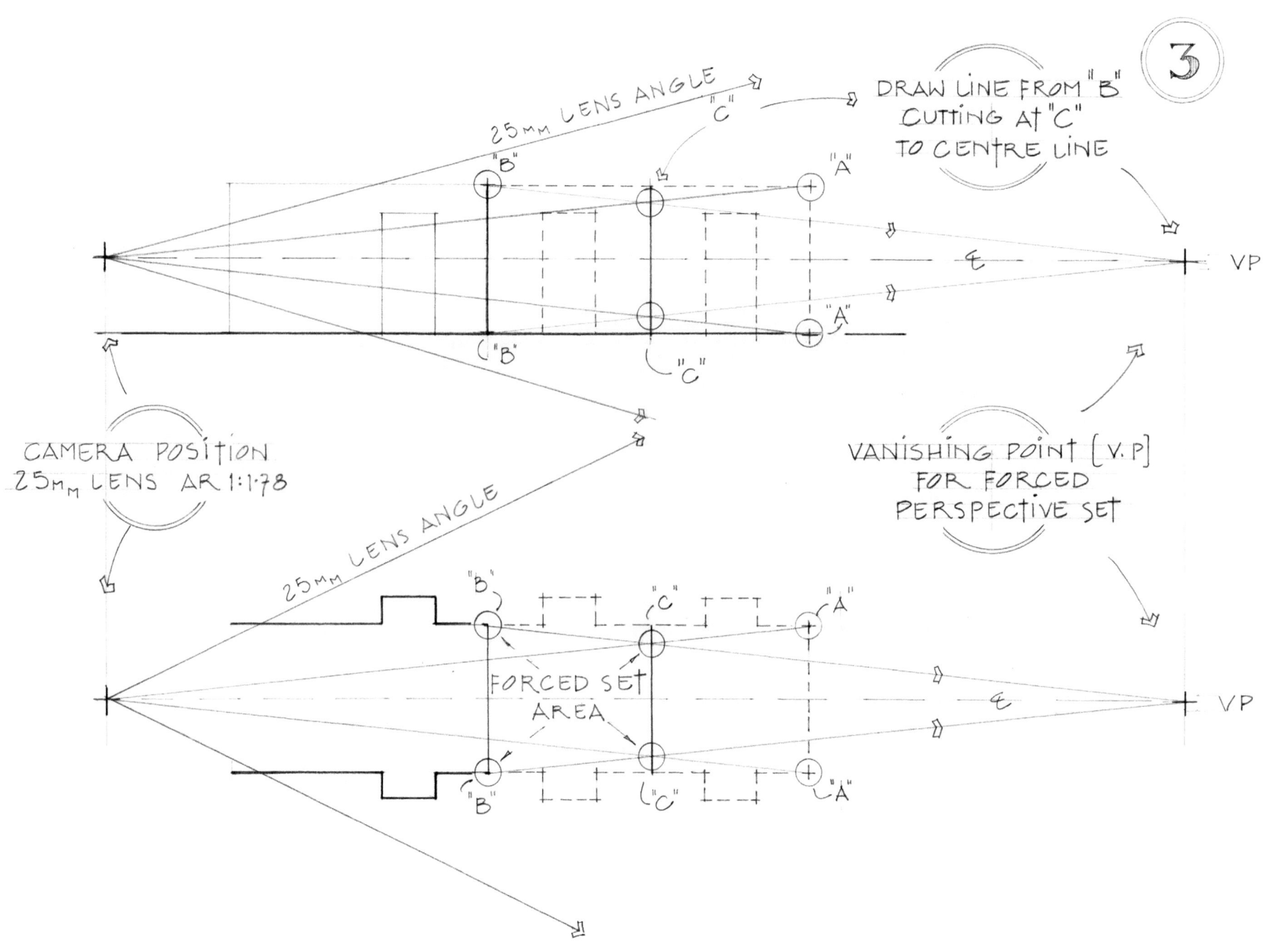

FORCED PERSPECTIVE — SET FORESHORTENING

④

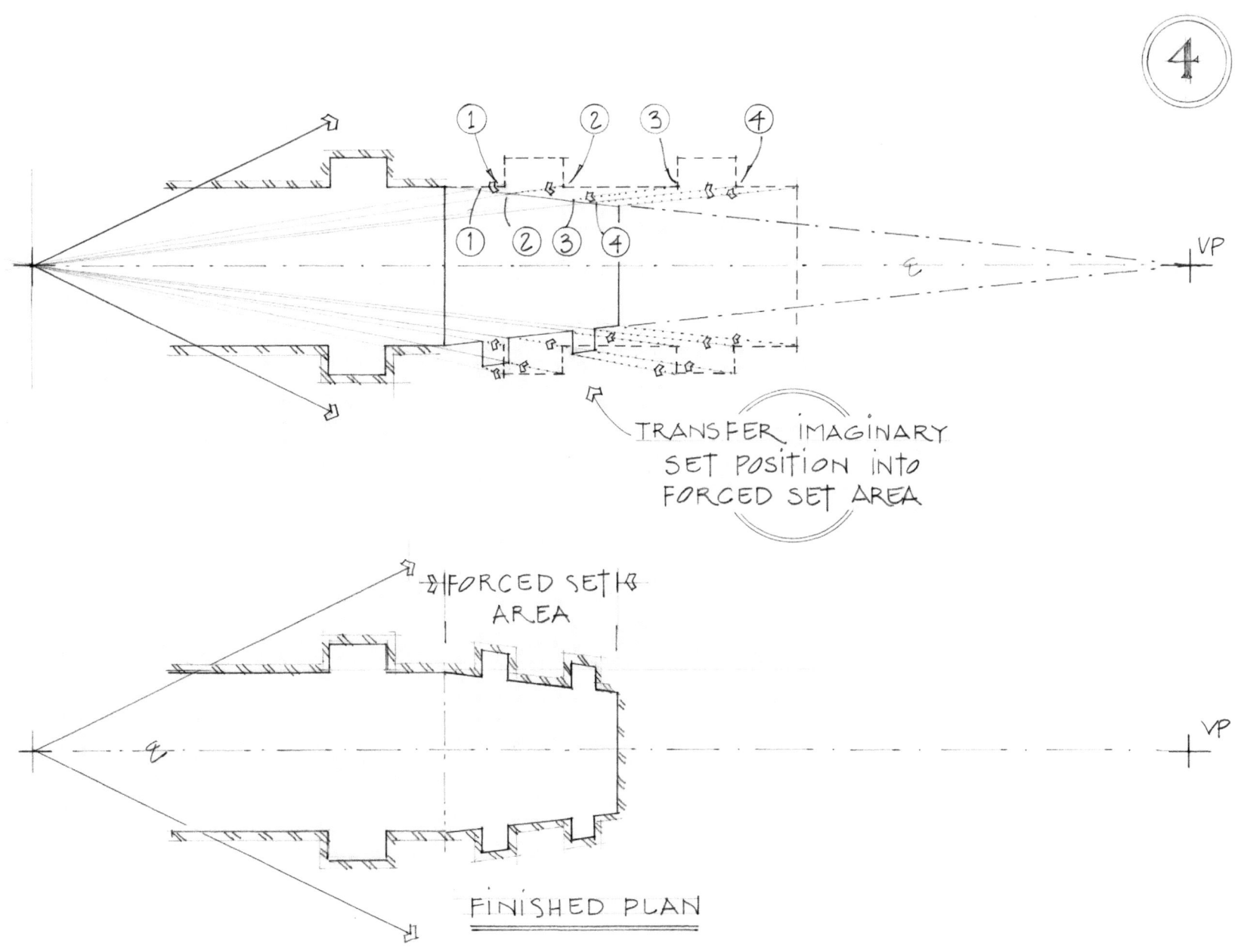

FORCED PERSPECTIVE - SET FORESHORTENING

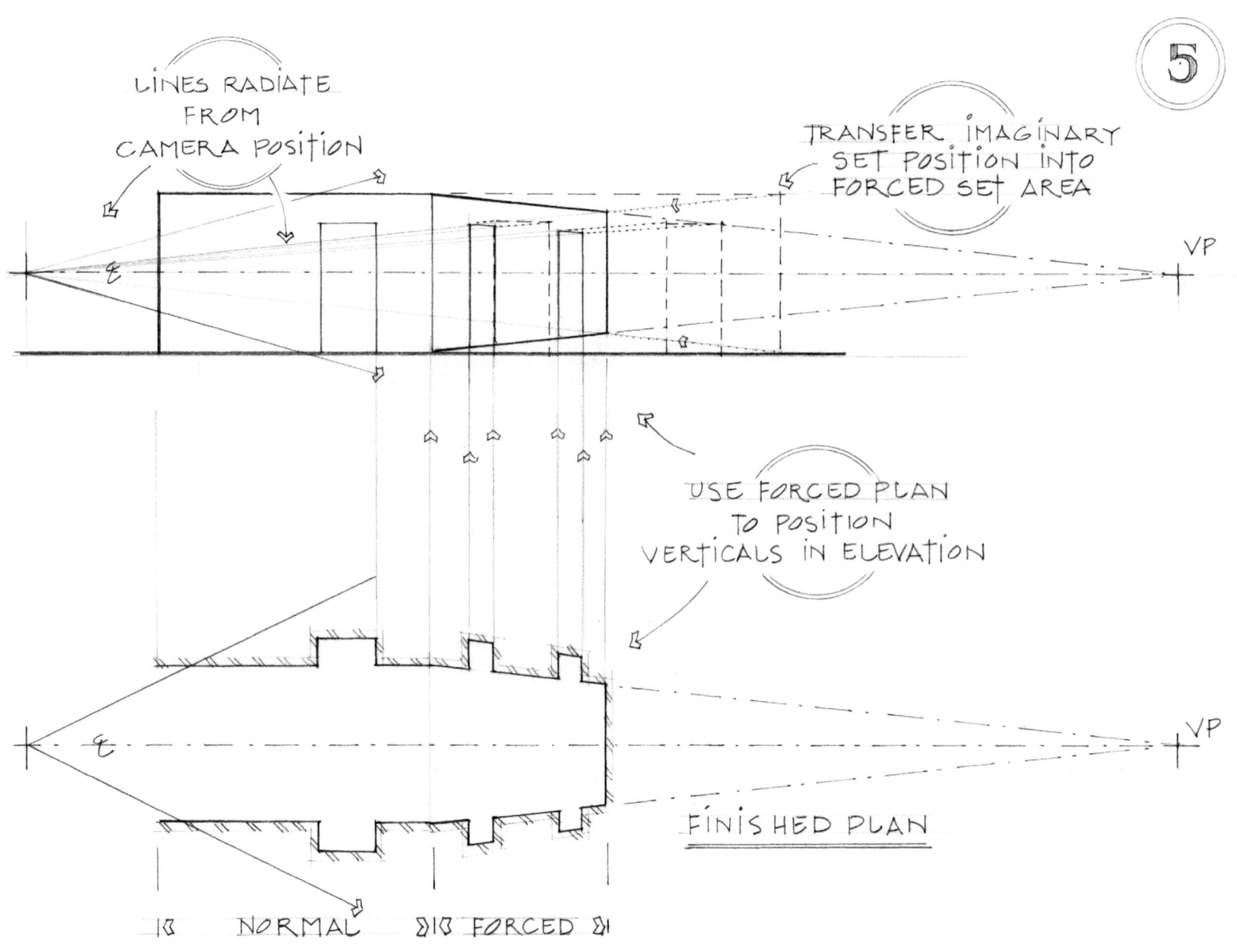

FORCED PERSPECTIVE - SET FORESHORTENING

— FINISHED PLAN & ELEVATION —

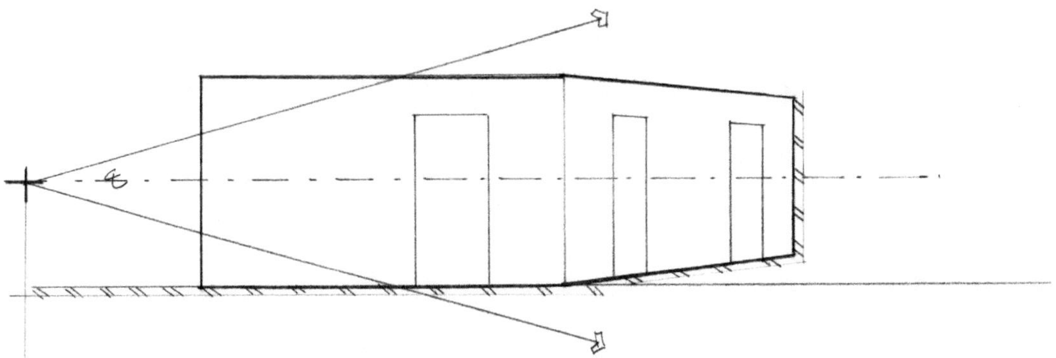

25mm LENS   AR 1:1.78

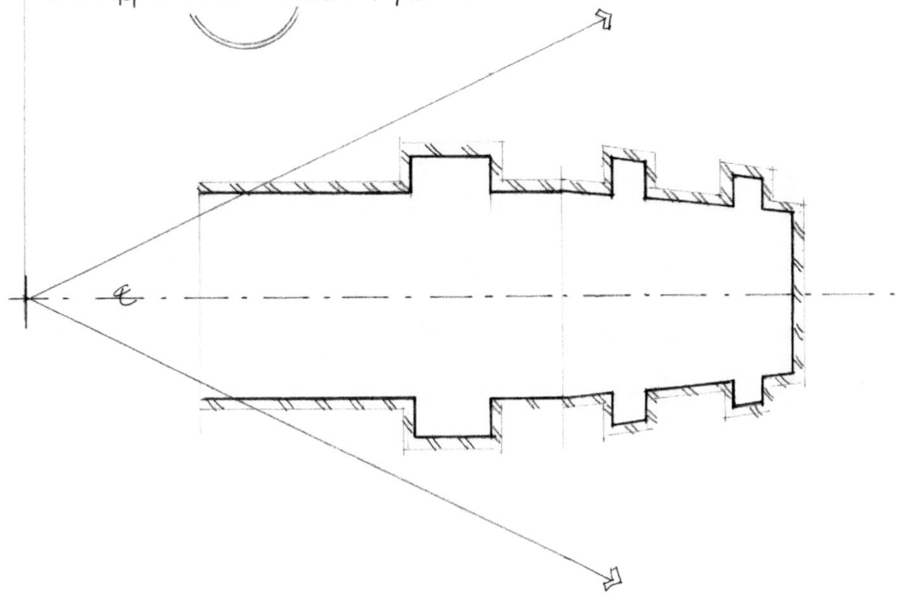

NB! ONLY ONE FIXED CAMERA POSITION WILL WORK! ARTISTES CAN ONLY BE IN "NORMAL" FOREGROUND SET

THE CLASSICAL ORDERS — DORIC [GREEK]

7TH CENTURY B.C.
CHARACTER: MASCULINITY & STRENGTH

- CAPITAL
  - ABACUS
  - ECHINUS
  - ANNULET

- ENTABLATURE
  - CORNICE
  - FRIEZE
  - ARCHITRAVE
- CAPITAL

2 DIA.

5½ DIA. — SHAFT

20 FLUTES [ARRISES]

- PEDIMENT
- STYLOBATE

PARTHENON

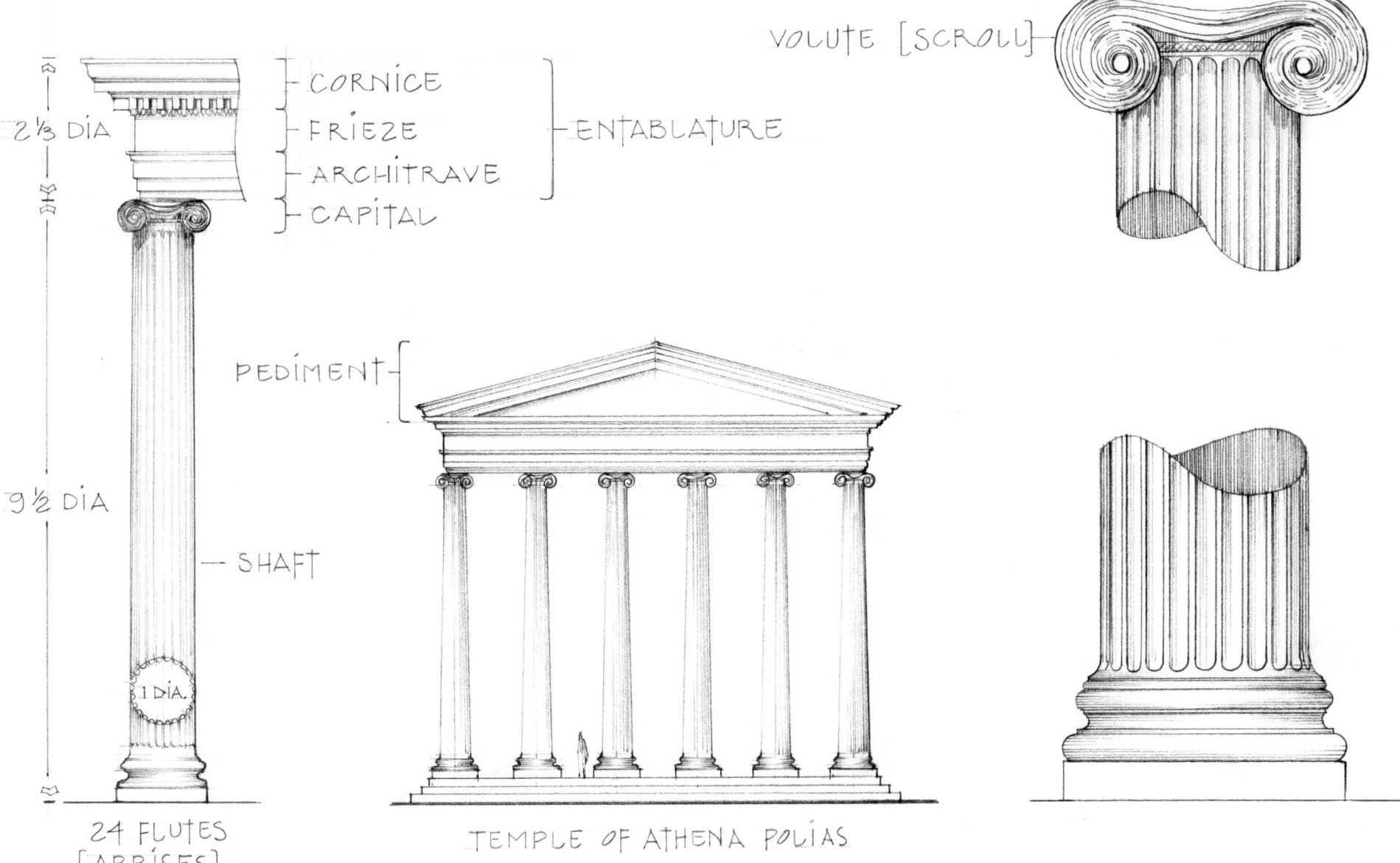

THE CLASSICAL ORDERS — CORINTHIAN [GREEK]

5TH CENTURY B.C.
CHARACTER: BARELY USED BY THE GREEKS & SOLELY FOR INTERIORS

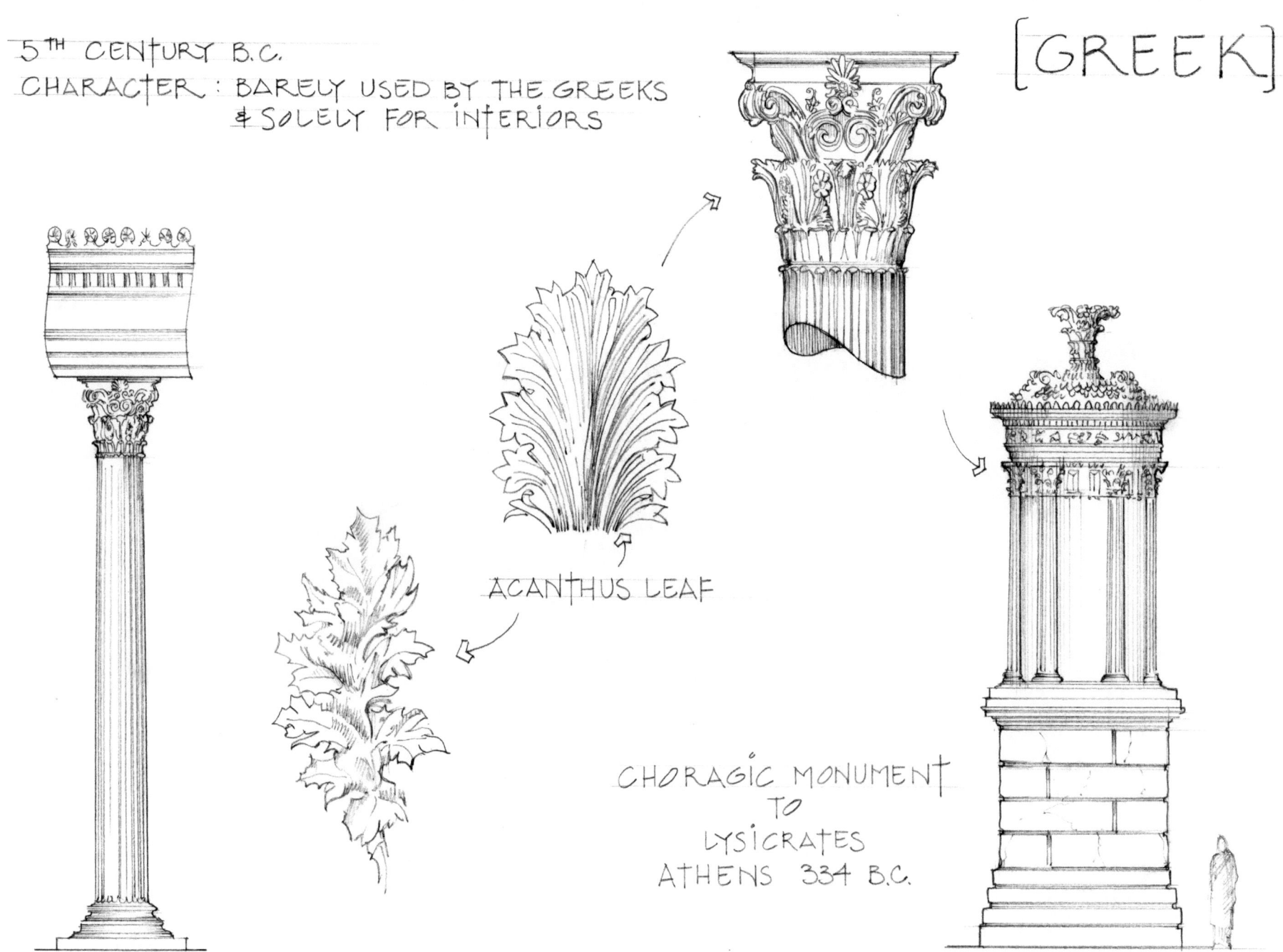

ACANTHUS LEAF

CHORAGIC MONUMENT TO LYSICRATES ATHENS 334 B.C.

THE CLASSICAL ORDERS - DORIC [ROMAN]

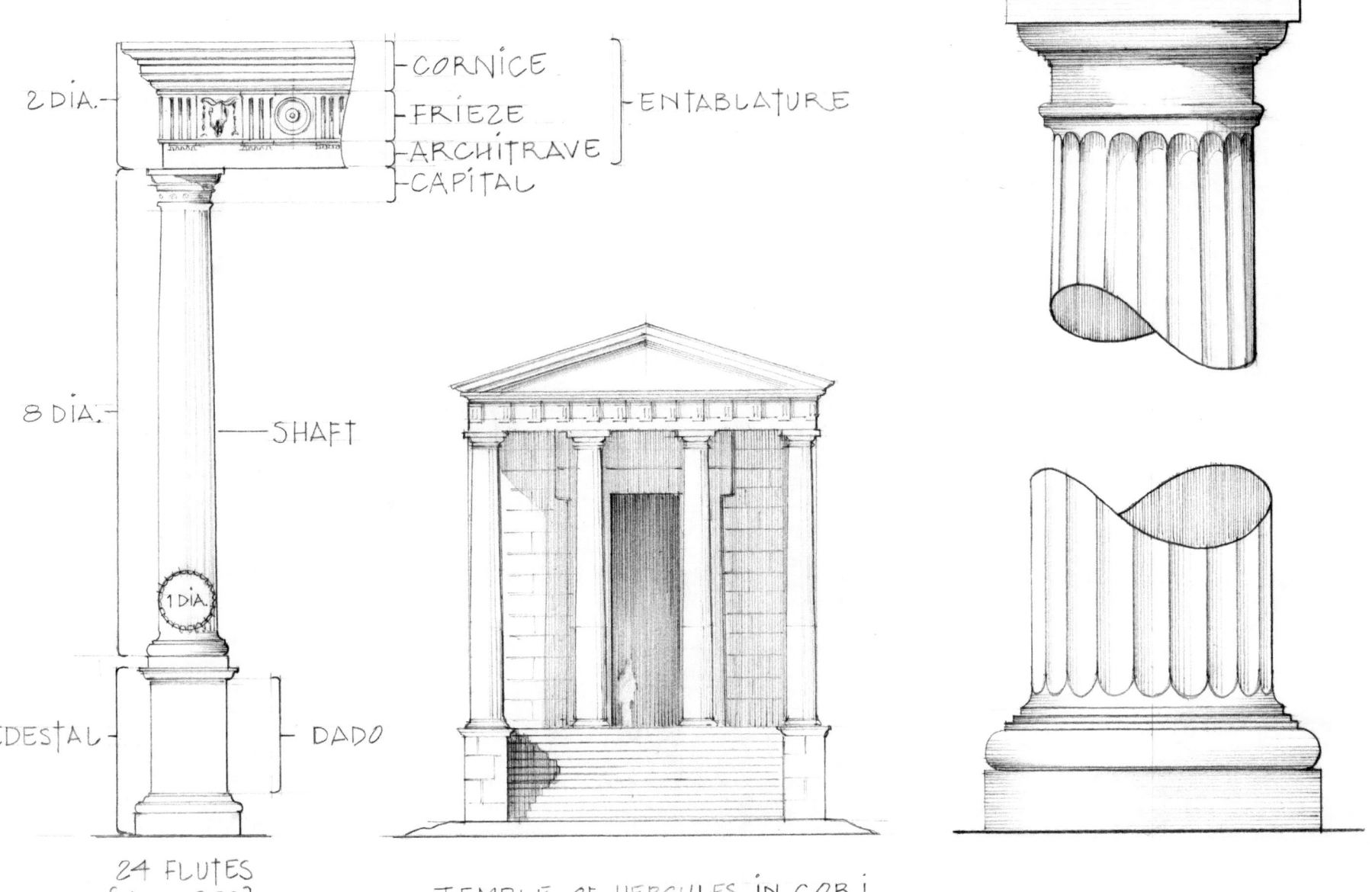

TEMPLE OF HERCULES IN CORI

24 FLUTES [ARRISES]

THE CLASSICAL ORDERS - TUSCAN [ROMAN]

1ST CENTURY B.C.
CHARACTER: SQUAT, STURDY & RUSTIC

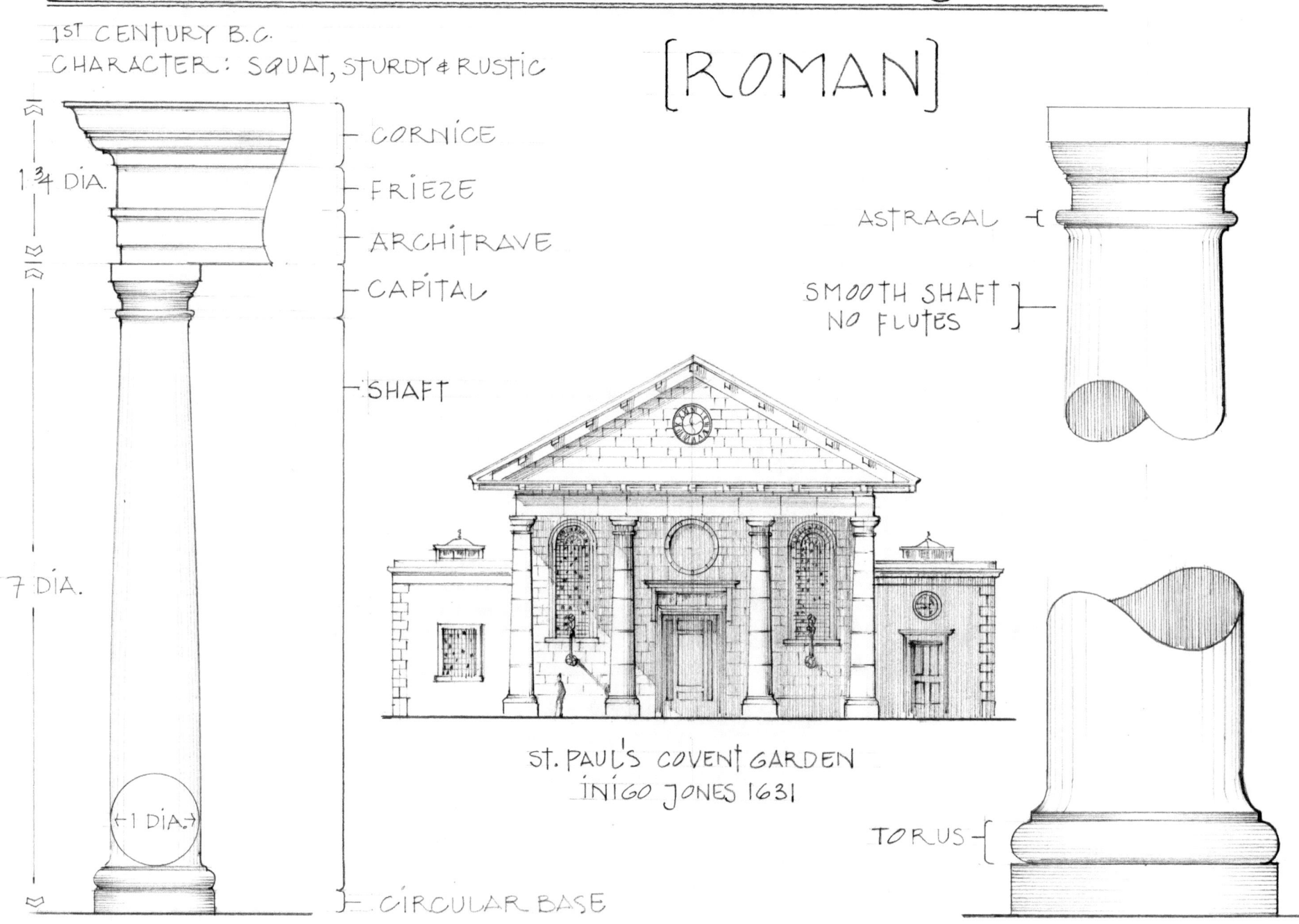

- CORNICE
- FRIEZE
- ARCHITRAVE
- CAPITAL
- SHAFT
- CIRCULAR BASE

1 ¾ DIA.
7 DIA.
1 DIA.

ASTRAGAL
SMOOTH SHAFT NO FLUTES
TORUS

ST. PAUL'S COVENT GARDEN
INIGO JONES 1631

THE CLASSICAL ORDERS — IONIC [ROMAN]

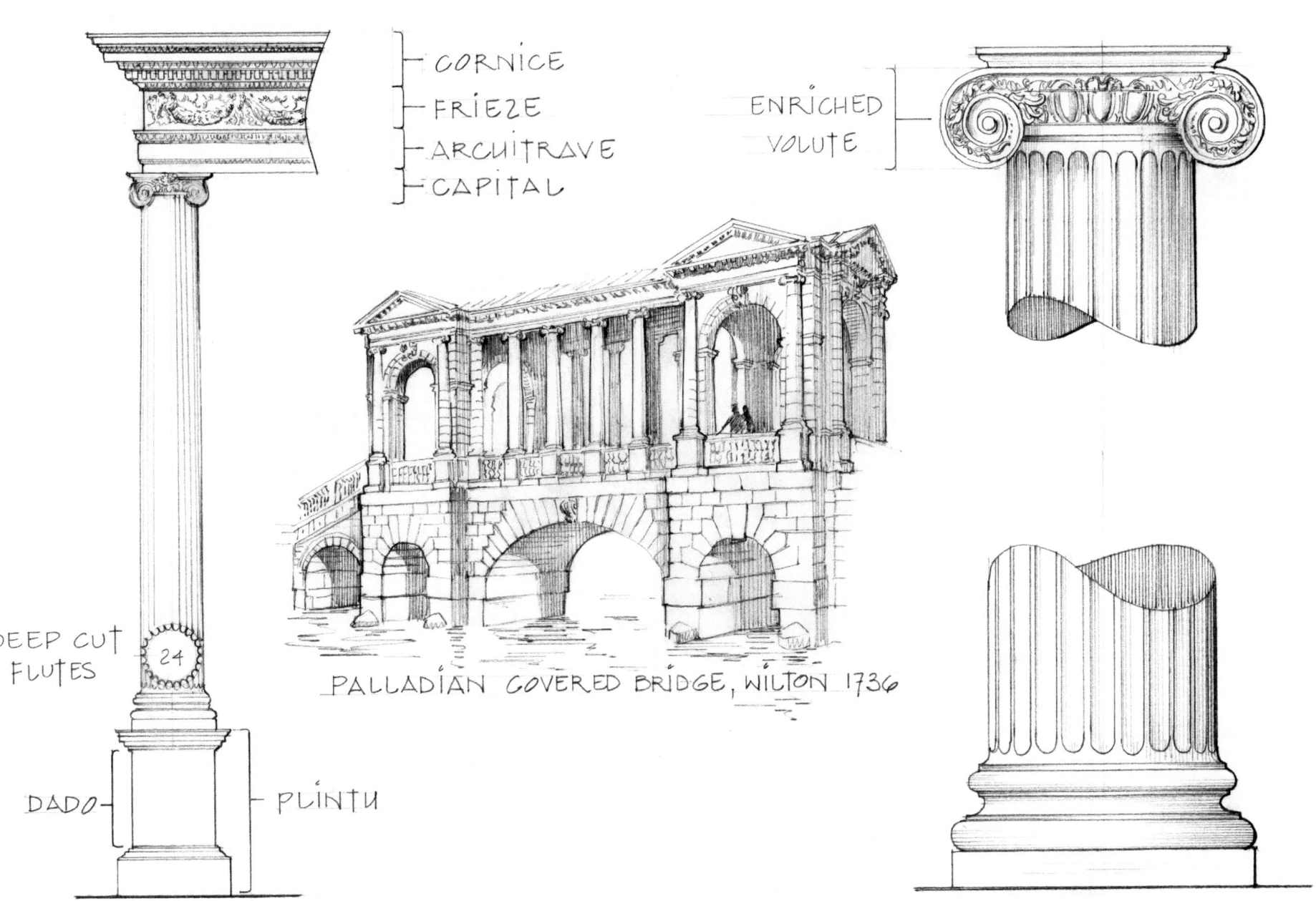

- CORNICE
- FRIEZE
- ARCHITRAVE
- CAPITAL

ENRICHED VOLUTE

DEEP CUT FLUTES 24

DADO — PLINTH

PALLADIAN COVERED BRIDGE, WILTON 1736

COLUMN MOUNTED ON PLINTH FOR EXTRA HEIGHT

THE CLASSICAL ORDERS — CORINTHIAN

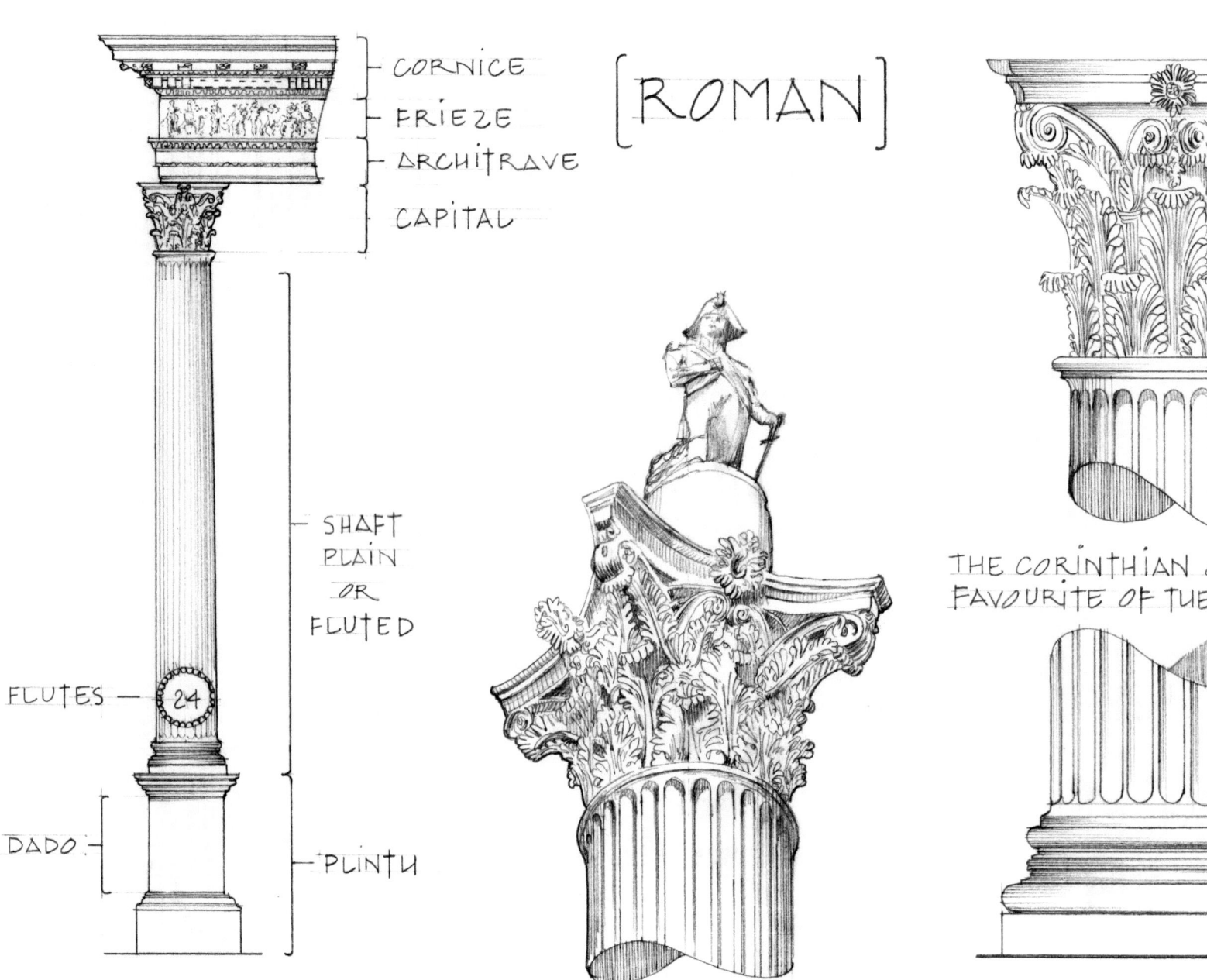

[ROMAN]

- CORNICE
- FRIEZE
- ARCHITRAVE
- CAPITAL

SHAFT PLAIN OR FLUTED

FLUTES

DADO

PLINTH

NELSON'S COLUMN — CAPITAL COPIED FROM TEMPLE OF MARS ULTOR, ROME

THE CORINTHIAN ORDER WAS THE FAVOURITE OF THE ROMANS

THE CLASSICAL ORDERS — COMPOSITE

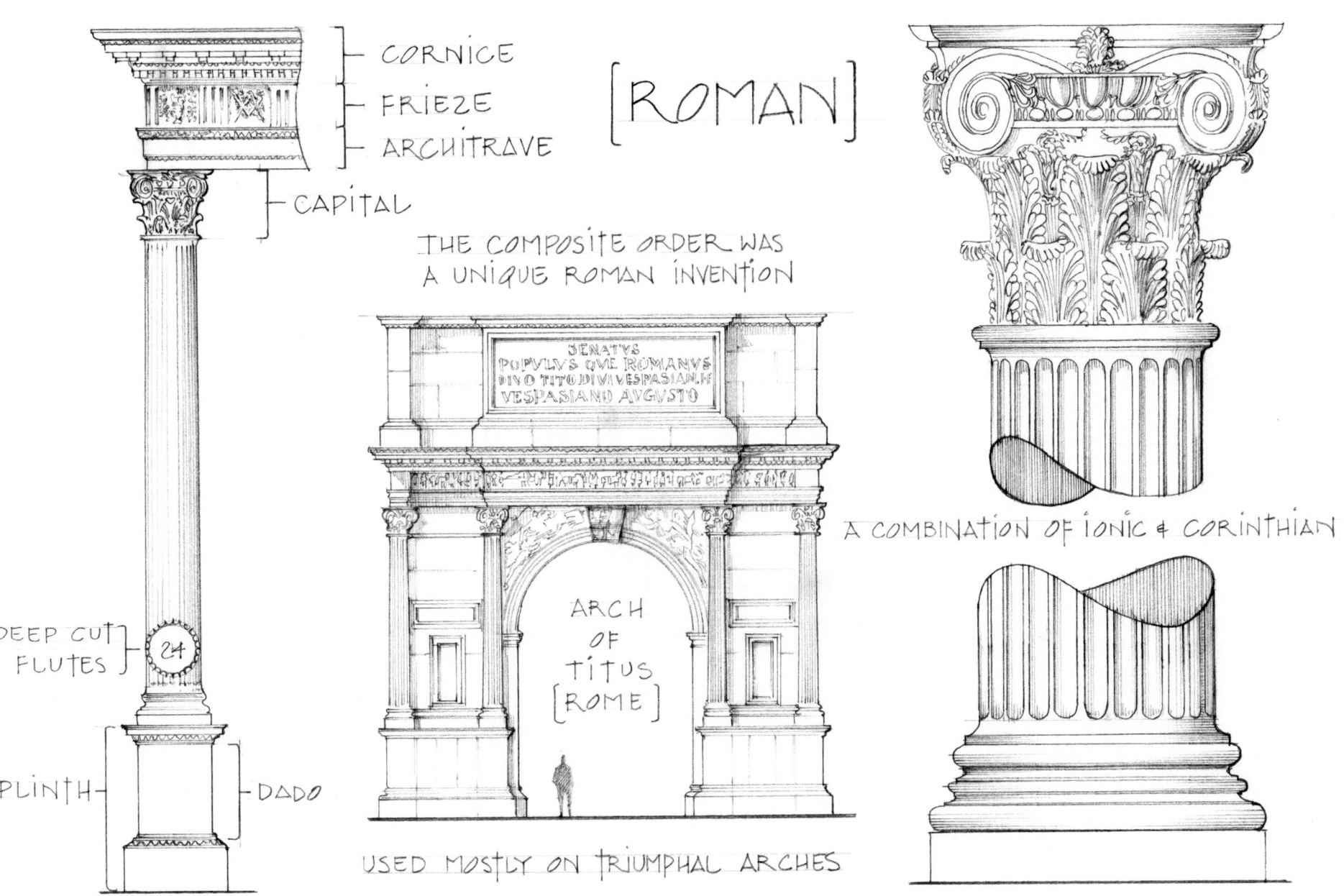

[ROMAN]

- CORNICE
- FRIEZE
- ARCHITRAVE
- CAPITAL

THE COMPOSITE ORDER WAS A UNIQUE ROMAN INVENTION

ARCH OF TITUS [ROME]

DEEP CUT FLUTES

PLINTH — DADO

A COMBINATION OF IONIC & CORINTHIAN

USED MOSTLY ON TRIUMPHAL ARCHES

ENTASIS OF COLUMN SHAFTS

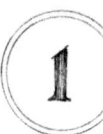

UPPER DIAMETER

THIS METHOD IS THE MOST OFTEN USED & IS KNOWN AS "THE CHONCOID OF NICOMEDES"

USE BASE RADIUS "r" ON ALL DIVISIONS

INCREASE THE NUMBER OF DIVISIONS FOR AN EASIER LINE TO DRAW WITH A FLEXIBLE CURVE OR FREEHAND

DIVIDE INTO EQUAL PARTS

BASE RADIUS 'r'

UPPER DIAMETER

BASE DIAMETER IS THE LARGEST & SHOULD NEVER BE EXCEEDED !

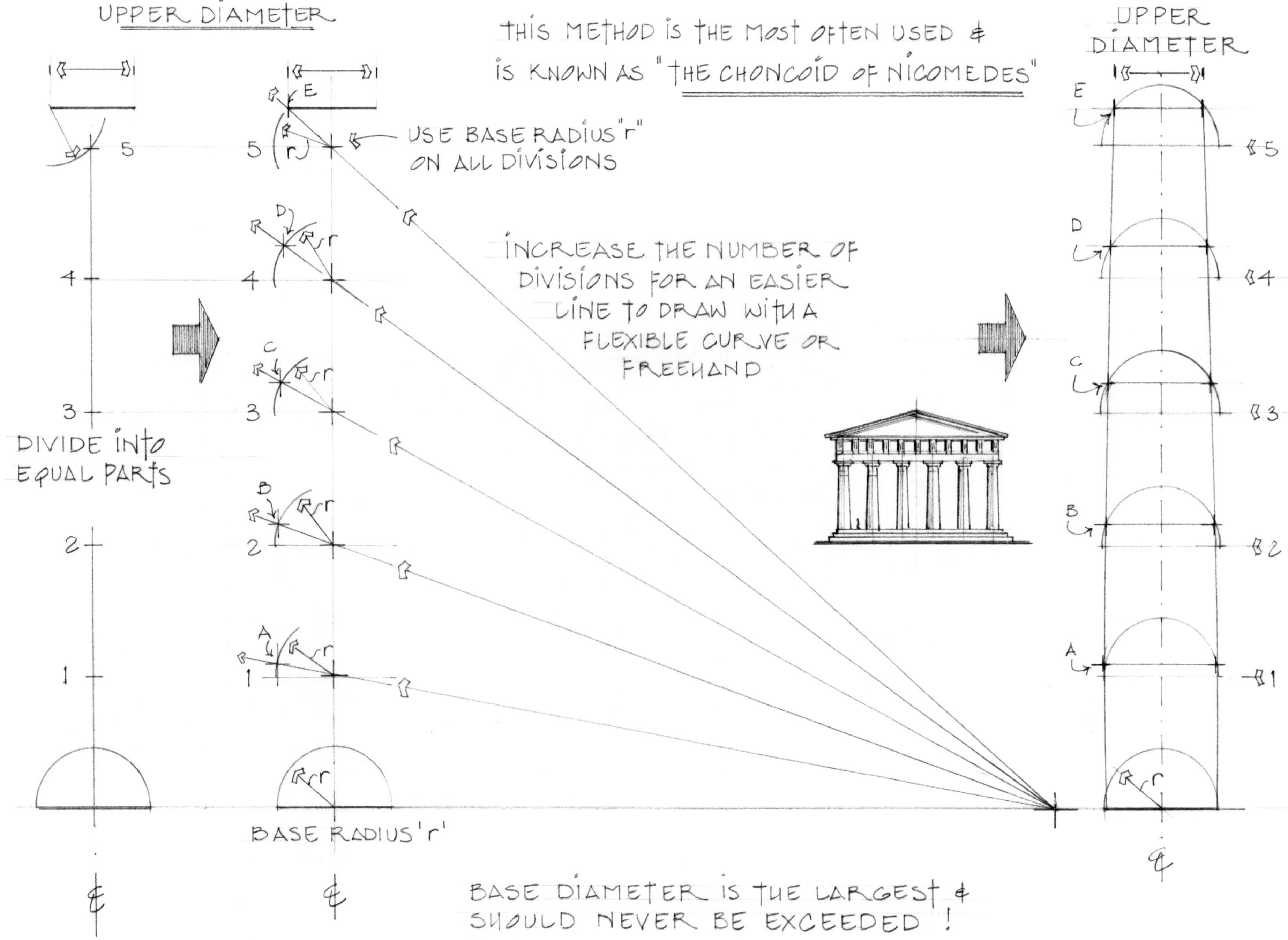

ENTASIS OF COLUMN SHAFTS

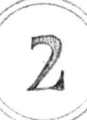

ENTASIS: THE CURVED SWELLING ON A COLUMN'S SHAFT.

OPTICALLY A STRAIGHT TAPER APPEARS TO CURVE INWARDS

THE SWELLING OF THE SHAFT COUNTERACTS THIS ILLUSION

THE ENTASIS MAY BE ON THE WHOLE SHAFT OR JUST THE UPPER TWO THIRDS

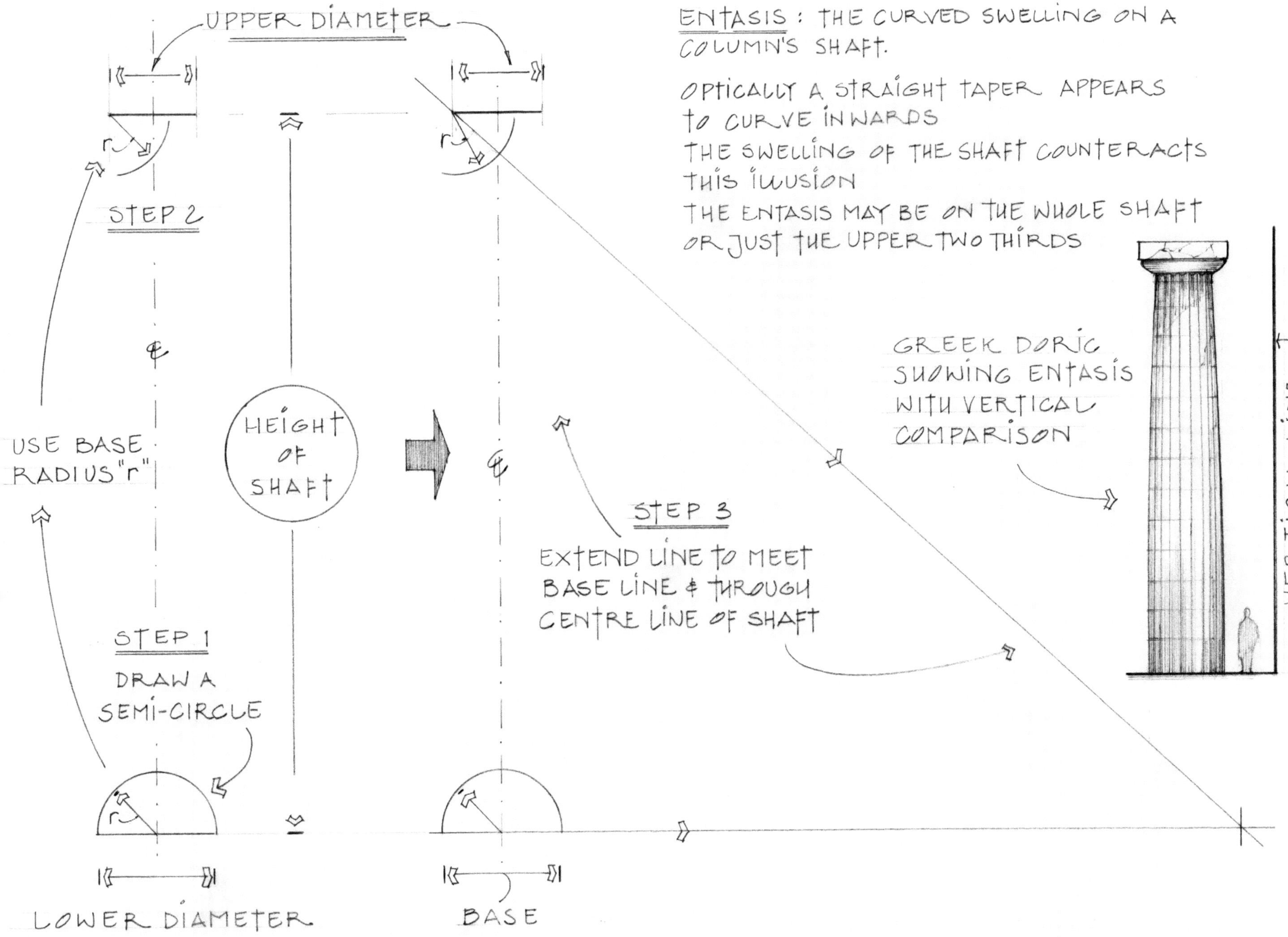

UPPER DIAMETER

STEP 2

USE BASE RADIUS "r"

HEIGHT OF SHAFT

STEP 1
DRAW A SEMI-CIRCLE

LOWER DIAMETER

BASE

STEP 3
EXTEND LINE TO MEET BASE LINE & THROUGH CENTRE LINE OF SHAFT

GREEK DORIC SHOWING ENTASIS WITH VERTICAL COMPARISON

VERTICAL LINE

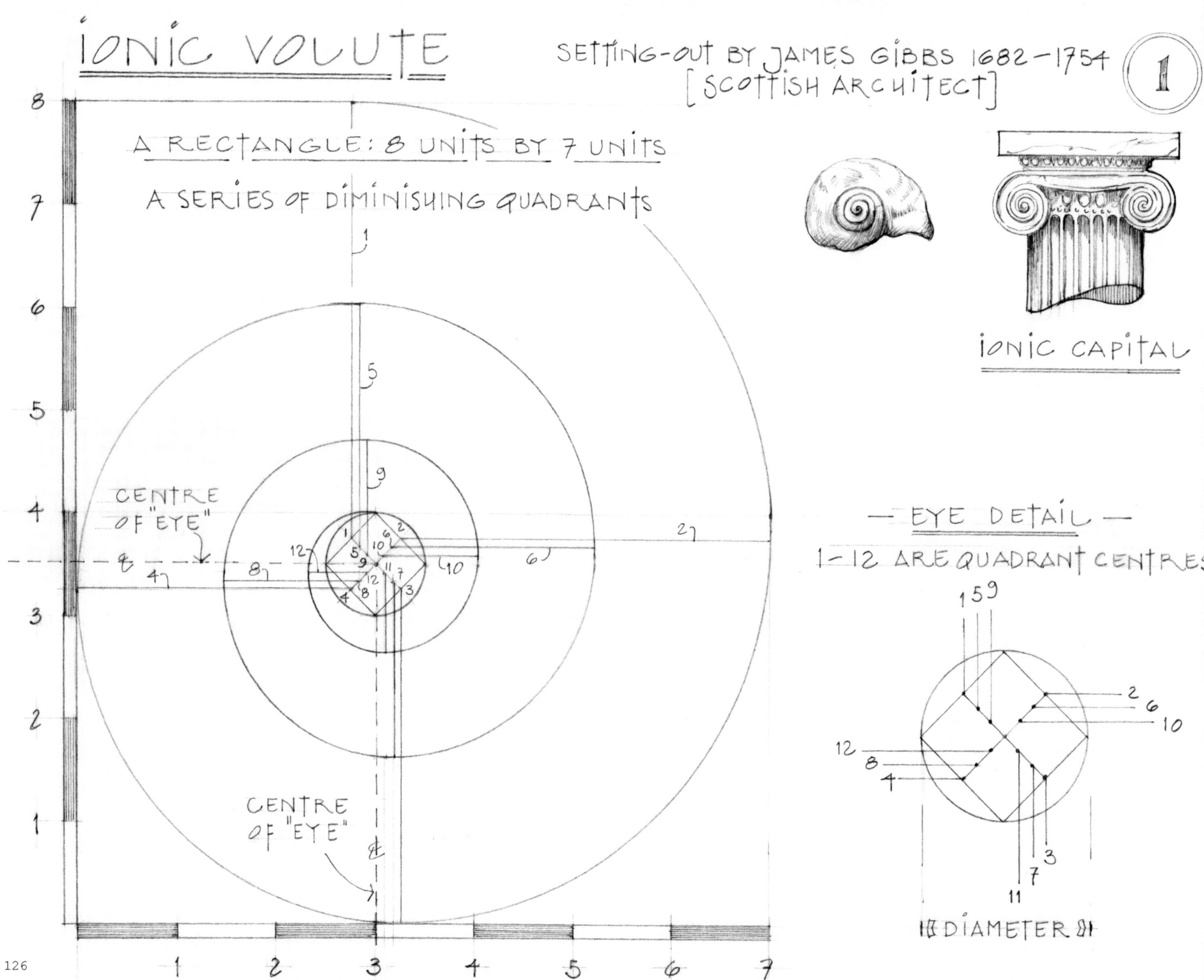

SPIRAL BASED ON QUADRANTS

DRAW A LINE & DIVIDE INTO 10 UNITS

"EYE" OF THE SPIRAL
2 UNITS = DIAMETER

THE 4 CORNERS OF THE SQUARE ARE **RADIAL POINTS**

COMPLETED — NOTE THE CONSTANT WIDTH ON EACH QUADRANT

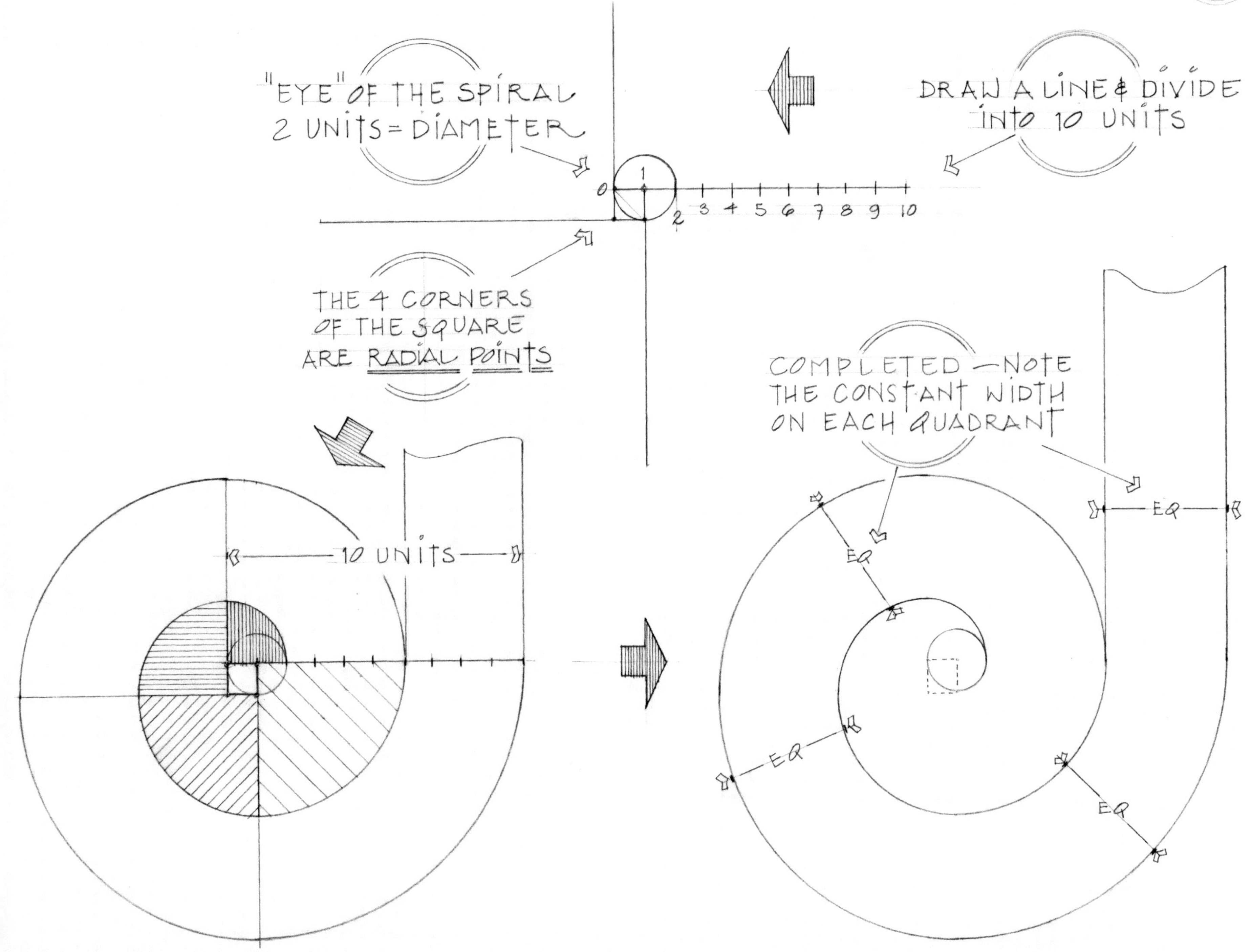

THE FIBONACCI SPIRAL — LEONARDO FIBONACCI
1170 – 1230

A CURVE THAT INCREASES CONSTANTLY WITHOUT EVER CHANGING ITS SHAPE

THE FIBONACCI SEQUENCE
1, 1, 2, 3, 5, 8, 13, 21, 34, 55 ⟶ ETC.

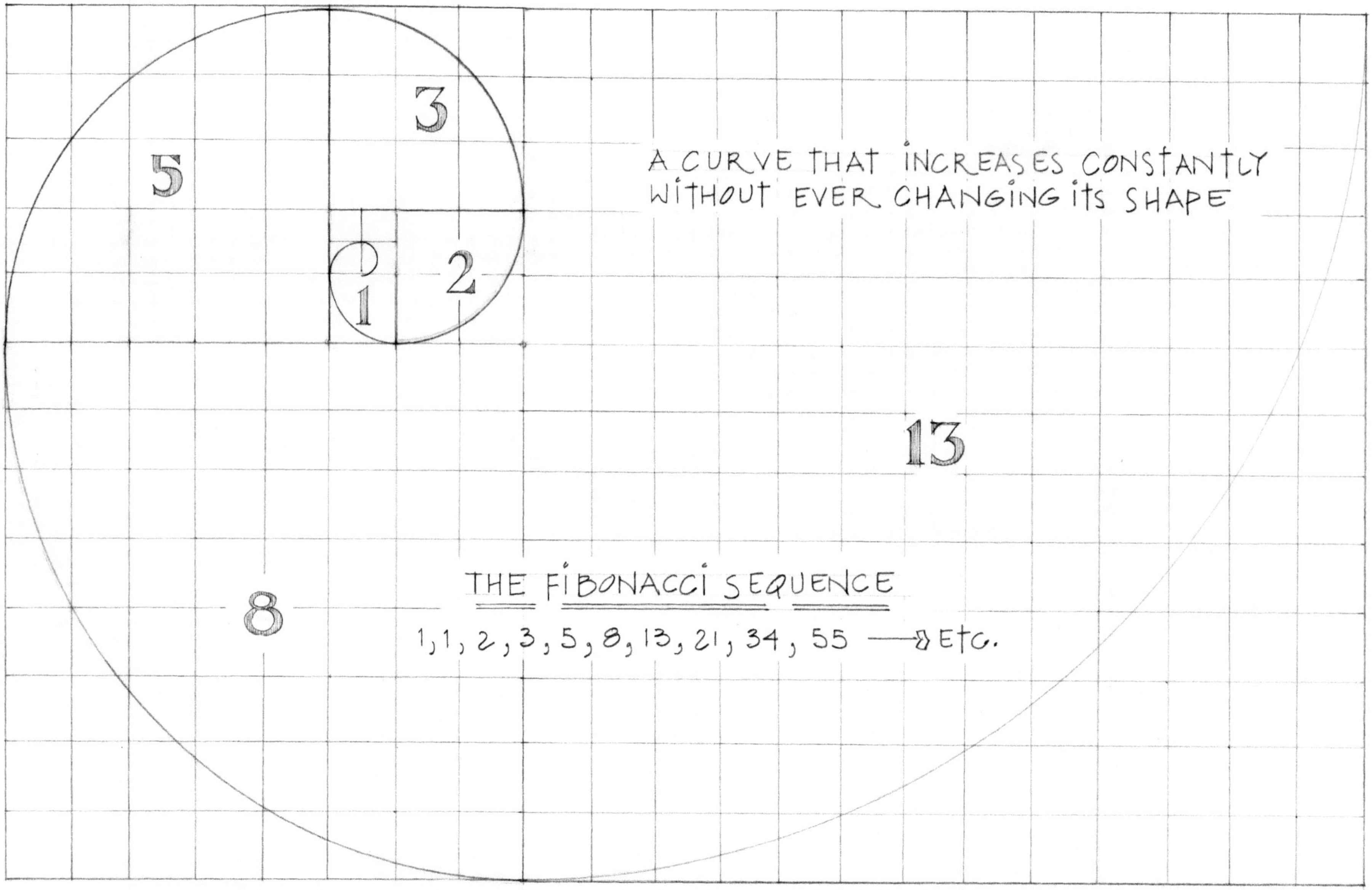

THE GOLDEN SECTION

DRAW A SQUARE OF ANY SIZE

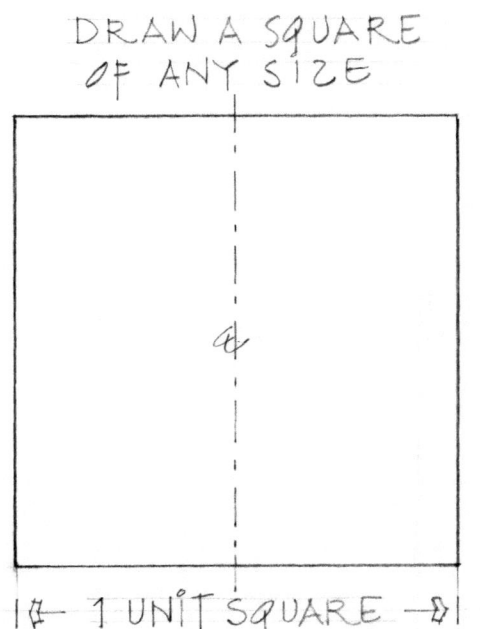

|← 1 UNIT SQUARE →|

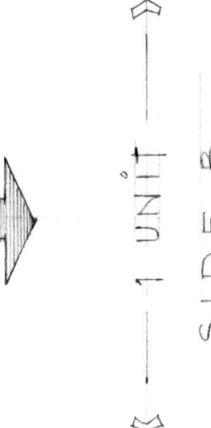

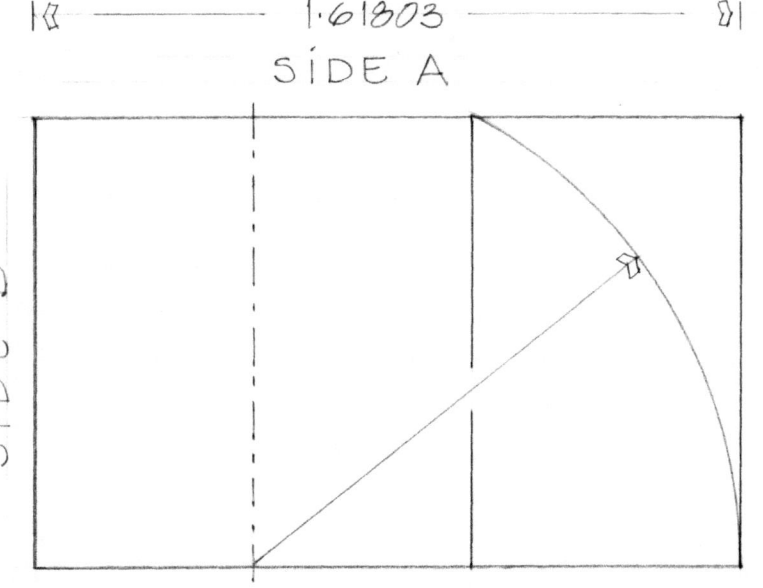

|← 1.61803 →|
SIDE A

SIDE B — 1 UNIT

A ÷ B IS THE SAME AS A+B ÷ A

THIS RATIO IS CALLED phi ϕ

ϕ = 1.61803....

ORIGINS ARE WITH THE ANCIENT GREEKS

AND

ANY CONNECTION TO THE NATURAL WORLD, ART OR ARCHITECTURE IS DEBATABLE

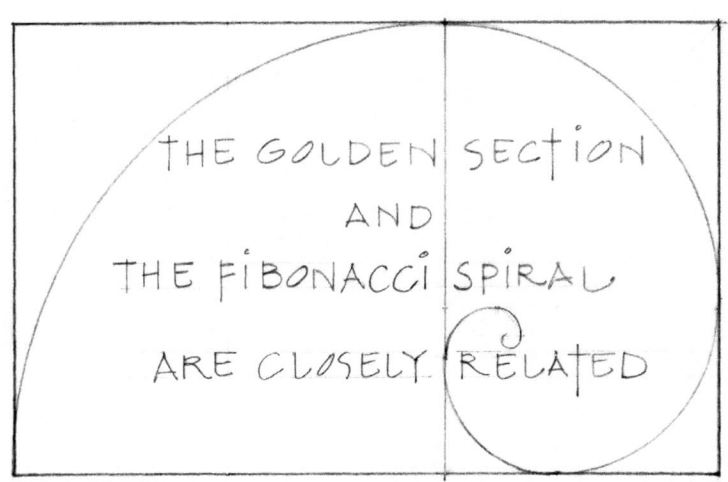

THE GOLDEN SECTION

AND

THE FIBONACCI SPIRAL

ARE CLOSELY RELATED

THE SPIRAL [HELIX]

THE HELIX IS THE BASIS OF A SPIRAL STAIRCASE

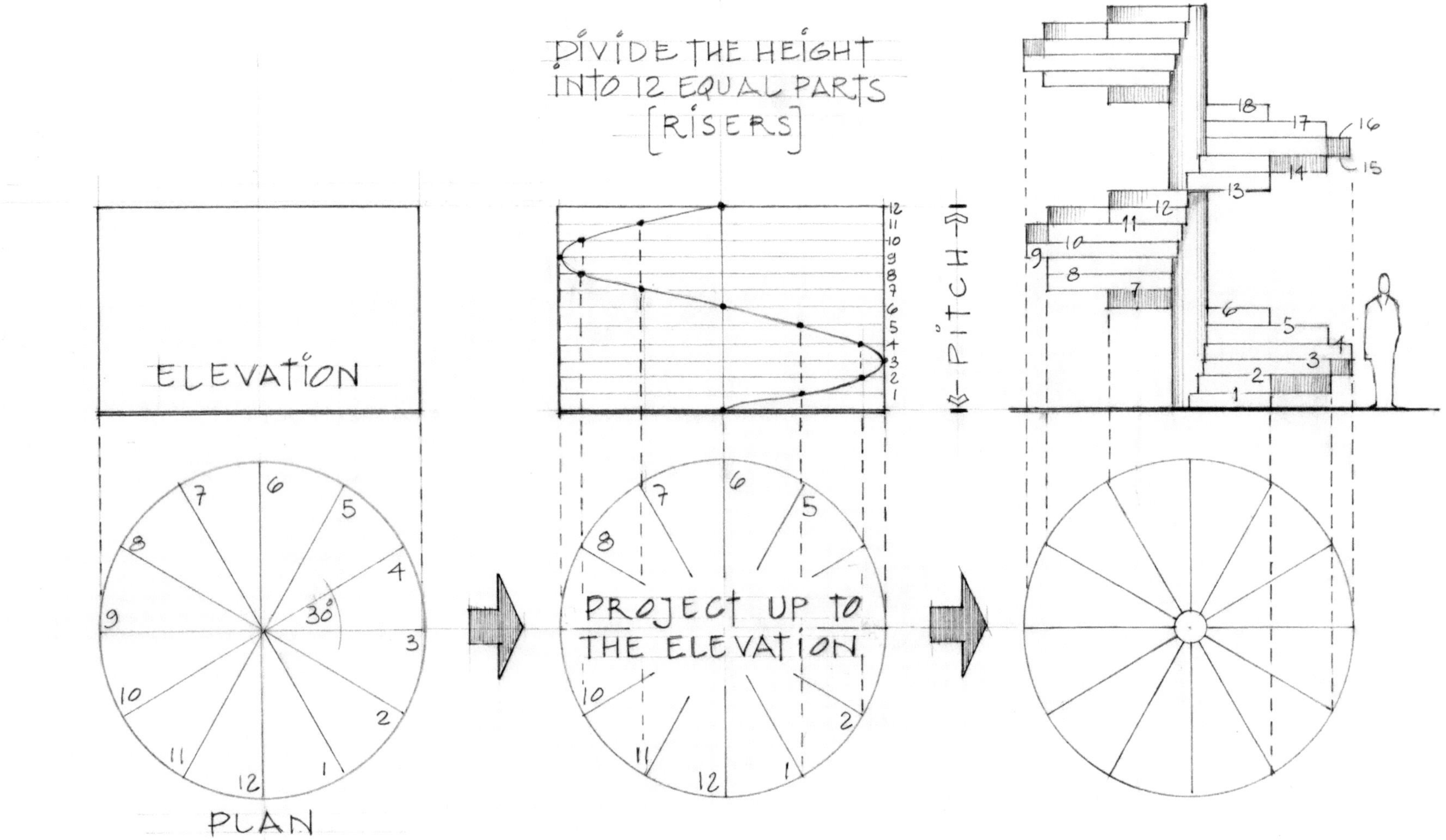

DIVIDE THE HEIGHT INTO 12 EQUAL PARTS [RISERS]

ELEVATION

PROJECT UP TO THE ELEVATION

PLAN

DRAW A CYLINDER IN PLAN AND THE ELEVATION ABOVE

DIVIDE THE PLAN INTO 12 PARTS

CHECK RISERS WILL GIVE SUFFICIENT HEADROOM!

SURVEYING — LOCATION INTERIORS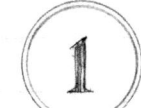

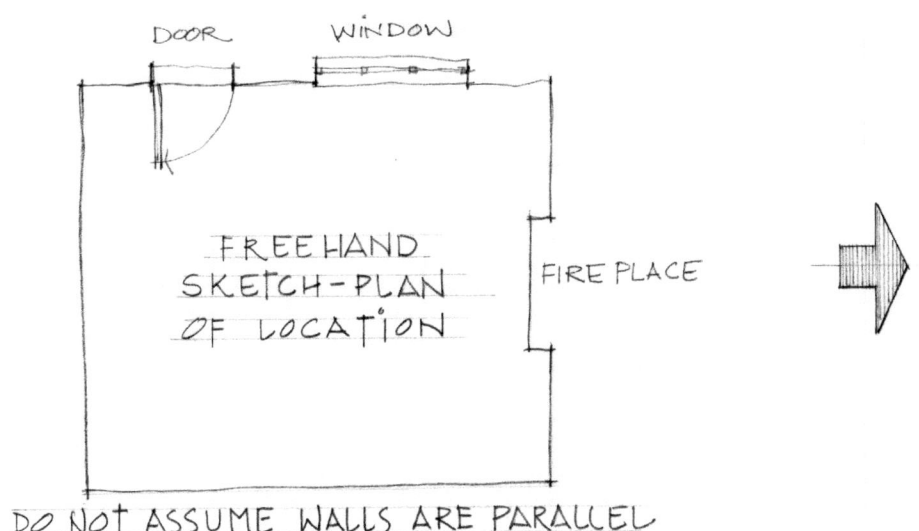

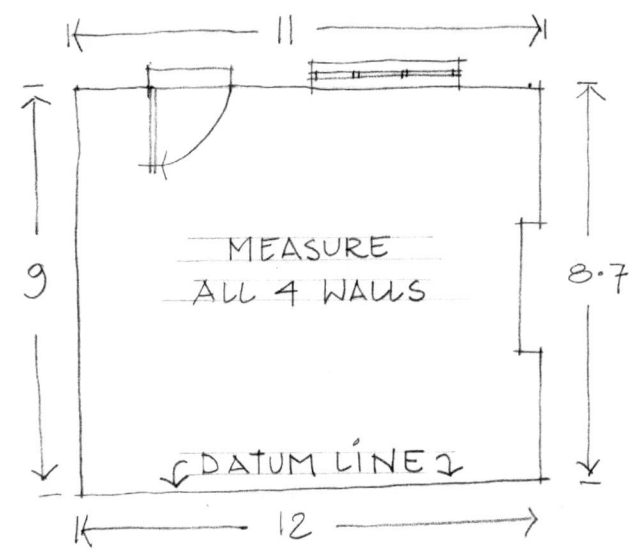

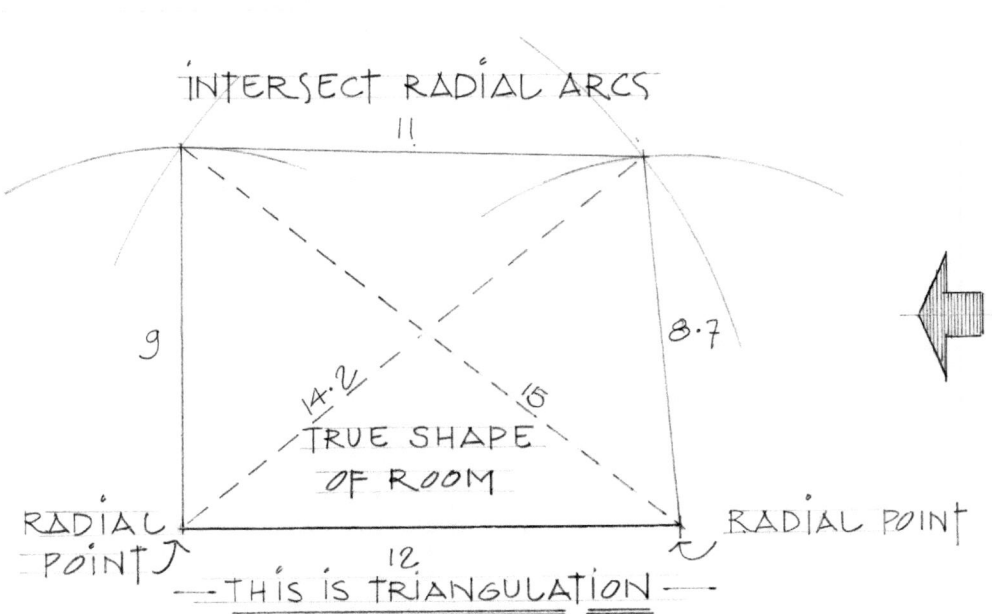

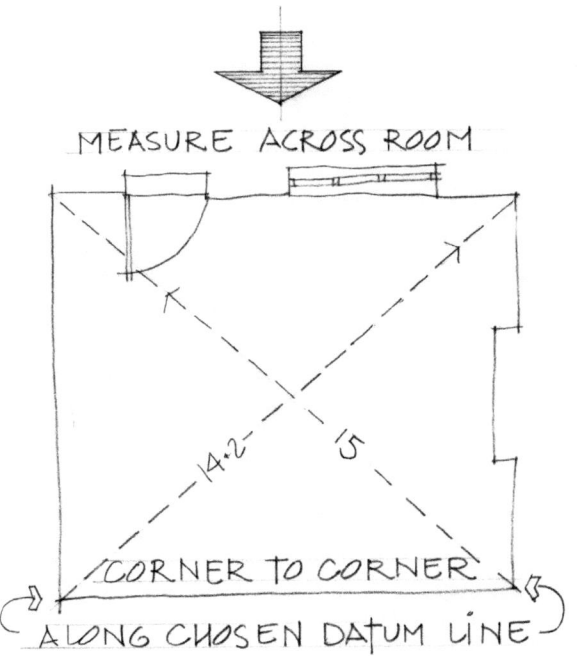

SURVEYING — LOCATION INTERIORS ②

— RUNNING DIMENSIONS —

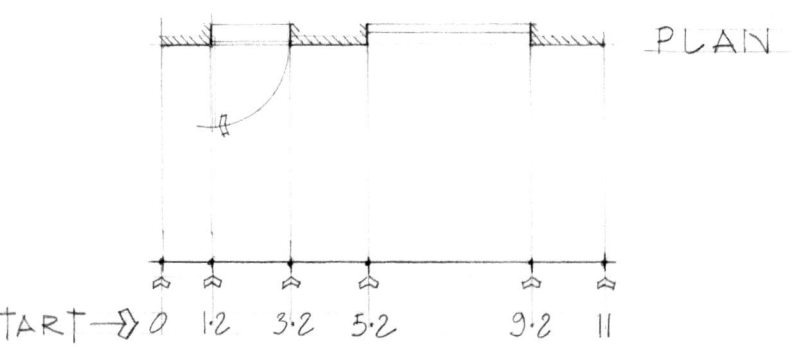

PLAN

START → 0 1·2 3·2 5·2 9·2 11

THIS WILL GIVE ACCURATE POSITIONS

THEN CHECK INDIVIDUAL DIMENSIONS

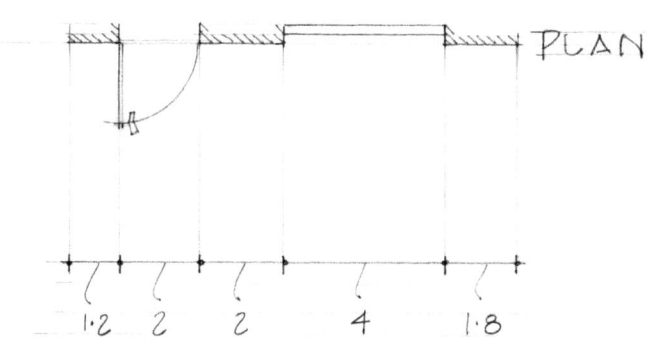

PLAN

1·2   2   2   4   1·8

MEASURE HEIGHT DIMENSIONS
[AT BOTH ENDS]

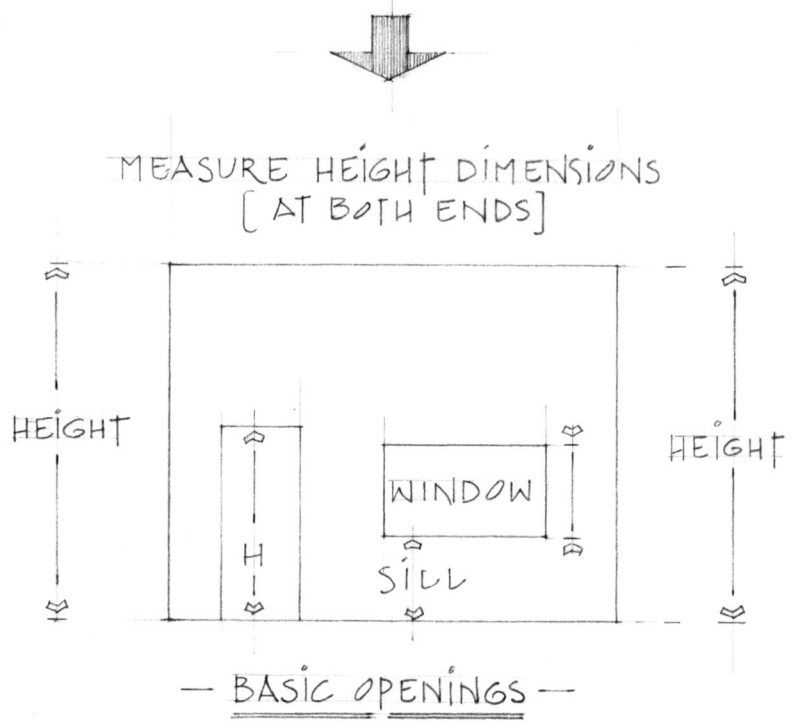

— BASIC OPENINGS —

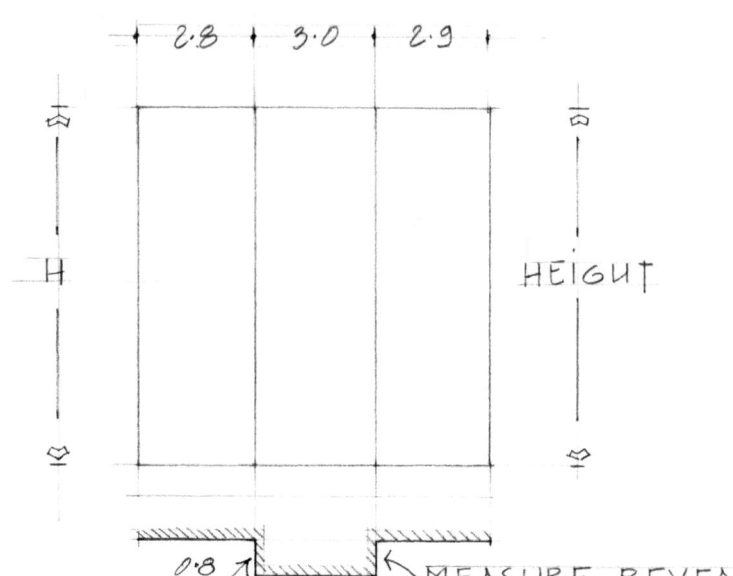

MEASURE REVEALS

SURVEYING — LOCATION INTERIORS ③

FINAL BASIC PLAN DRAWN TO A SCALE
[FOR INITIAL SURVEYS 1:50 or ¼"=1'-0"]

DRAW DETAILS &
ADD NOTES AS NECESSARY

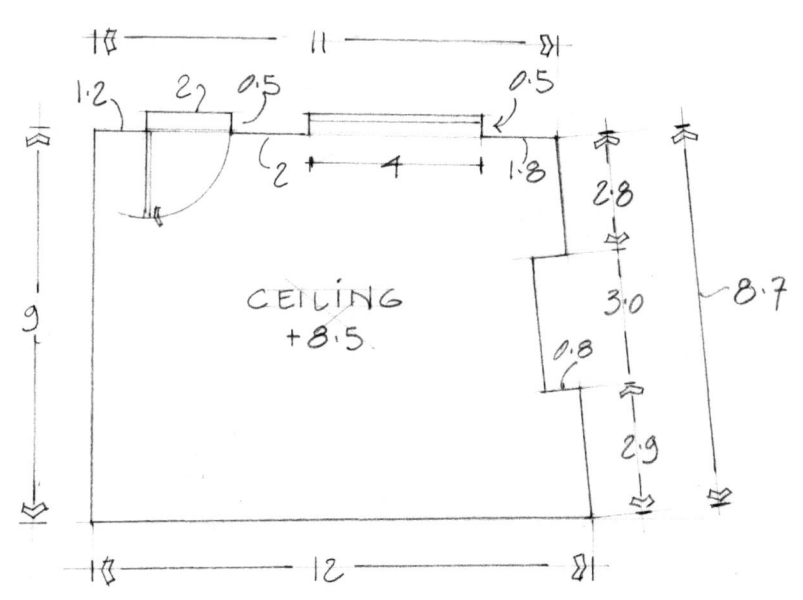

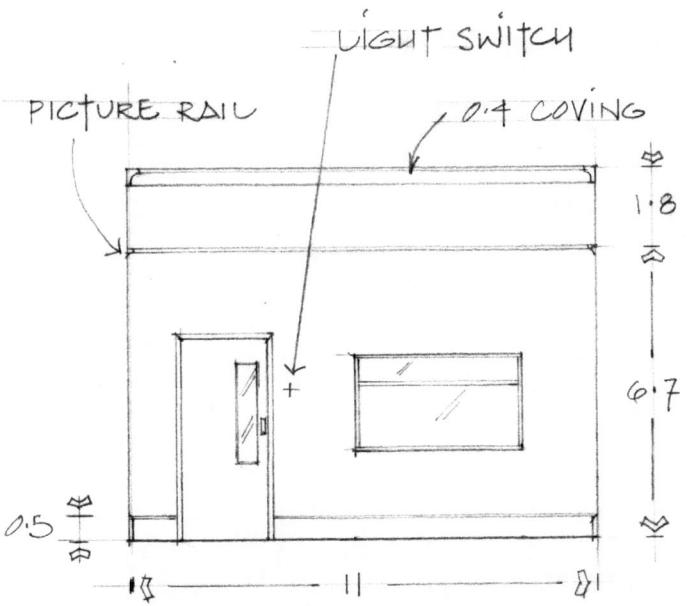

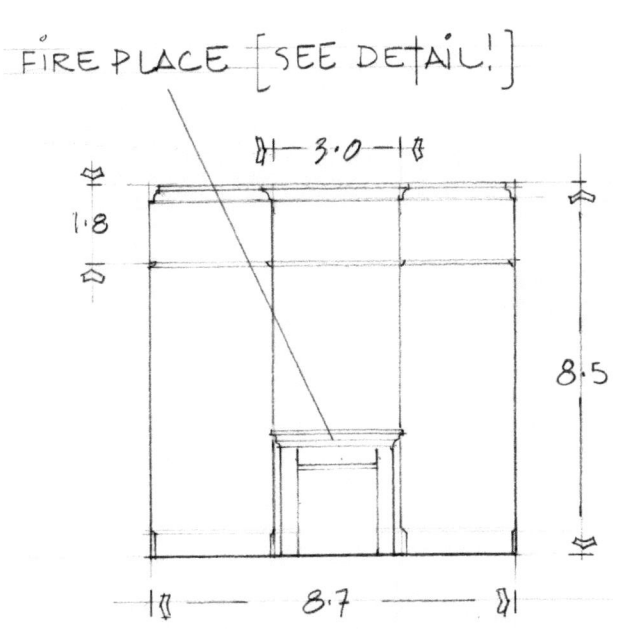

SURVEYING — LOCATION EXTERIORS

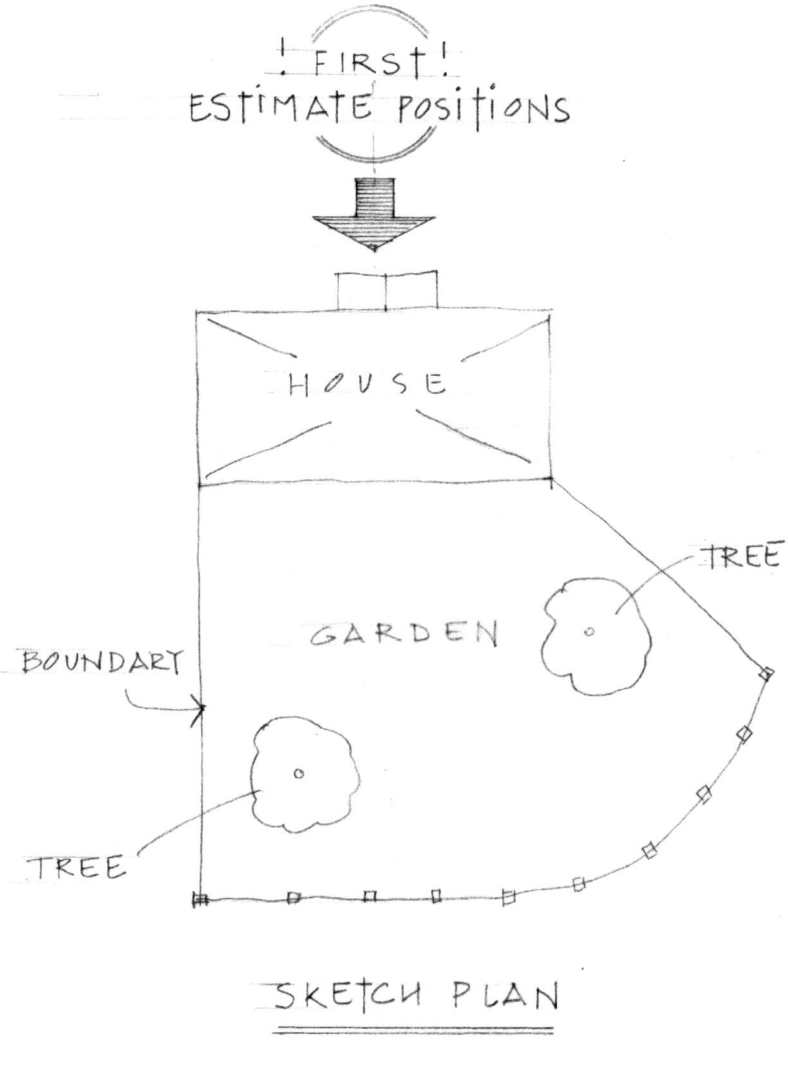

!FIRST! ESTIMATE POSITIONS

SKETCH PLAN

N.T.S. [NOT TO SCALE!]

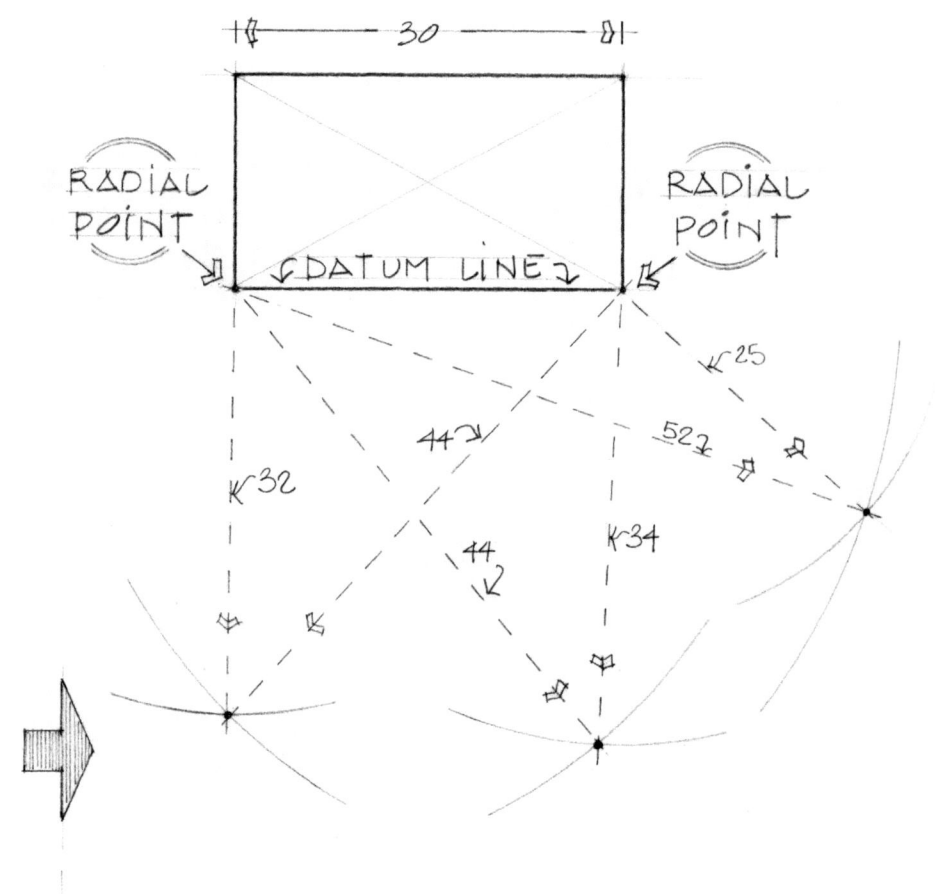

TRIANGULATE AS IN SURVEYING AN INTERIOR

NOW DRAW TO SCALE!

SURVEYING — LOCATION EXTERIORS (2)

TO DEFINE CURVE

EQUAL DIVISIONS ALONG FIXED LINE & MEASURE TO CURVE AT 90°

POSITION TREES IN SAME WAY [TRIANGULATE]

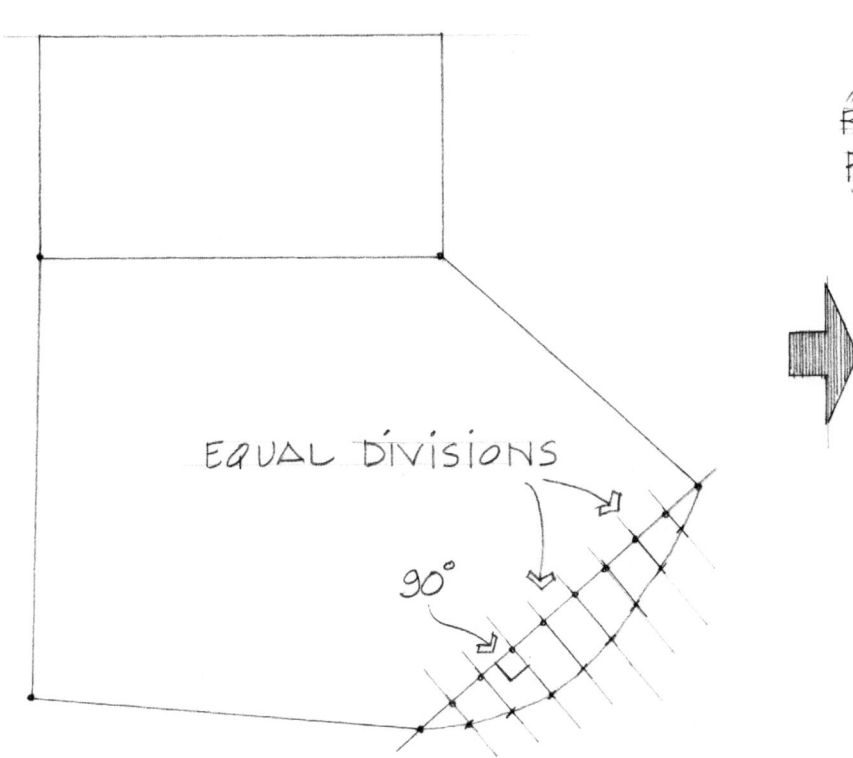

EQUAL DIVISIONS

90°

MORE REFERENCE POINTS GIVE MORE ACCURACY !!

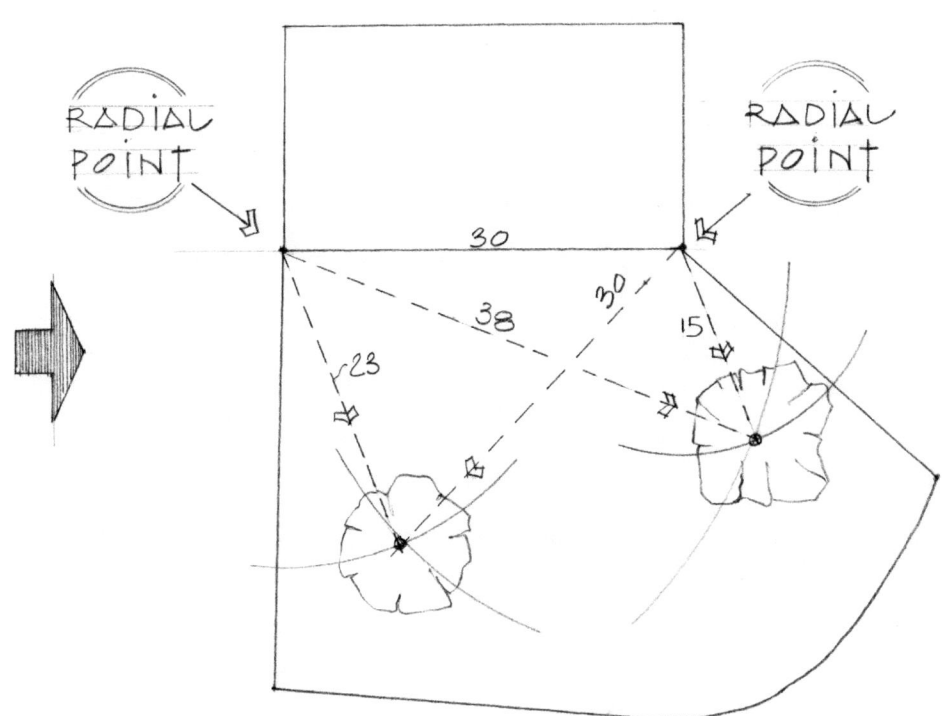

RADIAL POINT

RADIAL POINT

SURVEYING — LOCATION EXTERIORS

MAIN LOCATION PLAN
— SOUTH FARM, NORTH VILLAGE. —

FARM HOUSE

GARDEN

TREE

TREE

HERO ARMY TRUCK

BROKEN FENCE

MARK ORIENTATION

ADD DETAILS / NOTES ETC. AS REQUIRED

ADD SCALE
ESSENTIAL WHEN EMAILING
OR ENLARGING

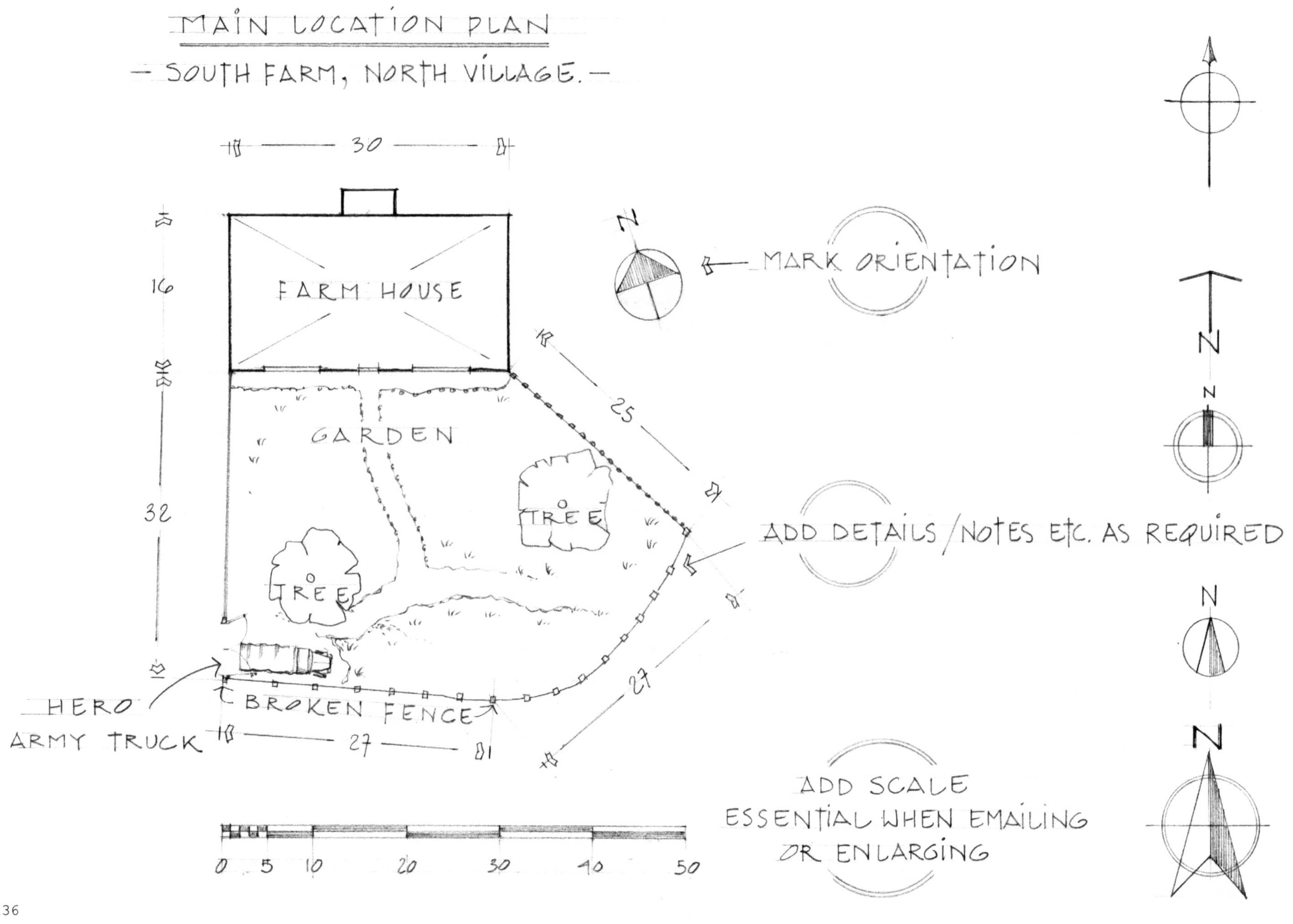

SURVEYING – LOCATION EXTERIORS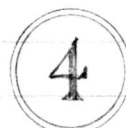

MEASURING HEIGHTS USING A SIMPLE CLINOMETER/INCLINOMETER

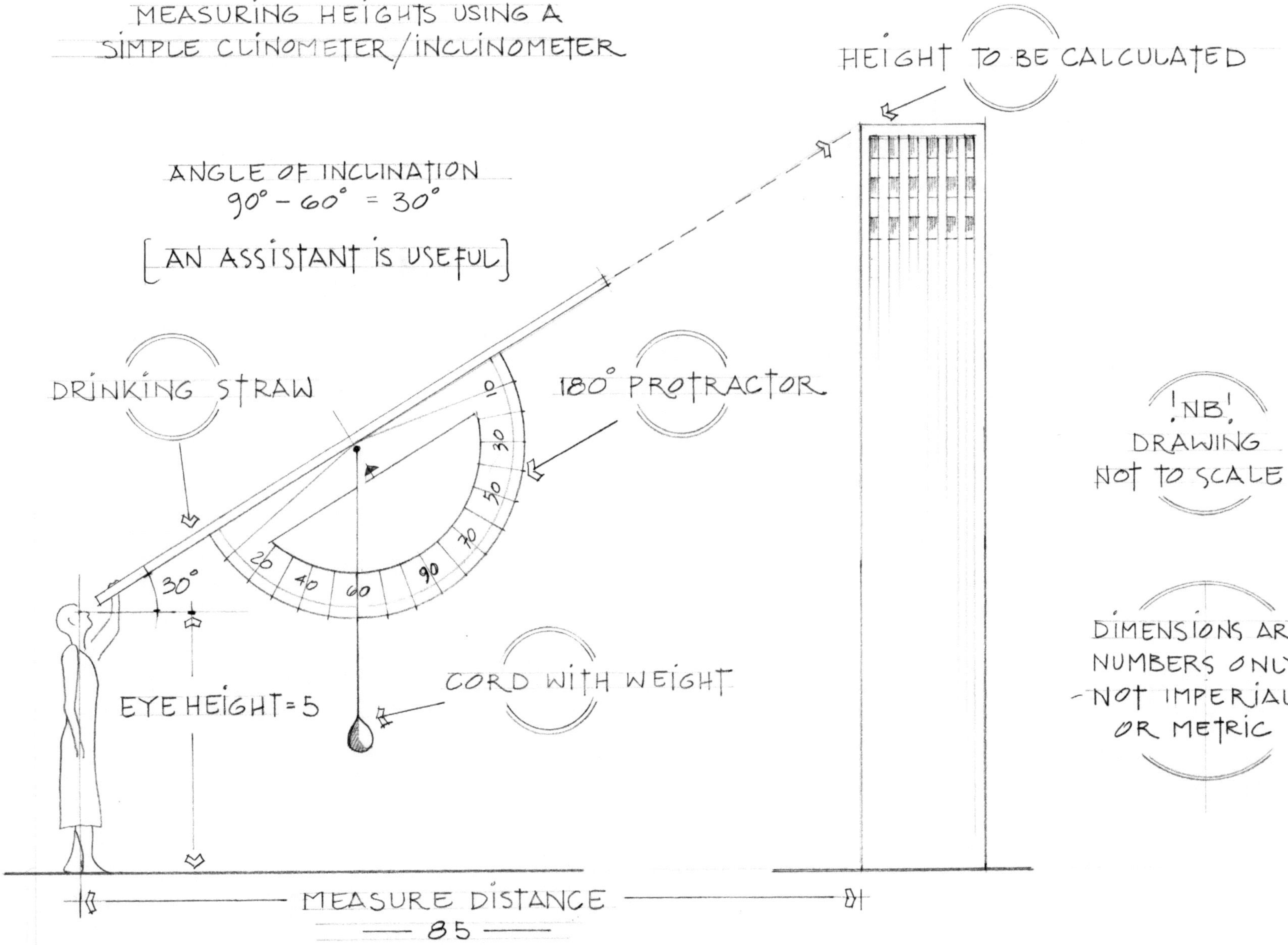

HEIGHT TO BE CALCULATED

ANGLE OF INCLINATION
90° − 60° = 30°

[AN ASSISTANT IS USEFUL]

DRINKING STRAW

180° PROTRACTOR

!NB! DRAWING NOT TO SCALE!

EYE HEIGHT = 5

CORD WITH WEIGHT

DIMENSIONS ARE NUMBERS ONLY – NOT IMPERIAL OR METRIC

MEASURE DISTANCE
85

SURVEYING - LOCATION EXTERIORS

CALCULATING HEIGHT ON DRAWING BOARD

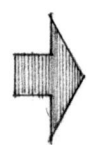 USING ANGLE OF INCLINATION = 30°
AND DISTANCE FROM BUILDING = 85
DRAW RIGHT ANGLED TRIANGLE TO SCALE

EYE HEIGHT + LENGTH OF OPPOSITE SIDE
= HEIGHT OF BUILDING = 54

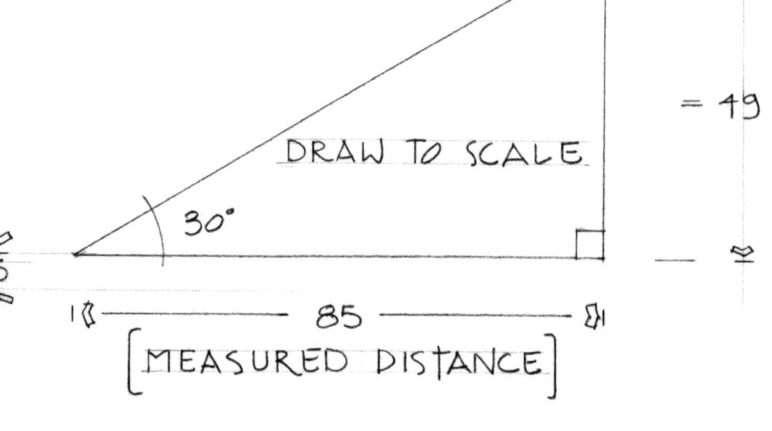

EYE HEIGHT = 5
[MEASURED DISTANCE] 85
DRAW TO SCALE = 49

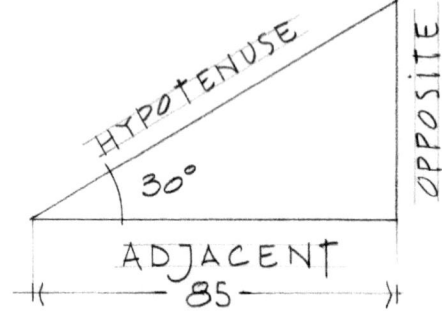

$\tan 30° = \dfrac{\text{OPPOSITE}}{\text{ADJACENT}}$ $\dfrac{\text{HYPOTENUSE}}{85}$

RE ARRANGE:

HEIGHT [OPPOSITE] = $85 \times \tan 30° = 49$

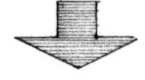

TO FIND TANGENTS USING MOBILE PHONE:

EG: $\tan 30°$ = CALCULATOR APP./SIDEWAYS/
ENTER: 30 / PRESS: Deg /
PRESS: tan
= 0.5773×85 [DISTANCE]
= 49.075 + EYE HEIGHT 5

HEIGHT OF BUILDING = 54.075

GLOSSARY

ABACUS

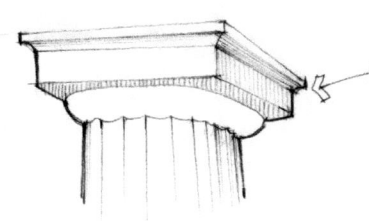

THE TOPMOST PART OF A COLUMN

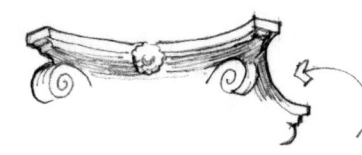

IT CAN ALSO BE HOLLOWED, NOT SQUARE

ACANTHUS

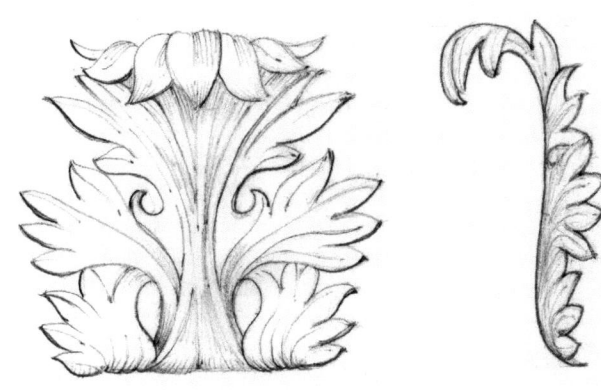

A STYLISED MEDITERRANEAN LEAF USED ON CORINTHIAN CAPITALS & MOULDINGS

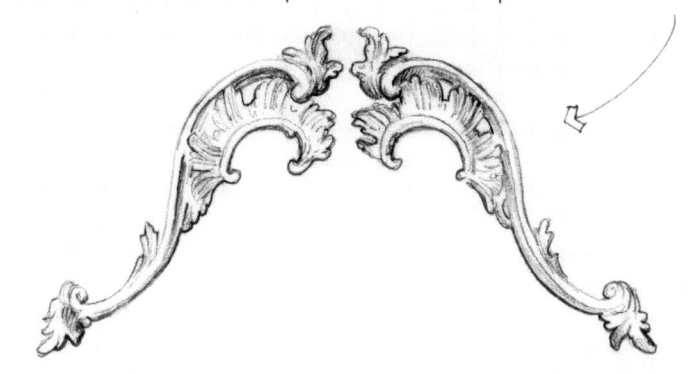

ALCOVE

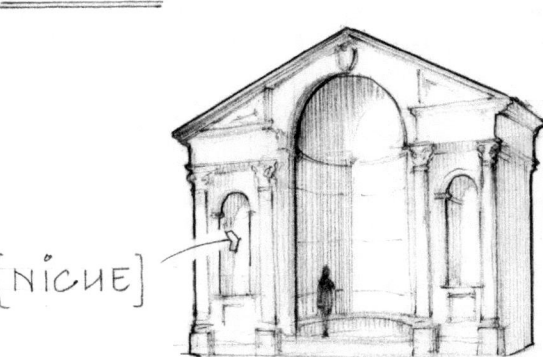

[NICHE]

A RECESS IN A BUILDING OR WALL

ANNULET

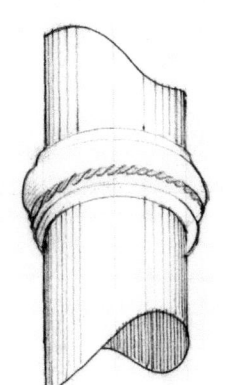

A MOULDING DECORATION AROUND A COLUMN

ARCHITRAVE

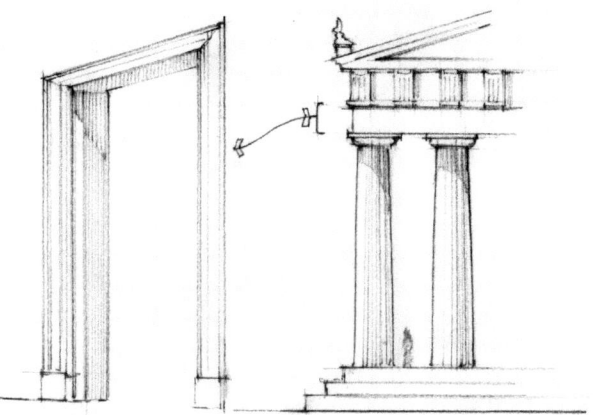

THE MOULDED FRAME SURROUNDING A DOOR OR WINDOW

DEVELOPED FROM THE LOWEST PART OF THE CLASSICAL ENTABLATURE

ARRIS

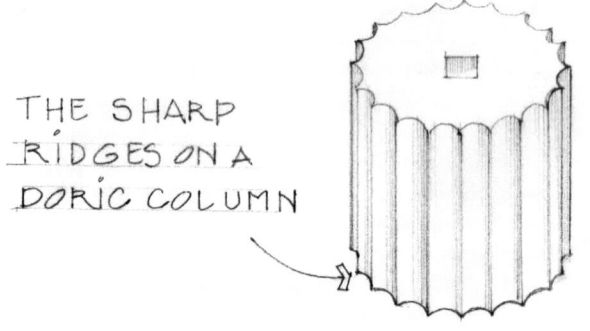

THE SHARP RIDGES ON A DORIC COLUMN

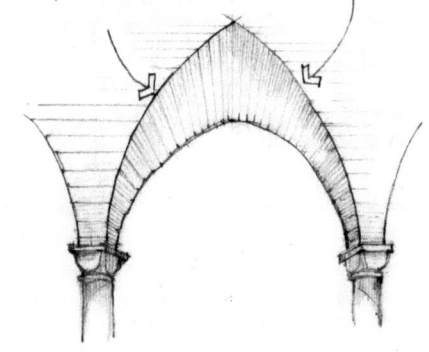

THE EDGE WHERE TWO SURFACES MEET AT ANY ANGLE

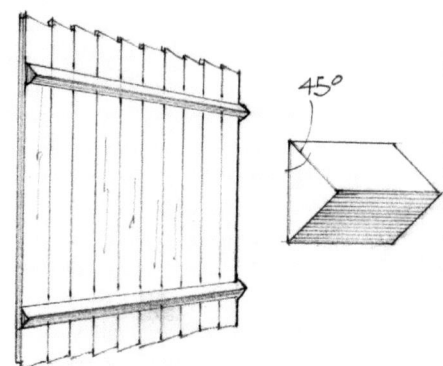

ARRIS-RAIL SUPPORTS A FENCE & ALLOWS WATER TO DRAIN AWAY

ASPECT RATIO [AR]

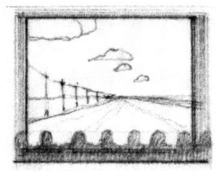
AR 1:1.33

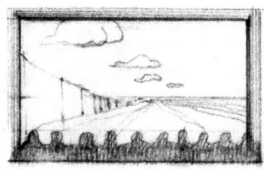
AR 1:1.85

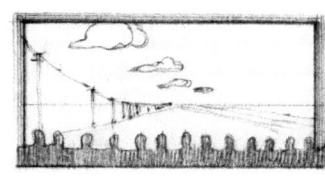
AR 1:2.35

DIVIDING THE WIDTH OF THE IMAGE BY THE HEIGHT GIVES THE ASPECT RATIO [AR]

APPLE BOX

A SERIES OF STACKING BOXES FOR RAISING PROPS, CAMERAS ETC.

ASTRAGAL

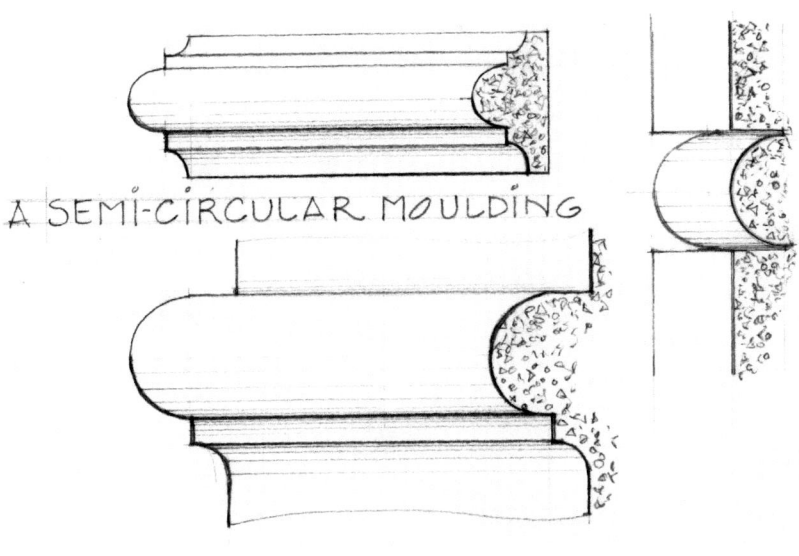

A SEMI-CIRCULAR MOULDING

ARCH A CURVED STRUCTURE SPANNING AN OPENING OR A SPACE

ATLANTES

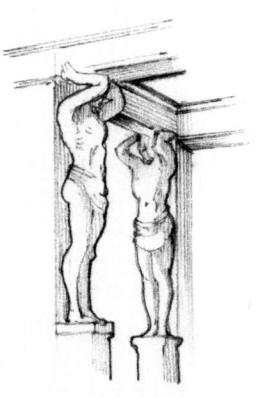

MALE FIGURES USED IN LIEU OF A COLUMN

AXONOMETRIC

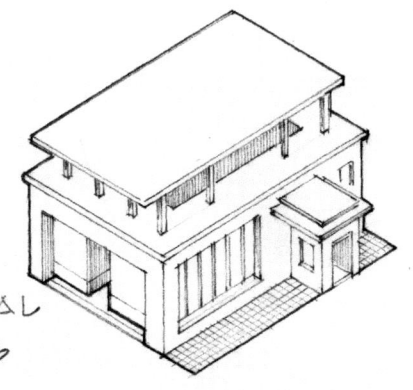

A THREE DIMENSIONAL MEASURED DRAWING

BACKING

A view seen through a window or opening. It can be painted or photographic.

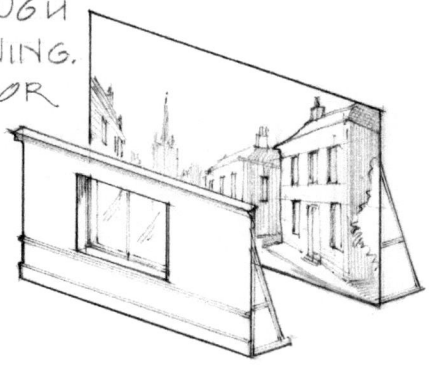

BEVEL

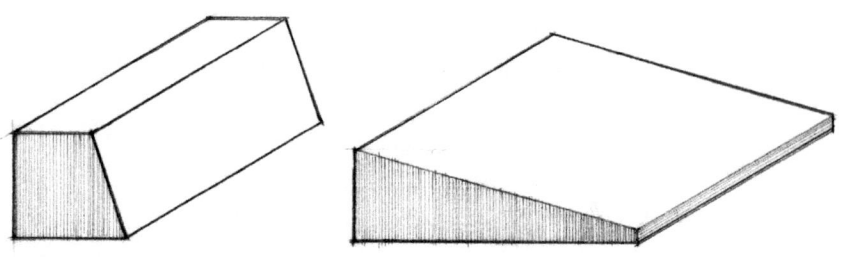

An edge that is not at right angles to either faces.
See "Chamfer"

BALUSTRADE

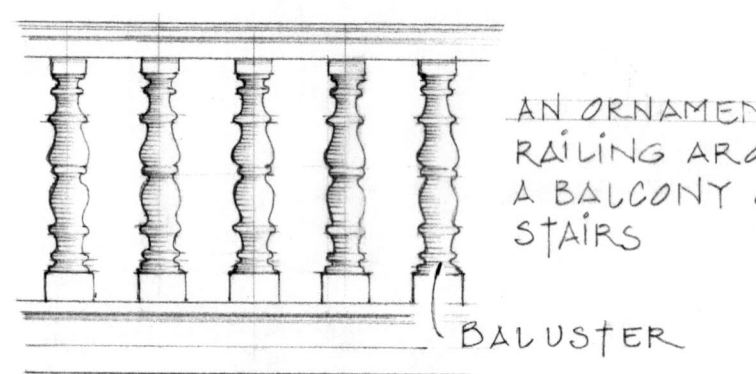

An ornamental railing around a balcony or stairs

BALUSTER

BARGE BOARD

On gable ends of roofs

Sometimes decorated

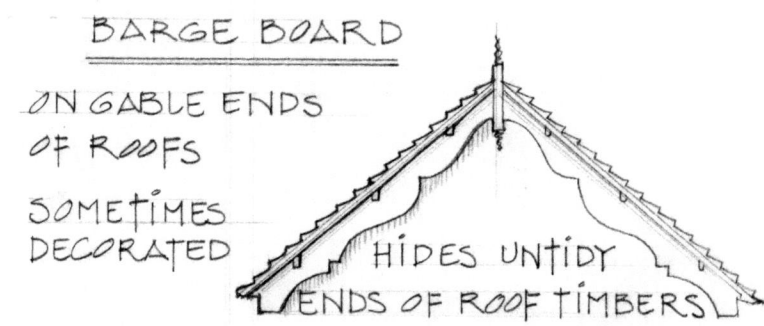

Hides untidy ends of roof timbers

BOSS

A feature covering joints on ceiling ribs

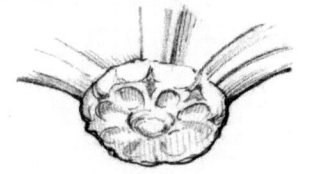
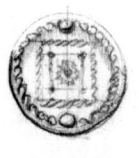
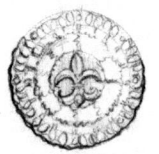

BOLECTION MOULDING

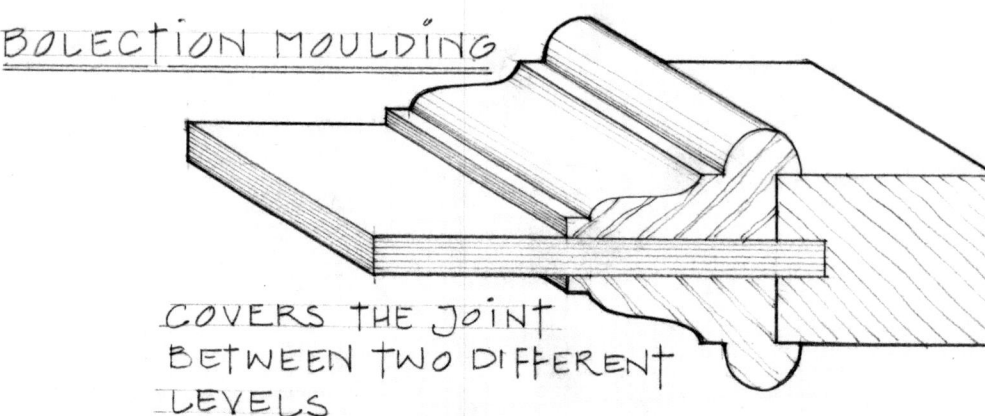

Covers the joint between two different levels

BULLSEYE

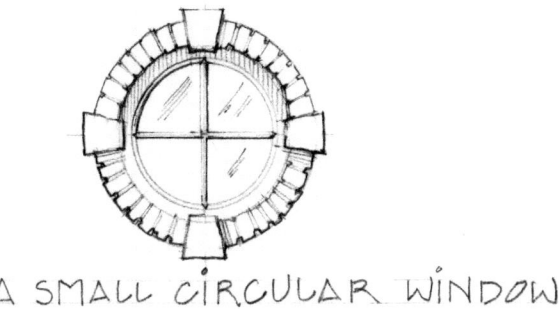

A SMALL CIRCULAR WINDOW

BUTTRESS

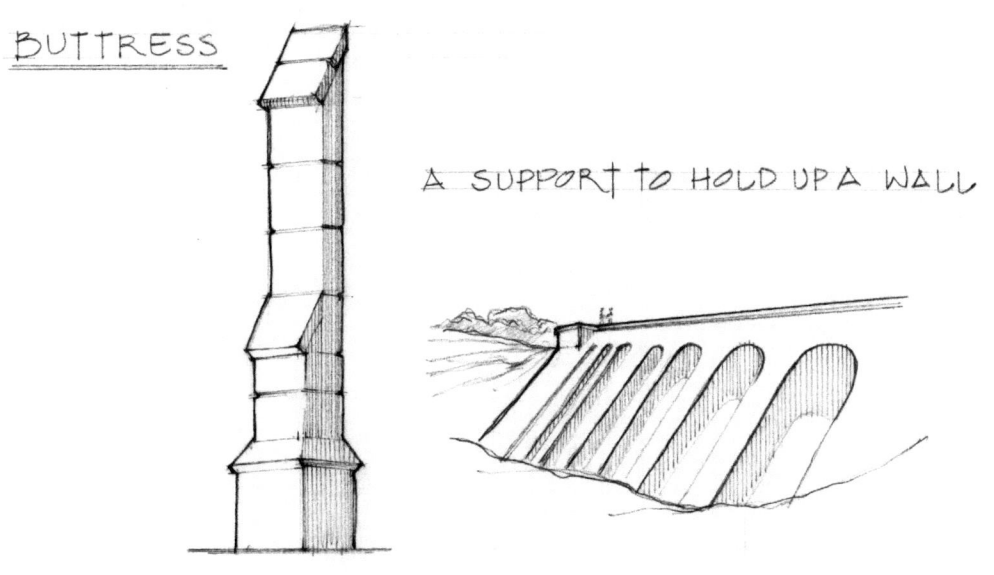

A SUPPORT TO HOLD UP A WALL

CANTILEVER

A PROJECTING PLATFORM OR SIMILAR, ANCHORED AT ONE END

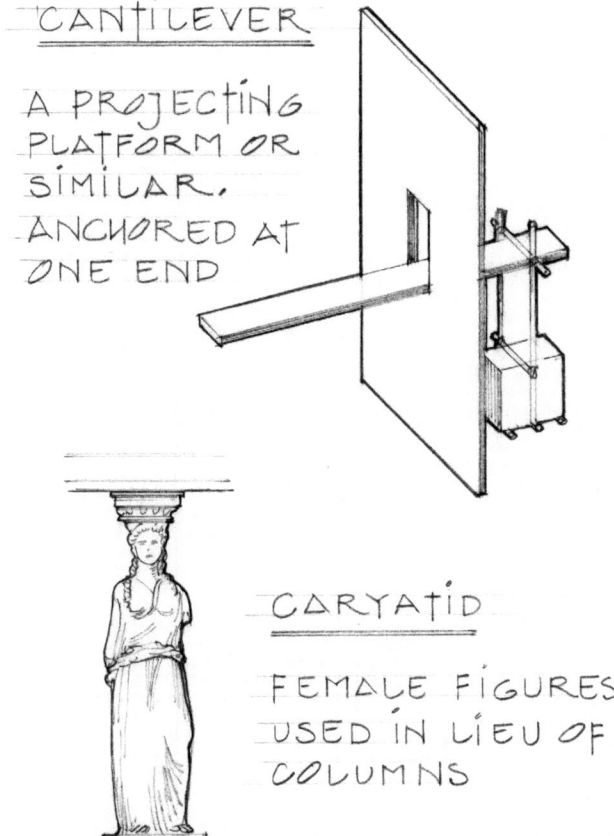

CAPITAL

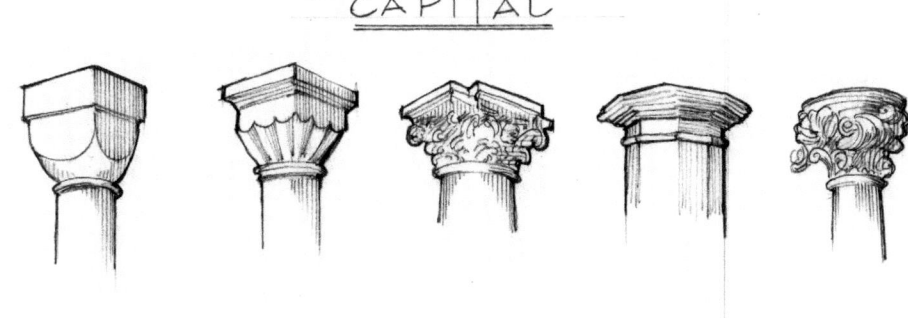

THE HEAD OF A COLUMN OR PILASTER

CARYATID

FEMALE FIGURES USED IN LIEU OF COLUMNS

CASTELLATION

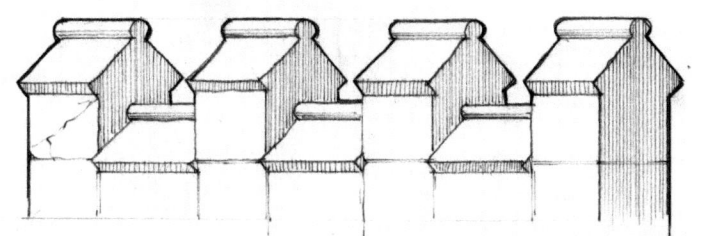

INDENTATIONS LIKE A CASTLE'S BATTLEMENTS

CHAIR RAIL

A MOULDING TO PROTECT WALLS FROM DAMAGE BY FURNITURE

AKA "DADO RAIL"

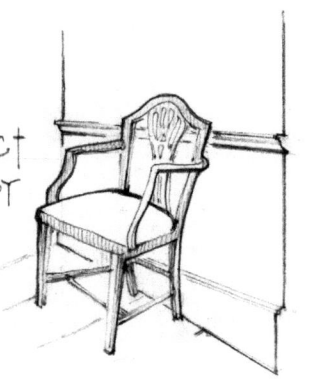

CHAMFER

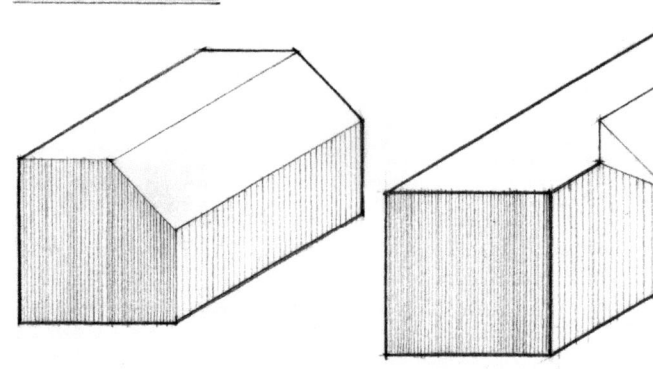

"STOP CHAMFER"

A PLANNED EDGE THAT IS AT 45° TO BOTH SIDES

CHEESE PIECE

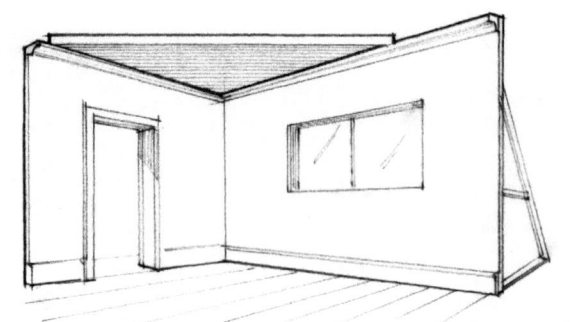

A WEDGE SHAPED CEILING PIECE

CORBEL

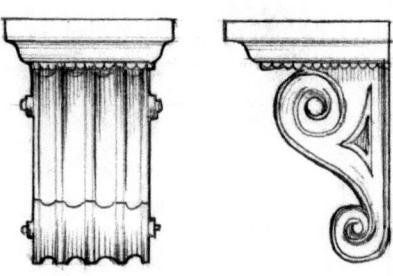

A SUPPORTING BRACKET

AKA "CONSOLE"

CORNICE

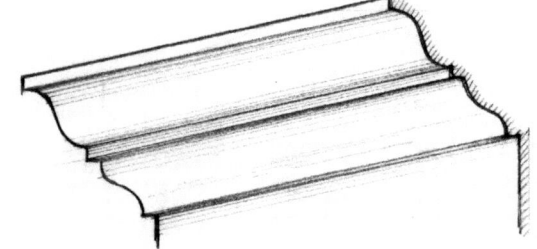

A MOULDING AT THE JUNCTION OF THE CEILING AND THE WALL

CROWS FOOT

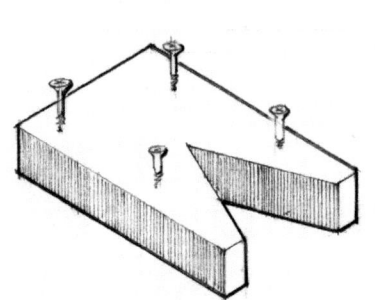

USED TO TRAP DRESSING AND PROPS TO FLOOR

CYCLORAMA

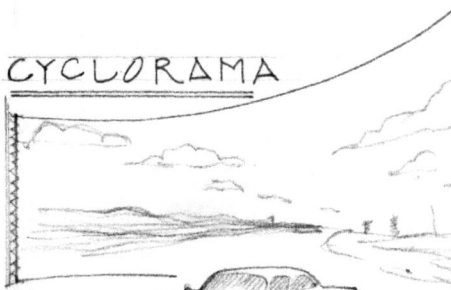

A LARGE CURVED BACKING [CYC]

DADO

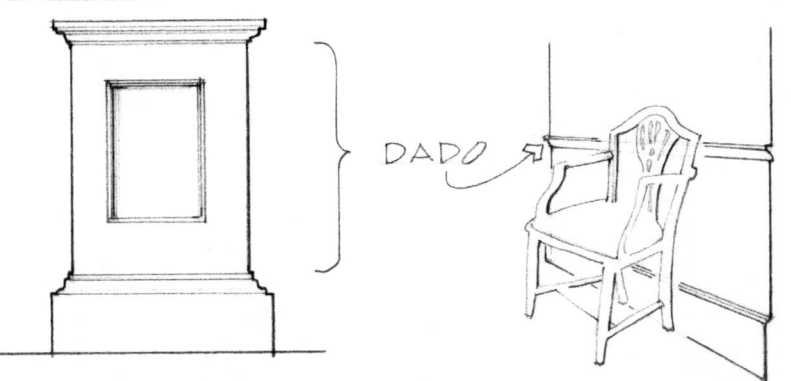

Originally part of a pedestal now known as the moulding at waist height

DENTIL MOULDING

A plain block moulding used in cornices

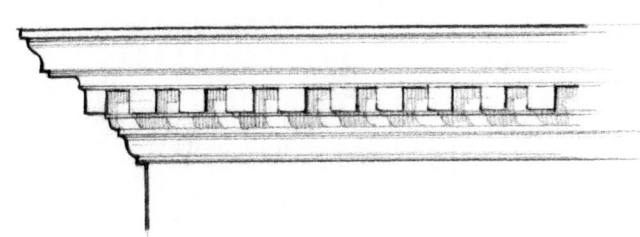

EGG AND DART

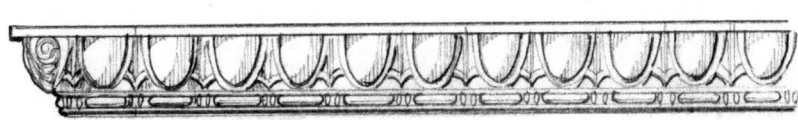

Moulding made up from egg and arrow head motifs. Represents life and death

FINIAL

An ornament on top of an object: a roof, furniture etc.

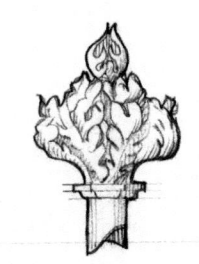 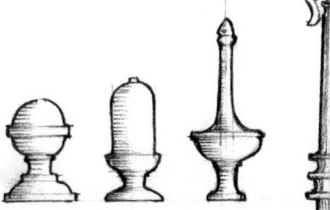

FLAT

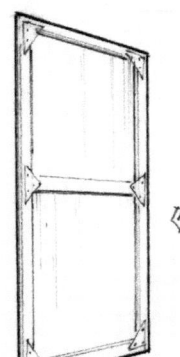

The basic element of scenery

This side not to camera!

DOUBLE CLAD FLAT

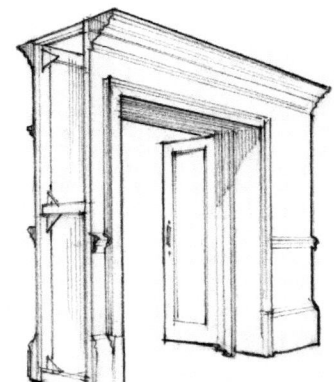

Shot from both sides built as one unit

FLOATER [U.S: WILD]

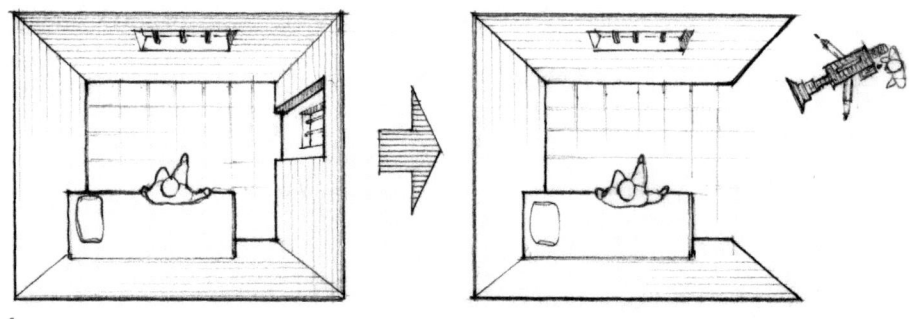

REMOVING A WALL TO ENABLE A CAMERA SET-UP

FRENCH BRACE

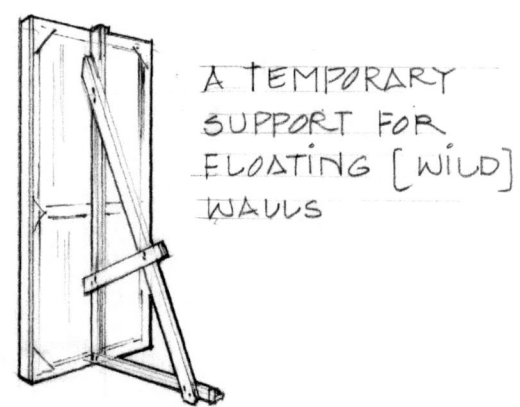

A TEMPORARY SUPPORT FOR FLOATING [WILD] WALLS

FRENCH CURVES

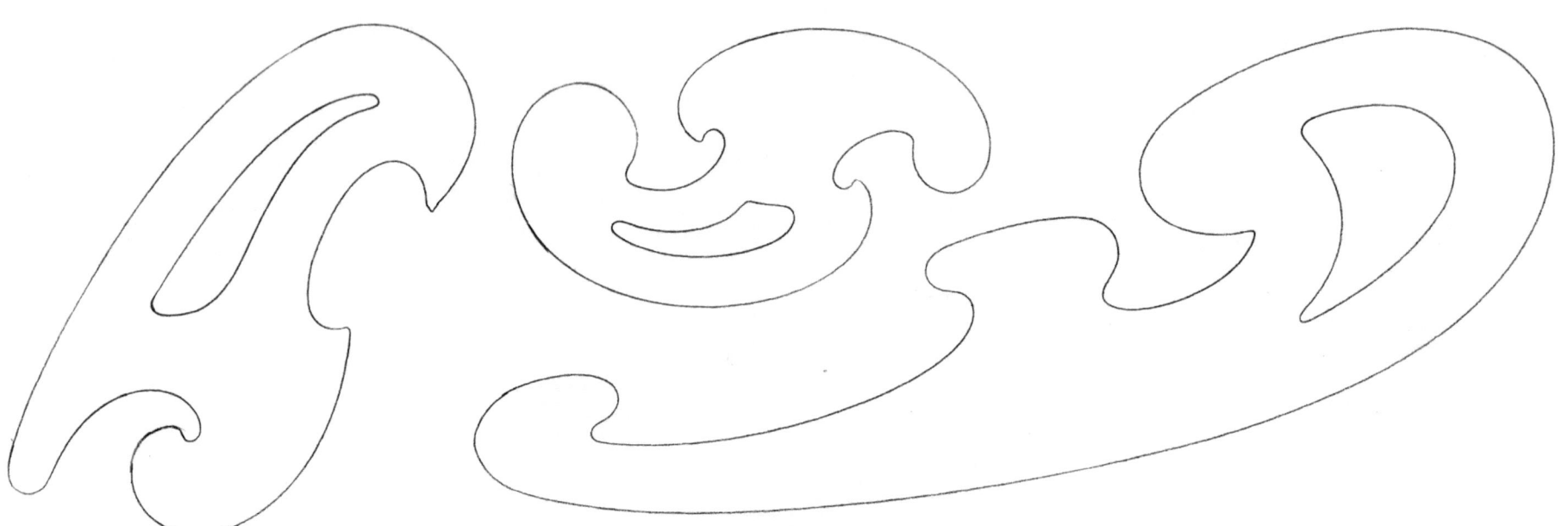

DESIGNED BY LUDWIG BURMESTER [1840-1927] A GERMAN SCIENTIST AND MATHMETICIAN USED FOR DRAWING SMOOTH CURVES OF VARYING RADII

GOING

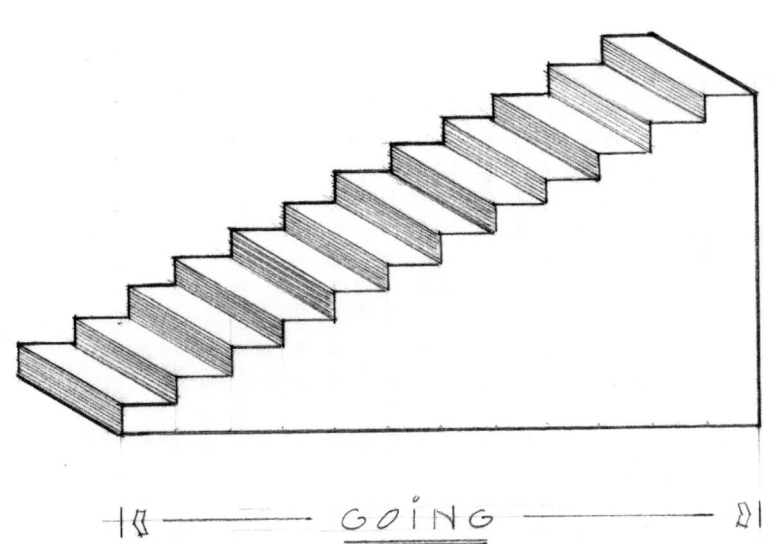

THE DISTANCE OF ALL THE TREADS COMBINED

GUILLOCHE

MEDIEVAL ORIGIN, BASED ON INTERLOCKING CIRCLES

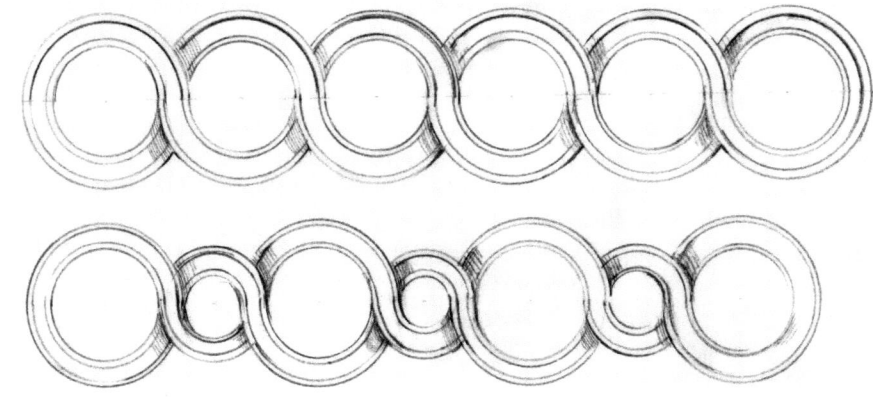

HEADER

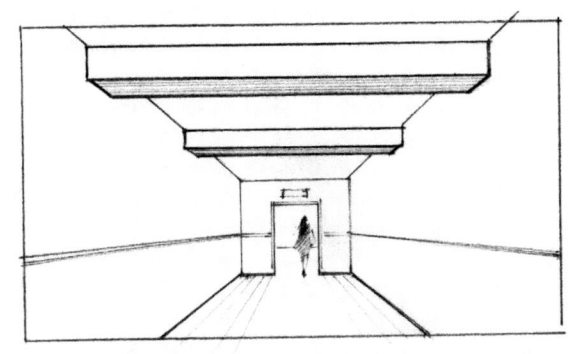

A USEFUL MEANS OF SUPPORTING CEILING PIECES

HERRINGBONE

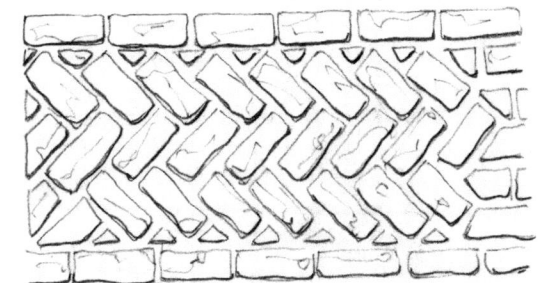

A 'V' SHAPED PATTERN USED ON FLOORS & BRICKWORK

PIN HINGE

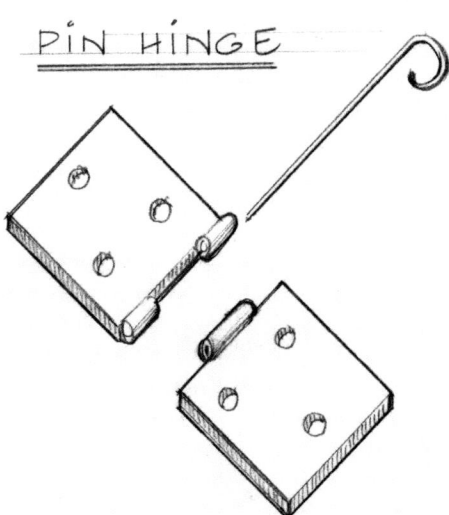

FOR QUICK RELEASE ON FLOATING (WILD) WALLS AND OTHER SCENERY

JAMB

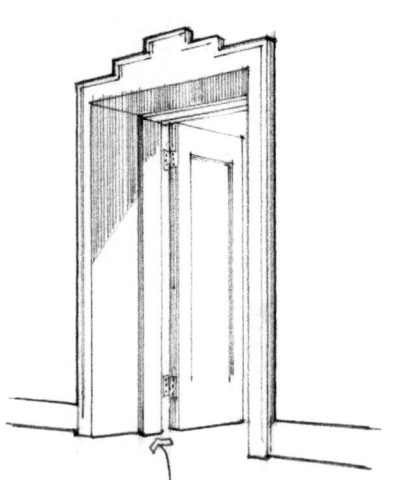

THE LINING AROUND A DOOR THAT HOLDS IT IN PLACE

JETTY

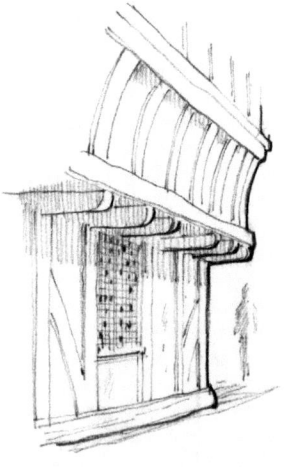

THE OVERHANG ON A WOODEN FRAMED BUILDING

JOCKEY

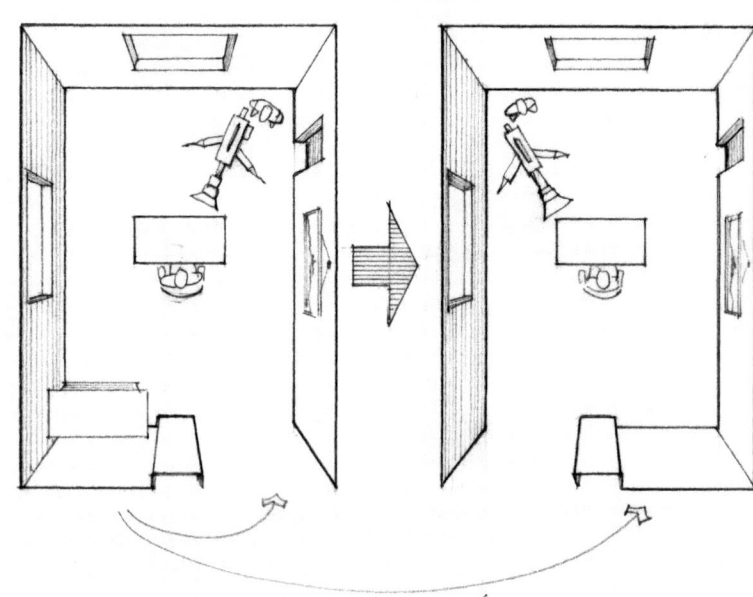

RE-USING A FLAT. IT CAN SAVE EXTRA BUILDING EXPENSE

JOG

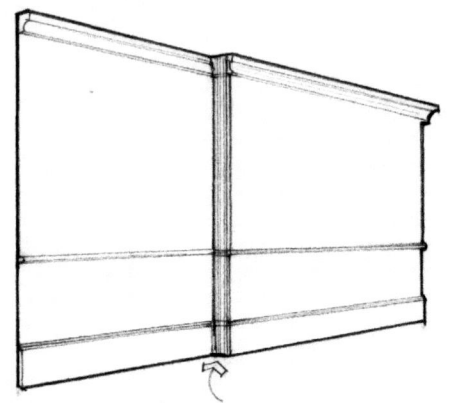

A SMALL CHANGE IN DIRECTION OF A WALL

JOIST

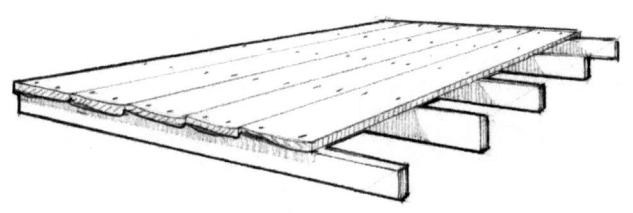

CARRIES THE FLOOR BOARDS BETWEEN THE WALLS

KEYSTONE

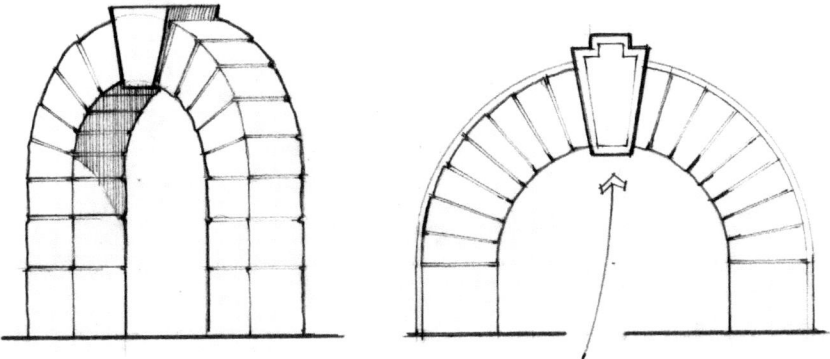

THE CENTRAL STONE OF AN ARCH

KEY PATTERN

A DECORATIVE BORDER
ORIGINS FROM ANCIENT GREECE

LAMBS TONGUE

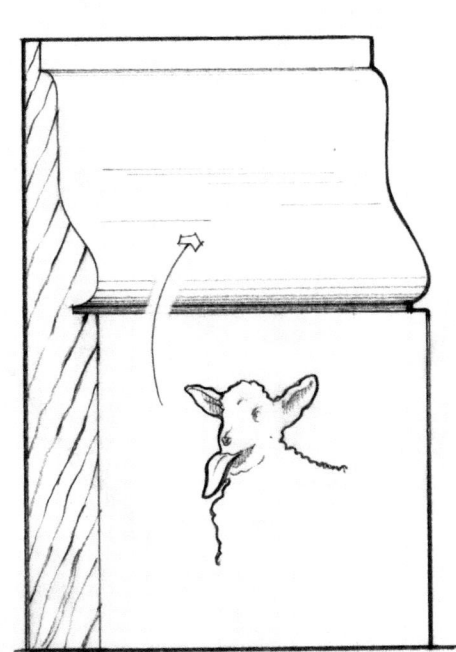

LOUVRE

SLOPING BOARDS OR GLASS ALLOWING AIR IN & KEEPING RAIN OUT

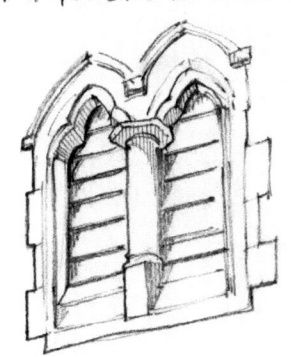

LINEN FOLD

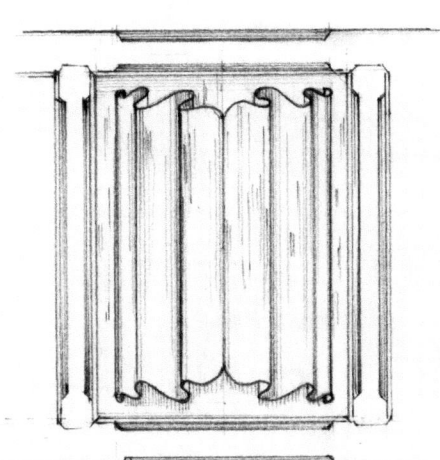

CARVED WOODEN PANELS IN THE FORM OF FOLDED LINEN CLOTH

MITRE

A JOINT MADE AT 90°

[ISOMETRIC PROJECTION]

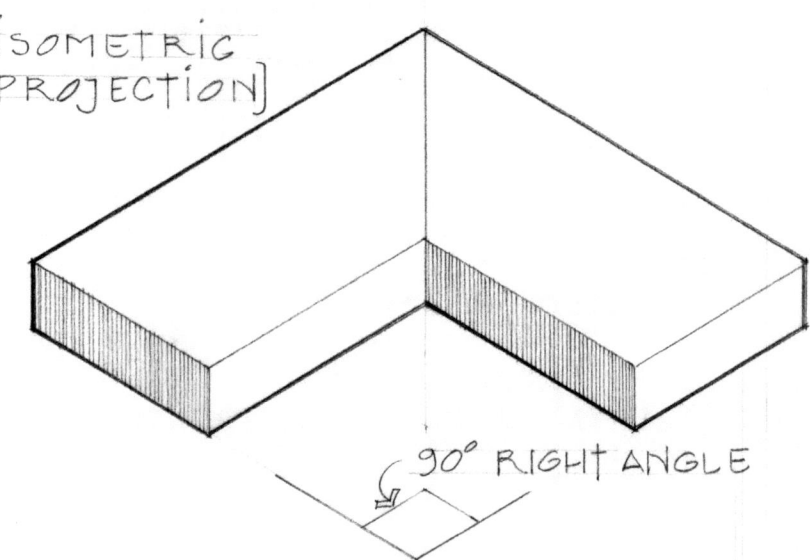

90° RIGHT ANGLE

MORTICE [AND TENON]

A SECURE JOINT

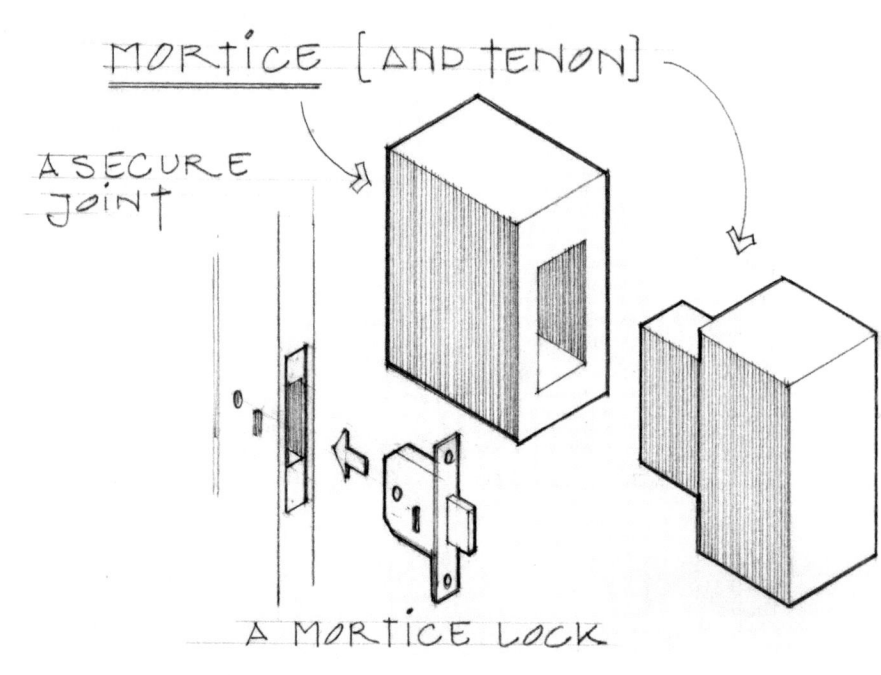

A MORTICE LOCK

MULLION

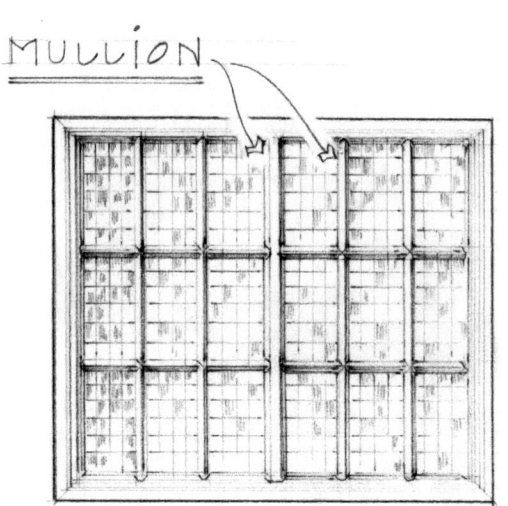

VERTICAL BARS BETWEEN THE GLASS PANES OF A WINDOW

MUNTIN

A.K.A: GLAZING BAR

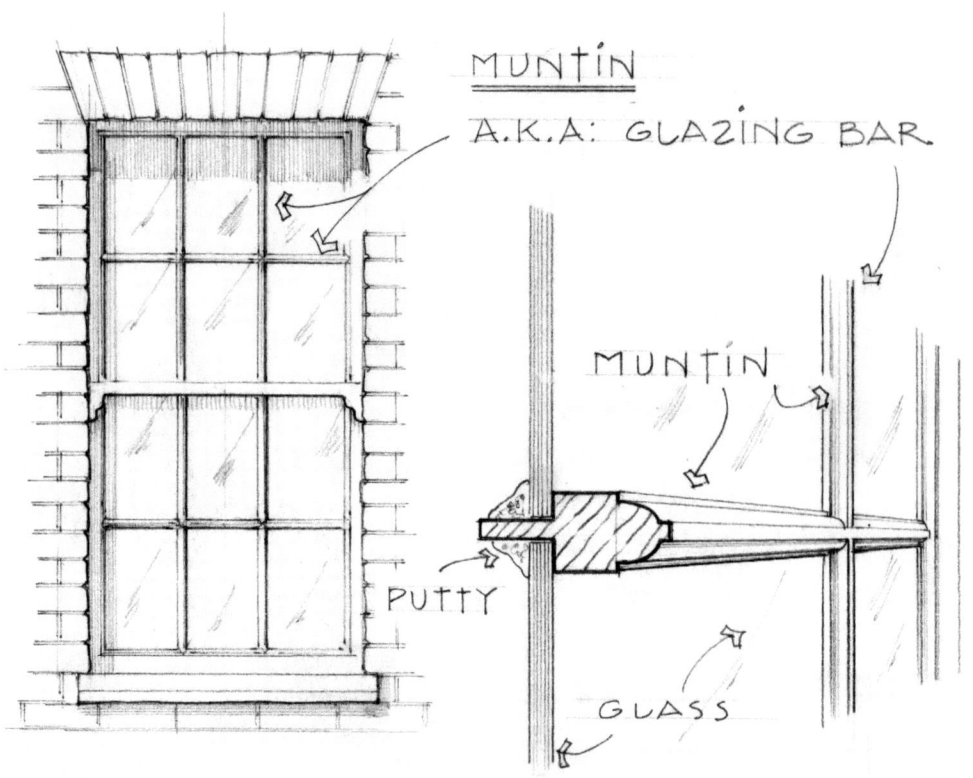

MUNTIN

PUTTY

GLASS

NAIL HEAD

SMALL PYRAMIDS IN A BAND.

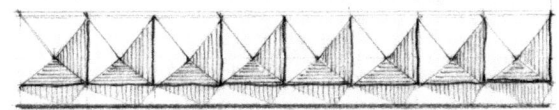

EARLY ENGLISH - NORMAN

NEWEL POST

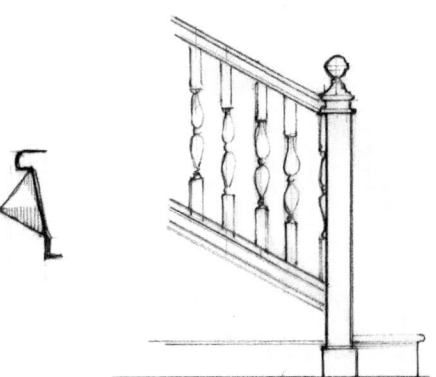
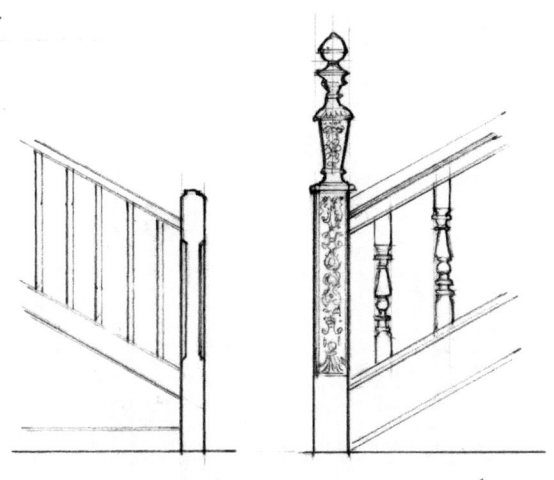

THE UPRIGHT POST THAT SUPPORTS THE HANDRAIL AND BALUSTERS

NICHE

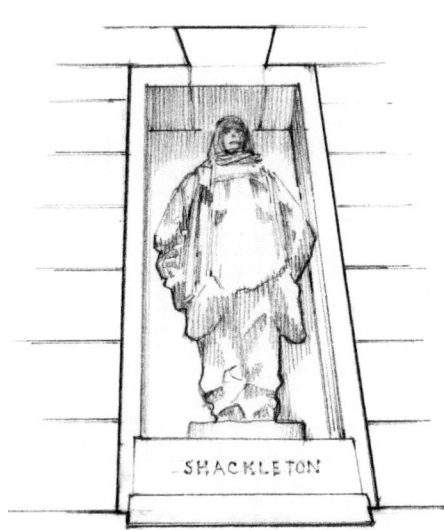

A RECESS IN A WALL FOR A STATUE OR DECORATION

OGEE

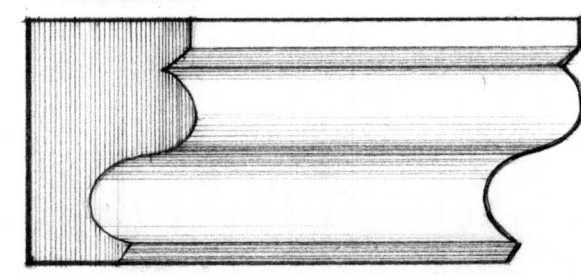

AN 'S' SHAPED CURVE

OVOLO

A ROUNDED CONVEX MOULDING

ORIEL WINDOW

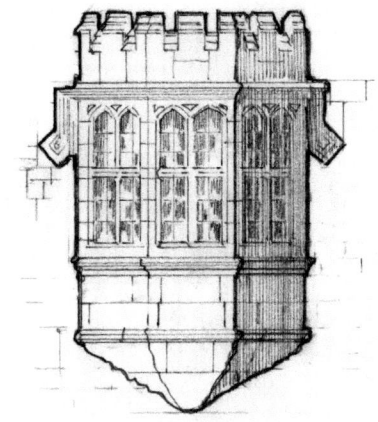

A BAY WINDOW ON AN UPPER FLOOR

PAGANINI'S ["PAGS"]

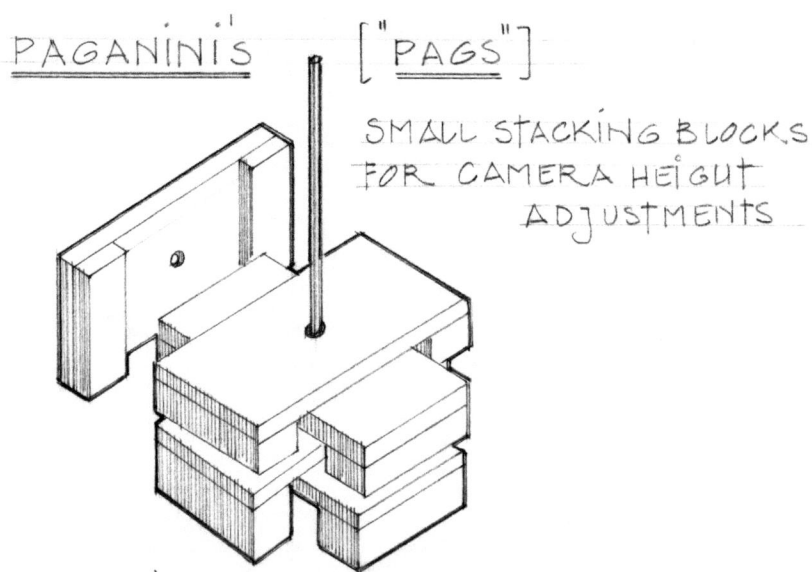

SMALL STACKING BLOCKS FOR CAMERA HEIGHT ADJUSTMENTS

NICCOLÒ PAGANINI [1782-1840] A GREAT ITALIAN VIOLINIST — TO ENABLE AUDIENCES TO SEE HIM [HE WAS NOT TALL] HE STOOD ON SMALL WOODEN BLOCKS....

PIER

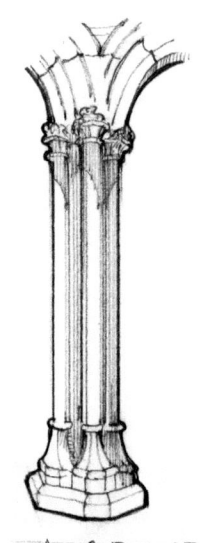

A GROUP OF COLUMN SHAFTS

PILASTER

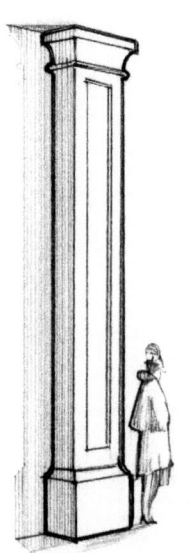

A RECTANGULAR COLUMN ATTACHED TO A WALL

PILLAR

A FREE STANDING STRUCTURE THAT CAN BE A SUPPORT FOR A BUILDING OR SIMPLY A MONUMENT OR ORNAMENT.

PLUG

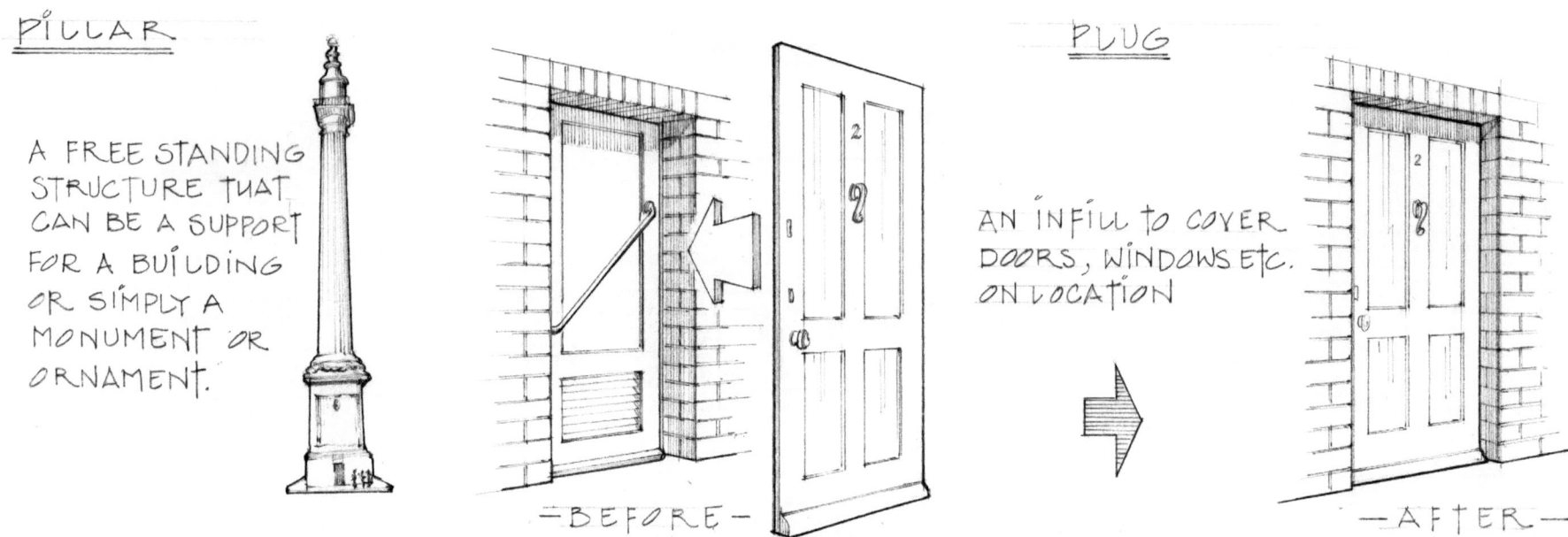

AN INFILL TO COVER DOORS, WINDOWS ETC. ON LOCATION

—BEFORE—   —AFTER—

QUIRK

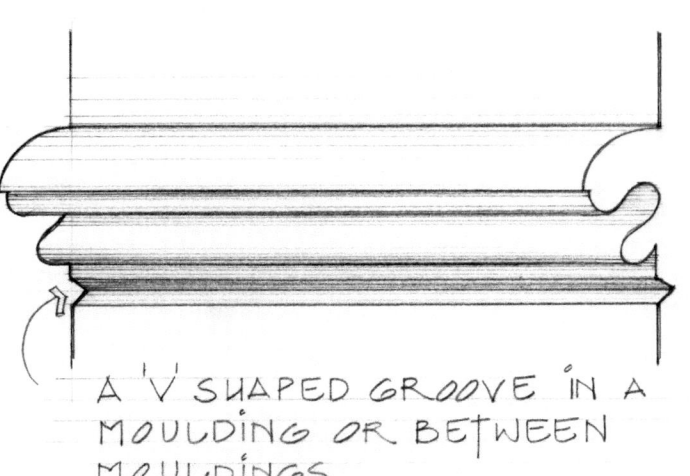

A 'V' SHAPED GROOVE IN A MOULDING OR BETWEEN MOULDINGS

QUOINS

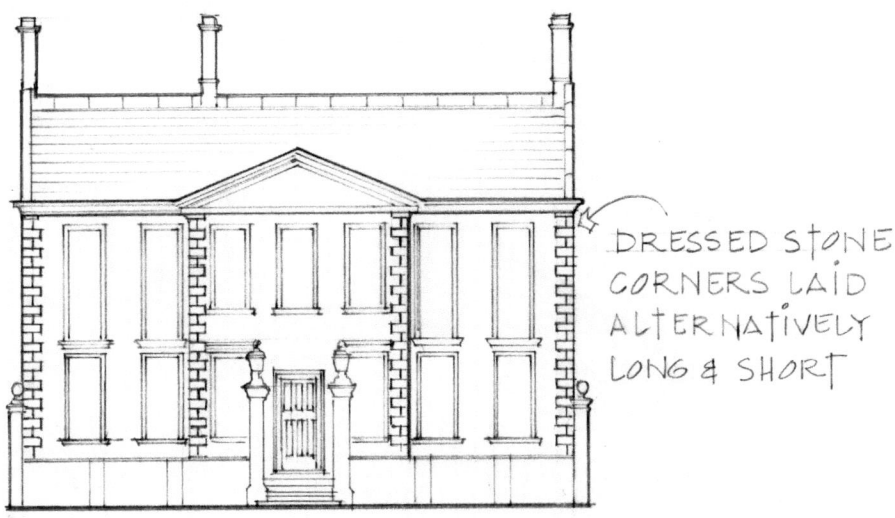

DRESSED STONE CORNERS LAID ALTERNATIVELY LONG & SHORT

QUADRANGLE

[QUAD]

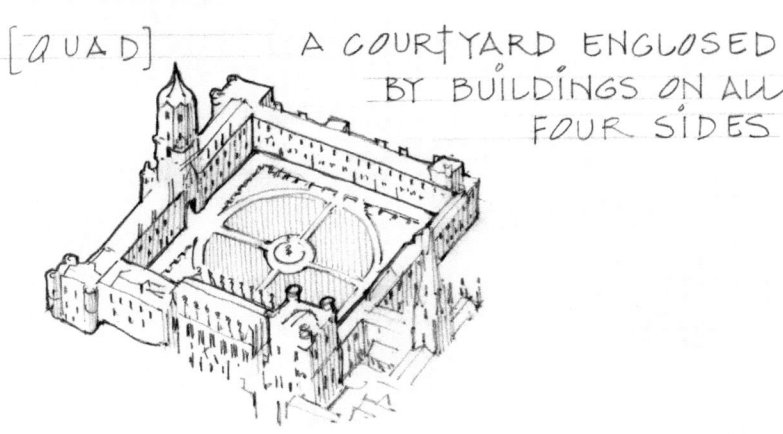

A COURTYARD ENCLOSED BY BUILDINGS ON ALL FOUR SIDES

MOSTLY FOUND IN SCHOOLS & COLLEGES

QUATREFOIL

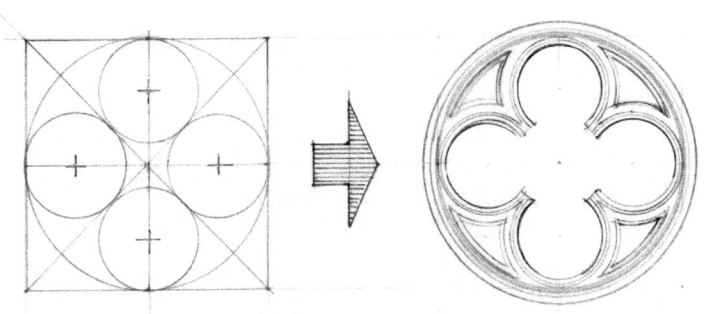

A FOUR-LEAFED SHAPED CURVE USED IN GOTHIC TRACERY. 'FOIL' IS FROM 'FOLIATED' - I.E. A LEAF FORM

REBATE

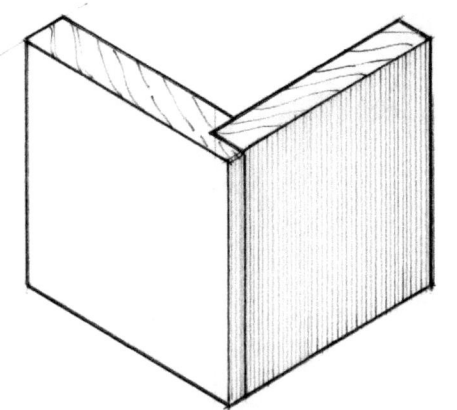

AKA: RABBET — A JOINT THAT HAS A STEP ON ONE PART.

REVEAL

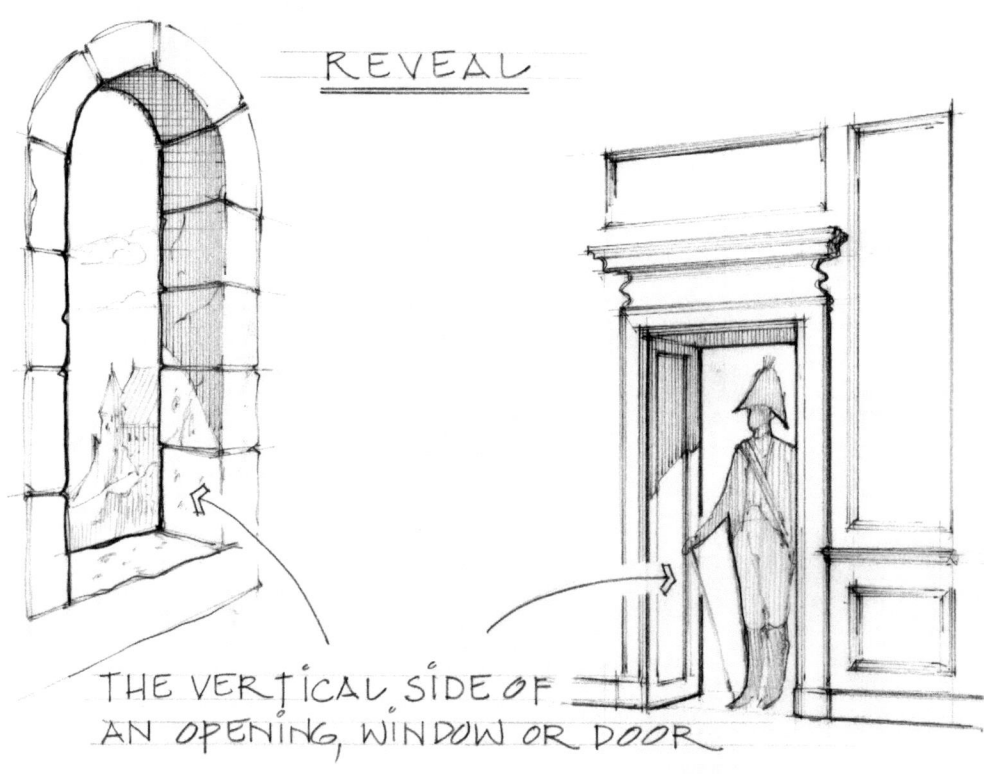

THE VERTICAL SIDE OF AN OPENING, WINDOW OR DOOR

RISER

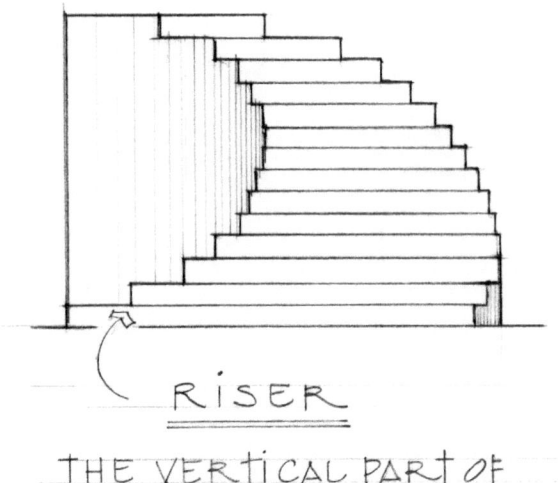

THE VERTICAL PART OF A STAIR OR STAIRCASE

ROSTRUM

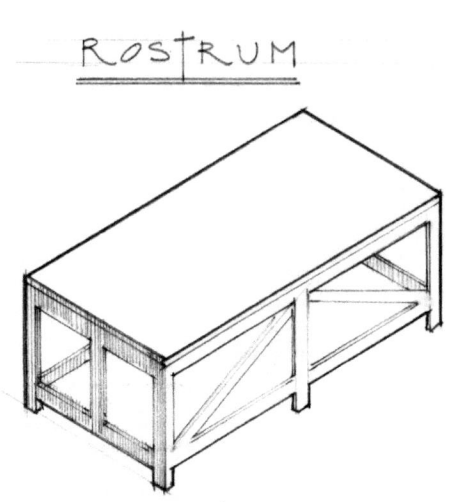

PLATFORMS OF VARYING HEIGHTS

RUSTICATION

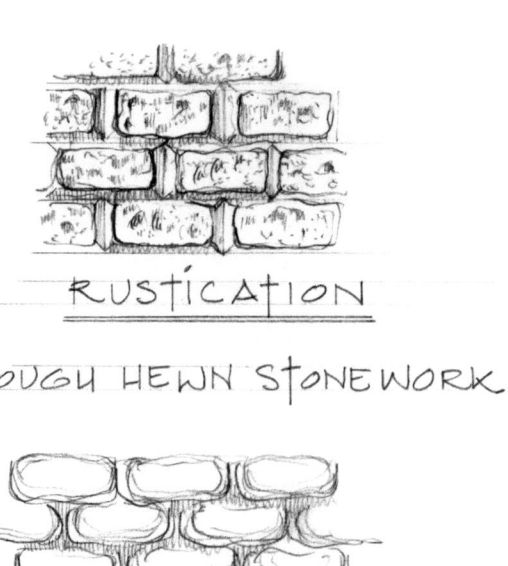

ROUGH HEWN STONEWORK

SCOTIA

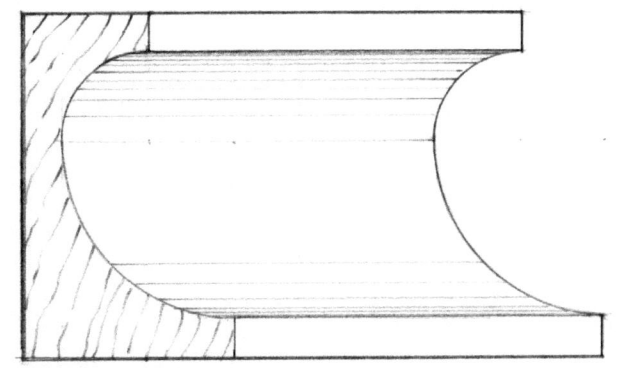

A CONCAVE MOULDING CASTING A STRONG SHADOW

SOFFIT

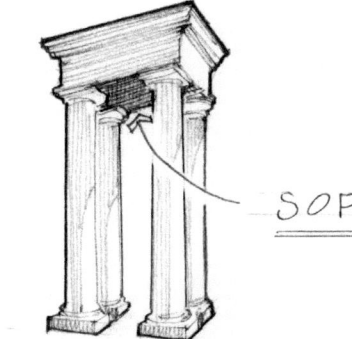

THE UNDERSIDE OF ANY ARCHITECTURAL ELEMENT

SOLOMONIC COLUMN

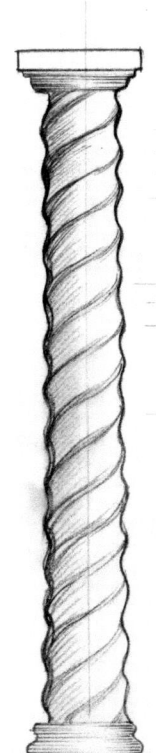

AKA: BARLEY-TWIST

A HELICAL SPIRAL THOUGHT TO ORIGINATE FROM THE TEMPLE OF KING SOLOMON

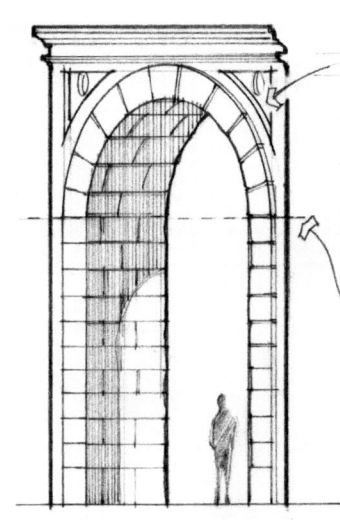

SPANDREL

THE TRIANGULAR SPACE BETWEEN AN ARCH'S APEX AND SPRING

SPRING

THE POINT WHERE AN ARCH SPRINGS FROM THE VERTICAL

STRINGER

THE HOUSING INTO WHICH THE RISERS AND TREADS ARE FIXED

SWINGER

A HINGED FLAT FOR EASY ACCESS

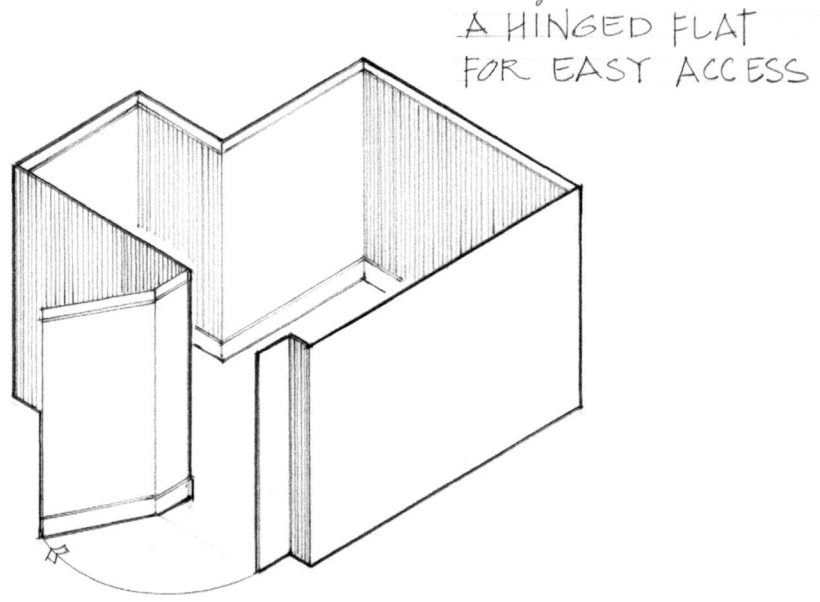

'T' SQUARE

USED WITH A BOARD FOR DRAWING PARALLEL LINES.

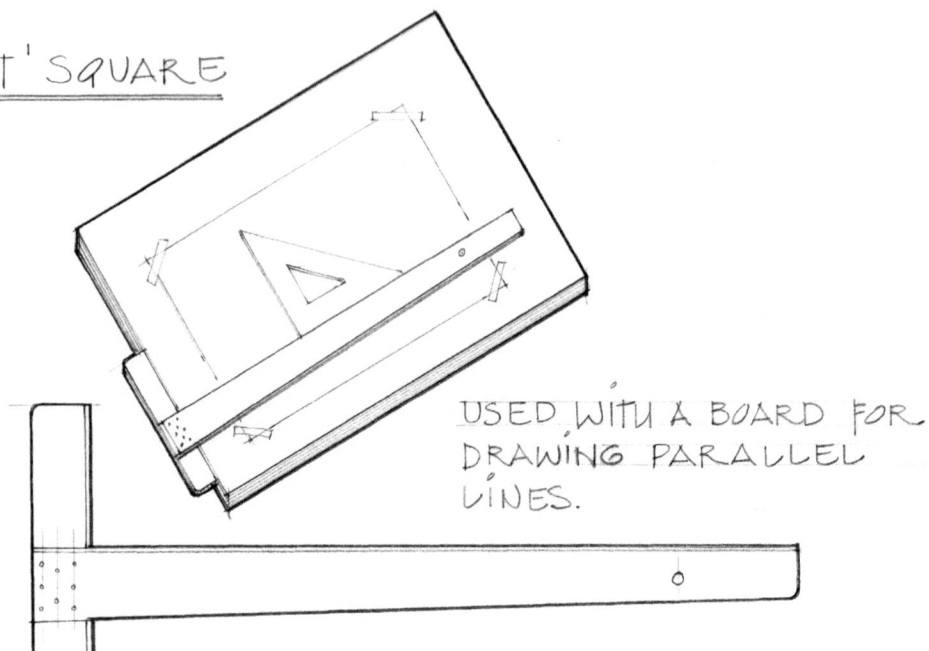

TORUS

A SEMI-CIRCULAR MOULDING

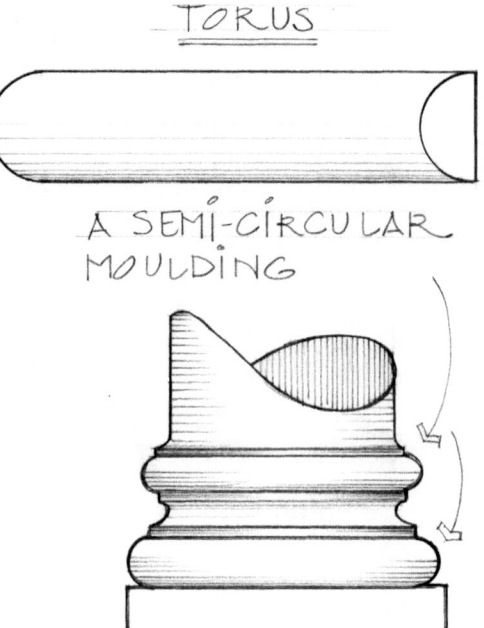

TRACERY

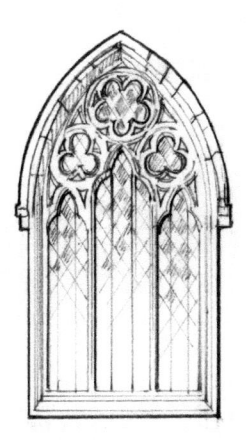
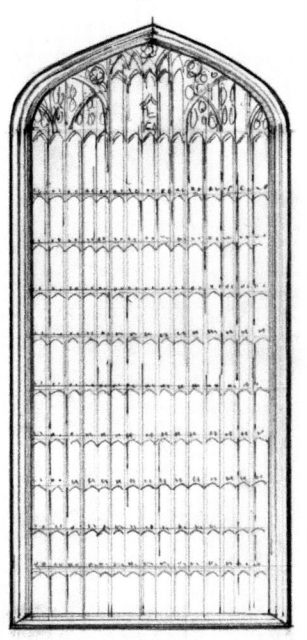

ORNAMENTAL STONEWORK OF ALL PERIODS OF GOTHIC ARCHITECTURE

TRANSOM

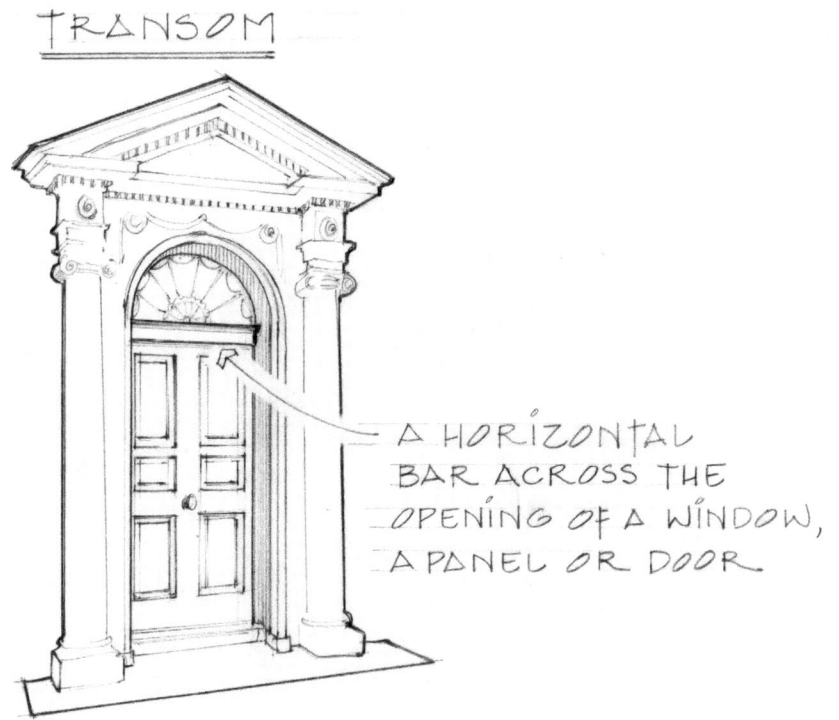

A HORIZONTAL BAR ACROSS THE OPENING OF A WINDOW, A PANEL OR DOOR

TRIANGULATION

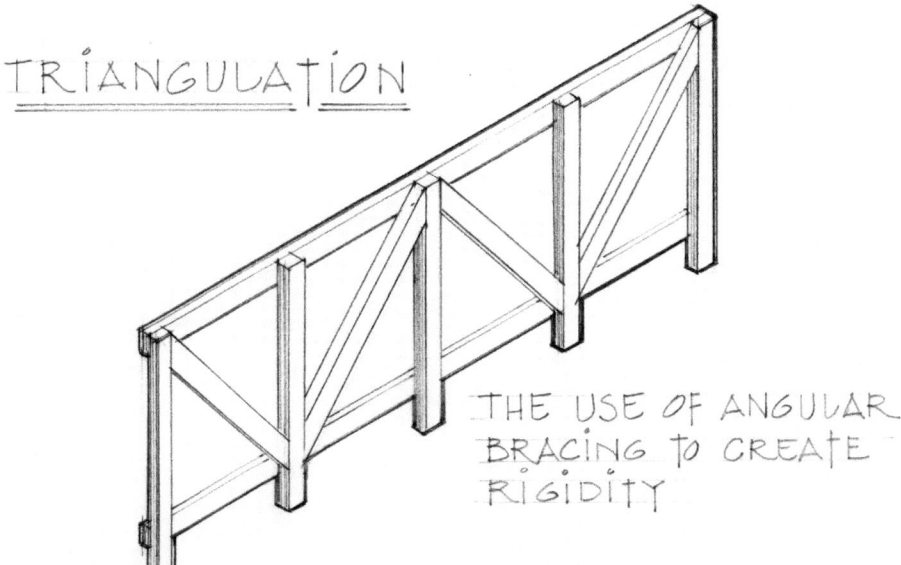

THE USE OF ANGULAR BRACING TO CREATE RIGIDITY

"TWO FOUR SIX"

A STACKING BLOCK TO RAISE CHAIRS/TABLES ETC.
2" – 4" – 6" [50mm – 100mm – 150mm]

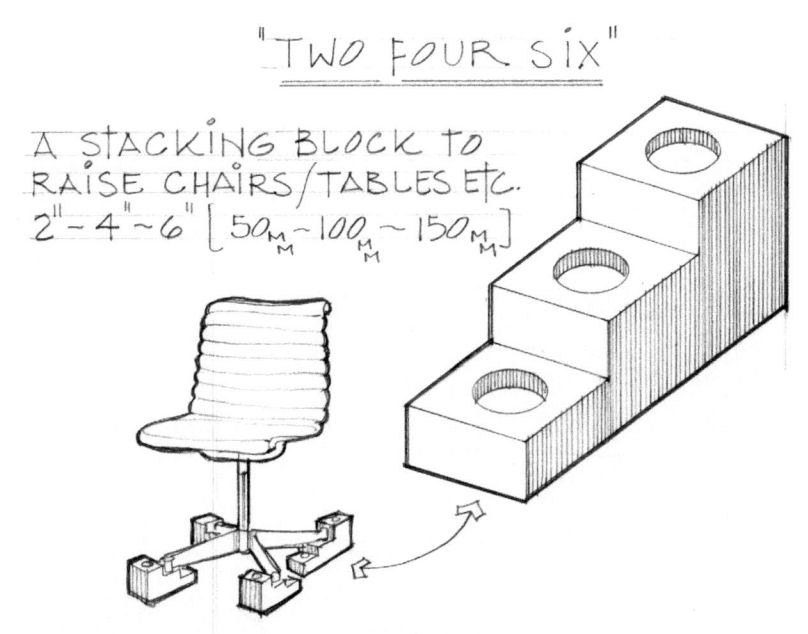

VOLUTE

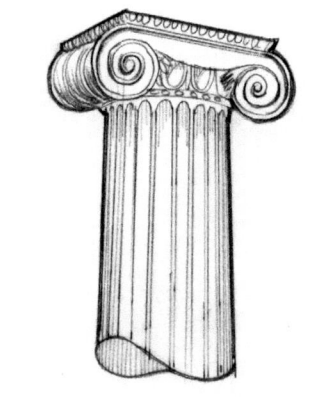

THE SPIRAL SCROLL ON AN IONIC CAPITAL

VOUSSOIRS

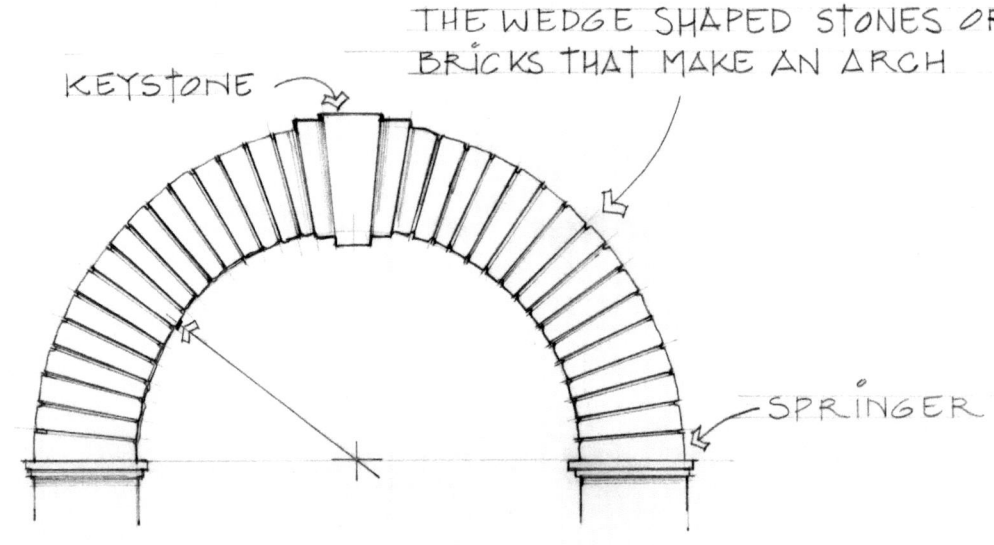

THE KEYSTONE AND SPRINGER ARE BOTH VOUSSOIRS

WAINSCOT

WOOD PANELLING

WINDBAG

A LIGHTWEIGHT CANVAS FLAT FOR CEILINGS OR BACKINGS

ZOETROPE

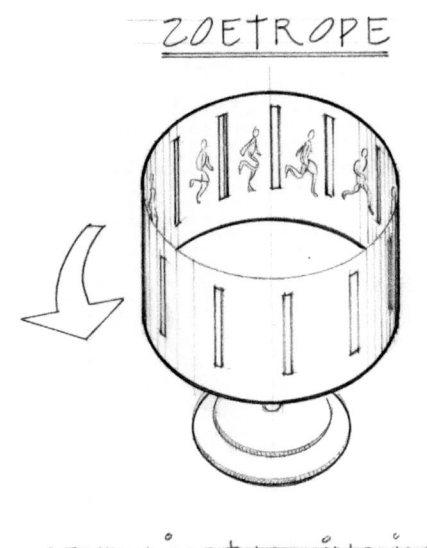

THE FIRST MOVING IMAGE

INDEX

A
ABACUS...................116, 139
ACADEMY 84
ACANTHUS................118, 139
ACUTE ANGLE...................32
ADJUSTABLE SET SQUARE.......3, 34
ALCOVE.......................139
ANNULET.................116, 139
APPLE BOX....................141
ARCH..........37 - 49, 123, 141
ARCHITRAVE........53, 56, 68, 116
117, 119, 120, 121, 122, 123, 140
ARRIS.........116, 117, 119, 140
ASPECT RATIO.............84, 140
ASTRAGAL.....55, 57, 66, 120, 141
ATLANTES.....................141
AXONOMETRIC..........70, 72, 141

B
BACKING......................142
BALUSTER......................63
BALUSTRADE...................142
BARGE BOARD..................142
BEAM COMPASS...................2
BEVEL........................142
BOLECTION MOULDING...........142
BOSS.........................142
BULLS EYE....................143
BUTTRESS.....................143

C
CANTILEVER...................143
CAPITAL.................116, 117
       119, 120, 121, 122, 123, 143
CARYATID.....................143
CASEMENT WINDOW...............57
CASTELLATION.................143
CAVETTO.......................65
CHAIR RAIL...................144
CHAMFER......................144
CHEESE PIECE.................144
CHORAGIC MONUMENT............118

CLINOMETER...................137
COMPASS........................2
CORBEL.......................144
CORINTHIAN (GREEK)...........118
CORINTHIAN (ROMAN)...........122
CORNICE.............68, 116, 117
119, 120, 121, 122, 123, 144, 145
CROWS FOOT...................144
CYCLORAMA (CYC)..............144
CYMA RECTA................65, 67
CYMA REVERSA..........44, 65, 67

D
DADO................68, 119, 121
                    122, 123, 145
DENTIL.......................145
DIMENSION LINES........10, 11, 13
DOG-LEG.......................60
DOORS.....................50 - 54
DORIC (GREEK)................116
DORIC (ROMAN)................119
DOUBLE CLAD..................145
DOUBLE MARGIN DOOR............53

E
ECHINUS......................116
EGG AND DART.................145
ELIPSE....................67, 72
ENGLISH BOND 64
ENTABLATURE........116, 117, 119
ENTASIS.................124, 125
ERASER SHIELD..................4

F
FIBONACCI SPIRAL........128, 129
FIELDED PANEL.................53
FINIAL.......................145
FLAT.........................145
FLEMISH BOND..................64
FLOATER (U.S. WILD).......18, 146
FLUTE(ARRIS)............116, 117
                  119, 121, 122, 123
FRENCH BRACE.................146

FRENCH CURVES................146
FRIEZE.............116, 117, 119
              120, 121, 122, 123

G
GLAZING BAR...................55
GOING.....................63, 147
GOLDEN SECTION...............129
GUILLOCHE....................147

H
HATCHING.......................8
HEADER.......................147
HEADING BOND..................64
HELIX........................130
HERRINGBONE..................147
HYPERBOLA.....................67

I
INCIDENCE (ANGLE OF).........105
INCLINOMETER.................137
IONIC (GREEK)................117
IONIC (ROMAN)................121
ISOSCELES TRIANGLE............32
ISOMETRIC.................69, 72

J
JAMB.........................148
JETTY........................148
JOCKEY.......................148
JOG..........................148
JOIST........................148

K
KEY PATTERN..................149
KEYSTONE.....................149
KITE WINDER...............59, 60

L
LAMBS TONGUE.................149
LEDGE AND BATTEN (DOOR).......51
LEDGE AND BRACE (DOOR)........52
LETTERING.................24, 25
LINEN FOLD...................149
LOCK RAIL.....................53
LOUVRE.......................149

INDEX

M
MECHANICAL PENCIL...............4
MEETING STILES.................54
MITRE........................150
MORTICE......................150
MULLION......................150
MUNTIN...................55, 150

N
NAIL HEAD....................151
NEWEL POST...............63, 151
NICHE........................151
NOSEING.......................63

O
OBLIQUE PROJECTION............71
OBTUSE ANGLE..................32
OGEE..................44, 47, 151
ORIEL WINDOW.................151
OVOLO....................65, 151

P
PAGANINI (PAGS)..............152
PARABOLA......................67
PARALLEL MOTION................1
PEDESTAL.....................119
PEDIMENT................116, 117
PIER.........................152
PILASTER.....................152
PILLAR.......................152
PIN HINGE....................147
PLAN........................7 - 18
PLANOMETRIC...............70, 72
PLINTH............121, 122, 123
PLUG.........................152
PROTRACTOR...................137

Q
QUADRANGLE...................153
QUATRE FOIL..................153
QUIRK........................153
QUOIN........................153

R
REBATE.......................154

REFLECTED CEILING PLAN........19
REVEAL.......................154
RIGHT ANGLE...................32
RISER.....................58, 154
ROSTRUM...........107, 108, 154
RUNNING DIMENSIONS...........132
RUSTICATION..................154

S
SCALE.......................5, 6
SCALENE TRIANGLE..............32
SCOPE..........84, 100, 101, 102
SCOTIA....................66, 155
SECTIONS.........12, 14, 16, 17
SET SQUARE.....................3
SHAFT.........116, 117, 119, 120
                   122, 124, 125
SILL......................56, 57
SKIRTING......................68
SLIDING SASH..............55, 56
SOFFIT.......................155
SOLOMONIC COLUMN.............155
SPANDREL.................63, 155
SPINDLE.......................63
SPIRAL............127, 128, 130
SPRING.......................155
SPRING BOW COMPASS.............2
STENCIL TEMPLATE...............4
STILE.........................55
STRETCHING BOND...............64
STRINGER.....................156
STYLOBATE....................116
SURVEYING...............131 - 138
SWINGER......................156

T
T SQUARE...................1, 156
TITLE BLOCK...............23, 26
TORUS........................156
TRACERY......................157
TRANSOM......................157
TREAD.........................63

TRIANGLE......................32
TRIANGULATION......131, 134, 157
TUSCAN.......................120
TWO, FOUR, SIX...............157

V
VANISHING POINT....73, 74, 75, 77
VOLUTE.........117, 121, 126, 158
VOUSSOIR.................37, 158

W
WAINSCOT.....................158
WILD (U.K. FLOAT).........18, 146
WINDBAG......................158

Z
ZOETROPE.....................158

T - #0052 - 230721 - C0 - 216/280/8 - PB - 9781138290334 - Matt Lamination